THE AMERICAN QUANTITY COOKBOOK:
Tracing Our Food Traditions

THE AMERICAN QUANTITY COOKBOOK:
Tracing Our Food Traditions

JANE YOUNG WALLACE
Editor, Institutions/VF Magazine
SPONSORING EDITOR

Published by
CAHNERS BOOKS INTERNATIONAL, INC.
221 Columbus Ave., Boston, Massachusetts 02116
Publishers of Institutions/VF Magazine

Library of Congress Cataloging in Publication Data
Main entry under title:

The American quantity cookbook.

"The core of materials in this book came from the
series of Bicentennial articles prepared by the
editorial staff of Institutions/vf magazine under the
guidance of Jane Young Wallace, editor."
    Includes index.
    1. Cookery for institutions, etc. 2. Cookery,
American. 3. Restaurants, lunch rooms, etc.—
United States—Directories. I. Wallace, Jane Young.
II. Institutions/volume feeding.
TX820.A534   641.5'72'0973   76-3419

Library of Congress Cataloging in Publication Data

ISBN 0-8436-2096-X

ISBN 0-8436-2096-X

Printed in the United States of America

*Cover credit: Brother Mateo, curator, Santa Barbara, Calif.
Mission; Jean Carey, Black Olive Commission, food stylist;
Madelin Schneider, West Coast editor,* Institutions/Volume
Feeding Magazine; *Barrie Schwortz, photographer.*

Contents

ACKNOWLEDGEMENTS

The core of materials in this book came from the series of Bicentennial articles prepared by the editorial staff of *Institutions/VF Magazine* under the guidance of Jane Young Wallace, Editor, with the cooperation of the art department, Ronald K. Hansen, Art Director, and Antonios Pronoitis, Director of the Art Department. Several of the food articles in the Bicentennial series were written by Eulalia Blair, Consulting Editor, and the recipes selected by her for the series are included in this book. Added to this basic core of materials are recipes sent by many of the members of the Foodservice Bicentennial Federation as a contribution to the magazine's presentation of the part played by the foodservice/lodging industry in the development of America.

To enlarge the work so that it could serve as a quantity cookbook reference to basic American dishes, recipes were also selected from the files of earlier issues of *Institutions/VF Magazine*. The recipes from the Federation members and many of the out-of-print classics were prepared for publication by Lola F. Townsend, a former member of the magazine's staff.

Grateful acknowledgement is due all of those who have helped to produce this authoritative collection of the recipes that are the basis of American quantity cuisine, together with information as to how and where these foods are being effectively presented today.

Jule Wilkinson
Book Editor
Institutions/VF Magazine

Foreword

The Bicentennial has presented both an opportunity and an obligation for the foodservice/lodging industry of America. As hundreds of thousands of Americans traveled the country soaking up their heritage, it became the industry's responsibility to serve them with care and quality.

It was for this reason that the editors of *Institutions/VF Magazine* created the Bicentennial Foodservice Federation in 1974. Two hundred operators from all sectors of the industry were chosen to guide the editors through the Bicentennial year.

On a rainy November afternoon in 1974, the Federation's first meeting was held. The location? Fraunces Tavern in New York, one of the nation's oldest restaurants, and the historic site where George Washington said farewell to his troops.

At this meeting, operators outlined their plans for the upcoming celebration and set up guidelines to help the editors. Beginning in January, 1975, the Magazine initiated a series on the historic aspects of food and lodging in the United States. Teams of editors and photographers literally criss-crossed the country, searching out the old, the well-known, and the typical.

From the blueberries of New England to the trout of Colorado, the potatoes of Idaho, the creole dishes of Louisiana, and the corn-on-the-cob of mid-America, recipes and serving ideas typifying the culinary heritage of our industry in America were collected.

Many were used in the Magazine, but because of space limitations, not all could be published. In this book, however, are both the recipes collected for the Magazine series and others sent to us by Bicentennial Foodservice Federation members exclusively for this salute to American foodservice. *The American Quantity Cookbook* is also designed to serve in the years ahead as a continuing reference to American food traditions and recipes.

Jane Wallace
Editor, *Institutions/VF Magazine*

As American As Apple Pie, Succotash, and Corn Flakes

A FASCINATING LIST of familiar dishes is as American as Thanksgiving or the Fourth of July. Some have an ancestry tracing back to Indian times and credit the creativeness of Colonial housewives. Others, just as American, mark their beginning at a later date. Some are the inventions of the past few decades.

Certainly, few items are as American as corn, beloved in all of its forms. The crop was strange to the early settlers, who learned the Indians' ways of dealing with the ground meal and samp (hominy) that they made from the corn after it dried. The Indians also demonstrated putting corn with beans for the dish that we still know as succotash.

Colonial women boiled cornmeal to prepare a simple thick mush. They also used the standby to devise more ambitious creations such as johnnycakes, spoonbread, and Indian pudding. The flour from wheat remained scarce throughout the country's formative years. This suggests why cornmeal, native and attainable, appears frequently—by itself in combination with flour—in the various recipes for Colonial breads.

Suffice to say that corn became as universally accepted by the American people as it was by the Indian tribes throughout the continent. Today, corn-on-the-cob maintains prestige as a favorite vegetable as does fresh, frozen, and canned corn in other styles. At the same time, the American-made corn flake stands out in its role as a breakfast cereal that traces its ancestry almost to the Mayflower.

The Indians of the Northeast grew a profusion of pumpkin and squash and had long since discovered a way to claim the sweet sap from the maple tree. But it was the imaginative Colonial housewife who recognized the possibilities that maple syrup offered for sweetening and flavor, and who found that pumpkin could provide the makings for a marvelous pie.

Our pies easily classify as one of the American traditions. The saying "As American as a piece of pie" is far from wrong. In this country pies are different. Natives entertain a certain attitude toward pie—partly fondness, partly pride—that just does not exist anywhere else.

True, other nations have their tarts and flans. And we know that the English enjoyed a version of mincemeat pie long before Tudor times. Still, none of these measures up to pie in American terms.

We cannot honestly lay claim to the invention of pie. But generations of American cooks deserve credit for the development of this delicacy to its present form. Pie-making challenged their creativity, artistry, and skill. Their imaginative efforts resulted in the quality of pastry, decorative touches, and the variety of fillings that we know today.

Flaky crust is one of the aspects that set American pies apart. Many believe that the Pennsylvania Dutch of early days were responsible for its development. Their culinary interests led them to improve on recipes brought from the homeland, and prompted them to experiment with their ample supplies of rendered lard.

Be that as it may, many of our pies do stem from New England or the Pennsylvania Dutch region. As the country grew, variety took on new dimensions according to the fruit and other pie materials indigenous to the new areas. Today's selections include cream pies and custards, pecan pies and chiffons, and still another offspring filled with ice cream. There are pies with two crusts, others with one; pies topped with streusel crumbs, fancy cutouts of pastry or swirls of meringue. It would take many a page to describe the enormous family of American pies.

Cooking and eating out-of-doors are another authentic part of the American way of life. The tradition of clambakes, barbecues, and other open-air feasts goes back a long way. For years they have been associated with group celebrations and used as a drawing-card to round up a large attendance at rallies, dedications, reunions, and similar outdoor affairs.

Clambakes typify the New England cookout. It involves cooking an assemblage of food items in a pit over hot stones. The menu usually includes lobster, chicken, ears of corn, and potatoes in addition to clams. Almost always, watermelon tops off the meal.

Familiar to everyone, the barbecue has a variety of meanings. It still applies to large outdoor feasts for one or more thousand people. But it also includes less backbreaking, modern applications that are better suited to smaller groups that can be served indoors as well as outside. It has to do with meat, poultry, or fish cooked over hot coals, either on a taut netting on a spit or within a covered pit. It also refers to special equipment used for this type of cookery and to the sauce that seasons or accompanies the food.

Newer interpretations permit taking advantage of the broiler and oven and allow introducing the sauce in a variety of ways. One procedure calls for braising the pieces of meat or poultry, using the barbecue sauce as liquid. Another prescribes broiling to brown the item, then basting with sauce, and continuing to broil and baste until the food is done. A third technique cooks the meat by itself and handles the sauce as an accompaniment.

Barbecue sauces are often based on catsup or some other form of tomato. They go from there to take on accents of horseradish, mustard, lemon, hot-pepper seasoning, and so on. Some hint of Mexican inspiration with chili, oregano, vinegar, and garlic. Others evidence an Oriental influence by combining such ingredients as ginger root, brown sugar, and soy. Still others include smoke-flavored salt or liquid smoke to simulate the taste that would come from an open fire.

Biscuits Go Back to the Revolution

As a nation, Americans are singularly fond of hot biscuits and other "quick" breads rarely seen in other parts of the world. Old records show that freshly baked biscuits were eaten as bread at the time of the American Revolution or even before. The event of the shortcake is not as well documented. But the writings of Roger Williams (the founder of Providence) reveal his wonderment at the profusion of wild strawberries that grew in the area. He goes on to tell that the Indians crushed them and mixed them with meal to make a strawberry bread. Goodness knows what that "bread" was like. But it may have held the idea that inspired some adventuresome pioneer cook to spoon berries over biscuits for the creation of our great American love, strawberry shortcake.

Many fruits grew naturally in this country when the land was new. Cranberries, for example, accompanied the turkey on that first Thanksgiving. From native species of grapes were developed our own Concord grape. Unlike European varieties, this hardy blue-black, slip-skin grape can adapt to almost any soil and withstand the abuse of cold winter weather. Americans are partial to its flavor found in many forms—grape juice, jelly, and preserves.

American inventiveness continues on. The ubiquitous ice cream cone came into being in 1904 and the Waldorf Salad but a few years before. The first ice cream cone was made during the St. Louis fair when a waffle vendor came to the rescue of a nearby ice cream stand that ran out of dishes. The enterprising vendor rolled one of his thin, wafer-like waffles into the shape of a cone. As it cooled it became firm and made a "dish" for ice cream that was good—and fun—to eat.

Credit for the creation of Waldorf Salad goes to Oscar Tschirky, who was maitre d' hotel of the Waldorf Hotel at the time it opened in New York City. The recipe first appears in the 1896 *Cookbook by "Oscar" Of The Waldorf*. It called for diced, unpeeled red apples, diced celery, and mayonnaise. Walnuts, generally regarded as a part of the original recipe, were actually added at some later date.

The nuts are still omitted by some. In their place may be added plumped raisins, pineapple chunks, halved and seeded grapes, julienne strips of dates, diced canned peaches, or segments of orange. Still another version of this salad calls for sprinkling portions with shredded sharp cheddar cheese. The typical American concoction lends itself easily to variations.

Christians vs. witches and the devil took firm root in New England folklore. Early settlers found evidence of providence in the new land's food from forest and shore. Hardships merely tested settlers' conviction and courage.

Delaware, Algonquin, Narraganset, and other Indian tribes aided the colonists. Maize was grown in patches with pumpkins and squash. Tomatoes came from the "weeds" found in those patches. Turkeys roamed the woods nearby and provided colonists with sport as they hunted them to shoot for food. Deer and other animals provided meat for the first New Englanders.

Clambakes—with lobsters, clams, maize, and sweet potatoes—became a new art in the culinary lives of colonists.

Succotash, made from dried beans and parched corn, was a staple in Colonial diets. The ground maize, or corn, was used for Indian pudding, corn bread, and hoe cakes.

Hoe cakes were usually a last resort to ward off hunger. Enough water was stirred into cornmeal to make a paste, which was cooked on a piece of metal, such as a hoe, and held over the fire until brown.

Cranberry bogs flourished in the Massachusetts Bay Colony; cranberries are still cultivated between New Bedford and Boston. The tart berries were cooked with meats. Later settlers learned to dilute the juice and add sugar to make a cranberry beverage. Some attribute the long lives of "Yankees" to their eating of cranberries, rich in vitamin C.

Tea, Symbol of Civilization

Sugar and tea were precious commodities brought by ship. Maple sugar provided makeshift sweetening for mush and breads. Tea, of course, was a symbol of civilization—together with the use of knives, forks, and spoons as tableware.

As trade between colonies grew, and the Portuguese settled along the Massachusetts coast to fish, the life-style of colonists centered more on commerce and "society." No laws regulated who could eat thin soup and who must eat thick soup, but wooden trenchers and sorghum remained earmarks of frontier life and hard times.

Swine were imported, and the Dutch settled on the edge of New England. Spicy pork dishes became an exotic treat—but were considered "foreign" by true New Englanders.

An English merchant family, the Cabots, fished for cod in the Grand Banks off Newfoundland. Eventually, the Cabots, the cod, and beans from Indian-taught colonists' fields all arrived in Boston.

The Irish moved into the Boston area along with the Italians. Potatoes greeted them. Long before, Sir Francis Drake took the first potatoes to Europe; other sailing ships brought them to New England where they flourished far from their origins in the Andes Mountains of Peru.

Hoe cakes and wooden trenchers gave way to steamed brown bread and china plates. Whaling flourished; ladies used whalebone stays and needles, lamps burned whale oil. Men trapped lobsters and fished for cod, haddock, and scallops. Tales of witches and the devil gave way to stories of the shrewd Yankee peddler and men who went "down to the sea in ships."

White House Menu Specialities in Mid-Century

Food ideas that governed menu making in the White House a bit later (about 1850) were revealed in *The White House Cook Book*, written by Mrs. F. L. Gillette and Hugo Ziemann, who had been a steward at The White House. Their recommendations for the proper sauce to accompany some frequently served entrees were:

SAUCES AND DRESSINGS.

With roast goose: apple sauce, cranberry sauce, grape or currant jelly.

With boiled fresh mackerel: stewed gooseberries.

With boiled blue fish: white cream sauce, lemon sauce.

With broiled shad: mushroom sauce, parsley or egg sauce.

With fresh salmon: green peas, cream sauce.

Pickles are good with all roast meats, and in fact are suitable accompaniments to all kinds of meats in general.

Spinach is the proper accompaniment to veal; green peas to lamb.

Lemon juice makes a very grateful addition to nearly all the insipid members of the fish kingdom. Slices of lemon cut into very small dice, and stirred into drawn butter, and allowed to come to the boiling point, served with fowls, is a fine accompaniment.

Other suggestions from the same source:

VEGETABLES APPROPRIATE TO DIFFERENT DISHES.

Potatoes are good with all meats. With fowls they are nicest mashed. Sweet potatoes are most appropriate with roast meats, as also are onions, winter squash, cucumbers, and asparagus.

Carrots, parsnips, turnips, greens, and cabbage are generally eaten with boiled meat, and corn, beets, peas, and beans are appropriate to either boiled or roasted meat.

Mashed turnip is good with roast pork and with boiled meats. Tomatoes are good with almost every kind of meat, especially with roasts.

WARM DISHES FOR BREAKFAST.

The following list of hot breakfast dishes may be of assistance in knowing what to provide for the comfortable meal called breakfast.

Broiled beef steak, broiled chops, broiled chicken, broiled fish, broiled quail on toast, fried pork tenderloins, fried pig's feet, fried oysters, fried clams, fried liver and bacon, fried chops, fried pork, ham and eggs fried, veal cutlets, breaded sausages, fricasseed tripe, fricasseed kidneys, turkey or chicken hash, corn beef hash, beef croquettes, codfish balls, creamed codfish, stewed meats on toast, poached eggs on toast, omelettes, eggs boiled plain, and eggs cooked in any of the various styles.

VEGETABLES FOR BREAKFAST.

Potatoes in any of the various modes of cooking, also stewed tomatoes, stewed corn, raw radishes, cucumbers sliced, tomatoes sliced raw, water cress, lettuce.

To be included with the breakfast dishes: oatmeal mush, cracked wheat, hominy or corn-meal mush, these with cream, milk, and sugar, or syrup.

RAISED BUCKWHEAT CAKES.

Take a small crock or large earthen pitcher, put into it a quart of warm water or half water and milk, one heaping teaspoonful of salt; then stir in as much buckwheat flour as will thicken it to rather a stiff batter; lastly add half a cup of yeast; make it smooth, cover it up warm to rise over night; in the morning, add a small, level teaspoonful of soda, dissolved in a little warm water; this will remove any sour taste, if any, and increase the lightness.

Not a few object to eating buckwheat, as its tendency is to thicken the blood, and also to produce constipation; this can be remedied by making the batter one-third corn-meal and two-thirds buckwheat, which makes the cakes equally as good. Many prefer them in this way.

GERMAN FRITTERS.

Take slices of stale bread cut in rounds,

or stale cake; fry them in hot lard, like crullers, to a *light* brown. Dip each slice when fried in boiling milk, to remove the grease; drain quickly, dust with powdered sugar, or spread with preserves. Pile on a hot plate, and serve. Sweet wine sauce poured over them is very nice.

HOMINY FRITTERS.

Take one pint of hot boiled hominy, two eggs, half a teaspoonful of salt, and a tablespoonful of flour; thin it a little with cold milk; when cold, add a teaspoonful of baking-powder, mix thoroughly, drop tablespoonfuls of it into hot fat, and fry to a delicate brown.

PARSNIP FRITTERS.

Take three or four good-sized parsnips. Boil them until tender. Mash and season with a little butter, a pinch of salt, and a slight sprinkling of pepper. Have ready a plate with some sifted flour on it. Drop a tablespoonful of the parsnip in the flour and roll it about until well-coated and formed into a ball. When you have a sufficient number ready, drop them into boiling drippings or lard, as you would a fritter; fry a delicate brown, and serve hot. Do not put them in a covered dish, for that would steam them and deprive them of their crispness, which is one of their great charms.

These are also very good fried in a frying-pan with a small quantity of lard and butter mixed, turning them over so as to fry both sides brown.

COOKED MEAT FOR MINCE PIES.

In order to succeed in having good mince pie, it is quite essential to cook the meat properly, so as to retain its juices and strength of flavor.

Select four pounds of lean beef, the neck piece is as good as any; wash it, and put it into a kettle with just water enough to cover it; take off the scum as it reaches the boiling point, add hot water from time to time, until it is tender, then season with salt and pepper; take off the cover and let it boil until almost dry, or until the juice has boiled back into the meat. When it looks as though it is beginning to fry in its own juice, it is time to take up, and set aside to get cold, which should be done the day before needed.

Next day, when the mince-meat is being made, the bones, gristle, and stringy bits should be well picked out before chopping.

MINCE PIES. No. 1.

The "Astor House," some years ago, was *famous* for its "mince pies." The chief pastry cook at that time, by request, published the recipe. I find that those who partake of it never fail to speak in laudable terms of the superior excellence of this recipe, when strictly followed.

Four pounds of lean boiled beef, chopped fine, twice as much of chopped green tart apples, one pound of chopped suet, three pounds of raisins, seeded, two pounds of currants picked over, washed and dried, half a pound of citron, cut up fine, one pound of brown sugar, one quart of cooking molasses, two quarts of sweet cider, one pint of boiled cider, one tablespoonful of salt, one tablespoonful of pepper, one tablespoonful of mace, one tablespoonful of allspice, and four tablespoonfuls of cinnamon, two grated nutmegs, one tablespoonful of cloves; mix thoroughly and warm it on the range, until heated through. Remove from the fire and when nearly cool, stir in a pint of good brandy, and one pint of Madeira wine.

Put mince-meat into a crock, cover it tightly, and set it in a cold place where it will not freeze, but keep perfectly cold. Will keep good all winter.

—*Chef de Cuisine, Astor House, N.Y.*

SYLLABUB.

One quart of rich milk or cream, a cupful of wine, half a cupful of sugar; put the sugar and wine into a bowl, and the milk lukewarm in a separate vessel. When the sugar is dissolved in the wine, pour the milk in, holding it high; pour it back and forth until it is frothy. Grate nutmeg over it.

CREAM FOR FRUIT.

This recipe is an excellent substitute for pure cream, to be eaten on fresh berries and fruit.

One cupful of sweet milk; heat it until boiling. Beat together the whites of two eggs, a tablespoonful of white sugar, and a piece of butter the size of a nutmeg. Now add half a cupful of cold milk and a teaspoonful of corn-starch; stir well together until very light and smooth, then add it to the boiling milk; cook it until it thickens; it must not boil. Set it aside to cool. It should be of the consistency of real fresh cream. Serve in a creamer.

STRAWBERRY SPONGE.

One quart of strawberries, half a package of gelatine, one cupful and a half of water, one cupful of sugar, the juice of a lemon, the whites of four eggs. Soak the gelatine for two hours in half a cupful of the water. Mash the strawberries, and add half the sugar to them. Boil the remainder of the sugar and the water gently twenty minutes. Rub the strawberries through a sieve. Add the gelatine to the boiling syrup and take from the fire immediately; then add the strawberries. Place in a pan of ice water, and beat five minutes. Add the whites of eggs, and beat until the mixture begins to thicken. Pour in the molds and set away to harden. Serve with sugar and cream. Raspberry and blackberry sponges are made in the same way.

BAKED CORN-MEAL PUDDING, WITH EGGS.

One small cupful of Indian meal, one-half cupful of wheat flour stirred together with cold milk. Scald one pint of milk, and stir the mixture in it and cook until thick; then thin with cold milk to the consistency of batter, not very thick; add half a cupful of sugar, half a cupful of molasses, two eggs, two tablespoonfuls of butter, a little salt, a tablespoonful of mixed cinnamon and nutmeg, two-thirds of a teaspoonful of soda added just before putting it into the oven. Bake two hours. After baking pudding for half an hour, stir it up thoroughly, then finish baking.

Serve it up hot, eat it with wine sauce, or with butter and syrup.

SWEET-POTATO PUDDING.

To a large sweet potato, weighing two pounds, allow half a pound of sugar, half a pound of butter, one gill of sweet cream, one gill of strong wine or brandy, one grated nutmeg, a little lemon peel, and four eggs. Boil the potato until thoroughly done, mash up fine, and while hot add the sugar and butter. Set aside to cool while you beat the eggs light, and add the seasoning last. Line tin plates with puff-paste, and pour in the mixture. Bake in a moderate but regularly heated oven. When the puddings are drawn from the fire, cover the top with thinly sliced bits of preserved citron or quince marmalade. Strew the top thickly with granulated white sugar, and serve, with the addition of a glass of rich milk for each person at table.

ROLEY POLEY PUDDING. (Apple.)

Peel, core, and slice sour apples; make a rich biscuit dough, or raised biscuit dough may be used if rolled thinner; roll not quite half an inch thick, lay the slices on the paste, roll up, tuck in the ends, prick deeply with a fork, lay it in a steamer, and steam hard for an hour and three-quarters. Or, wrap it in a pudding-cloth well floured; tie the ends, baste up the sides, plunge into boiling water, and boil continually an hour and a half, perhaps more. Stoned cherries, dried fruits, or any kind of berries, fresh or dried, may be used.

ROSE BRANDY.
(For Cakes and Puddings)

Gather the leaves of roses while the dew is on them, and as soon as they open, put them into a wide-mouthed bottle, and when the bottle is full, pour in the best of fourth proof French brandy.

It will be fit for use in three or four weeks, and may be frequently replenished. It is sometimes considered preferable to wine as a flavoring to pastries and pudding sauces.

American Culinary Art Aloft

Special menu promotions have helped airlines promote Bicentennial travel. United Airlines was one of the first to tie menus in with the Bicentennial.

United's Bicentennial menu series toasts the culinary art of America by taking recipes representative of American regional and national history and life-styles into the skies. Travelers in the "friendly skies" will be treated to these American favorites until the end of 1976.

Extensive research into the history of American foods was required before the program began. United appointed a task force of four Food Services Division officials, four executive chefs, and Trader Vic (Victor Jules Bergeron, longtime food consultant for the airline) to do the job.

Some of the group's findings were surprising. It seems that all was not tea, honey, and steak-time in the Revolutionary War period. Authentic Revolutionary War menus were more likely to feature boiled beef and steamed wheat, the "lean-years" meals for our nation's founding fathers and mothers. Obviously, today's airline passenger, no matter how dedicated to the Bicentennial theme, would not accept this fare.

Going back to the think-tank, the task force chose dishes that would celebrate all 200 years of American cookery. They drew ideas from many ethnic and regional groups.

Recipes were researched, developed, and taste-tested mainly in San Francisco, with some testing done in Chicago headquarters. A distinguished panel of United's executive chefs, John Wolfsheimer of San Francisco, Duri Arquisch of Salt Lake City, Edwin Wirz, and Herman Rothweiler of Chicago, directed the tasting and sampling.

Under their guidance, the task force narrowed 100 entrees down to nine. They were chosen not only on the basis of taste, eye appeal, uniqueness, and passenger acceptance, but also for operational and profit-oriented reasons.

"These items were selected for their application to in-flight service, practicality in freezing, market availability of some menu ingredients, and reconstitution ease," explained Robert Arnold, director of planning.

"We had to make sure that none of the items would up our cost parameters. Of course, that doesn't mean that we won't spend a little bit beyond the parameters to satisfy our customers!"

The Bicentennial entrees chosen include chicken creole, cowboys' barbecue beef, roast turkey stuffed with sage and apple dressing, Joe Booker stew, Cornish game hen Madeira with wild rice, Mike Fink's Mississippi jambalaya, Long Island duckling with wild rice and orange sauce, "smiling" beef stew, and scallop and noodle "pye."

Some items, because of cost, are not available in coach class. These more expensive entrees include the duckling, Cornish hen and jambalaya.

Supplementing the meals are "give-away" menus and inserts explaining the recipes' origins or historical points concerning the food or the region where it originated. United did not spare humor or creativity in developing these supplementary public-relations tools. For instance, menu covers reproduce original art, commissioned by United, depicting American scenes. Menu inserts are full of bits of the historical trivia and tales around which America was built.

United has also incorporated new methods of packaging these Bicentennial dishes. Stews are served in ceramic crocks (also used for regular pot pies), and Cornish hens arrive under clear, permanentware, bell-dome covers. Out of 51,000 meals United serves daily, about 6,000 are Bicentennial meals. Selection depends entirely on United's local operations' decisions.

United does not make any Bicentennial entrees in its own flight kitchens. Outside suppliers make the items according to specs approved by headquarters, based on the original task force chefs' recipes.

"There are no substitutions in any menu ingredient without our office's prior approval," states Arnold. "But that doesn't mean that we haven't instituted some changes already. We have modified some recipes for more eye appeal, water-release factors, maybe adding sauce."

United also makes available to all its flight kitchens a recipe book, newly revised, with a Bicentennial idea section. This lists recipes for menu accompaniments, such as breads and appetizers, all with an historical theme.

First Steps to Serving Nation on the Run

Institutions is grateful to Jack Welch, emeritus professor of foodservice and lodging management, for this special letter that looks back at the restaurant business at the turn of the century. In his letter, he takes us to the birth of the National Restaurant Association. He also offers some history of the fast-food chain based on some of his original photos of one of the very first.

Taken about 1902, pictures show the interior and exterior of "Boston Lunch No. 1" in Des Moines, Iowa, owned in partnership by Henry Scherer of Buffalo, New York, and my father, the late John W. Welch.

Together these men conceived the idea of a national chain of dairy lunches. Scherer would operate the eastern division, with headquarters in Buffalo, and my father the western division, with headquarters in Des Moines. The partnership was dissolved by Scherer's untimely death shortly after father had expanded the western division to Omaha and Lincoln, Nebraska, and to St. Joseph, Missouri. My father took over the operation of the western division as sole proprietor; but eventually he gave up the operations in Des Moines, Lincoln, and St. Joseph, as they required too much traveling on his part, and concentrated on the Omaha operation. By 1919, the Omaha operations consisted of 10 restaurants and a commissary.

Even at that time the restaurants seem to have had a "drive-in" feature, as is shown by the horses pictured outside the restaurant.

Father was an early member of Rotary International and was, for a number of years, chairman of the Round Table for Restaurant Operators at the International Conventions of that club. It was because of his wide acquaintance with the most prominent operators in the nation that the Kansas City Restaurant Association asked him to call a meeting there in 1919 for the purpose of founding the National Restaurant Association—badly needed then to solve problems developing from the aftermath of World War I and the disaster of Prohibition.

The meeting was held at the old Coates House in Kansas City. Here the NRA was born, and father was elected its first president. Myron Green of Kansas City was elected secretary.

A rash of "dairy lunches" developed between the late 1890s and the 1920s. The Boston Lunch, the Baltimore Lunch, John R. Thompsons', the Waldorf Systems and many others laid the foundation for chain restaurant—and later franchise—operations as we know them today.

As an aside, I have a strong feeling that the women of America had a lot to do with their popularity, since prior to prohibition their chief competitor was the "free lunch" in the corner saloon, and the dairy lunches served no intoxicating liquors. There is no record of Carrie Nation pole-axing a dairy lunch. I can envision her cohorts exhorting their menfolk to eat at the dairy lunches when they had to eat away from home to avoid contact with the "Demon Rum."

Prohibition sounded the death knell for the downtown areas, which were the stronghold of both saloons and the dairy lunches, although we were slow to recognize the full import of what was happening. Prior to 1919, for instance, Welch's Restaurants were 24-hour operations and did one-third of their sales volume between 7 p.m. and 6 a.m. When I made an operations analysis for my father in 1925, we were not taking in enough money between 8 p.m. and 6 a.m. to cover the night payroll!

Prohibition and the vast proliferation of automobiles following World War I—and the "dollar-down-dollar-when-we-catch-'em" credit expansion which was responsible for that proliferation (and, unless I miss my guess which is at the bottom of our present troubles, also)—had emptied the evening streets of the cities. Following close on its heels was the growth of radio, then television, which knocked out the last remaining evening activity—the theatre, both the movies and productions on the legitimate stage. Whatever evening activity remained centered in the speakeasy and suburban "road houses." Except in a few major cities like New York, Chicago, New Orleans, San Francisco, and Los Angeles, night life in the downtown areas was dead—and still is!

As a result of my 1925 operations analysis, I recommended to my father that we establish

American ingenuity when applied to native foods produces masterpieces. One irresistible example of America's culinary contributions to the world, is Fresh Strawberry Shortcake made with hot, feathery, buttered biscuits, and topped with whipped cream.

TIDEWATER

Right: Food at The Greenbrier, White Sulphur Springs, Va. is a legend in itself—historic favorites of the Tidewater prepared and served at their finest. Modern methods assure superior performance. A master detail sheet, with appropriate memos for each department, is drawn up for every scheduled food function. As a result, delighted guests are assured.

Below: Fieldstone fireplace, flanked by old cranberry scoops, dominates the dining room of McGrath's Restaurant, Plymouth, Mass. Waitresses carry small "beepers" in their pockets which chefs use to signal when orders are ready. Ernest McGrath finished the interior of this restaurant himself, "with the help of my wife Rose and a good carpenter."

NEW ENGLAND

Below: Sodas and sundaes rank with salads as America's important contributions to the world's cuisine. The banana split with its infinite possibilities for flavor combinations is probably the most exciting of the ice cream concoctions pictured here but well garnished sodas and sundaes have a large following, too.

Below. At The Lemon Tree, Lancaster, Pa., the cuisine is characterized as a "melting pot," though it is of an elegant order as it is drawn from fine dishes of all nations. (For a picture of the Windsor chairs and old farm implements used at The Lemon Tree as decorative elements, see p. 67.)

(For a picture of the Windsor chairs and old farm implements used at The Lemon Tree as decorative elements, see p. 67.)

Below: King's Arm Tavern, Colonial Williamsburg, a favorite dining place since Revolutionary times is noted especially for its Cream of Peanut Soup and Greengage Plum Ice Cream. Food is served by student waiters from the College of William and Mary who wear authentic costumes copied from pictures of 18th century servants.

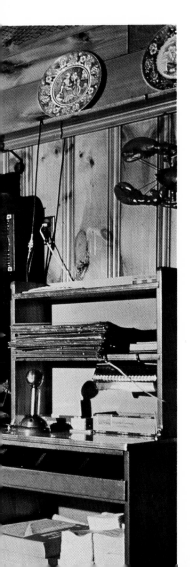

Right: Groups visiting Colonial Williamsburg enjoy menus like the one assembled here: Sally Lunn, baked in a turban mold, snap beans with peanuts, thick slices of rare prime rib, baked potatoes, and colorful arrangements of fresh fruit. Unusual serving dishes and platters are another element that sets Williamsburg cuisine apart.

Below: Peach Pie in an uncommon one-crust version topped with pastry stars is an effective item for a dessert display or for cart service. Pastry bells can be substituted.

An American invention that has become a menu classic, Waldorf Salad can be prepared in many variations of the original made-for-each-other combination of apples, celery, and walnuts.

Above: Current interpretations of America's adopted favorite, the barbecue, are easier to do. An example is the Herbed Lemon Barbecued Chicken, product, a cleverly seasoned sauce added to the chicken as it broils.

Above: New England Boiled Dinner, celebration of ingredients that kept without refrigeration through early winters, has as many admirers today, probably more since it appears less frequently. Presented as a well-seasoned combination of potatoes, carrots, onions, parsnips, turnips or rutabaga, cabbage, and corned beef, it can be counted on to sell out.

small, limited-menu restaurants at the intersections of the main highways on the fringes of Omaha, with ample parking facilities for cars—sort of a forerunner for today's "drive-in"! Even though I was careful to recommend only limited-menu restaurants—carefully avoiding any alcoholic connotation—my father refused to operate what he termed a "roadhouse." Had he followed my suggestions, we would have "sewed up" practically all of what is now the most valuable suburban commercial property in Omaha, perhaps also developing something along the McDonald's line in so doing. But, men like my father and Myron Green were good, solid, law-abiding, religious citizens to whom even the appearance of "evil" was anathema. May God rest their pious and straight-laced souls.

Sic semper gloria mundi!

Spices in Early America

In ancient times spices often played what we moderns would consider an extraordinary role in man's destiny. The search for better routes to the spice-rich lands of the East led to many of history's great explorations. Wars were fought over the spice islands. Spice fortunes financed much of the Renaissance in art.

Spices were important in the early life of our country, too—the daily life as well as the history and economy. As we prepare to celebrate our Bicentennial, the American Spice Trade Association offers the following compendium of historical glimpses of spices in early times.

Before discussing the Colonial era, it is worth remembering that:

*Spices were one of the prime objects of Columbus' voyages and thus the discovery of America.

*Columbus did not discover a shorter route to the Orient, but he did discover new spices in the Western World; e.g., red pepper and allspice.

*New York harbor was discovered by another sailor looking for a quicker route to the spice islands: Verrazano.

*Ponce de Leon's fountain of youth, in his words, "hath odour and savour of all spices...and they that dwell there and drink often of the well, they never have sickness and they seem always young." Result: discovery of Florida.

PEPPER AND THE FEDERAL BUDGET—Incredible as it sounds, there was a time in the years just after the Revolution when the duties on black pepper imports provided a significant share of the U. S. federal income! By the close of 1800, the Salem (Mass.) Federal Customs House had collected over $3 million in duties, much of it contributed by pepper from Sumatra. This was equal to about 5 percent of the average annual expenditures of the Federal Government during that period.

EARLY AMERICAN PEPPER MILLIONAIRES—Elihu Yale, who has a great university named for him, is said to have been the first American-born millionaire. Elias Hasket Derby of Salem, Mass., has also been referred to as "America's first millionaire." These two 18th century millionaires both made much of their fortunes in pepper trading. Yale started as a clerk of the East India Company in Madras. Elias Derby's ships sailed on 24,000-mile round trips to Sumatra to buy pepper directly without having to pay the middlemen.

FIRST PEPPER VOYAGE—The brig Cadet, Jonathan Carnes, master, returned to Salem (Mass.) in 1780 after a two year voyage to Sumatra, marking the opening of U. S. direct spice trading in the Orient. Profits of the voyage, 700 percent.

1,000 SPICE VOYAGES—Between 1780 and 1873, U. S. ships made nearly 1,000 spice voyages to the Far East returning with millions of pounds of spices to American ports. In 1805, re-exports of pepper alone (mostly to Europe) reached 7 million pounds.

EVERYDAY SPICES WERE PRECIOUS—Spices were highly valued commodities in 18th century America: vital to food preparation, essential as preservatives of food, and prized as medicines. Because of their close connection with medicine, and because they were so valuable, they were often sold in apothecary shops, such as the one now exhibited in Colonial Williamsburg, Va.

THE NECESSARY MORTAR AND PESTLE—Most tropical spices (cinnamon, cloves, pepper, nutmeg) were available to some degree in 18th century coastal cities, but were usually sold whole, to be cracked or ground at home. Whole spices retain their flavor much better and, as packaging was not refined and transportation was so slow, the ground spices would have lost much of their aroma by the time they had reached the ultimate consumer. That is why we find so many early-American spice mills, graters, and mortars and pestles in museums and, occasionally, in antique shops.

PHILADELPHIA PEPPERPOT SOUP SAVED THE DAY— Right in the worst part of the Revolutionary War, the story goes, Washington's soldiers were so hungry and depressed that their general asked his cook, a Philadelphian, to make a big pot of stew or soup, something that would be filling. There was little for the cook to put in the pot, though he did have tripe, some veal bones with much of the meat missing, potatoes, onions, and a fairly good collection of spices. He seasoned his soup with bay leaf, thyme, marjoram, parsley, red pepper, whole allspice, and cloves. Lovers of Philadelphia Pepperpot Soup still declare that is what won the war!

"MEETIN' SEEDS"—Fennel, dill, and caraway seeds, much grown in Colonial gardens, were called "meetin' seeds" because people brought them to church to nibble on during long sermons.

SWEET LAND OF LIBER-TEA—China tea was as popular as it was heavily taxed in America before the Revolution. Patriots, however, soon found they could brew delicious herb teas from mints, sage, and other garden herbs. Mace, cinnamon, lemon, rum, or honey were added. Patriotic news sheets of the period published long lists of recipes for these "liberty teas."

A NEW "TEA" FOR CHINA—One of the so-called "liberty teas" (herb teas) of the Revolutionary era which became extremely popular was sage tea. Shrewd Yankees even sold the Chinese on the idea to the point that when trade was resumed with China, the Orientals happily exchanged three pounds of tea for each pound of sage!

CALIFORNIA MUSTARD TRAILS— Padres along the Mission Trails, making their way through the unmapped 18th century California wilderness, trickled pocketsful of quick-growing mustard seeds as they explored. Within weeks, strips of golden mustard flowers assured them they were on the homeward-bound trail.

JEFFERSON INTRODUCED VANILLA— Among his many achievements, Thomas Jefferson introduced vanilla beans to this country. He had lived in France as minister to King Louis XVI and there tasted all manner of delectable, vanilla-flavored desserts. Since Jefferson loved entertaining, the 200 vanilla beans he brought home with him lasted less than a year. Among his papers is a letter he hurriedly wrote to a French friend begging him to send more beans. He explained "It (the vanilla bean) is unknown here."

FROM MARTHA TO GEORGE, WITH LOVE—Martha Washington's present to the General for the Christmas of 1776 was an amply spiced fruit cake. Appropriately, it arrived in Trenton on December 26 to help celebrate Washington's resounding Christmas day defeat of the British. Her recipe for this large cake called for 4 grated nutmegs; 1 tablespoon powdered mace; 1 tablespoon powdered cloves, and 2 tablespoons powdered cinnamon.

A SACK FULL OF SIMPLES—The colonial dames of Virginia had great faith in a tipple called Lady Hewitt's Water. The recipe called for 72 common and uncommon herbs and spices, the whole covered with sherry-sack and distilled. "There never was a better cordial in case of the greatest illness, two or three spoonfuls almost revive from death," said one early American herbal.

"T'AIN'T SO!" SAY CONNECTICUT YAN- KEES—The most famous American spice anecdote is that of the "wooden nutmeg," from which the state of Connecticut received its first nickname. The inference was that shrewd traders substituted wooden versions at a time when nutmegs were especially high priced. The truth, say loyal Connecticut-ers, is that a New London grocer simply whittled some nutmegs one day to pass the time and his intent was mistaken. The misnomer was finally put to rest when Connecticut officially became the "Constitution State" a few years ago.

A "TUSSIE MUSSIE"—The early American name for a bouquet of sweet herbs was "Tussie Mussie." Such a bouquet—and it is very colorful—arranged on a counter in the center of a table set for a party with early American glass and china, is bound to be a great success, a real conversation piece.

THE FIRST SPICE MILL—America's first commercial spice-grinding firm was established in Boston in 1821. Very possibly our first "convenience food," pre-ground and packaged spices, saved time and labor for early 19th century homemakers.

PEPPERCORN RENTS—Illustrating the great value of spices in early times was the "one peppercorn" annual fee for two acres of land rented to Millville (Pa.) Quakers by John W. Eves in 1794. The contract runs for 999 years—until 2793.

AMERICAN SAFFRON—Saffron, today our most costly imported spice, was grown locally in Pennsylvania for a time in the 18th century, primarily because the early German settlers prized a saffron-spiced breakfast cake, called "Swingfelder Cake."

CHILI POWDER INVENTED—No one is positive about the exact origin of chili powder, but it is believed that early 19th century English settlers in Texas developed it to simulate Mexican-style dishes, just as their countrymen had approximated native dishes in India with curry powder.

SAN FRANCISCO'S MINT—In the 18th century, long before it became San Francisco, that town was called El Paraga de Yerba Buena, "place of the good herb," because of its luxuriant mint.

CHARITABLE SPICES—"By the Order of the Common Council of Trustees for Establishing the Colony of Georgia in America...each person sent upon the Charity for his Maintenance in the Colony for one year shall have (among meats and other foods) 9 ounces of spice." Dated 1735.

NEW ORLEANS CUISINE—When France ceded Louisiana Territory to Spain in 1763, it laid the foundation for New Orleans cuisine: the French, with their love of herbs, shallots, onions; the Spanish, with a penchant for paprika, chilies, tropical spices, and herbs; Indians, who introduced gumbo file (sassafras powder); Africans, who brought "bene seeds" (sesame) and a taste for hot peppers.

IMPORTED SPICES—Robert Beverly, early 18th century Virginia historian, wrote about Colonial living: "...they have a great Plenty and Variety of Provisions for their Table; and as for Spicery, and other things that the Country don't produce, they have constant supplies of 'em from England..."

Six Special Lunches Help Children Celebrate

To celebrate the 200th birthday of the USA, schools, daycare centers, pediatrics wards—any foodservice operation catering to a young, captive audience—can now easily set up six very special American lunch parties. Each is based on a different event in U.S. history.

Each event has a menu and corresponding nutrition lesson for the classroom (or for children from about 10 through 14 years of age to enjoy on their own). Each theme kit provides artwork for menu covers and ideas for costumes, decorations, music, and games. All help promote the lunch.

The kits for the six lunches use such themes as the Boston Tea Party, the Alamo, the Gold Rush. They are provided by a group of advisory boards working with the Nutrition Action Committee of the California School Food Service Association. Sponsoring the program and making kits available to operators on a first-come basis are the California Milk Advisory Board, the California Raisin Advisory Board, the Potato Board, and the Cling Peach Advisory Board.

This same group has previously sponsored similar ventures promoting holiday lunches. The programs were enormously popular, having been adopted by approximately 70,000 schools and instititions in one year.

Each menu is a type "A" lunch.

The nutrition package includes the cover designs for six menus, six lesson plans for grades four to six, plus special adaptations of the Gold Rush and President's Table (which also have posters) for use at the junior and senior high school levels.

Menu cover samples, or masters, are simple black and white line drawings that can be reproduced in the quantities needed on the schools' duplicating or multilithing equipment. These line drawings then lend themselves to coloring in the classroom with paints or crayons. Several of the menus open up and contain amusing puzzles dealing with nutrition, as well as more serious lessons.

Several manufacturers and distributors of food products asked sponsors' permission to reprint the kits for customers, using their own identification. The American School Foodservice Assn. also supplies the kits.

Foodservice/Lodging for the Founding Fathers

TIDEWATER IS THE coastal Atlantic land from Chespeake Bay's northern end, near the mouth of the Potomac River and Jones Falls, along the Maryland shore to the James River.

This triangle was the first area colonized by the English. Until television homogenized much of American culture, the hills of Virginia and West Virginia still echoed the accents of the England of Elizabeth I.

The earliest settlers were lazy and quarrelsome. Those who survived adopted Indian foods. Maize and venison were staples of their diet. Later, Lord Baltimore sent two ships of carefully picked colonists.

Pigs soon ran wild, and trading began in earnest. Tobacco was planted as a cash crop. Trade in slaves joined the trade in sugar, rum, and tobacco.

Today, corn remains a dietary staple. Corn oysters or fritters, hominy, and corn bread are menu favorites.

Peanuts, for soup and as an integral part of creamed onions, are used often. Fried tomatoes, green or ripe, are also special favorites.

Molasses still flavors some dishes, especially gingerbread, or as syrup for fried mush.

Maryland blue crabs are eaten just after moulting as soft-shell crabs. Steamed crabs are layered with seaweed and a blend of spices sold as "crab boil." Hard-shelled crabs, when they weight 6 oz. or more, are eaten with gusto at crab feasts.

At such feasts the table is covered with a paper runner or newspaper. Diners get bibs and mallets with claw-crackers. Then, steamed crabs are dumped in the middle of the table. Tankards of beer are the sole accompaniment.

Virginia is noted for hams. Salt-cured or smoked until firm, these dominated the winter and spring diets of early settlers. Several 17th century diaries recorded wishes for "a good leg of mutton" instead of ham.

Terrapins were caught and used for stews. Arguments rage over the "proper" ingredients for a traditional burgoo. But Kentuckians have the edge in being more adventurous with kettle contents.

And, of course, oysters have been beloved since Tidewater folks took their first steps off the boats. Fritters, stew, and fried oysters are only a beginning. Oyster pie, a pot pie, may be an entree or first course. Scalloped oysters are a luncheon favorite. And at the oyster roast, bushels of oysters are served with only salt, pepper, and butter. Accompaniments are fried oysters, raw oysters on the half shell, and oyster stew.

Haussner's Restaurant
Baltimore, Md.

It's the busiest kitchen in Baltimore, serving more than 2,000 meals a day in the 463-seat dining room.

Haussner's, founded in 1926, plans to help celebrate the nation's Bicentennial with its own 50th anniversary. Sales are "well over $3 million," according to Frances Haussner, widow of founder William H. Haussner.

Called "Mom" by family and employees, Mrs. Haussner is in the restaurant every day to greet customers and keep in touch with operations. Her sons-in-law, Stephen George and Jerome Zaras, run the restaurant.

George manages the front of the house and Zaras does all purchasing. Family-owned, Haussner's began with German specialties made from scratch and continues that tradition to this day, along with more than 50 seafood entrees.

It takes 1-1/2 tons of flour each week for the 12 kinds of pie, five kinds of cake, and 13 other sweet goods (plus breads) served in the restaurant. A retail bakery counter in the entrance to the dining room also enjoys brisk trade.

Customers arriving on winter nights are kept warm as they line up outside by 11 heaters; that gas costs 77 cents per hour. The laundry bill is more than $80,000 annually. But profits are checked roughly by customer count.

"We keep track of costs and know when we hit our break-even point in terms of customer count per month," says George. "We want the high volume business, but we don't skimp on quality."

Meticulous records of all costs, complete inventory, customer count, and local conditions are kept. Secret of success, avows Mrs. Haussner, is "waste not."

About 50 percent of the 219 full-time staff can walk to the restaurant. Some employees are retired now; others have worked at Haussner's for 40 years. They enjoy a pension plan; medical, health, and life insurance; even paid vacations. No deductions are taken from the workers' wages for any of these "fringes."

Haussner's was designed by a local architect, Prentis Browne. Decor includes more than 650 paintings; most noteworthy are the sections of "Pantheon de la Guerre," the largest painting in the world. Numerous pieces of sculpture are on display in the nooks and archways of the big dining room. In fact, it is hard to find a bare spot. Mrs. Haussner considers the restaurant a museum for her favorite organization, the Boys Club of the Salvation Army.

Johns Hopkins Medical Institutions
Baltimore, Md.

The first teaching hospital in the United States, Johns Hopkins Medical Institutions, was set up in 1889 with a $3.5 million endowment. It has 1,000 beds; 30,000 people pass through its doors daily. A Sargent painting of the four famous founding physicians hangs in Welch Medical Library.

Classroom teaching and bedside care go hand-in-hand in a unique combination of the English "lecture education" and the German "practicum." The Flexner Report, which became the blueprint for medical schools across the land, was based on the Johns Hopkins system of teaching and practice.

And 7,500 patients, staff and visitors are fed each day. Two of the largest rotating ovens in the country are in the kitchen, reports Don Cruise, food production manager.

Hot food preparation is staffed by 21 people, with four in the bakery and eight in the salad and pantry area. Training is handled by three staff persons and the line supervisors in the Nutrition Department.

Labor costs jumped recently due to a new union contract negotiated at the end of 1974. Food preparation is a combination of "from scratch" and pre-prepared items integrated into the system.

Breakfast and lunch are offered for three hours each; dinner is served during a two-and-a-half hour period. A vending operation takes over when the cafeteria is closed.

Seafood is a popular menu feature. Two foodservice operations are run by the Women's Board, but major patient and staff foodservice is managed by ARA Food Services Company.

Various events and promotions originate

from the Nutrition Dept. Last spring saw a Mardi Gras celebration, complete with Dixieland band and employees wearing New Orleans-style costumes. During last summer, the Baltimore Orioles came in to sign autographs in the cafeteria. A "look and learn" exhibit with foods from local manufacturers is featured this winter.

"We are a community; we serve the community," sums up Ronald DeMatteo of the administrative staff. "Johns Hopkins is so large, so well known, so unique—we want to provide service and care for all who come to us."

The Greenbrier
White Sulphur Springs, W. Va.

"Life as it should be," wrote one journalist in an attempt to describe The Greenbrier. But Truman Wright, retiring vice-president and managing director, sums it up simply as, "Ladies and gentlemen serving ladies and gentlemen."

Every large property must maintain certain ideals, for resorts are like people—the character and personality of an operation is what makes it stand out from the multitude. Built in 1910-1913, The Greenbrier established characteristics of gracious service and excellent food.

Much of the decor, done by Dorothy Draper in the mid-1940s, is part of The Greenbrier personality. Service is attentive, with a one-to-one ratio of staff to guests.

Income from food sales in 1973 accounted for about 4 percent of parent company Chessie System's $1.1 billion operating revenues. And food sales were about 30 percent of gross revenue for The Greenbrier; the kitchen operates in the black as a profit center.

Executive Food Director Hermann Rusch runs the kitchen, the pastry shop, and the bakery in traditional style. He oversees 50 chefs and 25 apprentices. Minimum apprentice training takes 27 months.

Basic curriculum for the culinary apprentice and training program at The Greenbrier was developed by a committee of men who had apprenticed in the great kitchens of Europe.

The first requirements that Rusch impresses on new apprentices are, "Hours are not usual office hours. Stability of emotions is necessary."

Although Rusch is a stern taskmaster, he is fair in giving praise for outstanding work as well as criticism for sloppy work.

Wright pushed for the first bar ever opened in The Greenbrier; it paid for itself and was operating in the black by the end of the first year.

Meetings and conventions account for 80 to 85 percent of business. John C. (Jack) Horton, director of convention sales, says about 60 percent of the bookings are annual repeat business.

"We have bookings into 1999. I know we can deliver whenever I promise special service. Personnel here go out of the way to help each other," Horton says.

"All bookings come through my office," he adds. "We coordinate rooms, menus, prices, and meeting spaces. Flowers, special items (from roosters to a truckload of monkeys), and all details are handled here. At the end of a telephone conversation or visit, we can write a letter of confirmation defining everything. It's a matter of offering organization along with space and the usual services."

New Vice-President and Managing Director John Lanahan notes, "The average meeting runs three and a half days. There will be 10 to 1,100 people. We encourage guests to relax, whether they are here for a checkup at the medical clinic or for business meetings."

Colonial Williamsburg Foundation
Williamsburg, Va.

George Washington slept here. So did Patrick Henry, Thomas Jefferson, and other patriots who shaped the 13 colonies in the United States of America.

From its early 17th century beginnings, Williamsburg grew to become the capital of the Virginia Colony. It replaced Jamestown as the capital in 1699, but in 1780 the capital moved to Richmond.

In 1926, John D. Rockefeller, Jr. supported and financed restoration of the historic area of Williamsburg.

It covers 173 acres, with the College of William and Mary at the western end and the capital at the eastern end.

Colonial Williamsburg is straight out of the 18th century, with 88 restored buildings and 50 more that have been carefully rebuilt on their original sites. This was one of the earliest planned cities. It includes numerous craft shops, with artisans in 18th century costume who employ hand methods in their work.

King's Arms Tavern, favored by Revolutionary patriots, today is noted for cream of peanut soup and greengage plum ice cream. Average check is $8. Waiters are students at the College of William and Mary; they wear the garb of 18th century servants. William Cini, manager of the 210-seat operation, describes the service as modified French.

Christina Campbell, a short woman with a "little turned-up Pug nose," ran an 18th century tavern that still flourishes today. This 188-seat dining spot was a favorite of George Washington. Salmagundi Salad, similar to today's chef salad, is still on the menu, 200-plus years later. Richard Hammond, manager, reports a check average of $8 for a menu which emphasizes beef and seafood.

Josiah Chowning put up both man and beast at his "ordinary," but today's fare is only for modern man. A garden, open for summer dining, supplements the 98 indoor seats.

Minstrels entertain during dinner with 18th century ballads. Manager Allan Knaggs describes decor as, "18th century, a bit more rustic than King's Arms and Campbell's." Food here is lighter, with emphasis on sandwiches. The average check is about $6.50.

General forecasting is done yearly. Up to 17 tons of meat and 11 tons of seafood are used per year. Flatware is used at a rate of about 4,000 dozen pieces annually.

Vice-President Sebastion DiMeglio, who is also director of hotels and restaurants, says, "We use historical information and advance room reservations as a basis for forecasting. Precise records of number of meals served and menu items ordered are maintained in each restaurant on a daily basis. Chefs and managers use this information for preparation of menu items. This is a fairly accurate means of knowing how much of each menu item to prepare."

They Collected a Village

Collectors of Americana indulge themselves amassing coins, books, documents, art, autographs, and other memorabilia. Fred and Ethel Noyes moved their sights up and collected buildings. The Historic Towne of Smithville, N.J., is the result.

Growing up in southern New Jersey, Ethel Noyes became highly conversant with the history and folklore of the region. With regret, she viewed the passing of the simple, graceful, agrarian way of life. In an attempt to preserve some of that American past for future generations, the Noyes' embarked upon a salvage and restoration program of almost unimaginable proportions.

Beginning with the purchase of the Smithville Inn, built in 1787, in 1952 the Noyes' began charting a project that has occupied their energies for more than 20 years. Seeking out and collecting the neglected antique buildings of New Jersey, they have unravelled the endless red tape required to transport buildings. They have carefully and thoughtfully engineered the actual transportation of these buildings, more than 90 now, to the Smithville site, currently more than 2,300 acres at the tip of the pine barrens and just above the Mason-Dixon line, 12 miles south of Atlantic City.

Transportation of a building alone, before beginning meticulous restoration and refurbishing, can mean an investment of $3,000 to $10,000.

The original Smithville Inn was a run-down, one-room stagecoach inn when purchased by the Noyes'. They refurbished it and turned it into a restaurant; it has grown to a total of nine rooms.

The original room of the Inn, the Port Republic Room, has a low ceiling and its original floor. The walls are decorated with early documents and "carriage paintings" from the Noyes collection. Now extremely rare outside collections, "carriage paintings" are American primitive painting.

Visited by winter sleighing parties, traveling Quakers, and stagecoach passengers, the Inn became particularly popular after the War of 1812.

Of the hospitality and food, a descendant of the Smith family wrote, "In the attic could always be found large pans of scrapple and links upon links of homemade sausage. By their side were turkey, geese, and ducks, tame or wild, ready to cook at a minute's notice. Large quantities of doughnuts in stone crocks and jars of preserves were also waiting to be eaten by the hungry guests. In the smoke house there were a dozen or more hams, and in the cellar could always be found clams, oysters, and terrapin. An abundance of everything and a hearty welcome was given to all. Guests registered their names on the weather boards, and these names remained long after the writers had passed beyond."

At the Smithville Inn today, waitresses in appropriate garb of the late 1700s and early 1800s serve regional specialties: oyster pie, country ham on cornbread with chicken, country sausages with apple fritters and syrup, or roasted Absecon duckling. American antiques decorate the walls: handcarved duck decoys and whales, clipper-ship models, wood plaque signs.

Caroling programs and other events take place regularly in the Historic Towne of Smithville at the Inn or in one of three additional restaurants. Encouraged by the popularity of the Inn, the Noyes' built the Lantern Light Inn, the Quail Hill Inn, and the Spread Eagle Tavern. Combined, the restaurants can serve 1,850 diners.

The restaurants are located in a complex including shops, a motel, an airfield. Most recent addition: "The Old Village," a reconstructed town designed to capture the flavor of a crossroads community of southern New Jersey in the early 1800s. Plans on the drawing board include a large motel, suitable for conventions, and a golf course.

When "The Old Village" opened last May 2, New Jersey Governor Brendan Byrne attended with a number of Congressmen. The event was recognized with statewide fanfare and a number of local proclamations. "The Old Village" has more than 50 restored buildings—a grist mill, a clam house, a Quaker meeting house, a cobbler shop, and a one-room schoolhouse. It is inhabited by costumed residents who perform appropriate tasks. A stagecoach sits in the town. On the local lake, a "Bugeye" boat, used to catch oysters in the 19th century, is lashed to the dock.

Last October, the Historic Towne of Smithville was purchased by the American Broadcasting Company's Leisure Group II as part of the ABC Scenic and Wildlife Attractions Division. The Noyes' still administer the operations through a corporation which they have set up.

"If you can't do one thing well, don't do it," is one of Ethel Noyes favorite sayings. So when she and her husband Fred created the Historic Towne of Smithville, they lavished care to preserve the authenticity of the buildings while evoking the warmth and charm of a vanishing American past.

Through a museum of buildings, Smithville preserves a part of the American heritage for future generations—and some of the values of America's vanishing rural farmland. And, it carries forward traditions of friendly food-service.

Tidewater Recipes

CHEESE AND OLIVE BALLS

Chefs at Williamsburg make these appetizers ahead and freeze until bake-and-serve time.

Yield: about 36

Ingredients

CHEESE, CHEDDAR, SHARP, grated	8 ounces
BUTTER, at room temperature	4 ounces
PASTRY FLOUR	1-1/2 cups
PAPRIKA	1/4 teaspoon
SALT	1/4 teaspoon (approx.)
PIMIENTO-STUFFED SPANISH GREEN OLIVES	36

Procedure

1. Blend together cheese and butter.
2. Sift in flour, paprika, and salt. Blend to make a smooth dough.
3. Pinch off a small piece of dough; press flat and wrap around an olive. Continue until all olives are wrapped in dough.
4. Bake in oven at 350°F. for 10 to 15 minutes, until golden.

CORN OYSTERS

Yield: about 1 dozen

Ingredients

FRESH CORN, scraped	1 quart
SIFTED FLOUR	1-1/2 cups
EGGS, beaten	4
CREAM	1/3 cup
SALT	1 teaspoon
PEPPER	1/4 teaspoon

Procedure

1. Combine all ingredients; stir until well mixed.
2. Portion with No. 16 scoop.
3. Fry in deep fat at 365°F. until golden brown, about 3 minutes.
4. Serve with honey or cream gravy, if desired.

BEEF AND PORK PASTRIES

*"Popular for large luncheon groups,"
agree chefs at Williamsburg.*

Yield: 900 pastries

Ingredients

GROUND BEEF	30 pounds
GROUND PORK	30 pounds
ONIONS, LARGE, finely chopped	24
CELERY, finely chopped	6 stalks
SALT	1-1/2 cups
POULTRY SEASONING	3 teaspoons
SAGE, rubbed	3 teaspoons
DRY MUSTARD	6 tablespoons
WHITE PEPPER	9 tablespoons
MONOSODIUM GLUTAMATE	1 cup
BEEF STOCK, hot	6 quarts
INSTANT MASHED POTATO FLAKES or GRANULES	3 pounds
FRESH BREAD CRUMBS	3 pounds
EGGS, beaten	3 dozen
PIE SHELLS, unbaked, 6-inch	900
PASTRY CRUSTS, 7-inch	900
EGG WASH	as needed

Procedure

1. Place ground beef and pork in a large brazier or tilt fryer. Cook ground meat until it begins to brown.
2. Add chopped onions, celery, and salt. Cook until meat is thoroughly browned and onions are transparent.
3. Add remaining seasonings and beef stock. Heat until liquid begins to simmer. Remove from heat.
4. Stir in dry potato flakes. Mix in bread crumbs. Add beaten eggs; mix thoroughly. Allow mixture to cool.
5. Place 6 ounces of meat mixture in each pie shell and cover with pastry crust. Seal edges; crimp. Brush top crusts with egg wash. Make 2 or 3 slits, each about 1 inch long in top crusts.
6. Bake in oven at 375°F. for about 20 to 30 minutes, or until well browned.

BASIC CREAM OF NUT SOUP
*(Williamsburg chefs use a basic recipe,
then add the nuts.)*

Yield: about 2 gallons

Ingredients

CELERY, chopped	3 cups
ONION, chopped	1 pint
BUTTER	1 pound
FLOUR	3 cups
CHICKEN STOCK, hot	2 gallons
CHICKEN BASE	as needed
SALT	as needed
MONOSODIUM GLUTAMATE	as needed
WHITE PEPPER (optional)	as needed

Procedure

1. Saute celery and onion in butter until tender. Add flour to make a roux. Cook roux to pale gold. Gradually whip in stock. Simmer for 30 minutes.

2. Season to taste with chicken base, salt, monosodium glutamate, and pepper.

3. Strain.

CREAM OF ALMOND SOUP

1. Add 2 quarts light cream or half-and-half, and about 2 teaspoons almond extract to Basic Cream of Nut Soup. Heat to serving temperature but do not boil.

2. Add blanched almonds to each portion just before serving.

CREAM OF PEANUT SOUP

1. Add 2 quarts light cream or half-and-half, and about 1 pound chunky peanut butter to Basic Cream of Nut Soup. Heat to serving temperature, stirring until peanut butter dissolves. Do not boil.

2. Garnish with salted peanuts before serving, if desired.

EASTERN SHORE CHOWDER

Yield: 300 portions

Ingredients

THINLY SLICED POTATOES	1 gallon
FISH STOCK	8 gallons
SALT	4 ounces
WORCESTERSHIRE SAUCE	1/2 cup
LIQUID HOT PEPPER SEASONING	1 teaspoon
BUTTER or MARGARINE	6 pounds
DICED ONION	1 gallon
SLICED CELERY	1/2 gallon
FLOUR	6 pounds
CREAM, HEAVY	1 gallon
HADDOCK, cooked	10 pounds
ALASKA KING CRABMEAT, cooked	5 pounds
REGULAR CRABMEAT, cooked	2 pounds

Procedure

1. Cook potatoes with just enough fish stock to cover; add salt, Worcestershire sauce, and liquid hot pepper seasoning. Simmer until potatoes are tender.

2. Melt butter; saute onion and celery until transparent. Stir in the flour to make a roux; cook 5 to 6 minutes, but do not brown. Add the remaining stock gradually, whipping or stirring until thickened and smooth. Cook 10 minutes.

3. Add mixture; blend with a paddle.

4. Heat the cream and combine with chowder base. Adjust seasonings.

5. Flake and chop fish and crabmeat; add to chowder. Keep hot until serving time. Do not boil.

FISH HOUSE PUNCH

"The longer it's in the refrigerator, the better the flavor," say people at Williamsburg.

Yield: 4-1/2 gallons

Ingredients

WATER	6 quarts
BROWN SUGAR	3 pounds
LEMONS	54
PINEAPPLE JUICE	2 No. 5 cans
DARK RUM	6 fifths
COGNAC	3 fifths
PEACH BRANDY	1 pint

Procedure

1. Boil water and sugar just until syrup is clear.
2. Peel lemons, then squeeze juice from lemons.
3. In glass or china container, combine syrup, lemon peel, and juice. Let stand overnight.
4. Remove lemon peel. Add remaining ingredients to syrup.
5. Refrigerate until serving time. Serve over crushed ice.

LEEK AND POTATO SOUP

Yield: 50 servings

Ingredients

LEEKS, diced	8 pounds
ONIONS, diced	6
BUTTER	8 ounces
FLOUR	6 ounces
CHICKEN STOCK, hot	2 gallons
POTATOES, diced	4 pounds
CHICKEN BASE	4 ounces
SALT	as needed
PEPPER	as needed
MONOSODIUM GLUTAMATE	as needed
LIGHT CREAM or	
HALF-AND-HALF	2 quarts

Procedure

1. Saute leeks and onions in butter until tender. Stir in flour to make a roux. Cook until roux is pale gold. Whip in chicken stock. Simmer 10 minutes.
2. Add potatoes; simmer about 2 minutes, or until tender.
3. Add chicken base.
4. Season to taste with salt, pepper, and monosodium glutamate.
5. Stir in cream; heat to serving temperature but do not boil.

PLANTATION PICKLED SHRIMP REMOULADE

Yield: 24 servings

Ingredients

MINCED CELERY	1-1/2 cups
CHOPPED ONION	1-1/2 cups
MINCED PARSLEY	1-1/2 cups
CHOPPED DILL PICKLE	1-1/2 cups
MINCED GARLIC	2 tablespoons
PREPARED HOT MUSTARD	3-1/2 cups
HORSERADISH	1/3 cup
VINEGAR	1/2 cup
SALAD OIL	1/2 cup
COOKED SHRIMP	6 pounds
SHREDDED LETTUCE or	
GREENS	3 quarts

Procedure

1. Combine all ingredients except shrimp and lettuce. Mix well and chill.
2. Arrange 4 ounces of shrimp on 1/2 cup of shredded lettuce; top with 1/2 cup of Remoulade Sauce.

Pickle Packers International, Inc.

SQUASH MEDLEY

Yield: 100 1/2-cup servings

Ingredients

SLICED or CHOPPED ONIONS	3 quarts (3-3/4 pounds)
BUTTER	3-1/2 pounds
SQUASH, CANNED	4 No. 10 cans
or	
FROZEN	18 pounds
TOMATOES	1 No. 10 can
CHEESE, grated	3 pounds
SALT	6 tablespoons
PEPPER	1 teaspoon
BREAD CRUMBS	2 quarts

Procedure

1. Saute onions in half the butter.
2. Combine sauteed onions with squash, tomatoes, cheese, salt, and pepper. Place 1/4 of the mixture into each of 4 greased steam table pans.
3. Melt remaining butter in a large skillet. Add bread crumbs and stir until nicely browned.
4. Sprinkle evenly over top of each pan.
5. Bake in oven at 350°F. for 30 minutes.

Atlanta Public Schools

CORNISH GAME HEN MADEIRA

Yield: 6 servings

Ingredients

ONION, small, finely diced	1
VEGETABLE OIL	1 tablespoon
BUTTER	1 tablespoon
COOKED WILD RICE	2 cups
COOKED WHITE RICE	1 cup
CORNISH GAME HENS, 16 to 18 ounces each, partially boned	6
BUTTER	as needed
SALT	to taste
PEPPER	to taste

Procedure

1. Saute onion in oil and butter over low heat. Do not brown. Add rice and mix well. Adjust seasoning and cool.

2. Divide stuffing into 6 equal portions and fill game hen cavities. Rub with butter and season with salt and pepper.

3. Roast in oven at 350°F. for about 1 hour, or until tender and golden in color.

4. Serve with Sauce Madeira.*

*SAUCE MADEIRA

Yield: 6 servings

Ingredients

SHALLOT, finely chopped	1
CHOPPED FRESH MUSHROOMS	1/2 cup
VEGETABLE OIL	1 tablespoon
BUTTER	2 tablespoons
MADEIRA	1/2 cup
BEEF CONSOMME	2 cups
RED CURRANT JELLY	1 tablespoon
FLOUR mixed with	2 tablespoons
COGNAC	2 tablespoons
SALT	to taste
PEPPER	to taste

Procedure

1. Saute shallot and mushrooms in oil and 1 tablespoon butter over low heat. Do not brown.

2. Add wine and reduce mixture to 1/4 of its volume. Add consomme and jelly and boil again.

3. Add flour-cognac mixture slowly, stirring constantly with a wire whip until smooth. Reduce heat and simmer for 15 minutes. Adjust seasoning.

4. Stir in the remaining tablespoon of butter and strain.

United Airlines Food Services Library

POT ROAST OF BEEF

Yield: 25 servings

Ingredients

FLOUR	2 cups
SALT	1 tablespoon
PEPPER	1 tablespoon
BEEF ROAST	15 pounds
FAT or OIL	1 cup
ONIONS, MEDIUM SIZED, diced	3
BAY LEAVES	2
TOMATO PUREE	1 No. 10 can
TOMATOES	1 No. 10 can

Procedure

1. Mix together flour, salt, and pepper. Dredge meat in seasoned flour.

2. Heat fat in deep roasting pan. Brown meat on all sides in the hot fat.

3. Add remaining ingredients.

4. Roast in oven at 350°F. for about 4 hours, or until meat is well done.

POACHED EGGS AMERICAN
The Greenbrier, White Sulphur Springs, West Va.

Yield: 1 portion

Ingredients

IDAHO POTATO, LARGE, BAKED	1
EGG, poached	1
CHEDDAR CHEESE RAREBIT	2 ounces
WHIPPED CREAM	2 teaspoons
PARSLEY	1 bunch

Procedure

1. Cut 1-inch slice from top of large baked potato. Scoop out potato. Do not break skin.

2. Combine mashed potato with Cheddar Cheese Rarebit. Blend well.

3. Refill potato. Top with poached egg.

4. Cover with whipped cream and glaze.

5. Serve with Fried Parsley.

TO PREPARE PARSLEY

Wash and dry parsley. Fry in oil for a few seconds. Drain. Sprinkle with salt. Serve on napkin next to the potato.

MARYLAND CRAB CAKES
A favorite at ARA's Eastern establishments

Yield: 50 2-ounce cakes

Ingredients

CRABMEAT, FRESH	4 pounds, 8 ounces
SOFT BREAD CRUMBS	15 ounces
EGGS, beaten	1-1/2 cups
MILK	1 cup
CHOPPED PARSLEY	3 tablespoons
DRY MUSTARD	1-1/2 teaspoons
SALT	1-1/2 teaspoons
CELERY SEED	1/2 teaspoon
SEAFOOD SEASONING BLEND	1/2 teaspoon
WORCESTERSHIRE SAUCE	1-1/2 tablespoons

Procedure

1. Mix together crabmeat and bread crumbs.
2. Combine eggs and milk; add parsley and seasonings.
3. Combine crabmeat mixture and egg mixture. Chill for 30 minutes.
4. Form into 2-ounce cakes; portion with a No. 20 scoop.
5. Fry cakes in deep fat at 375°F. until golden.
6. Drain well. Serve hot.

FRIED TOMATOES

Yield: 2 portions

Ingredients

TOMATO, LARGE, FIRM, RIPE or GREEN	1
SUGAR	1/2 to 1 teaspoon
FLOUR	1 tablespoon
SALT	1/8 teaspoon
PEPPER	dash
BACON FAT or BUTTER	3 tablespoons

Procedure

1. Core tomato; cut into 1/2-inch slices. Sprinkle a little sugar on each side of each slice.
2. Mix flour with salt and pepper. Coat tomato slices with seasoned flour.
3. Saute tomato slices in hot fat until golden on each side.
4. Serve with brown or cream gravy, if desired.

SCALLOP AND NOODLE "PYE"
(Scallops in Natural Shell)

Yield: 6 servings

Ingredients

NOODLES, FRESH	1 pound
FINELY CHOPPED ONION	1 tablespoon
BAY SCALLOPS	1-1/4 pounds
WHITE WINE, DRY	1/2 cup
CREAM SAUCE	1 cup
CREAM, HEAVY	1/2 cup
TERIYAKI SAUCE	2 tablespoons
CHEESE SAUCE	6 tablespoons
PAPRIKA	to garnish

Procedure

1. Cook fresh noodles in plenty of water until al dente. Cool.
2. Cut into no longer than 2-inch pieces. Butter and season lightly, divide evenly into 6 natural scallop shells. Make a well in center of dish.
3. Saute onions and scallops in butter over medium heat; douse with white wine. Reduce liquid a bit. Add cream sauce, heavy cream, and Teriyaki Sauce. Season with salt and pepper. Divide into the pre-prepared scallop shells with the noodles. Cover top of each with 1 tablespoon of Cheese Sauce and sprinkle with a bit of paprika.
4. Bake in oven at 325°F. until cheese bubbles.

United Airlines, Food Services Library, Trader Vic's

FISH LOAF

Yield: 250 portions

Ingredients

SALMON or OTHER CANNED FISH	28 pounds
WHOLE EGGS, beaten	2-1/2 dozen
BREAD CRUMBS, soft	2-1/2 gallons
TOMATOES, CANNED	5 quarts
CHOPPED PARSLEY	2-1/2 cups
CHOPPED ONION	2-1/2 cups
CELERY SALT	3 tablespoons
FAT, melted	2-1/2 cups
SALT	to taste

Procedure

1. Mix all ingredients carefully. Place in greased steam table pans.
2. Combine bread crumbs and melted fat. Top pans with bread crumbs.
3. Bake in oven at 375°F. for approximately 45 minutes. Cut in squares.
4. Serve with real or mock hollandaise sauce. Garnish with parsley.

Washington, D. C.

BREAST OF CHICKEN IN CASSEROLE A LA HOMESTEAD

Yield: 24 portions

Ingredients

3-POUND CHICKENS, uncooked	24
FLOUR	2 cups
PAPRIKA	1 tablespoon
SALT	to season
PEPPER	to season
BUTTER	1 pound
SHORTENING	1 pound
SAUCE	
FLOUR	3/4 cup
MILK	1 quart
CREAM (20%)	1 quart
SHORTENING	as above
SEASONINGS*	1/2 cup
BOTTLED BROWNING SAUCE	2 tablespoons
SALT	to season
PEPPER	to season
MUSHROOMS, FRESH, cut julienne	1 pound
HAM, cooked, cut julienne	3/4 pound

*This seasoning is a commercial preparation containing water, hydrolyzed plant proteins, monosodium glutamate, and caramel flavoring.

Procedure

1. Roll chicken breasts in flour seasoned with salt, pepper, and paprika.

2. Place butter and shortening in braising pot, and when hot, sear chicken breasts until a golden brown, turning occasionally—approximately 10 minutes.

3. Cover braising pot, and place chicken in oven at 350°F. Cook until chicken is fork-tender.

4. Remove chicken from pot. Keep hot.

5. Make sauce in pan in which chicken was cooked. (Pour off excess fat).

6. Add 3/4 cup flour to equal amount of fat in pan. Stir well and cook until a golden brown.

7. Combine milk and cream; heat; gradually add to flour mixture, stirring well with wire whip.

8. Add seasonings, kitchen bouquet, and salt and pepper to season.

9. Cook thoroughly until all trace of raw starch disappears.

10. Saute mushrooms julienne in 2 ounces shortening.

11. Add mushrooms and ham julienne to the sauce.

12. Blend thoroughly, and bring to simmering point. Reduce heat.

13. Place breast of chicken in preheated, greased individual casserole.

14. Pour hot sauce over chicken. Serve immediately.

BAKED CHICKEN AND NOODLE CASSEROLE

Yield: 50 5-ounce portions

Ingredients

STEWING CHICKENS, 5 POUNDS EACH	2
BUTTER	2 cups
ALL-PURPOSE FLOUR	3 cups
WHOLE MILK	1 gallon
CHICKEN STOCK	2 quarts
MUSHROOMS, CANNED, SLICED	2 cups
SALT	2 tablespoons
WHITE PEPPER	1/2 teaspoon
GROUND NUTMEG	1/2 teaspoon
BREAD, cut in 1/4-inch cubes	1 pound
BUTTER, melted	4 ounces
EGG NOODLES, MEDIUM, uncooked	1 pound

Procedure

1. Simmer chicken until tender. Remove from stock and cool.

2. Cut chicken meat in 1/2- to 3/4-inch cubes.

3. Cook noodles in boiling salted water. Drain and wash in cold water.

4. Melt butter; add flour and blend well.

5. Gradually add milk and chicken stock, stirring constantly with wire whip. Add salt, pepper, and nutmeg.

6. Cook until sauce is thick and the starch thoroughly cooked.

7. Add diced chicken and bring to simmering point. Add sliced mushrooms.

8. Stir in the cooked noodles. Add more seasoning if necessary.

9. Toss bread cubes in melted butter.

10. Put approximately 5 ounces chicken-noodle mixture into each individual, greased casserole dish. Top with buttered bread.

11. Bake in oven at 400°F. until bread is a golden brown.

Note

Chicken fat may be substituted for some of the butter in the sauce.

Turkey may be used in place of chicken.

Maryland

COURONNE (MOLD) OF BRANDIED PEACHES

Yield: 12 portions

Ingredients

VANILLA ICE CREAM	2 quarts
MACAROONS, crushed	12
LADYFINGERS, crushed	12
PEACHES, FRESH	12
PEACH BRANDY	
HOT APRICOT-PEACH BRANDY SAUCE	
APRICOT PUREE	1 pint
PEACH BRANDY	4 tablespoons
SPONGE CAKE	

Procedure

1. Place vanilla ice cream in round mold. See that it is kept frozen hard until used. Combine crushed macaroons and ladyfingers with enough peach brandy to make a stiff paste. Remove pits from peaches, and fill cavity with the paste. Keep peaches in their original shape and marinate them in peach brandy in refrigerator for 2 hours.

2. Combine apricot puree and peach brandy, and bring to a boil.

3. Remove ice cream from mold. Place on a round of sponge cake 1/2 inch thick. Arrange peaches in center of mold, and decorate.

Pour Hot Apricot-Brandy Sauce over the Peach Mold.

The Homestead, Hot Springs, Va.

FROSTY FUDGE PIE

Yield: 1 10-inch pie

Ingredients

WHOLE EGGS	4 (only)
GRANULATED SUGAR	2 cups
MARGARINE, melted	1/3 cup
CHOCOLATE, melted	3 squares
CHOPPED NUTS	1 cup
VANILLA	1 teaspoon
PIE SHELL, unbaked	1

Procedure

1. Beat eggs until light. Add sugar gradually and blend well.

2. Add other ingredients and mix thoroughly.

3. Place mixture in unbaked pie shell. Bake in oven at 350°F. for 35 to 40 min. Do not overbake.

4. Cool. Serve with whipped cream or ice cream.

Note

The filling will not crack on top if baked in a glass pie dish.

Arlington, Virginia

LADY BALTIMORE CAKE

Yield: 5 10-inch layer cakes

Ingredients

RAISINS, CALIFORNIA SEEDLESS	2 pounds
SHERRY	1 cup
WALNUTS	15 ounces
CHERRIES, CANDIED	1 pound
SUGAR	2 pounds
WATER	1 cup
CORN SYRUP, LIGHT	1 pint
SALT	1/4 ounce
EGG WHITES	1 pound, 1 ounce (16)
VANILLA	2 tablespoons
ALMOND EXTRACT	2 teaspoons
LEMON JUICE	2 tablespoons
GRATED LEMON PEEL	2 teaspoons
CAKE LAYERS, WHITE, (10-inch)	10 layers

Procedure

1. Chop raisins; add sherry and marinate at least 1 hour. Drain well.

2. Chop nuts and cherries; add drained raisins.

3. Boil sugar, water, corn syrup, and salt together to 242°F., keeping pan covered first 5 minutes.

4. Whip egg whites stiff; pour syrup into beaten whites, beating constantly until thick and glossy. Beat in flavorings, lemon juice, and peel.

5. To 2/3 of the fluffy frosting, add raisin-nut mixture.

6. Split the cake layers in half horizontally. Use 4 thin layers to assemble each cake and fill with fruited frosting. Frost top and sides with remaining plain frosting.

California Raisin Advisory Board

ORANGE WINE CAKE

Yield: 6 10-inch layer cakes, 2 layers each

Ingredients

BUTTER	3 pounds
GRANULATED SUGAR	2-3/4 pounds
WHOLE EGGS	24 (only)
VANILLA	4 ounces
PECANS, chopped	3 pounds
SIFTED CAKE FLOUR	6 pounds
SOUR MILK	1-1/2 quarts
ORANGE RIND, from	4 oranges
SALT	1 ounce
RAISINS	3 pounds
SODA	2-1/2 ounces

Procedure

1. Cream butter, sugar, and orange rind until mixture is light and fluffy. Reduce speed on electric mixer and add eggs.

2. Combine soda, sour milk, and vanilla. Add flour alternately with the milk, having the mixer at very low speed. Blend well.

3. Bake in well greased and floured layer cake tins, 10 inches in diameter, in oven at 350°F. for about 25 minutes.

4. Remove from tins and allow to cool on cooling racks.

5. Put layers together with Butter Cream Icing flavored with sherry.

Williamsburg, Virginia

CHICKEN LOAF

Yield: 28 portions

Ingredients

DICED ONION	1 cup
DICED CELERY	1 cup
SLICED MUSHROOMS	3 cups
BUTTER or MARGARINE	6 tablespoons
CHICKEN, cooked, diced	1-1/2 pounds
EGGS, beaten	5
MILK	1 quart
CHICKEN BROTH	1-1/2 quarts
SALT	to taste
PEPPER	to taste
BREAD CRUMBS	1-1/2 quarts
BUTTER or MARGARINE, melted	3/4 cup

Procedure

1. Saute onion, celery, and mushrooms in 6 tablespoons butter.

2. Beat eggs. Add milk and chicken broth, then the sauteed vegetables and chicken.

3. Fold in the bread crumbs. Taste. Add salt and pepper.

4. Pour into a greased steam table pan. Top with melted butter.

5. Bake in oven at 350°F. for 1 hour or until set.

6. Serve with Giblet Gravy or Mushroom Sauce.

The Frances Virginia Tea Room, Atlanta, Ga.

FRESH PORK BARBECUE

Yield: 4 gallons barbecue sauce, 600 portions

Ingredients

PORK LOIN of FRESH PORK HAM, cooked, cubed 1/2 inch	200 pounds
BARBECUE SAUCE	
HOT STEAK SAUCE, 6-OUNCE BOTTLE	12
VINEGAR	3 quarts
WORCESTERSHIRE SAUCE	1 pint
PREPARED MUSTARD	1 cup
ONION, minced	2 pounds
TOMATO PUREE	1 pound, 10 ounces
WATER	3-1/2 gallons
SUGAR	1 pound

Procedure

1. Chop cooked pork into 1/2-inch pieces.

2. Combine ingredients for Barbecue Sauce and bring to a boil.

3. Pour sauce over meat and simmer gently for 2 hours. The long simmering develops a rich flavor.

4. With a No. 16 scoop, serve on bun or toast.

Duke University, Durham, N.C.

PEANUT BUTTER FINGERS

Yield: 200 pieces

Ingredients

BUTTER	2 cups
SUGAR	2 cups
BROWN SUGAR, firmly packed	2 cups
EGGS	4
PEANUT BUTTER	1-1/3 cups
SODA	2 teaspoons
SALT	1 teaspoon
VANILLA	1 teaspoon
FLOUR	4 cups
ROLLED OATS OR ROLLED WHEAT	4 cups
ICING	
EVAPORATED MILK	1 cup (approximately)
CONFECTIONERS' SUGAR	4 cups
PEANUT BUTTER	1 cup

Procedure

1. Cream butter and sugars. Add eggs. Mix well. Add peanut butter, soda, salt, and vanilla. Mix well. Stir in flour and rolled oats.

2. Spread in prepared 26-inch by 18-inch pan. Bake in oven at 350°F. for 20 to 30 minutes.

3. Cool and ice.

4. To prepare icing, add enough milk to powdered sugar and peanut butter to make mixture smooth enough to spread. Spread on cake and cut to finger length, 1-inch by 3-inch.

Note

These freeze well.

Atlanta Public Schools

FRENCH CREAM CHERRY PIE

Yield: 6 10-inch pies

Ingredients

MILK	2 quarts
SUGAR	1 pound, 4 ounces
MARGARINE	4 ounces
WHOLE EGGS	5 (only)
CORNSTARCH	9 ounces
SALT	1/4 teaspoon
CHERRIES, CANNED, PIE	1 No. 10 can
SUGAR	2 pounds
PIE SHELLS, baked	6
MERINGUE	
EGG WHITES	2 cups (16)
SUGAR	16 ounces
SALT	1/2 teaspoon

Procedure

1. Mix one-half of the cornstarch with the 1-1/4 pounds sugar. Add a little of the cold milk and blend well.

2. Scald the remaining milk in small steam-jacketed kettle or double boiler. Add cornstarch mixture to it, stirring with wire whip.

3. Cook until mixture is thick and free of any raw starch taste. Add margarine. Beat eggs. Pour some of hot mixture over eggs, stirring constantly, and add to hot mixture in kettle. Stir with wire whip.

4. Cook 5 to 7 minutes. (This is the custard mixture for pies.)

5. Drain cherries. Heat cherry juice. Combine remainder of cornstarch with the 2 pounds sugar. Add to hot cherry juice, stirring rapidly.

6. Cook until mixture is thick and transparent. Add fruit and mix well. Half-fill baked pie shell with cherry filling. Pour custard filling over cherry mixture.

7. Top with meringue while filling is still warm. Brown meringue in oven at 375°F. for 10 to 12 minutes or at 425°F. for 4-1/2 to 6 minutes. One quart whipped cream may also be used as topping.

Duke University, Durham, N. C.

Pilgrims Discover American Foods

IT IS A PROUD tradition—foodservice lodging. Not like the Old World's, where inns and restaurants came after the town. Instead, in our own tradition, having led the way across the frontier, the restaurant and inn were already open for business when permanent settlers arrived. The Harvey Girls, The Brown Palace, The Palmer House, The Waldorf, and the Astor are all a familiar part of our social history.

Our concept of eating out is uniquely American. It is no surprise then that, even after 200 years, 44 percent of the entire world's eating out is done in America! When celebrating America's 200-year milestone, what better place is there to begin the celebration than the land of Pilgrims—New England?

Another First at Concord

Mike Barnes never had a reputation for throwing a big party, but he has one of historic proportions now.

Barnes is Service Systems' 32-year-old New England vice-president of operations, who prepared and served 8,600 box lunches to marching bands, government and military officials, and volunteers at the official Bicentennial kick-off in Concord, Mass., last April.

It was an unusual undertaking for a company that specializes in school, college, and in-plant feeding around New England. But Barnes and Neil Hooper, director of operations for central New England, wanted to give it a try for their own special reasons.

"New Englanders have their own style and their own thinking," says Barnes. "They are proud and love their traditions. We wanted to be sensitive to that, so we went very hard after the parade contract.

"We wanted some recognition, too," he adds, "so we made a no-profit bid because it was something we really wanted to do. We're glad we did."

Preparation began the day before the event at Service Systems' Worcester commissary. Thirty-one employees worked until 10:30 p.m. pre-producing all the sandwiches necessary to feed 6,000 hungry band members, 700 top officials at a sit-down VIP luncheon, and assorted parade volunteers.

Inside each box lunch were two sandwiches

(ham and roast beef), potato chips, orange drink, and fruit. Cost: $1.36 per lunch.

For the VIP luncheon, the town of Concord (by then strapped for funds) settled on stacked roast beef sandwiches, a petit four, salad, and coffee. Cost: $2.25 per plate. A local bank donated champagne.

"Cold cuts and champagne," chuckles Barnes. He was not chuckling at the time. "We tried pre-setting the first bottle of champagne. But when we set them out with loosened corks, all the bottles started exploding. The National Guard, responsible for security, thought guns were going off each time the corks popped. So we ran around putting all the corks back in the bottles."

That wasn't the end of it. His 24 Girl Scout volunteers, Barnes discovered too late, were all under age 18 and couldn't legally serve the champagne.

"So, three other people and I served the champagne to the 700 guests! We just ran like crazy. These things always happen; it wouldn't be any fun if they didn't," he says good-naturedly.

As expected, preparation at the Worcester commissary went without a hitch. With the sandwiches made up by 10:30 p.m. and loaded onto four refrigerated trucks by 3 a.m., Barnes and eight Service Systems' employees made their midnight ride to Concord. They arrived at the celebration site by 4:30 a.m., making their way through the first of the day's eventual 125,000 visitors.

Distribution of box lunches began at 9:30 a.m. The 140 buses, carrying members of 75 bands from around the country, were lined up on several main roads of the town, awaiting the lunches. It was a simple matter for the Service Systems' trucks to ride alongside the buses, distributing the exact number of lunches pre-marked on each bus.

With the box lunch distribution under way, Barnes raced over to Concord's Minute Man Armory with 24 Girl Scouts in tow to set up for the Honored Guest luncheon. As well as he can recall, with the exception of the champagne incident, the luncheon went smoothly.

"We're rather surprised we pulled it off as well as we did," he reflected a month after the fact.

Would he do it again?

"Oh yeah," he said unhesitatingly. "It was

fun. I got wrapped up in it all. Sometimes the day-to-day institutional feeding business can get monotonous.

"The Bicentennial performance is what all of our training is pointed toward. It's at events like that where we put our careers to the test."

Wayside Inn
South Sudbury, Mass.

"One autumn night, in Sudbury town, . . .
The windows of the wayside inn
Gleamed red with fire-light through the leaves . . .
Built in the old Colonial day,
When men lived in a grander way . . .
'Listen my children and you shall hear of the midnight ride of Paul Revere.. . .'"

> *Tales of a Wayside Inn,*
> *by Henry Wadsworth Longfellow.*

Old records neglect to pinpoint the exact date and first name of the grandson of John Howe who received consent of the Selectmen to keep a "hous of entertainment for travelers" just after King Philip's War.

Iron was scarce; lead was used for bullets in fighting the Indians. The old inn was built with mortized joints and wooden pegs, no nails.

In 1716 David Howe got a regular license for a house of entertainment. The inn remained a property of the Howe family for more than a century. Then Edward Lemon bought it in 1897. By 1923, when Henry Ford bought the inn from Lemon's widow, the name had changed from Howes Tavern to Red Horse Tavern (1746) to Wayside Inn (1863).

Ford restored the property; in 1945 he deeded it to the Wayside Inn Corp., a non-government, non-profit, educational trust. When fire destroyed much of the inn in 1955, the Ford Foundation granted money for the three-year restoration. Finally, in 1973 the inn was declared an historic site.

Barbara Deveneau, whose family settled in the area about the same time the Howes did, is assistant to today's innkeeper. She attended Redstone School, made famous in "Mary Had a Little Lamb." The schoolhouse was moved from Sterling, Mass., to the Wayside Inn property in 1927.

History and hospitality are equally important at Wayside Inn. The nine trustees are practical men who work at following the charter. In fact, the entire town encourages the inn and the trustees to maintain their perspective on early American history. As a result, this area has zip code 01776.

"We always made a profit on food, drink and lodging," says Francis Koppeis, innkeeper. Which is not to say that charges are exorbitant for hospitality. "We price for a fair, but small, profit on hospitality; that profit is used for maintenance of display rooms and hostesses who talk with people here to 'just look around'. Our charges are made to enhance the sense of value received."

Durgin-Park Restaurant
Boston, Mass.

Soon after Peter Faneuil built his market near the Boston waterfront in 1742, a warehouse went up nearby. It was on the second floor of this warehouse that Durgin-Park originated.

Eldredge Park, John Durgin, and John Chandler bought the eating establishment that had "just grown there for the past 50 years or so." A few years later Park and Durgin died. Chandler ran the place under their names; his grandson, Jerry, came up in the business.

Yankee food was, and is, the rule here. Roast beef, boiled lobster, baked beans, boiled dinners, and Indian pudding are staples served with corn bread and clam chowder. Cod fish and men wearing hats are also as much a part of the dining scene at Durgin-Park as the waitress who tells you what you are going to eat.

Today's menu is about the same, except for prices, as it was when James Hallet bought the place just after World War II.

The decor has changed slightly in the past five years. Instead of only the long tables for 20, some small tables for four line the wall in one dining room. The change in seating took away some of the original 250 seats. But Saturday nights have increased to five turns instead of "about four."

Hallet's philosophy is the same as that of Durgin and Park: "The best advertising is plenty of food on the eating table."

Mayflower Seafood Restaurant
Plymouth, Mass.

"We had been suppliers of fish for many years. In 1960 I looked for ways to diversify. We opened the Mayflower with 145 seats, all in the self-service dining area. The first year we cleared a profit of $1,000." Gordon Howland, owner, sums up 14 years of hard work and good management.

"Best quality fish and seafood at lowest possible price goes on our menu. You'll never get any of that 'public be damned' business here."

Howland opened the service dining room in 1966 as a separate area from the rest of the operation. The 75 seats are at small tables and a few banquettes. Emphasis is on gracious dining.

Howland insists he can't boil water, "but I can criticize madly." Lobsters from Howland's farm in Maine are cooked in a 4-foot tank filled with salt and sea water. High pressure steam provides heat.

"We have a different way to evaluate," says Manager Tony Costa. "We look at total hours of labor. If that number is too high for our customer count in a given week, the next week those labor hours are back in the kind of ratio we want to see."

Service plates, striking blue glassware, and oyster forks all vanish out the door as diners leave. Howland believes thieving soon will reach the point that imprinted silver and attractive table tops are things of the past.

"Most of our customers are not local. They all want a souvenir to take home." Howland says in disgust. And he adds that profits for 1974 were the lowest since that first year of operation. "Tourists!"

McGrath's Restaurant
Plymouth, Mass.

Ernest McGrath and his uncle began business in another location as Dearn & McGrath. They had 30 seats when they opened in 1946, fresh out of the Navy.

There was not much by way of competition then. "Clambakes were popular. We catered those in a pavilion down by the Town Wharf," McGrath remembers.

A small cruise ship sailed out of Boston, to Plymouth and Providence. McGrath catered clambakes for those passengers. At about the end of this period, McGath threw the "world's largest clambake."

"Then, as now, Thomas Mitchell was our chef. We put up a circus tent, set up three serving lines and fed 7,500 people. That was quite a day. We fed those people clams, lobsters, corn-on-the-cob, sweet potatoes, and clam stew. Dessert was watermelon with coffee," McGrath recalls.

By this time the 30-seat operation was too small. McGrath & Dearn were known for clambakes. They expanded the pavilion into a 350-seat, rustic-style restaurant. Shore dinners and lobster dinners sold for about $2.50. "Now," McGrath says, "we are lucky to buy lobster for that price."

Dearn died in 1966 and McGrath took over the whole business. Catering and clambakes became a thing of the past. "I can't be two places at once," McGrath explains. "I was hooked on running a restaurant; I concentrated on that because I enjoy it."

Today's menu includes the shore dinner, but with Irish potatoes instead of the sweets. A recent weekend ad in Brockton, about 40 miles away, brought in 500 extra people for shore dinners.

McGrath sells about 100,000 pounds of lobster and 5,000 pounds of scallops annually. "We may serve 800 to 1,000 people a day in the summer. Most are visitors. We take special care of local people; that's why we stay open in the winter. Our winter lunch check runs $4," says McGrath.

Locke-Ober Cafe
Boston, Mass.

Winter Place is an alley, just a short block from the Boston Commons, where Frank Locke served plain Maine fare, steak and lobster. Next door, Louis Ober served Parisian cuisine. During the hottest part of their rivalry, in 1890 or thereabouts, dinners cost 75 cents between 1 and 4 p.m.

In 1894 liquor dealers bought both businesses, cut down partitions, and threw the key into Boston Harbor. Emil Camus was introduced as manager, and the name of the place was Winter Place Tavern. The next new owner introduced the Ward Eight, grenadine in a whiskey sour, to celebrate the election of a favorite customer. Ownership passed to the Locke-Ober Company.

The Men's Bar, with stools hung onto the mahogany bar by wrought iron supports, has the essential nude painting of "Mademoiselle Yvonne." The legend of the lady is a far cry from her pot-boiler reality, but patrons have delighted in telling her story since its invention by headwaiter Charlie Koechling in the late 1800s.

This was the era when waiters prided themselves on their "drug store" set-up. All the condiments for the ritual of eating raw oysters were set out on a snowy cloth on a ledge at the waiter's station.

William F. Harrington, today's general manager and president of Locke-Ober, maintains good control of his staff. Executive chef Dean J. Lynch, who is also food and beverage director, graduated from the Culinary Institute of America and worked in clubs and hotels before coming to Boston. The kitchen is run European-style, with 23 cooks and chefs. Harrington, Lynch, and night manager Paul Queenan take a physical inventory once each month. Lynch does the purchasing of all foods and liquor.

Waiters take pride in their work. "Our waiters work for Locke-Ober; there is no idea of doing the customer a favor. We are all in this business to serve customers, maintain traditional high standards, and make money in the process." Lynch sees to it that those standards are high; he works with the staff to see that they know how to maintain them.

"It is our high standards, good food, and good service, that attract and satisfy our prime customer," says Lynch.

Menus change with the seasons. Lunch menus offer 20 to 25 entrees, with six on a daily special. Daily averages are 275 lunches and one-and-one-half turns for dinner.

The first floor Men's Bar still is male dominated. "We gotta allow women in here now," grumbles one bartender. Furnishings and layout maintain the masculine image. A beautifully etched glass door reads "toilet" and leads to the only public phone on that floor as well as the men's room.

On the second floor the atmosphere changes dramatically. This is the place for dining in mixed company. Pace is leisurely. Up one more flight of stairs is another change. These are conference rooms where good food and discreetly attentive service take second place to business.

"Tradition." Harrington and Lynch nod wisely.

New England Recipes

THE COO WOOW

(The Wayside Inn declares this to be the oldest cock-tail in the country.)

Yield: 1 portion

Ingredients

LIGHT RUM	2 ounces
GINGER BRANDY	1 ounce
CRUSHED ICE	as needed

Procedure

1. Combine all ingredients in cocktail shaker.
2. Stir or shake for 30 seconds.
3. Strain and serve in a low-ball glass.

Wayside Inn

BOG FOG

Yield: 2 portions

Ingredients

CRANBERRY JUICE COCKTAIL	4 ounces
ORANGE JUICE	4 ounces
VODKA	2 ounces
ICE	as needed

Procedure

1. Mix together cranberry juice cocktail, orange juice, and vodka. Pour into on-the-rocks glasses with ice.

TO BOIL A LOBSTER

The only lobster fit to boil is a live lobster, agree New Englanders. Plunge live lobsters into boiling water. Add a few strands of seaweed or use half sea-water/half fresh water for extra flavor, if desired. As soon as shell and claws turn bright red, lobster is done. Cooking time is about 5 to 7 minutes per pound.

CLAM CHOWDER

Yield: about 1 gallon

Ingredients

SALT PORK or BACON, chopped	1/2 pound
CHOPPED ONION	1 cup
CLAM JUICE	2 No. 5 cans
POTATOES, peeled, cubed	1-1/2 pounds
SALT	1 teaspoon
WHITE PEPPER	1/2 teaspoon
CHOPPED CLAMS	1 pint
CREAM, LIGHT or HALF-and-HALF	3 pints
BUTTER PATS	as needed

Procedure

1. In steam-jacketed kettle or large pot, saute salt pork until transparent. Add onion; saute until golden.
2. Add clam juice, potatoes, salt, and pepper. Boil for about 20 minutes, until potatoes are tender.
3. Add clams and cream. Heat through but do not boil.
4. Float a butter pat on top of each portion.

HALIBUT WITH DILL PICKLE SAUCE

Yield: 50 portions

Ingredients

HALIBUT FILLETS, 1 inch thick	12 pounds
COMMERCIAL SOUR CREAM	3 quarts
CHOPPED DILL PICKLES	1 pint
CHOPPED GREEN ONIONS	1 pint
CHOPPED GREEN PEPPER	1 cup
CHOPPED PARSLEY	3/4 cup
LEMON JUICE	3/4 cup
DRY MUSTARD	1 tablespoon
BASIL	1 tablespoon
SALT	1 tablespoon
PEPPER	1 teaspoon

Procedure

1. Arrange halibut in greased baking pans.
2. Combine all remaining ingredients and pour over fish.
3. Bake in oven at 350°F. for 30 minutes.
4. Garnish with dill pickle slices and parsley sprigs.

Pickle Packers International, Inc.

ROAST TURKEY

Yield: 10 portions

Ingredients

TURKEY, 8 to 10 POUNDS	1
SALT	as needed
PEPPER	as needed
BUTTER	1/4 cup
DICED SOUP GREENS (CELERY and ONION)	1 cup
CHICKEN STOCK	1 quart
CORNSTARCH	3 teaspoons

Procedure

1. Season turkey with salt and pepper. Rub turkey with butter and place in a roasting pan in oven at 400°F. After 1/2 hour, reduce heat to 325°F.

2. Add vegetables to pan for gravy. When turkey is tender and well browned,* remove from roasting pan.

3. Brown vegetables in roasting pan on top of stove. Add chicken stock. Let boil well. Thicken with cornstarch.

4. Strain gravy and season to taste.

*The roasting time of a young 8 to 10 pound turkey should be 2-1/2 to 3 hours. Baste and turn bird to all sides for even roasting.

Note

Serve with Apple-Sage Dressing and Cranberry Puff.

United Airlines Food Services Library

BOSTON BURGER

Yield: 1 portion

Ingredients

HAMBURGER	1
ONION BUN	1
BOSTON BAKED BEANS	1 scoop
CHEDDAR CHEESE	1 slice
LETTUCE LEAF	1
ONION	1 slice
TOMATO WEDGE	1
KOSHER PICKLE	1 slice
FRENCH FRIES	one order

Procedure

1. Broil the hamburger and place on half of a toasted onion bun topped with baked beans, and the slice of cheddar cheese. Glaze in the salamander.

2. On the other half of toasted onion bun, place one crisp lettuce leaf topped with the onion slice, tomato wedge, and kosher pickle. Serve with french fries next to the hamburger.

Ilikai, Hawaii

APPLE-SAGE DRESSING

Yield: 6 portions

Ingredients

CHOPPED ONION	1/4 cup
CHOPPED CELERY	1/4 cup
BUTTER	1 teaspoon
CHICKEN BASE	1/2 teaspoon
FRENCH ROLLS, diced	6
APPLE, peeled, sliced	4 ounces
SAGE	to taste
POULTRY SEASONING	to taste
SALT	to taste
PEPPER	to taste
EGG, slightly beaten	1

Procedure

1. Saute onion and celery in butter.

2. Add chicken base (dissolved in water) and the bread, apples, and seasonings. Mix and remove from fire.

3. Add egg; mix well. Place mixture in a stainless steel pan. Bake in oven at 350°F. for 20 minutes.

Note

Use to accompany Roast Turkey.

United Airlines Food Services Library, Duri Arquisch

LAMB SPARERIBS WITH PICKLE SAUCE

Yield: 25 portions

Ingredients

LAMB SPARERIBS	16 pounds
WATER	1-1/2 cups
DRY MUSTARD	2 teaspoons
LIGHT MOLASSES	2 cups
PICKLE RELISH	2 cups

Procedure

1. Arrange ribs in baking pans. Bake in oven at 325°F. for 1 hour. Pour off excess fat.

2. Combine water, mustard, light molasses, and pickle relish. Spoon molasses sauce over ribs and continue baking for 1-1/4 hours, basting frequently.

Pickle Packers International, Inc.

BOSTON BAKED BEANS

(The Durgin-Park recipe calls for California pea beans and constant watching.)

Yield: 10 entree portions

Ingredients

DRY BEANS	2 pounds
BAKING SODA	1 teaspoon
SALT PORK with RIND	1 pound
ONION, MEDIUM-SIZED	1
SUGAR	1/2 cup
SALT	4 teaspoons
DRY MUSTARD	2 teaspoons
PEPPER	1/2 teaspoon
MOLASSES	2/3 cup
WATER, hot	as needed

Procedure

1. Soak beans overnight in enough cold water to cover to depth of 2 inches above beans.

2. In the morning, add baking soda; parboil for 10 minutes. Rinse beans in colander under cool running water.

3. Cut salt pork into 1/2-inch squares. Place half of pork squares on bottom of 2-quart bean pot.

4. Add whole onion, then drained beans. Add remaining pork squares.

5. Mix all remaining ingredients with about 1 pint hot water. Pour over beans.

6. Bake in oven at 300°F. for 6 hours. Add more hot water as needed to keep beans moist during cooking. (Beans should never be flooded and never be dry.)

Durgin-Park, Boston

NEW ENGLAND BOILED DINNER

Yield: 25 portions

Ingredients

CORNED BEEF ROUNDS or BRISKETS	10 to 12 pounds
WATER	as needed
ONIONS, MEDIUM-SIZED	6
GARLIC CLOVES (optional)	2
BAY LEAVES	3
BLACK PEPPERCORNS	16
CLOVES	6
MUSTARD SEED	1 teaspoon
SALT PORK, cut in 1-inch cubes (optional)	1/2 pound
CARROTS	2 pounds
PARSNIPS, cut up	2 pounds
POTATOES, MEDIUM-SIZED	25 (about 6-1/2 pounds)
TURNIPS or RUTABAGAS, quartered	1 pound
CABBAGE, MEDIUM-SIZED HEADS, cored, cut into wedges	5

Procedure

1. Cover corned beef with water in steam-jacketed kettle or large pot. Bring to a boil. Reduce heat; simmer 10 minutes.

2. Skim off foam. Add garlic, onions, cloves, peppercorns, bay leaves, mustard seed, and salt pork. Simmer for about 3-1/2 hours, or until meat is tender.

3. Add carrots, parsnips, potatoes, and turnips. Cook for about 20 minutes, until almost tender.

4. Remove meat and slice for service.

5. Add cabbage to kettle; cook 15 minutes or just until cabbage is tender crisp.

SQUASH WITH RUBY STUFFING

Yield: 24 portions

Ingredients

WINTER SQUASH (ACORN, HUBBARD, or BUTTERNUT)	12 to 14 pounds
SALT	as needed
PEPPER	as needed
CRANBERRIES, chopped	3 pounds
APPLES, cored, chopped	2 pounds
ORANGES, peeled, diced	1 pound
BROWN SUGAR	12 ounces
BUTTER or MARGARINE, melted	12 ounces

Procedure

1. Cut squash into 24 equal serving portions; remove seeds, but leave rind on.
2. Place squash with rind up in oiled baking pans. Bake in oven at 350°F. for 40 minutes.
3. Turn squash so rind is on bottom. Lightly sprinkle squash with salt and pepper.
4. Mix together cranberries, apples, oranges, and brown sugar.
5. Portion cranberry mixture onto squash portions; use a No. 24 scoop.
6. Drizzle about 1 tablespoon melted butter over stuffing on each portion.
7. Bake stuffed squash in oven at 350°F. for 20 to 30 minutes longer, until apples and squash are tender.

CORN BREAD

Yield: 21 to 24 portions

Ingredients

SUGAR	3/4 cup
EGGS	2
FLOUR	2 cups
CORN MEAL	1 cup
BAKING POWDER	1 tablespoon
SALT	3/4 teaspoon
MILK	1-1/2 cups
BUTTER, melted	1 tablespoon

Procedure

1. Beat sugar and eggs until frothy.
2. Sift together flour, corn meal, baking powder, and salt. Stir flour mixture into egg mixture.
3. Beat in milk and melted butter.
4. Turn batter into well-buttered pan, about 10-inch by 20-inch.
5. Bake in oven at 400°F. until browned on edges, about 25 minutes. Cut into squares to serve.

PATRIOT'S PICKLE BREAD

Yield: 4 loaves

Ingredients

FLOUR	3 quarts
SUGAR	2 cups
BAKING POWDER	1/3 cup
SALT	1/4 cup
BUTTER, softened	1 pound
CHOPPED DILL PICKLE	2-2/3 cups
CHOPPED NUTS	2 cups
CHOPPED PIMIENTO	1/2 cup
MILK	3 cups
EGGS, beaten slightly	8

Procedure

1. Sift together flour, sugar, baking powder, and salt.
2. Add butter and mix with paddle one minute at low speed.
3. Mix in pickle, nuts, and pimiento. Add milk and eggs; blend lightly.
4. Divide batter into 4 greased 9-inch by 5-inch by 3-inch loaf pans. Smooth tops.
5. Bake in oven at 350°F. for 55 to 65 minutes. Cool in pans.

Pickle Packers International, Inc.

HONEY DRESSING

Yield: about 5 gallons

Ingredients

VINEGAR	1-1/2 gallons
SUGAR	12 cups
HONEY	9 cups
DRY MUSTARD	1 cup
PAPRIKA	1 cup
CELERY SALT	3 cups
CELERY SEED	1-1/2 cups
SALAD OIL	3 gallons
HONEY	3 cups
ONION JUICE	1-1/2 cups

Procedure

1. Combine vinegar, first amount of honey, sugar, mustard, and paprika in large pot. Boil until mixture begins to thicken, about 30 to 45 minutes.
2. Allow vinegar mixture to cool.
3. Mix together oil, second amount of honey, onion juice, celery salt, and celery seed.
4. Then gradually whisk oil mixture into vinegar mixture.

GINGER PUMPKIN SOUFFLE

Yield: 2 portions

Ingredients

CANNED PUMPKIN	1/2 cup
BROWN SUGAR	1 tablespoon
MOLASSES	1 tablespoon
GROUND GINGER	1/4 teaspoon
GROUND ALLSPICE	1/8 teaspoon
SALT	dash
BUTTER	1 tablespoon
EGG YOLKS, beaten	2
EGG WHITES	2
SUGAR	1 tablespoon
SALT	dash
CANDIED GINGER	as needed

Procedure

1. Cook together the pumpkin, brown sugar, molasses, ginger, allspice, salt, and butter. Stir and cook until butter melts and mixture is hot.

2. Slowly stir pumpkin mixture into beaten egg yolks, return mixture to pan and cook 2 minutes over low heat, stirring constantly. Remove from heat; let cool slightly.

3. Whip egg whites until soft peaks form; add sugar and salt. Whip until glossy stiff peaks form.

4. Fold pumpkin mixture into whipped egg whites. Turn into 2 buttered souffle dishes. Place in pan of water 1 inch deep.

5. Bake in oven at 350°F. for about 25 minutes, or until knife inserted near center comes out clean. Garnish with candied ginger.

CRANBERRY PUFF

Yield: 6 portions

Ingredients

APPLE, SMALL	1
CARROT, SMALL	1
CRANBERRIES	12 ounces
SUGAR	1 tablespoon
ORANGE JUICE	2 ounces
COCONUT	1 teaspoon
CREAM SAUCE	1 tablespoon
BREAD CRUMBS	1 teaspoon
EGG WHITES	2
SUGAR	1 teaspoon
EGG YOLKS	3

Procedure

1. Grind apples, carrots, and cranberries through fine meat grinder. Add the sugar, orange juice, and coconut.

2. Cook very slowly for 20 to 30 minutes.

3. Remove from heat and add the cream sauce and bread crumbs.

4. Whip egg whites with 1 teaspoon sugar (do not whip too stiff) and fold into the cranberry-fruit mixture. Add the egg yolks.

5. Place in buttered baking dish (muffin dish) and bake in oven at 350°F. until done, about 35 minutes.

Note

Use to accompany Roast Turkey with Apple-Sage Dressing.

**United Airlines Food Services Library,
Duri Arquisch**

APPLE PAN DOWDY

(This is very similar to apple pie, says the Durgin-Park recipe.)

Yield: 8 to 10 portions

Ingredients

PASTRY	2 pounds (about)
APPLES, MEDIUM-SIZED, peeled, cored	24
SUGAR	2 cups
MOLASSES	1 cup
GROUND CINNAMON	2 teaspoons
GROUND NUTMEG	2 teaspoons
SALT	1/2 teaspoon
BUTTER, cut into small pieces	1/3 cup

Procedure

1. Line a 2 inch deep, 10- or 12-inch pan with half the pastry.

2. Slice or coarsely chop apples. Mix apples with remaining ingredients, except pastry and butter. Spread apple mixture evenly in pan. Dot with the butter pieces.

3. Roll out remaining pastry; place over apples. Cut small slits in top crust to allow steam to escape.

4. Bake in oven at 350°F. for about 1 hour, or until crust is golden. Serve warm.

Durgin-Park, Boston

FRUIT BETTY

Yield: 35 portions

Ingredients

PIE, FILLING and CRUST	3 quarts
BROWN SUGAR, No. 9, light	3/4 quart
LEMON RIND	2 teaspoons
LEMON JUICE	3 tablespoons
WATER, hot	1/2 cup
BUTTER, melted	1/2 cup

Procedure

1. Grease a large pan. Cut leftover pie into small pieces.

2. Add brown sugar, lemon rind and juice, water, and butter.

3. Bake in covered pan in oven at 350°F. for 1-1/2 to 2 hours, or steam, covered, until done, approximately 1/2 hour in steamer.

4. Serve with Lemon, Orange, or Foamy Sauce.

Arlington, Virginia

BAKED INDIAN PUDDING

Yield: 2 quarts

Ingredients

MILK, hot	5 cups
BLACK MOLASSES	1/2 cup
SUGAR	1/4 cup
LARD or BUTTER	1/4 cup
SALT	1/4 teaspoon
BAKING SODA	1/4 teaspoon
EGGS	2
MILK, hot	5 cups

Procedure

1. Mix first amount of hot milk with remaining ingredients, except second amount of hot milk. Beat until thoroughly mixed.

2. Turn into well-greased baking crock or souffle dish.

3. Bake in oven at 425°F. until mixture boils. Then stir in remaining hot milk.

4. Reduce heat to 275°F. Bake pudding for 5 to 7 hours, until set like custard and knife inserted near center comes out clean.

5. Serve warm with vanilla ice cream.

The Inns and Taverns of New York

AMONG THE EARLIEST recorded historical events in New York State was one in which white settlers were saved by foodservice, an "eat-all" dinner given for the Onandaga Indians by the settlers.

The dinner was planned as a cover for the escape of the settlers who had come to the area hoping to stay, but learned after a few months that they were about to be massacred. The dinner, which took place on May 17, 1656, was a success as the Indians, having accepted the challenge to eat all the food set before them, became so comatose that they were not aware that their intended victims had departed. The tale of "the Eat-All Diner" is retold in *The Tavern Lamps Are Burning*, by Carl Carmer.

The reputation for unique approaches to foodservice demonstrated in that event has been maintained throughout the centuries since both in New York City and the six regions into which the state divides.

The size of the state in itself encouraged varied styles in menus and lodgings. The growing conditions and sources of food supplies changed with the regions so that there was no single cuisine that could represent all of New York State. The six regions can be considered as follows: (1) The Hudson, The Catskills, The Taconics; (2) The Adirondacks, The St. Lawrence; (3) The Mohawk Valley, The Erie; (4) The Finger Lakes; (5) Western New York, and (6) The Southern Tier.

The distances that had to be covered in the state led to the development of the inns which made stagecoach and river packet trips possible, first for settlers, later for traders, and finally for homesteaders traveling from the port of New York City through New York State to the frontier beyond.

Later the "drummers" who brought goods from the city for buyers in the state's six regions kept the inns filled and encouraged steady improvement in accommodations. Special resorts were established at about that time in the many scenic areas of the state for the city dwellers who needed a pleasant place to go during the summer. Many of these continue to operate successfully today.

But New York City must be given the credit for playing host to Washington and his generals at a crucial point in the development of this country.

Revolutionary Taste Sensations

The torch held by the famous lady in Manhattan's harbor never shone on George Washington. But behind New York's frieze of 20th-century skyscrapers nestle inns that witnessed America's revolution—and still carry on the spirit of '76.

Fraunces Tavern
New York City

The echoes of George Washington's 1783 farewell to his officers remain at Fraunces Tavern, where the commander-in-chief often liked to sup. The tavern's owner, Samuel Fraunces, had a winsome young daughter named Phoebe.

Now, Phoebe had an Irish lover, a redcoat with a more than ordinary interest in the general's diet. He poisoned some peas Phoebe was to serve to Washington and to General Putnam. When she discovered the plot, Phoebe turned her lover in—and he was hanged at Bowling Green.

Reputedly the "oldest continuously operating tavern in the English-speaking world," Fraunces opened in 1762 as Queen's Head Tavern. Even then, location was key to foodservice/lodging success: the Queen's Street site was on the Boston Post road, in the Wall Street district.

In the early days of the United States, all place names honoring royalty were changed. Queen's Street became Pearl Street, in reference to the oyster shells that paved it. And Fraunces put his own name to his tavern.

One of New York's largest buildings until 1800, the inn naturally played host to many important functions. A few months after the Boston Tea Party, the Sons of Liberty met at Fraunces. They proceeded to New York's harbor—and dumped tea from a British ship.

New York's Chamber of Commerce and its first hospital were conceived at Fraunces. In the 19th century, the tavern almost fell prey to the fire that burnt most of New York City—up to one block from Fraunces. (Like the New York Tea Party, the fire has been overshadowed in popular history by another city's event.)

More recently, a building next to the tavern was bombed. Fraunces had to close for a mere three days, and its damaged annex was soon re-opened.

In fact, the inn has seen so much history that part of it is now a museum. The Sons of the Revolution in New York State bought the building in about 1905 and tried to restore it to its original state. They display such treasures as Lafayette's blood-stained scarf in a third-floor exhibit area, and guide tours to the Long Room, where Washington bade his famous farewell, and another second-floor room that housed our first State Department and part of the original Treasury Dept.

But Fraunces is also very much a restaurant. Guided by the Norden family since 1937, the inn has been expanded to about 400 seats in six dining rooms. Robert Norden, who took over operations from his father in 1960, carefully maintains the Colonial atmosphere. Service plates feature George Washington's picture; dining room walls have pictures from the tavern's museum; and the menu includes such traditional dishes as Baked Chicken a la Washington.

Operating a restaurant in a museum has special problems, Norden confides. For example, the building has very thick walls—some showing bits of shell, mud, and hair used in the original construction—that complicate any attempts to run in new water lines. Then there are the school children who troop in and out.

But the 250 to 300 customers who lunch and sup at Fraunces each weekday come for the food, spending an average of $8 to $9 for it. Norden takes pride in his popular daily special—usually fish, such as striped bass with orange sauce or red snapper or shad roe, that he selects at the nearby Fulton Fish Market each morning.

"Basically, my customers come here to have a business lunch," Norden says. "It's a great place to eat and discuss their business."

Many Wall Street groups are Fraunces' regulars. And the restaurant caters such functions as retirement parties. But with the interest in American history generated by the Bicentennial, tourist interest could add 10 percent to sales.

During the Bicentennial, Norden offers a Colonial special each day, priced at about $6. These menu offerings include dry-cured ham, curry, Brunswick stew, Indian pudding, apple cobbler.

Norden is also featuring Fish House punch, which was created in 1732. A strong, sneaky drink, it starts with a rum base to which lemon juice and peach brandy are added.

Like Fish House punch, the history of Fraunces Tavern has a strong, subtle, irresistible appeal.

"Usually I'm so busy I don't think about those things," Norden says. "But sometimes I do, and I feel warm. Sometimes I sit at Lafayette's desk. Or I run my hand over the back of a chair and think, 'Washington might have sat here'."

Milleridge Inn
Jericho, N. Y.

Concern for the dignity of men of property inflamed Colonial Americans. One indignity that enraged them was "Quartering," forcing residents to give room and board to British soldiers. Among the houses so inflicted was the Milleridge, home during the Revolutionary War period of Elias Hicks.

Hicks and his Jericho neighbors were Quakers, who first settled the area in 1653. Mary Willets began the Milleridge house with two rooms in 1672.

By 1783, the nearby turnpike had become a major road. To forestall the opening of bars and grog houses, Hicks opened his house to travelers, caring for as many as 20 a night. He served them simple fare—stews, fish, meat, and home-baked bread—and lodged them.

As new highways were built, Jericho returned to repose. The old Hicks house continued to be a private home, with additions making it a stately white clapboard mansion, until well into the 20th century.

Now, the Milleridge Inn is one of the most famous eating places on Long Island. Bought by the Murphy family 12 years ago, it is an extremely large *a la carte* restaurant—with seats for more than 1,000 people. Manager Jack Terzi estimates that Milleridge's 300 employees serve at least 12,000 people during the inn's seven-day week, with an average cover of $4 at lunch and $7 to $8 at dinner.

One of the original rooms of the house remains as a dining area, called the Willets Room. Two dining rooms at the back are also old, with newer rooms at the front. The bar area was created out of a former lean-to that served as the barn. Upstairs rooms are set up for small parties. The entire structure is replete with old pictures and artifacts and Colonial-type fireplaces.

The Milleridge attracts family business. Weekends are always jammed, and the inn serves an estimated 4,500 patrons on Mother's Day alone. It pulls in customers from New York City, and—since it is in the middle of Long Island—it attracts many business meetings.

Guests can enjoy traditional menu fare, such as pot roast. But most popular are prime rib, mushrooms stuffed with shrimp and crab, and fresh trout stuffed with shrimp and crab.

But Milleridge Inn is more than a restaurant. Shortly after the Murphy family took over, they began to create a village of gift shops by moving old buildings to the site. Among the items sold: Milleridge's own breads and bakery products.

"People can browse as well as eat," observes Terzi. "They can spend an hour or an afternoon."

Born and raised near Jericho, Terzi takes pride in the old building and in the Murphy's efforts to maintain it. He concedes that it takes a lot of money. One big problem: the old structure's heavy beams and flooring must be supported by a spider web of beams in the basement. That complicates any necessary repairs or replacements on the old plumbing and electrical systems.

Yet it is the inn's past that helps assure a proud future.

"There's a growing interest in historical places," Terzi believes. "People are looking for roots. Everybody is looking to belong to something."

The Old '76 House
Tappan, N. Y.

Now it can be told: the noble words of our Declaration of Independence trace their origins to a bar.

On July 4, 1774, the citizens of Orangetown met at the Yoast-Marble Tavern, now the Old '76 House. Still loyal to the crown but distressed by some Colonial practices, they drafted the Orangetown Resolutions. Two years later, some of their concepts were incorporated into that other document, also signed on July 4.

Built in 1733, the Old '76 House was an overnight stop for the Albany-New York stagecoach run. It became a favorite gathering place for the Hudson Valley Command under General Greene in 1780. A plaque near the bar lists some of the men who drank there: General Washington, General Lafayette, Alexander Hamilton and—the patron most connected with the tavern—John Andre.

This British spy plotted with Benedict Arnold to turn the fort of West Point over to the redcoats in 1780. Major Andre was captured across the river from Tappan with the sinister plans in his boot. He was kept at the Old '76 House until his fate was decided. Then he was taken to a nearby hill and hanged.

The tavern today recalls that event. The room where Major Andre was "imprisoned" has been kept virtually intact—with the addition of a painting showing the condemned man leaving for the gallows. On the left side of the doorway separating the tavern's two dining rooms is a picture of "Major Andre, the Spy;" on the right is a picture of "Benedict Arnold, the Traitor"—hanging upside down.

The present owners look upon the tavern as a trust. Thomas McCabe and Thomas Ciganek bought the property two years ago, leaving management to Mark Ciganek and Ingo Schneider. They have added to the memorabilia housed there.

"We have a genuine interest in American history," says Mark Ciganek. "The restaurant is not 100 percent commercialized, and that's a big thing these days. In other words, we're trying to keep something the way it was.

"Although the placed is owned, the history dictates it belongs to everyone," he adds.

The only remodeling done was to put in a wall to block the view of the kitchen from the dining room. And, although the Old '76 House is open only for dinner, Ciganek often comes in during the day to let groups interested in history look around.

Most interest centers in the tap room, reportedly the most original in the U.S., which dates back to 1755. Proud features are cocktails named for Major Andre and Benedict Arnold.

Far from being kept on bread and water, Major Andre was well served. So are the 525 patrons who come to the 130-seat restaurant each week.

The Old '76 House specialty starts with a shrimp cocktail, prepared by the same cook— famous for his tangy sauce—for the past 20 years. The $10.75 meal also includes steak, salad, vegetables, potatoes, rolls, dessert, and beverage.

The menu presents the new with the old. To one side are listed the three credit cards accepted. On the other side are old rules of the inn: "No more than five to sleep in one bed. No boots to be worn in bed. Organ grinders to sleep in wash house. No dogs allowed upstairs. No rum allowed in kitchen. No razor grinders or tinkers taken in."

Having that kind of historical reference makes the Old '76 House a special restaurant. Ciganek likes to sit there alone after closing, finding a peaceful feeling by getting in touch with our Revolutionary War past.

New York Recipes

BENEDICT ARNOLD COCKTAIL

Yield: 1

Ingredients

FRESH LEMON JUICE	1 ounce
GRENADINE	1 ounce
BLACK CHERRY BRANDY	1 ounce
VODKA	1-1/2 ounces
TEQUILA	1-1/2 ounces

Procedure

1. Place ingredients into a mixing glass and ice. Shake vigorously.

2. Pour into a large metal mug. Garnish with a large wedge of lime.

Note

The Old '76 House bills this drink as "a traitor's delight."

The Old '76 House

MAJOR ANDRE COCKTAIL

Yield: 1

Ingredients

CREAM, HEAVY	2 ounces
CREME DE ALMOND	1/2 ounce
CREME DE CACAO (WHITE)	1 ounce
FRENCH ARMAGNAC	1 ounce

Procedure

1. Measure all ingredients into a mixing glass. Shake lightly. Strain.

2. Pour into a large stem glass.

(Drink was developed to reflect the characteristics of Major Andre: artistic, gentle, esthetic.)

The Old '76 House

COLD CREAM OF CELERY SOUP

Yield: 3 quarts

Ingredients

CELERY ROOT	
(2 pieces, cleaned, cut small)	1 pound
CHOPPED ONION	1/2 pound
BUTTER	2 ounces
CHICKEN STOCK	1/2 gallon
CHICKEN BASE	2 ounces
RICE FLOUR	3 ounces
CREAM, LIGHT	6 ounces
WATER	6 ounces
EGG YOLKS	3
CREAM, HEAVY	4 ounces
MILK	1 pint
CREAM, WHIPPED	1/2 quart
PORT WINE	4 ounces
CELERY ROOT, grated	1/2 pound

Procedure

1. Saute celery root and onion in butter until golden brown.

2. Add chicken stock and chicken base to sauteed celery and onion. Stir well and let simmer for 1 hour.

3. Mix rice flour, light cream, and water together to a smooth consistency.

4. Add this slowly to the cooking stock, stirring constantly.

5. Mix egg yolks and heavy cream. Add to stock, stirring constantly. Let simmer for 1/2 hour.

6. Strain mixture through china cap and let chill.

7. Add milk and port wine. Fold in whipped cream so that it does not break up. Add grated celery root and mix well.

8. To serve, sprinkle with chopped chives.

Top of the Park Restaurant

Above: Fraunces Tavern successfully promotes original American flavors to today's Wall Street brokers. Recipes in use were researched from original Colonial versions, then adapted for today's methods and ingredients. The professionalism of Samuel Fraunces, who was so respected that George Washington named him Steward of the Presidential Household in 1789, prevails today.

Right: When Fraunces took over the tavern in 1770, the building was already 51 years old. Bits of oyster shell, mud, and hair used in original construction can still be seen in walls.

NEW YORK

Right: The fifes and drums of the Revolutionary War still echo at the Old '76 House, Tappan, N. Y. The bar was installed in 1755 and was part of the inn when George Washington and Alexander Hamilton met there to plan battle strategy.

Above: The room in the Old '76 House where British spy John Andre was held captive is a lure for history buffs. Painting shows Andre on way to be hanged.

Left: Milleridge Inn, Jericho, N.Y. is an authentic example of the way inns developed as the population of New York grew and travel through the state increased. (More pictures on next page.)

Milleridge Inn has grown from a private home welcoming a few travelers into a foodservice complex serving 1000 people a day. Also added is this village of old shops relocated on the Milleridge site and a popular browsing spot.

Above: One of the first additions to the original two-room house contained a large cooking fireplace. Utensils typical of those used to cook the meals of travelers arriving by stagecoach at the Jericho, N. Y. stop are items of decorative and historical interest today.

Left: The intimate dining areas, enhanced by unusual Colonial artifacts, reflect the friendly atmosphere that has prevailed at the Inn since its earliest days.

LONG ISLAND DUCKLING

Yield: 8 portions

Ingredients

LONG ISLAND DUCKLINGS, 5-1/2 POUNDS	2
SALT	to taste
PEPPER	to taste
VEGETABLE GREENS, diced (SOUP GREENS)	1 pound
MEAT STOCK	1 pint
BROWN VEAL STOCK	1 cup
ORANGES	3
LEMON JUICE	1 tablespoon
CURRANT JELLY	2 tablespoons
SHERRY	1/2 cup
CORNSTARCH	2 teaspoons
MARASCHINO CHERRIES	8
ORANGES, sectioned	2
CHOPPED PARSLEY	to garnish

Procedure

1. Roast well-seasoned ducklings in oven at 400°F. for 45 minutes.

2. Drain off excess fat. Add diced soup greens. Reduce oven temperature to 350°F. and continue baking 1-1/4 hours longer or until ducklings are well done.

3. Remove ducklings from pan.

4. Add meat stock, brown veal stock, juice of the oranges, lemon juice, and currant jelly to the pan. Strain.

5. Add sherry and lightly blanched julienne of orange rind. Thicken mixture with cornstarch dissolved in small amount of water. Season to taste.

6. Cut ducklings into portion size and place 3 orange sections and halved maraschino cherries on top. Pour gravy over the ducks and sprinkle with chopped parsley.

United Airlines Food Services Library

HERBED LEMON BARBECUED CHICKEN

Yield: 48 portions

Ingredients

LEMON JUICE	2-2/3 cups
WATER	2-2/3 cups
CATSUP	2 cups
DARK BROWN SUGAR, (packed measure)	3/4 cup
PAPRIKA	1/2 cup
ONION POWDER	1/2 cup
CORNSTARCH	1/4 cup
SALT	2-1/2 tablespoons
OREGANO LEAVES	2 tablespoons
GARLIC POWDER	4 teaspoons
GROUND RED PEPPER	1 tablespoon
POWDERED MUSTARD	2 teaspoons
THYME LEAVES	2 teaspoons
COOKING OIL	1 cup
PARSLEY FLAKES	1/4 cup
CHICKENS, quartered (2-1/2-pound size)	12
SALT	2-1/2 tablespoons

Procedure

1. Combine lemon juice, water, catsup, brown sugar, paprika, onion powder, cornstarch, first amount of salt, oregano, garlic powder, red pepper, mustard, and thyme; blend well.

2. Stir in oil. Cook and stir until mixture thickens, about 3 minutes.

3. Remove from heat; stir in parsley flakes. Cool; set aside.

4. Sprinkle both sides of chicken pieces with remaining salt.

5. Broil chicken about 30 minutes, turning often.

6. Brush with the barbecue sauce; continue to broil, turning and brushing frequently with the sauce, until chicken is tender, about 15 to 20 minutes.

CHICKEN MOMI

Yield: 20 portions

Ingredients

CHICKEN BREASTS, halved	20 8-ounce halves
CHICKEN MOMI DRESSING	prepare 1 recipe
SALT	to taste
COOKING OIL	as needed
PINEAPPLES	10
HONEY	8 ounces
SESAME SEED, toasted	1/3 cup

Procedure

1. Remove all bones from chicken breasts.

2. Fill cavities with Chicken Momi Dressing. Salt chicken breasts and cook in oil on sheet pan in oven at 350°F. for 1 hour, or until brown and tender.

3. Split pineapples in half lengthwise. Remove cores only. Section meat of pineapples with grapefruit knife and leave as you do with a grapefruit, segments free but in place.

4. Slice chicken into 4 cuts, re-form breast, and place on top of pineapple. Take scant tablespoon of honey and glaze over top of each chicken breast. Sprinkle with toasted sesame seeds.

5. Bake in oven at 400°F. for 10 to 15 minutes.

Service Systems Corporation

DRESSING FOR CHICKEN MOMI

Yield: 20 portions

Ingredients

GROUND VEAL	2 pounds
GROUND PORK	2 pounds
STALE WHITE or FRENCH BREAD, soaked in cream (half-and-half)	1 cup
FINELY CHOPPED ONION	1/2 cup
EGGS, beaten slightly	8
SOY SAUCE	8 ounces
GINGER	2 teaspoons
CAYENNE PEPPER	1/4 teaspoon
MONOSODIUM GLUTAMATE	1/2 teaspoon
CHOPPED WATER CHESTNUTS OR BEAN SPROUTS	2 cups

Procedure

Blend all ingredients.

Service Systems Corporation

LOBSTER SAUCE*

Yield: 2 portions

Ingredients

FRESH LOBSTER	2 pounds
BUTTER	1 tablespoon
SHALLOT, chopped	1
DRY SHERRY	1 cup
CREAM, HEAVY	1/2 cup
SALT	1 teaspoon
BLACK PEPPER, freshly ground	to taste
CREAM SAUCE	2 tablespoons

Procedure

1. Cut the lobster into 6 or 8 pieces.

2. Saute cut lobster in butter for 3 or 4 minutes. Add shallot, 1/2 cup sherry, cream, salt, and pepper. Cover tightly and cook for 20 minutes. Remove lobster and save it for another meal.

3. Cook remaining liquid until it is reduced to one half. Add cream sauce and stir until thickened. Season with salt and pepper and add remaining 1/2 cup of sherry. Strain through cheesecloth.

*To be served over any poached fish.

Top of the Park Restaurant

HOT REUBEN TURKEY SANDWICH

Yield: 96 sandwiches

Ingredients

CORNED BEEF, PRECOOKED	6 pounds
TURKEY ROLL, DARK	6 pounds
SAUERKRAUT	1 No. 10 can
CHEESE, SWISS	5 pounds (20 slices to pound)
KAISER ROLLS, PUMPERNICKEL	96

Procedure

1. Slice corned beef on slicer into 1/2-ounce slices. Use 2 slices for each sandwich.

2. Slice turkey into 1-ounce slices on slicer set on 8.

3. Place 1 ounce turkey on bun; top with 1 ounce corned beef, 1 ounce drained kraut, and 1 slice of cheese. Top with bun half.

4. Heat in convection oven at 350°F. for 2 to 3 minutes, or until cheese melts.

Westminster Choir College

BAKED EGGPLANT MOUSSAKA

Yield: 10 to 12 portions

Ingredients

EGGPLANT, MEDIUM- to LARGE-SIZED	2 or 3
OIL or VEGETABLE SHORTENING	1/2 cup
BUTTER or MARGARINE	1/4 pound
GROUND LAMB or BEEF	1-1/2 to 2 pounds
ONIONS, chopped	2 small or 1 large
CATSUP	1/2 cup
SALT	to season
PEPPER	to season
WHITE SAUCE	
BUTTER	1-1/2 tablespoons
CORNSTARCH	2 tablespoons
SALT	to taste
MILK	3 cups
EGGS	4
CATSUP, diluted in a little water	1 tablespoon
CINNAMON	1/2 teaspoon

Procedure

1. Wash eggplant and cut in 1/2-inch slices. Sprinkle with salt and let stand in a bowl for 1/2 hour, then rinse and dry in towel.

2. Melt oil and butter together. Oil cookie sheet with some of this mixture. Place slices of eggplant close together on the cookie sheet, brushing the tops with oil-butter mixture. Bake in pre-heated oven at 350°F. for about 15 minutes. Remove from oven.

3. Place a tablespoon of oil-butter mixture in a frying pan and cook meat, onions, catsup, salt, and pepper for about 10 minutes, until slightly brown.

4. Make a white sauce by heating butter and stirring in cornstarch and salt until mixture bubbles. Add milk gradually and heat until thickened.

5. Beat eggs and add a small quantity of white sauce, mixing well. Add this mixture to remaining sauce, along with the diluted catsup.

6. Oil the bottom and sides of a 12-inch by 9-inch baking pan with the oil-butter mixture.

7. Divide the eggplant into three portions and the meat into 2 portions. Spread one layer of eggplant on bottom of baking pan. Top with a layer of meat. Alternate layers of eggplant and meat, ending with eggplant layer. Pour the white sauce over the layers and sprinkle top with 1/2 teaspoon cinnamon.

9. Bake in oven at 325°F. for 3/4 to 1 hour until nicely browned.

Note

If any oil-butter mixture is left, it may be added before baking, if desired.

Peter Gust Economou—The Park Lane

HUNGARIAN BEEF ON NOODLES

Yield: 50 portions

Ingredients

STEW BEEF, cut 1 inch	15 pounds
ONION, diced	3 pounds
SHORTENING	3/4 cup
BAY LEAVES	2
GARLIC CLOVES, grated	3
SALT	1 ounce
PAPRIKA	6 tablespoons
TOMATOES	1 No. 10 can
WATER	1-1/2 quarts
FLOUR	1 pound
NOODLES	3 pounds

Procedure

1. Saute onion and beef in shortening.

2. Add next five ingredients and simmer 1 to 1-1/2 hours. Thicken with flour and water mixture.

3. Cook noodles according to package directions.

4. Serve beef mixture over noodles.

Note

Rice can be used instead of noodles.

MOHAWK CHOWDER

Yield: 32 servings, about 1 cup each

Ingredients

FORDHOOK LIMA BEANS, FROZEN	2-1/2 pounds
CHICKEN BROTH	2 quarts
CORN, CREAM-STYLE	2 quarts
CLAMS, CHOPPED	5 15-ounce cans
or	
OYSTERS, FRESH, shucked	1-1/4 quarts
HALF-AND-HALF	2 cups
WHITE PEPPER	1/2 teaspoon
SALT	as needed
PARSLEY, chopped	as needed

Procedure

1. Cook lima beans in broth until tender.
2. Add corn, oysters, half-and-half, and pepper. Heat through (or until oysters curl). Salt to taste.
3. Serve garnished with parsley.

**California Frozen Vegetable Council
FCB/PR**

CAVIAR MOLD

Yield: 7-1/2-inch by 4-inch by 2-1/4-inch mold

Ingredients

CAVIAR	4 to 6 ounces
GELATINE, UNFLAVORED	2 tablespoons
WATER, cold	1/4 cup
CHICKEN BROTH	14 ounces
DRY SHERRY	1/4 cup
EGGS, hard-cooked	4
FINELY CHOPPED GREEN ONIONS	3/4 cup

Procedure

1. Soak gelatine in cold water, then dissolve in boiling broth.
2. When cool, add sherry and pour thin covering in bottom of mold. Chill until set.
3. Carefully spread portion of caviar over this and barely cover with broth mixture. Chill until set.
4. Very finely chop egg whites and yolks separately. Add layer of egg whites and cover with broth. Chill.
5. Add layer of egg yolks and cover with broth. Chill.
6. Add layer of green onions. Chill.

7. Repeat the process with layers of each item, adding broth and chilling after each layer. Refrigerate overnight.
8. Before serving, carefully turn out on tray. Sprinkle top with a little fresh lemon juice and decorate with very thin slices of 1 lemon. Serve cold with thinly sliced french or italian bread. (Do not use crackers or rounds.)

Peter Gust Economou—The Park Lane

GREEK SALAD

Yield: 10 to 12 portions

Ingredients
DRESSING

OLIVE OIL	1 cup
WINE VINEGAR	1/2 cup
VERY FINELY CHOPPED FRESH BASIL	1 teaspoon
FINELY CRUMBLED OREGANO	1 teaspoon
SALT	2 teaspoons
FRESHLY CRUSHED BLACK PEPPER	1/2 teaspoon
FRESH LEMON JUICE	1-1/2 ounces
SALAD	
HEARTS of ICEBERG LETTUCE	1
TOMATO WEDGES	3
CUCUMBER, thinly sliced	3 slices
GREEN ONION, thinly sliced, quartered	1
GREEK OLIVES	4 or 5
FETA CHEESE	4 or 5 small chunks
ANCHOVY STRIPS	3 to 5

Procedure

1. Combine first 7 ingredients. Shake well. Chill.
2. After salad is arranged, shake dressing well and put two to three tablespoonfuls on each order.

Note

This salad has to be prepared on individual plates or in bowls with ingredients for one serving as follows: Arrange hearts of lettuce attractively in center of plate or bowl. Alternate tomato wedges and cucumber slices around lettuce. Arrange the remaining ingredients on top of the salad.

Peter Gust Economou—The Park Lane

WALDORF SALAD

Yield: 100 1/2-cup portions

Ingredients

DICED CELERY	1 No. 10 can
MAYONNAISE	3 cups
SOUR CREAM	2 cups
SALT	3 tablespoons
APPLES, diced, unpeeled	1-3/4 gallons (8 pounds)
WALNUTS, coarsely chopped	3 cups (1 pound)

Procedure

1. Wash celery. Rinse; drain well.
2. Combine mayonnaise, sour cream, and salt; blend.
3. Combine celery and apples. Add dressing; toss to mix. Add walnuts just before serving.

CONGEALED CRANBERRY SALAD

Yield: 100 servings

Ingredients

GELATIN, LEMON FLAVOR	1 box, 24 ounces
GELATIN, CHERRY FLAVOR	1 box, 24 ounces
HOT WATER (180°F.)	3 quarts
COLD WATER	2 quarts
CRANBERRY SAUCE, WHOLE	1 No. 10 can
CELERY	1/2 pound
ORANGE SECTIONS, CANNED	2-1/2 pounds
PECANS, MEDIUM-SIZED	1/2 pound

Procedure

1. Dissolve gelatin in hot water. Mix in whole cranberry sauce.
2. Add cold water and stir well.
3. Chill and allow to thicken slightly.
4. Chop celery in chopper
5. Rinse orange sections with cold water and drain; cut by hand into 1/2-inch pieces.
6. When gelatin is slightly thickened, add celery, orange sections, and pecans. Mix well.
7. Pour mixture into individual molds. Refrigerate to congeal.
8. Serve on lettuce leaf.

Westminster Choir College

CONCORD ICE CREAM PIE

Yield: 6 10-inch pies

Ingredients

CORN FLAKE CRUMBS	3 quarts
SUGAR	1 cup
CINNAMON	2 teaspoons
BUTTER or MARGARINE, melted	1 pound
ICE CREAM, VANILLA	2 gallons
CONCORD GRAPE PRESERVES	3 quarts
LEMON RIND, grated from	6 lemons
SLICED APPLES, CANNED, chopped	1-1/2 quarts

Procedure

1. Mix crumbs, sugar, cinnamon, and butter. Press mixture firmly and evenly into six buttered 10-inch pie pans. Chill.
2. Soften ice cream. Spoon a layer of the ice cream into each pie shell, allowing about 2-1/2 cups per pie. Spread evenly in crumb crusts.
3. Combine preserves, lemon rind, and chopped apples; mix; divide mixture into two equal parts. Use one part to spread over the ice cream in each pie shell.
4. Top with remaining ice cream, again allowing about 2-1/2 cups per pie.
5. Drizzle remaining fruit mixture over ice cream. Freeze until hard.
6. When ready to serve, cut into portions while frozen hard. Allow to stand for a few minutes before serving.

Variation

For fruit mixture, combine 3 quarts of concord grape preserves with the grated rind from 4 oranges and 2-1/4 quarts sliced fresh strawberries. Mix and use as in recipe above. Sprinkle 2 cups coconut on pies, dividing evenly. Freeze.

OLD-FASHIONED STRAWBERRY SHORTCAKE

Yield: 100 shortcakes

Ingredients

FRESH STRAWBERRIES	18 quarts
SUGAR	4 pounds
BISCUIT MIX	6 pounds
SUGAR (optional)	1 cup
CREAM	3 pounds
WHIPPED CREAM or	
TOPPING	as needed

Procedure

1. Wash berries; remove hulls.

2. Slice berries, leaving some of them whole, if desired. Or, slice about one-half of the berries and crush the remainder. Spread prepared fruit in shallow containers; sprinkle with first amount of sugar; let stand for at least an hour.

3. Combine biscuit mix and remaining sugar; add cream to biscuit mix. Mix until soft dough forms.

4. Turn out on lightly floured board. Knead about 10 times. Roll out to 1/2-inch thickness. Cut out biscuits using a 3-inch cutter. Place on baking sheets.

5. Bake in oven at 450°F. for 10 to 15 minutes, or until golden brown.

6. Split biscuits. Spoon sweetened berries over bottom half. Cover with top half of biscuit; spoon berries over top. Garnish with whipped cream or topping.

PEACH PIE

Yield: 2 10-inch, or 3 9-inch pies

Ingredients

ELBERTA PEACHES, SLICED	1 No. 10 can
SUGAR	2 cups
FLOUR	1 cup (4 ounces)
GROUND CINNAMON	1 teaspoon
BUTTER or MARGARINE	1/4 cup (2 ounces)
ALMOND EXTRACT	1-1/2 teaspoons
GRATED LEMON RIND	2 teaspoons
LEMON JUICE	4 teaspoons
PIE PASTRY DOUGH	as needed

Procedure

1. Drain peaches well, reserving syrup.

2. Combine sugar, flour, and cinnamon. Add reserved syrup and butter. Cook and stir until mixture thickens and boils.

3. Add almond extract, lemon rind, lemon juice, and the drained peaches.

4. Line pie pans with pastry.

5. Divide peach filling evenly into pie shells. Bake in oven at 400°F. for 30 to 35 minutes.

6. Cut stars, bells, or other desired shapes from rolled-out pastry. Bake separately; arrange on top of baked pies.

7. Serve pie with whipped cream, sour cream, or ice cream, if desired.

Note

If desired, close pie with top crust (plain or lattice) and bake as directed.

Cumberland Trail to Adventures in Dining

PHILADELPHIA WAS not only the cradle of American independence, but also where some of our traditional American food favorites had their beginning. Philadelphia pepper-pot soup, according to legend, was invented for George Washington and his troops during their long winter at Valley Forge. This hearty soup of tripe spiced with both red and black pepper is today fortified with dumplings or potato cubes.

Philadelphia was also noted for its excellent ice cream as far back as 1782. The first recipe for ice cream found in the U.S. is in a 1792 Philadelphia cookbook. Even today, Philadelphia maintains its reputation.

But Philadelphia could not contain the American spirit for very long. Adventurous settlers trekked westward through the Cumberland Gap. As they explored "Kaintuck," they encountered new foods and started new customs.

Benjamin Franklin gave up printing for politics. Daniel Boone, Meriwether Lewis, and George Rogers Clark won their first fame in these mountains and river valleys.

The Dutch joined Scots and English along the Appalachian Trail, through the mountains into Penn's Woods. Germans settled in Pennsylvania and Ohio. This area witnessed one of the earliest blends of varied European cuisines in the American melting pot.

Wild game was plentiful on the Cumberland Trails. Cows, sheep, and goats came with the settlers.

Hospitality was a matter of survival as well as courtesy. Religious groups and Germans influenced eating habits. Stage coach lines brought "civilization" to dining tables of the inns.

Today, bear steak and terrapin stew are curiosities; wild game is served in private homes. Cider and dried apples are still popular. Sausage, fried chicken, and beer share honors with pickles. Corn is still a source of bread and moonshine.

Old Original Bookbinders
Philadelphia, Pa.

An Indian cemetery in back of the restaurant dates to 1682, when William Penn landed. Samuel and Sarah Bookbinder opened their restaurant about 160 years later near the docks on the Delaware River. Lunch was the main business; Sarah rang a bell to let the neighborhood know when to come in and eat. Today that bell is just inside the doorway of the restaurant.

Great and famous people dined at Old Original Bookbinders. But the wholesale merchants of Dock Street, the produce men and the fish merchants, came for lunch when Sarah rang the bell each day. Today such merchants still come in for lunch, often at the same tables, day after day.

John Taxin, himself a Dock Street produce merchant, bought Old Original Bookbinders in 1941. Today he and his son, Albert, have 180 employees for their 400-seat operation plus private dining rooms in frequent use. Lunch checks average $4.20.

"We are an institution, not just a restaurant," declares John Taxin.

The Lemon Tree
Lancaster, Pa.

Roy Reifsnyder bought The Lemon Tree in 1970 and turned the summer kitchen of the old (circa 1800) farmhouse into another dining room.

Antique silver, candles, Windsor and Hitchcock chairs set off the sophisticated and varied menu.

Bill Roberts, chef, and Richard Brooks, assistant chef, use fresh produce from local farms as well as the garden outside the restaurant's back door.

Reifsnyder and Roberts like to restructure classic recipes for Continental cuisine. They use the same ingredients to prepare the dish another way. "We serve provocative foods," says Roberts.

"Finicky," is the way Reifsnyder describes himself. He and the chefs seam veal, prepare vegetables only to order, bone their own ducks, and insist that waitresses ask whether diners prefer sauce on the plate or masking the food.

Four small dining rooms seat a total of 90. Average check, including wines and liquor, is about $12. Waitresses have only four tables per station.

"Our success is due to our good staff," declares Reifsnyder.

Plain & Fancy
Bird-in-Hand, Pa.

Lancaster County, Pa., must surely be the destination of more bus tours than any other spot in the world. Plain & Fancy Farm and Dining Room is in the heart of Lancaster County and the land of the Pennsylvania Dutch.

Local Mennonite and Amish farm women come in to cook for Plain & Fancy. "They cook just like they do at home," say Robert and Ruth Lapp.

Bob Lapp finished the dining room interior himself. Service is family style. Since the 1959 opening, business has grown rapidly; about 75 percent is repeat customers. On its biggest day ever, Plain & Fancy served 2,800 people.

The menu varies from day to day but always includes: two beef entrees, such as beef and noodles; chicken, and ham. A lower-cost entree is also available daily; ham loaf is a favorite. Patrons buy their meal tickets at the counter before going into the dining room.

Long tables, for 12, are filled with several groups. "We introduce people to one another as we seat them," explains Mrs. Lapp. "The waitresses have three tables to a station. With this kind of seating, and family-style service, turnover can be speedy."

John Wanamaker
Philadelphia, Pa.

In 1911 John Wanamaker opened his department store in its present downtown location. President Taft was there to dedicate the building.

The largest pipe organ in the world and a metal eagle with more than 2,000 separate feathers were brought into the main store from the 1904 Exposition in St. Louis. An Italian marble fountain, weighing five tons, was installed in the Grand Crystal Tea Room of the Philadelphia store.

Downtown Wanamaker's still offers a tea menu. Service is for one hour in the afternoon, except during the Christmas season when tea is served for two hours in the Crystal Room.

The Crystal Room, still the largest dining room in Philadelphia, has 22,000 sq. ft. and seating for 1,400. The average check is about $2.25. Chandeliers of Waterford and Lalique crystal give this room its name.

Downstairs in the contrasting Dairy Bar, a soft serve called Wanafrost is very popular. Check average at this snack bar is 88 cents.

Chef Ed Lamberter recently took over the kitchen from Chef Jean Chevral at the main store. Ten branch stores all use the same menu, but the main store maintains individuality. Foodservice Director William Farren explains, "Our customers come here to spend the whole day shopping. Wednesday is ladies' day in downtown Philadelphia."

Hotel Hershey
Hershey, Pa.

Hotel Hershey is a "grand resort hotel" with a 300-seat dining room, 75 percent occupancy rate, tennis courts, and all the amenities.

Built in the 1930s to provide employment for townspeople and stave off the Depression, the hotel also fulfilled Milton Hershey's dream. Hershey saw a picture of a Caribbean hotel and dreamed of one almost like it overlooking the town.

"Groups and conventions comprise only 50 percent of the business; families and individuals also enjoy choosing a meal/lodging plan suited to their need," says Donald Pierson, managing director.

The dinner dances and Sunday brunch bring in local people as well as travelers and hotel guests. "An 18-day cycle menu is served in the dining room," reports Chef Rupert Gruber. Dinner checks average $12.

Schmidt's Sausage Haus
Columbus, Ohio

Promotion is the key to success with this restaurant, which began as a packing house and sausage factory.

Schmidt's, owned by the J. Fred Schmidt Packing Co., is in a restored area called the German Village. By 1966, the third generation of Schmidts decided to capitalize on their sandwich business made famous by the state fair.

Menus are die-cut beer steins, which promote draft beer and two top-selling sandwiches from the state fair. Bratwurst *und* chips comes "state-fair style." The Bahama Mama is a smoked sausage served hot with German-style potato salad. Of course, kraut is offered as a side dish. Pies and pastries are displayed in cases by the entrance.

Frank Massaro, director of marketing and promotion, says the restaurant has a lunch check average of about $2.50; "dinner is more." Promotions include "Fasching," a festival similar to Mardi Gras in the spring; St. Patrick's Day; wooden pennies for souvenirs, and special pricing on retail sales. "We also pass out hundreds of menus and placemats," says Massaro.

The Oktoberfest is such a big festival that it moved from the German Village out to the state fairgrounds. Craftsmen display their art; dancers and musicians come to perform; people gorge on sausage sandwiches and beer from the Schmidt's concession.

The Shakers
Pleasant Hill, Ky.
The Golden Lamb Inn
Lebanon, Ohio

Although Shakers have vanished from the village of Pleasant Hill and the Golden Lamb Inn in Lebanon, their influence remains in many areas of these operations.

Shakers, a sect which differed from Quakers, believed in a simple creed: "Give your hands to work and your heart to God." These celibate communities had only converts, no children.

At Pleasant Hill, near Harrodsburg, Ky., the annual Shaker festival each September includes an apple butter "stir." Visitors within the hand-stacked rock fences may help stir the apples as they cook into apple butter. A total of 60 rooms for overnight guests are scattered among nine buildings. The Trustee's House, used for registration and greeting guests, also has a 120-seat dining room.

Menus include a special "Shaker dish of the day," as well as country-style foods. "The average check is about $4; three meals for one day average less than $14 per person," reports Mrs. Harold P. Kremer, director of foodservice. Temperance still prevails in the village.

Charles Dickens once visited The Golden Lamb. Upset because the innkeeper refused to serve him brandy, Dickens complained that the other beverages available on the menu were unfit to drink.

Lee and Michael Comisar, Cincinnati restaurateurs, bought the Golden Lamb in 1969. They still serve the simple, delicious fare offered in Shaker days. Now, however, wines, brandy and other spirits are offered.

As Ohio's oldest inn, The Golden Lamb is noted for a Shaker museum.

Cumberland Trail Recipes

PENNSYLVANIA DUTCH APPETIZER TRAY

Yield: 25 servings

Ingredients

FRANKFURTERS, quartered (about 3 pounds)	25
WHOLE CLOVES	as needed
WINE VINEGAR	2 cups
SALAD OIL	1 cup
GARLIC CLOVES	2
SALT	to taste
PEPPER	to taste
SAUERKRAUT, drained (6-pound, 3-ounce can)	1
SOUR CREAM	2 cups
CHOPPED ONION	1 cup
CELERY SEED	2 teaspoons
BEETS, diced, cooked or CANNED	1 quart
CHOPPED ONION	1/2 cup
PREPARED HORSERADISH	1 tablespoon
MAYONNAISE	1/2 cup
POTATO SALAD	
DILL PICKLES	
CUCUMBER SLICES	
COTTAGE CHEESE and CHIVES	

Procedure

1. Cook frankfurters in boiling water 10 minutes; drain and cool. Stud with cloves.
2. Combine vinegar and oil; beat well. Add frankfurters, garlic, salt, pepper. Chill 1 hour.
3. Meanwhile, to half of kraut, add cream, 1 cup onion, and celery seed; mix well and chill.
4. To remaining kraut, add beets and 1/2 cup onion.
5. Combine horseradish and mayonnaise; mix well. Add to kraut-beet mixture; mix well. Chill.
6. Arrange frankfurters and kraut mixtures on tray. Surround with remaining ingredients.
7. Serve with rye bread, pumpernickel bread, an assortment of cheeses.

TOMATO BOUILLON, ORANGE BLOSSOM WHIP

"The Orange Blossom Whip used with this recipe is original with us, and rarely fails to invite pleasing comments."

Yield: 35 to 40 bouillon cups

Ingredients

TOMATO SOUP, CANNED	2 No. 5 cans
WATER	1-3/4 quarts
ORANGE BLOSSOM WHIP	
WHIPPED CREAM	2-1/2 cups
GRATED ORANGE RIND, from	3 oranges

Procedure

1. Mix the 2 cans of tomato soup with an equal amount of water.
2. Heat to boiling point and season.
3. Garnish top of each cup of soup with Orange Blossom Whip.

SHAKER HERB SOUP

Yield: about 1 gallon

Ingredients

BUTTER	4 ounces
CELERY, thinly sliced	1 quart
CHERVIL, FRESH, minced	1/2 cup
CHOPPED FRESH CHIVES	1/2 cup
MINCED FRESH SORREL	1/2 cup
MINCED FRESH TARRAGON	2 teaspoons
CHICKEN BROTH	1 gallon
SALT	1 tablespoon
SUGAR	2 teaspoons
PEPPER	1 teaspoon
NUTMEG, grated	as needed
CROUTONS	as needed
CHEESE, grated	as needed

Procedure

1. Melt butter in stock pot or steam-jacketed kettle. Add celery and all herbs. Saute gently for 3 minutes.
2. Add broth, salt, sugar, and pepper. Simmer for 20 to 30 minutes.
3. To serve, place croutons in bowl and sprinkle with nutmeg. Ladle in soup. Top with the cheese.

SNAPPER SOUP

Yield: approximately 1 gallon

Ingredients

VEAL KNUCKLE	3-1/2 pounds
CHICKEN FAT or BUTTER	1 cup
ONIONS, finely chopped	3
CELERY RIBS, chopped	2
CARROTS, diced	2
THYME	1/4 teaspoon
MARJORAM	1/2 teaspoon
CLOVES, WHOLE	3
BAY LEAF	1
SALT	to taste
PEPPER	to taste
FLOUR	1 cup
BEEF BROTH	3 or 4 quarts
TOMATOES, strained	2 cups
SNAPPER TURTLE, MEAT,	1
SHERRY	2 cups
LIQUID HOT PEPPER SEASONING	dash
LEMON SLICES	3
EGG, hard-cooked, chopped	1

Procedure

1. Have knuckles broken into 2-inch pieces.
2. Place knuckles in a roasting pan and add the chicken fat or butter, onions, celery, carrots, thyme, marjoram, cloves, bay leaf, salt, and pepper.
3. Bake in oven at 400°F. until brown.
4. Remove from oven and add flour, mixing well. Bake 30 minutes longer.
5. Pour browned mixture into a large soup kettle; add the broth and tomatoes and cook slowly for 3-1/2 hours.
6. Cook snapper turtle. Cut meat into small pieces.
7. Combine the snapper meat with 1 cup of sherry, salt to taste, the liquid hot pepper seasoning, and lemon slices; simmer for 10 minutes.
8. Strain the soup and combine the two mixtures. Add the chopped egg and the balance of the sherry and serve immediately.

Old Original Bookbinders

PEPPER-POT SOUP

Yield: 24 servings

Ingredients

CHICKEN BOUILLON CUBES	18
WATER, boiling	4-1/2 quarts
BAY LEAVES	3
SALT	1 tablespoon
GROUND BLACK PEPPER	2 teaspoons
DRIED THYME LEAVES	1/2 teaspoon
HONEYCOMB TRIPE	3 pounds
BACON	1/2 pound
CHOPPED ONION	1-1/2 cups
DICED GREEN PEPPER	3 cups
CELERY STALKS, sliced	6 stalks
POTATOES, pared, cubed	1-1/2 quarts
ALL-PURPOSE FLOUR	3/4 cup
CREAM, LIGHT	1-1/2 cups
SALTINE CRACKERS	

Procedure

1. Dissolve bouillon cubes in water. Add next five ingredients. Bring to boil; skim surface; then simmer, covered, for 1-1/4 hours.
2. Cook bacon until crisp; drain and crumble.
3. In bacon fat, saute onion, green pepper, and celery until onion is transparent.
4. Add with potatoes and crumbled bacon to soup. Simmer, covered, 30 minutes, or until meat and vegetables are tender.
5. Beat together flour and cream. Stir into soup. Simmer about 10 minutes, or until flavors are blended.
6. Serve 1-1/4 cup servings with saltine crackers.

DUNKER HILL PICKLE DIP

Yield: 2 quarts, 25 2-ounce servings

Ingredients

SOUR CREAM	1-1/2 quarts
CHOPPED DILL PICKLES, drained	3 cups
LEMON JUICE	1/4 cup
INSTANT MINCED ONION	1 tablespoon
DILL WEED	1 tablespoon
SALT	1 teaspoon
WHITE PEPPER	1/2 teaspoon
GARLIC SALT	1/2 teaspoon

Procedure

1. Combine all ingredients; mix until blended.

Pickle Packers International, Inc.

PHILADELPHIA PEPPER POT SOUP

Yield: 50 servings

Ingredients

HONEYCOMB TRIPE	3 pounds
CHICKEN STOCK, hot	2-1/2 gallons
BUTTER	10 ounces
ONION, MEDIUM DICE	2 pounds
FLOUR	as needed
SALT	1 tablespoon
WHITE PEPPER	1 teaspoon
SWEET MARJORAM	1 teaspoon
GREEN PEPPER, MEDIUM DICE	1 pound
POTATOES, peeled, diced 1/4-inch	3-1/2 pounds

Procedure

1. Cut tripe in 1/2-inch cubes. Cover with part of the chicken stock and cook slowly until tender.

2. Melt butter in soup pot. Add onion and saute until tender. Add flour to make roux and cook 8 to 10 minutes. *Do not brown.*

3. Reserve sufficient stock to blanch green pepper and to cook potatoes. Add balance of stock gradually to roux, stirring until slightly thickened and smooth. Add seasonings when soup reaches a boil; reduce heat and simmer.

4. Blanch green pepper in boiling chicken stock for 5 minutes.

5. Cook potatoes in lightly salted stock until nearly tender.

6. When tripe and potatoes are done, add to soup with water in which they were cooked.

7. Drain blanched green pepper and add to soup.

Old Original Bookbinder's

BAKED STUFFED PORK CHOPS

Yield: 8 servings

Ingredients

MARGARINE	1/3 cup
FINELY CHOPPED CELERY	1/2 cup
MINCED ONION	1/2 cup
CHICKEN BOUILLON CUBES	2
HOT WATER	2 cups
DAY-OLD BREAD, cubed	1/2 pound
EGG, slightly beaten	1
POULTRY SEASONING	1 teaspoon
PEPPER	1/4 teaspoon
PORK CHOPS (1 inch thick, with pocket)	8
SALT	to taste
PEPPER	to taste
MARGARINE	3 tablespoons
WATER	1/2 cup

Procedure

1. Melt 1/3 cup margarine and simmer celery and onion in it until tender, but not brown.

2. Dissolve bouillon cubes in hot water. Pour over bread. Add egg, celery, onion, and seasonings. Mix well.

3. Sprinkle pork chops with salt and pepper. Stuff with bread dressing, using about 2 tablespoons per chop. Melt 3 tablespoons margarine in skillet over low heat; brown chops until rich golden brown on both sides, 15 to 20 minutes. Place chops in greased casserole. Meanwhile, start heating oven to 350°F.

4. Add 1/2 cup water to drippings in skillet; stir to loosen brown bits; pour over chops. Bake, covered, for 45 minutes. Uncover; bake 5 minutes, or until fork-tender.

Note

This popular bread dressing, from Chef Bill Turner, is delicious served with chicken or turkey.

The Cincinnati Milacron Cafeteria

COLD MARINATED SALMON

Yield: approx. 35 servings

Ingredients

SALMON FILLETS, FRESH	8 to 10 pounds
ONION, thinly sliced	1 pound
VINEGAR	2 cups
SUGAR	1/2 cup
PICKLING SPICES	
(tied in a bag)	2 tablespoons
SALT	1/2 tablespoon
PEPPER	1/2 tablespoon

Procedure

1. Tie salmon in cheesecloth.
2. Place in enough water in pan to cover the salmon. Add remaining ingredients. Steam-cook for 1/2 hour.
3. Place in refrigerator and let stand overnight to marinate.

Old Original Bookbinder's

POACHED EGGS WITH CANADIAN BACON AND GREEN ASPARAGUS A LA BENEDICT

Yield: 12 portions

Ingredients

HOLLANDAISE SAUCE	1 pint
EGGS	24
CANADIAN BACON	24 slices
TOAST, trimmed	12 slices
ASPARAGUS, FRESH GREEN	48 spears
MASHED POTATOES	1 quart
TRUFFLES, CANNED,	
thinly cut	2 ounces

Procedure

1. Prepare hollandaise sauce.
2. Poach eggs. Broil bacon. Make toast. Cut each slice of toast diagonally.
3. Place diagonally-cut toast halves in bottom of greased individual casseroles.
4. Add 2 slices of bacon, then 2 poached eggs.
5. Lay 2 asparagus spears on both sides of the eggs, and parallel with the sides of the casserole.
6. With pastry bag, make a rosette of mashed potatoes at each end of casserole.
7. Place casserole in oven at 375°F. and heat thoroughly.
8. Top poached eggs with hollandaise sauce.
9. Garnish with slice of truffle. Serve at once.

MOSTACCIOLI

Yield: 6 servings

Ingredients

CHOPPED GREEN PEPPER	1/3 cup
CHOPPED ONION	2 tablespoons
SHORTENING	2 tablespoons
GROUND BEEF	3/4 pound
TOMATOES	1 No. 303 can
TOMATO SAUCE	1 cup
BAY LEAF	1/2
SALT	2 teaspoons
PEPPER	1/4 teaspoon
MOSTACCIOLI NOODLES,	
cooked, drained	1/2 pound
CHEESE, SHARP	
PROCESSED, sliced	1/2 pound
CHEESE, PARMESAN,	
grated	2 tablespoons

Procedure

1. Saute green pepper and onion in shortening until tender; add the meat and cook until browned. Stir in tomatoes, tomato sauce, and seasonings. Simmer 15 minutes. Remove bay leaf.
2. In a shallow, greased 2-quart casserole, place layer of noodles, meat mixture, and sharp processed cheese; repeat layers. Sprinkle with parmesan cheese. Bake in oven at 350°F. for 30 minutes.

Note

This can be prepared early in the day or the day before, then refrigerated and baked. Add an extra 10 minutes to the baking time. This casserole improves if it stands about 10 minutes after it is removed from the oven.

The Cincinnati Milacron Cafeteria

DUTCH GREEN BEANS

Yield: 4-gallon pan making 100 3-ounce portions of this popular vegetable

Ingredients

BACON, cooked, chopped	20 slices
CHOPPED ONION	1 pint
GREEN BEANS, CANNED	4 No. 10 cans
VINEGAR	1 pint
BACON FAT	1 cup

Procedure

1. Cook bacon. Cool and chop into fine pieces.
2. Cook onion in a little of the bacon fat.
3. Place beans in steam kettle or steamer and heat thoroughly. Add bacon, bacon fat, onion, and vinegar. Heat to boiling point.
4. Reduce steam, and serve.

PARSLEYED RICE

Yield: 6 servings

Ingredients

MARGARINE	1/4 cup
FINELY CHOPPED GREEN ONIONS, with tops	1/4 cup
DICED GREEN PEPPER	1/4 cup
SLIVERED ALMONDS, UNBLANCHED	1/4 cup
RICE, LONG GRAIN, uncooked	1 cup
CHICKEN STOCK*	2 cups
SALT	1/2 teaspoon
COARSELY CHOPPED PARSLEY	1/2 cup

*Two bouillon cubes dissolved in 2 cups boiling water may be used.

Procedure

1. Melt margarine in heavy saucepan.

2. Add sliced green onions, diced green pepper, slivered almonds, and uncooked rice. Stir over low heat until rice is coated with margarine and is golden.

3. Add chicken stock and salt. Bring to rolling boil. Cover with tight lid and cook on low heat for 30 minutes, or until rice is tender. (If preferred, place in covered pan in oven at 350°F. for the same length of time.)

4. Fold chopped parsley into cooked rice.

The Cincinnati Milacron Cafeteria

SWEET AND SOUR RED BEETS

Yield: about 1 gallon

Ingredients

BEETS, SLICED	1 No. 10 can
VINEGAR	1 quart
SUGAR	2 pounds
SALT	1 tablespoon
PEPPER	1 teaspoon
ONIONS, MEDIUM-SIZED, sliced	2

Procedure

1. Drain beets, place in large bowl.

2. Combine remaining ingredients in saucepan; bring to a boil. Reduce heat and simmer for 2 minutes.

3. At once pour hot mixture over beets.

4. Refrigerate for at least 6 hours.

TOMATO PUDDING*

Yield: 8 servings

Ingredients

BROWN SUGAR, packed	1/2 cup
TOMATO PUREE	2 10-ounce cans
BUTTER or MARGARINE, melted	1/2 cup
CUBED FRESH BREAD, (1/2 inch)	1-1/2 cups
SALT	1/2 teaspoon

Procedure

1. Add brown sugar to tomato puree and cook for 5 minutes.

2. Melt butter and pour over bread cubes until absorbed.

3. Pour puree over bread cubes. Add salt and combine.

4. Bake in oven at 375°F. for 45 minutes.

*Old Ohio Farm Dish

John C. Friese, Ohio State University

SCALLOP OF SWEET POTATOES AND APPLES

Yield: 35 portions

Ingredients

SWEET POTATOES, MEDIUM-SIZED	18
APPLES, TART, MEDIUM-SIZED	5
BROWN SUGAR, packed	1 cup
SALT	4 tablespoons
BUTTER	1 cup

Procedure

1. Cook potatoes in skins until well done. Peel and slice 1/8 inch thick. Wash, peel, and slice apples.

2. Arrange 1/3 of the potatoes in the bottom of a greased baking pan. Add 1/2 of the sliced apples.

3. Sprinkle with brown sugar and salt. Dot with butter.

4. Repeat layers, ending with the sweet potatoes. Dot with butter.

5. Bake in oven at 350°F. for 30 minutes or until apples are tender.

Note

For variety, sprinkle raw cranberries between the layers and over the top before baking.

Kaase's Restaurant, Akron, Ohio

SHAKER JOHNNY CAKE

(Originally called "journey cake" because travelers carried the crisp bread along to "dunk" in cider at mealtime)

Yield: 18 portions (36 pieces)

Ingredients

CORN MEAL	1 quart
BAKING SODA	2 teaspoons
SALT	1-1/2 teaspoons
BUTTERMILK*	1 pint
MOLASSES	1 cup
SUET, finely chopped	12 to 16 ounces

*Substitute 1 pint regular whole milk and 2 teaspoons vinegar.

Procedure

1. Mix together corn meal, soda, and salt. Blend in buttermilk and molasses until smooth. Then fold in the suet.

2. Spread in 18-inch by 26-inch baking pan. Bake in oven at 400°F. for about 20 minutes. Crust should be crisp.

SALLY LUNN

(Popular from Virginia's coast to farms and Shaker communities of Kentucky and Ohio)

Yield: 1 loaf, 10-inch round

Ingredients

MILK	1 cup
BUTTER	1/2 pound
SUGAR	3 tablespoons
SALT	2 teaspoons
YEAST, FRESH CAKES	1-1/2 ounces
EGGS, beaten	5 ounces
FLOUR	6 cups
BUTTER, soft	as needed

Procedure

1. Scald milk. Stir in butter, sugar, and salt.

2. When mixture has cooled to lukewarm, crumble in yeast. Stir in eggs. Gradually beat in flour. Place dough in a well-greased bowl. Cover.

3. Let rise in warm place until doubled in bulk. Punch down. Knead lightly.

4. Place in a well-greased 10-inch turban mold or angel food tube pan. Brush top with soft butter. Let rise until almost double in bulk.

5. Bake in oven at 350°F. for about 50 minutes, or until golden. Brush top with soft butter.

CORN FRITTERS

Yield: 25 portions

Ingredients

SIFTED BREAD FLOUR	1-1/2 quarts
BAKING POWDER	1/2 cup plus 1 tablespoon
GRANULATED SUGAR	1 cup
SALT	1 tablespoon
MILK	2 cups
WHOLE EGGS	6
CORN, WHOLE KERNEL, CANNED	1-1/2 quarts

Procedure

1. Mix together the first four ingredients.

2. Add milk to the well-beaten eggs. Then gradually add to dry ingredients.

3. Stir in the kernel corn.

4. Use a level No. 40 scoop for each fritter. Fry in deep fat until a golden brown.

Damon's, Cleveland Heights, Ohio

GURKEN SALAT

(One version of Pennsylvania Dutch cucumber salad.)

Yield: about 1 quart

Ingredients

CUCUMBERS, MEDIUM-SIZED, peeled, sliced	14
ONIONS, MEDIUM-SIZED, thinly sliced	5
SALT	1/3 cup
SOUR CREAM	3/4 cup
VINEGAR	1/3 cup
CHOPPED PARSLEY	1/2 cup
PEPPER	1/4 teaspoon

Procedure

1. Combine cucumbers and onions in large bowl. Sprinkle with salt. Place a plate on top, so it fits on vegetables without extra space. Weight the plate with a can or bottle. Let stand for about 45 minutes.

2. Drain well.

3. In small bowl, whip sour cream and vinegar until smooth. Add sour cream mixture, parsley, and pepper to cucumbers and onoins. Stir to mix. Serve at once.

LIME GLOW SALAD

Yield: 8 individual molds or 1 6-inch mold

Ingredients

GELATIN, LIME FLAVOR	1 6-ounce package
WATER, boiling	2 cups
WATER, cold	1 cup
CRUSHED PINEAPPLE, drained	1/2 cup
COTTAGE CHEESE, drained	1/2 cup

Procedure

1. Dissolve gelatin in boiling water. Add cold water. Pour 1-1/2 cups of gelatin mixture into mold that has been rinsed with cold water. Chill until firm. Let remaining gelatin mixture stand at room temperature.

2. Combine drained pineapple and cottage cheese; spread over firm gelatin and pour remaining gelatin over pineapple and cheese layer. Chill until firm.

3. Unmold and garnish with endive or lettuce.

The Cincinnati Milacron Cafeteria

ORANGE DELIGHT SALAD

Yield: 1 6-inch mold

Ingredients

GELATIN, ORANGE FLAVOR	1 6-ounce package
WATER, boiling	2 cups
WATER, cold	1-1/2 cups
MINIATURE MARSHMALLOWS	1 cup
MANDARIN ORANGES, drained	1 11-ounce can
COCONUT, SHORT SHRED	1/2 cup (scant)
MINT SPRIGS	to garnish

Procedure

1. Dissolve gelatin in boiling water. Add cold water.

2. Line bottom of 6-inch mold with 1/4 cup marshmallows and 1/4 cup coconut. Cover with 1/4 of the gelatin. Chill until firm. Add oranges to remaining gelatin. Let stand at room temperature.

3. Spread 1/2 of the remaining marshmallows and 1/2 of the remaining coconut over firm gelatin, cover with 1/2 of the remaining gelatin. Chill until firm.

4. Repeat for third layer. Chill until firm.

5. Unmold on crisp lettuce. Garnish with sprig of mint.

The Cincinnati Milacron Cafeteria

CABBAGE RELISH

Yield: 6 to 8 servings

Ingredients

GRANULATED SUGAR	1 cup
CIDER VINEGAR	1/2 cup
SALT	1-1/2 teaspoons
SHREDDED CABBAGE	1 quart
GREEN PEPPER, MEDIUM-SIZED, chopped	1

Procedure

1. Mix sugar, vinegar, and salt together. Pour over cabbage and green pepper. Let stand 1/2 hour to develop flavor.

The Cincinnati Milacron Cafeteria

NOEL ANISE DROPS

Yield: 7 dozen

Ingredients

FLOUR	1-3/4 cups
BAKING POWDER	1/2 teaspoon
SALT	1/2 teaspoon
EGGS	3
GRANULATED SUGAR	1 cup
ANISEED	1 tablespoon

Procedure

1. Sift flour with baking powder and salt.

2. Put eggs and sugar in mixer bowl and beat for 10 minutes on medium speed.

3. Add the flour mixture and beat another 3 minutes. Add aniseed and blend quickly.

4. Drop by teaspoonfuls, 2 inches apart, onto greased and floured cookie sheet. Let set overnight.

5. Bake in oven at 325°F. for 10 to 12 minutes. Remove from cookie sheets immediately.

Note

For best eating, store cookies in an airtight container for a few days.

The Cincinnati Milacron Cafeteria

Above: First choice of most Midwest patrons is roast prime rib, nowhere given better treatment than at Chicago's Stockyard Inn. With the closing of the stockyards, The Stockyard Inn no longer has a ready-made clientele. However, the continued service of high quality beef and an aggressive advertising campaign has permitted the establishment to carry on.

Right: At Old Original Bookbinders, seafood is the most frequently selected menu item. Expert "openers" speed service of patron selections from the extensive list of shellfish specialties.

Left: One of the take-off points for the Cumberland Trail, Philadelphia has many foodservice establishments with long histories. Old Original Bookbinders, started before 1850, was located near the Delaware River docks and drew its clientele from workers there. Great and famous people also dined there as the historical memorabilia that line the stairway to the private dining rooms attest. Bookbinders' collections of historic objects has become so sizable, they have taken over the gun shop next door (pictured here) to display them.

Above: The melting pot cuisine of the Midwest is especially evident in Chicago. One of the ethnic cuisines developed early was Italian. The Como Inn is noted for authentic Italian food and decor. The owners return regularly to Italy to search for food and design ideas. In many cases, enthusiasm for The Como Inn has been passed down from one generation to the next among regular patrons of the 450-seat restaurant.

Right: The Berghoff Restaurant, familiarly known just as Berghoff's by most Chicagoans, is another ethnic success. With a menu that got its start as pre-Prohibition free lunch (items chosen primarily as an accompaniment for nickel beer though whiskey was also offered at 15¢ a shot) the offerings were expanded during Prohibition. Adding to its original German base, the menu lists 40 hearty entrees a day, 75 to 100 entrees a week. Here waiter Pete Pappas, wearing the European type uniform that is standard at Berghoff's, serves John Berghoff, third generation owner.

Below and Bottom of page: Seafood specialties from all parts of the country are equally superlative, though far from their native habitat, when served in Chicago's Cape Cod Room. Artifacts related to the New England fishing fleet as well as old-time cooking utensils contribute to decor.

Above: Windsor chairs and old farm implements used in the lounge set the stage for patrons of The Lemon Tree in Lancaster, Pa. Traditional Shaker furnishings are used in the other rooms.

14K CAKE

Yield: 8 servings

Ingredients

EGG WHITE	1
CREAM of TARTAR	1/4 teaspoon
SUGAR	2 tablespoons
ALL-PURPOSE FLOUR	1-1/3 cups
SUGAR	3/4 cup
CINNAMON	1/2 teaspoon
SALT	3/4 teaspoon
BAKING SODA	1/2 teaspoon
BAKING POWDER	1/4 teaspoon
SALAD OIL	3/4 cup
EGG YOLK	1
GRATED MEDIUM CARROTS	1-1/4 cups
VANILLA	1/2 teaspoon

Procedure

1. Pre-heat oven to 350°F. Grease and flour bottom of 9-inch by 2-inch round pan.

2. Combine egg white and cream of tartar; beat until soft mounds begin to form, then beat in the 2 tablespoons sugar. Beat until very stiff peaks are formed. Set aside.

3. Sift flour once, measure, and sift into mixer bowl with 3/4 cup sugar, cinnamon, salt, baking soda, and baking powder.

4. Add salad oil and egg yolk. Beat at low speed for 1 minute, then at medium speed for 1 minute.

5. Add carrots and vanilla and beat at medium speed for 2 minutes.

6. Fold in egg white mixture.

7. Pour into prepared pan and bake in oven at 350°F. for 40 to 45 minutes. Set pan on cake rack for 5 minutes. Remove cake from pan and finish cooling on cake rack. Frost top and sides with 14K Icing. (See next column.) Chill.

The Cincinnati Milacron Cafeteria

14K ICING

Yield: icing for one 14K cake

Ingredients

SMOOTH COTTAGE CHEESE*	2/3 cup
SIFTED CONFECTIONERS' SUGAR	1-3/4 cups
MARGARINE	1/4 cup
COCONUT	3/4 cup
CHOPPED PECANS	1/4 cup
RAISINS	1/4 cup
VANILLA	3/4 teaspoon

*If smooth cottage cheese is not available, place other cottage cheese in blender and blend until smooth.

Procedure

1. Cream the cottage cheese, sugar, and margarine until light.

2. Fold in remaining ingredients. Spread on cake.

The Cincinnati Milacron Cafeteria

LEMON CHESS PIE

Yield: 1 8-inch pie

Ingredients

PIE SHELL, 8-inch, with fluted rim, unbaked	1
SUGAR	7/8 cup
ALL-PURPOSE FLOUR	1/3 cup
YELLOW CORN MEAL	2 tablespoons
SALT	1/4 teaspoon
BUTTER or MARGARINE, softened	1/3 cup
LEMON RIND, grated from	2 lemons
LEMON JUICE	1/4 cup
WATER, boiling	1 cup
EGGS	4

Procedure

1. Heat oven to 400°F.

2. Sift the dry ingredients into bowl of electric mixer. Add butter and mix well. Add lemon rind, lemon juice, and boiling water and mix well. Add eggs and beat just enough to mix eggs smooth. Pour into prepared unbaked pie shell.

3. Bake in oven at 400°F. for about 30 minutes, or just until pie is beginning to puff. A knife inserted about halfway between rim and center should come out clean.

4. Cool on cake rack. Let pie cool to room temperature before cutting.

The Cincinnati Milacron Cafeteria

SANTA'S FAVORITE TOFFEE

Yield: 2 pounds

Ingredients

SUGAR	2-1/2 cups
DARK CORN SYRUP	1-1/2 cups
COCOA	1/4 cup
CREAM, HEAVY	1 cup
CREAM, LIGHT	1 cup
SALT	1 teaspoon
BUTTER	6 tablespoons
VANILLA	1 teaspoon

Procedure

1. Combine sugar, syrup, cocoa, creams, salt, and 3 tablespoons of the butter in heavy saucepan. Cook over low heat, stirring occasionally, until mixture forms firm ball (250°F.). Stir in remaining butter a little at a time; add vanilla.

2. Pour into well buttered 8-inch square cake pan. Cool slightly. Cut in small squares with oiled scissors or sharp knife. Wrap pieces in plastic wrap.

The Cincinnati Milacron Cafeteria

NO-BAKE COOKIES

Yield: 4 dozen

Ingredients

SUGAR	2 cups
COCOA	2 teaspoons
MILK	1/2 cup
BUTTER	1/2 cup
ROLLED OATS	3 cups
PEANUT BUTTER	1-1/2 cups
COCONUT	1 cup
CHOPPED NUTS	1 cup
VANILLA	1 teaspoon

Procedure

1. Combine sugar, cocoa, milk, and butter in saucepan. Bring to a boil and boil for 1 minute.

2. Place rolled oats, peanut butter, coconut, and chopped nuts in large bowl.

3. Pour hot mixture over dry ingredients, add vanilla. Mix thoroughly. Drop by spoonful on waxed paper.

Note

White or brown sugar, or half of each, may be used.

The Cincinnati Milacron Cafeteria
Rachel Rorick

EARLY AMERICAN GINGER CUTOUTS

Yield: 30 cookies

Ingredients

SIFTED FLOUR	2-3/4 cups
BAKING SODA	1/2 teaspoon
GINGER	1 teaspoon
CINNAMON	1/2 teaspoon
CLOVES	1/2 teaspoon
SALT	1/2 teaspoon
BUTTER	1/2 cup
DARK BROWN SUGAR, firmly packed	1/4 cup
DARK MOLASSES	3/4 cup
EGG, beaten	1
WATER, hot	1 teaspoon
VINEGAR	1 teaspoon

Procedure

1. Preheat oven to 350°F.

2. Sift dry ingredients together.

3. Cream butter and sugar. Add molasses and egg, beating until smooth. Mix in sifted dry ingredients; then add water and vinegar and blend well.

4. Chill dough two hours or overnight.

5. Roll out on lightly floured board to 1/4-inch thickness and cut with gingerbread man and animal cookie cutters.

6. Place on cookie sheet and bake about 15 minutes. When cooled, decorate with various butter frostings.

PUMPKIN PIE

Yield: 1 8-inch pie

Ingredients

EGGS	2
PUMPKIN	1-1/3 cups
MAPLE SYRUP	3 tablespoons
SALT	1/4 teaspoon
MILK	1 cup
PUMPKIN PIE SPICES	1/2 teaspoon
SUGAR	1/2 cup
PIE SHELL, 8-inch, unbaked	1

Procedure

1. Beat the eggs slightly. Add remaining ingredients and mix well. Pour mixture into an unbaked 8-inch pie shell with a fluted rim.

2. Bake in oven at 425°F. for 30 minutes.

The Cincinnati Milacron Cafeteria

MRS. CLAUS' FUDGE

Yield: 64 1-inch pieces

Ingredients

GRANULATED SUGAR	4 cups
EVAPORATED MILK	1-2/3 cups
BUTTER	1 cup
SALT	1 teaspoon
SEMI-SWEET CHOCOLATE PIECES	2 cups
MARSHMALLOW CREAM	1 pint
VANILLA	1 teaspoon
CHOPPED BLACK WALNUTS or PECANS	1 cup

Procedure

1. Butter sides of a heavy 3-quart saucepan. In it combine sugar, evaporated milk, butter, and salt.

2. Cook over medium heat to soft ball stage (236°F.), stirring frequently.

3. Remove from heat; add remaining ingredients. Beat until chocolate is melted and blended. Pour into buttered 9-inch by 9-inch by 2-inch pan. Score in squares while warm. Cut when firm. Decorate with candied cherries or nuts if desired.

The Cincinnati Milacron Cafeteria

HOLIDAY GEMS

Yield: 3-1/2 dozen

Ingredients

BUTTER	1/2 cup
CREAM CHEESE	3 ounces
FLOUR	1 cup
CHERRY or APRICOT JAM	1 cup
CONFECTIONERS' SUGAR	as needed

Procedure

1. Cream butter and cheese together. Gradually work in flour. Chill.

2. Roll out paper-thin on floured board or pastry cloth. Cut with 2-1/2-inch round cutter. Spread with jam. Fold two edges to center, overlapping slightly. Press down lightly with thumb. Place on greased cookie sheet.

3. Bake in oven at 375°F. for 15 minutes. While warm, sift confectioners' sugar over the top.

Note

These fragile cream cheese cookies are ideal for holiday entertaining.

The Cincinnati Milacron Cafeteria

CHRISTMAS STOLLEN

Yield: 1 large crescent or loaf

Ingredients

FLOUR	5 cups
ACTIVE DRY YEAST	2 packages
SUGAR	1/2 cup
SALT	2 teaspoons
CARDAMOM, GROUND	1/4 teaspoon
MACE	1/4 teaspoon
MILK	3/4 cup
WATER	1/2 cup
BRANDY	1 tablespoon
BUTTER	1/2 cup
EGGS	2
CHOPPED, BLANCHED ALMONDS	1/2 cup
CANDIED CHERRIES	1/2 cup
MIXED CANDIED FRUITS	1/2 cup
CURRANTS	1/2 cup
RAISINS	1/2 cup
BUTTER	1 tablespoon

Procedure

1. Mix 1-1/2 cups flour with yeast and next 4 ingredients.

2. Heat liquid ingredients and 1/2 cup butter until warm.

3. Gradually add liquids to dry ingredients. Beat two minutes at medium speed. Add eggs and 1/2 cup flour. Beat two minutes at high speed.

4. Stir in additional flour (3 cups) until dough begins to leave the sides of the mixing bowl. Turn onto lightly floured board and knead until elastic, about 10 minutes. Place in lightly greased bowl, turning once to grease surface. Cover, let rise in warm place until double in bulk, about 1 hour. Punch down. Let rise again until almost double, 30 to 45 minutes.

5. Turn dough onto lightly floured board and flatten. Sprinkle nuts and fruit over dough and knead them into it. Pat into an oval about 8 inches by 12 inches. Spread with 2 teaspoonfuls soft butter. Fold lengthwise, press folded edge in place so it cannot spring open. Place on greased baking sheet. Brush with 1 teaspoon melted butter. Let rise until almost double, about 40 minutes. Bake in oven at 375°F. for 30 to 35 minutes.

6. While warm, frost with confectioners' icing and decorate, or sprinkle with confectioners' sugar.

The Cincinnati Milacron Cafeteria

PECAN PIE

Yield: 1 8-inch pie

Ingredients

SUGAR	1 cup
SALT	1/2 teaspoon
BUTTER, melted	3 tablespoons
EGGS, slightly beaten	4
WHITE CORN SYRUP	1 cup
VANILLA	2 teaspoons
CHOPPED PECANS	1/2 cup
PIE SHELL, 8-inch, unbaked	1

Procedure

1. Mix sugar and salt. Stir in butter and eggs. Blend in syrup and vanilla. Put pecans in pie shell and pour in filling.

2. Bake in oven at 325°F. for 30 minutes or until done.

The Cincinnati Milacron Cafeteria

LEMON SQUARES

Yield: 4 dozen

Ingredients
DOUGH

SIFTED FLOUR	2 cups
BUTTER	1 cup
SUGAR	1/2 cup

FILLING

SUGAR	2 cups
FLOUR	4 tablespoons
BAKING POWDER	1 teaspoon
FRESH LEMON JUICE	1/2 cup
EGGS, slightly beaten	4

Procedure

1. Preheat oven to 375°F.

2. Mix first 3 ingredients together and press into 15-1/2-inch by 10-1/2-inch by 1-inch (jelly roll) greased pan, pressing firmly against sides.

3. Bake in oven at 375°F. for 20 minutes. *Do not overbrown.* Remove from oven; cool 10 minutes.

4. Mix all filling ingredients together and pour over baked crust.

5. Return to oven immediately and bake 25 minutes more.

6. Remove from oven and cool slightly (about 10 minutes).

7. Sift confectioners' sugar over top. Cool completely, then cut into squares.

8. Store in airtight container.

The Cincinnati Milacron Cafeteria

LITTLE ANGEL FRUIT CAKES

Yield: 18

Ingredients

RAISINS, LIGHT or DARK	1 cup
COARSELY CHOPPED NUTS	1 cup
CHOPPED CANDIED FRUITS	1 cup
SHERRY or ORANGE JUICE	1/4 cup
EGGS	2
GRANULATED SUGAR	1 cup
BUTTER or MARGARINE, softened	1/2 cup
SIFTED ALL-PURPOSE FLOUR	1 cup
BAKING POWDER	1 teaspoon
SALT	1 teaspoon
WINE SYRUP	
WHITE CORN SYRUP	1/3 cup
SHERRY or MUSCATEL	1/3 cup

Procedure

1. Combine first 4 ingredients. Let stand.

2. In mixer bowl, beat next 3 ingredients until light and creamy. Remove beaters and add next 3 ingredients all at one time. Stir quickly with spoon until smooth. Stir in nuts and fruits.

3. Spoon into paper cups set in muffin tins. Bake in oven at 325°F. for 30 to 35 minutes. Avoid overcooking.

4. Cool. Brush each cake with Wine Syrup. Let stand until thoroughly cold before storing in airtight containers. Cakes should age at least several days.

The Cincinnati Milacron Cafeteria
Zita Vondermeulen

CHEESE ALMOND DREAM

Yield: 20 whole slices (1-pound loaf, thinly sliced)

Ingredients

CHEESE, SHARP CHEDDAR, melted	1/2 pound
BACON SLICES, chopped, crisp-cooked	6
ONION, SMALL, finely chopped	1
SLIVERED ALMONDS, sauteed	4 ounces
MAYONNAISE	1 cup
WORCESTERSHIRE SAUCE	2 teaspoons
SALT	to taste
PEPPER	to taste

Procedure

Mix all ingredients together and spread thickly on trimmed, thin slices of a home-style bread; cover with foil and freeze. When needed, cut in strips and heat in oven at 350°F. for 10 minutes. Delicious.

The Cincinnati Milacron Cafeteria

SHOO-FLY PIE

Yield: 20 servings

Ingredients

CRUMB PORTION

SIFTED ALL-PURPOSE FLOUR	3 cups
GRANULATED SUGAR, CANE or BEET	1-1/2 cups
BUTTER	2/3 cup
SALT	2 teaspoons
NUTMEG	1 teaspoon
CLOVES	1 teaspoon
CINNAMON	2 teaspoons

LIQUID PORTION

MOLASSES	2 cups
CORN SYRUP	2 cups
CORNSTARCH	1 tablespoon
EVAPORATED MILK	2 cups
EGGS	4

Procedure

1. Measure or scale crumb portion into mixer and mix to crumb consistency.

2. Measure or scale all of liquid portion into container and stir well. Measure or scale liquid portion into 9-inch by 1-1/2-inch unbaked pie shells.

3. Place crumb portion on top of liquid which has been scaled into pie shells. Bake in oven at 425°F.

APPLE BROWN BETTY

Yield: 25 4-ounce portions

Ingredients

APPLES, FROZEN	1 gallon
WATER, warm	1/2 cup
NUTMEG	1 tablespoon
SALT	1/2 teaspoon
SUGAR	3 cups
BUTTER, melted	1/4 cup

TOPPING

BREAD CRUMBS	3 cups
CINNAMON	2 teaspoons
SALT	1/2 teaspoon
BUTTER, melted	1/2 cup

Procedure

1. Combine the first 6 ingredients.

2. Place mixture in greased baking pans.

3. Combine all ingredients for topping and spread over top of apples.

4. Bake in oven at 350°F. for 45 to 60 minutes.

5. Serve with whipped cream.

BAKED PRUNE WHIP

Yield: 54 portions

Ingredients

COOKED, PITTED, CHOPPED PRUNES	2 quarts
SUGAR	2 pounds
EGG WHITES	3 cups
LEMON JUICE	6 tablespoons
SALT	2 teaspoons

Procedure

1. Put all ingredients in mixing bowl and beat until stiff enough to form peaks, but not dry.

2. Spread mixture in two ungreased baking pans, and place in pans containing 1/2 inch hot water.

3. Bake in oven at 325°F. for 60 to 70 minutes, or until a knife inserted comes out clean.

4. Remove pudding pans from hot water.

5. Allow pudding to cool and set before cutting into 3-inch squares.

6. Serve with Custard Sauce.

YULE LOGS

Yield: 32 bars

Ingredients

GRANULATED SUGAR	1/2 cup
LIGHT CORN SYRUP	1/2 cup
PEANUT BUTTER	1/2 cup
VANILLA	1 teaspoon
CRISP RICE CEREAL	3 cups
SALTED PEANUTS	1 cup

Procedure

1. Combine sugar and syrup. Cook, stirring constantly, until mixture comes to a rapid boil. Remove from heat.

2. Stir in peanut butter and vanilla. Immediately pour syrup over cereal and peanuts which have been mixed together. Stir gently to coat. Pat into buttered 8-inch by 8-inch by 2-inch pan. Cool. Cut into bars.

The Cincinnati Milacron Cafeteria

CRANBERRY SALAD

Yield: 6 servings

Ingredients

GELATIN, STRAWBERRY FLAVOR	1 3-ounce package
SUGAR	1/2 cup
WATER, boiling	1 cup
WATER, cold	1/2 cup
ORANGE, MEDIUM-SIZED	1/2
CRANBERRIES, RAW	1/4 pound
CHOPPED CELERY	1/2 cup
DICED APPLES	1/2 cup

Procedure

1. Dissolve gelatin and sugar in boiling water. Add cold water.

2. Remove seeds from orange but do not peel. Grind cranberries and orange; mix into gelatin mixture. Chill.

3. When gelatin mixture begins to thicken, fold in celery and apples. Turn into pan or individual molds. Chill until firm.

4. Unmold on crisp lettuce and garnish with mayonnaise if desired.

The Cincinnati Milacron Cafeteria

PINK ANGEL DIVINITY

Yield: 5 to 6 dozen pieces

Ingredients

GRANULATED SUGAR	3 cups
LIGHT CORN SYRUP	3/4 cup
WATER	3/4 cup
SALT	1/2 teaspoon
EGG WHITES	2
GELATIN, STRAWBERRY FLAVOR (reserve 1 tablespoon to tint coconut)	3 ounces
VANILLA	1 teaspoon
CHOPPED PECANS	1 cup
FLAKED COCONUT, tinted pink*	1/2 cup

*To tint coconut, place coconut and 1 tablespoon gelatin in glass jar, cover, and shake until colored.

Procedure

1. Combine sugar, corn syrup, water, and salt in buttered, heavy, 2-quart saucepan. Cook over medium heat, stirring constantly, until mixture boils. Then cook without stirring to hard ball stage (250°F.). Remove from heat.

2. Beat egg whites in large bowl of mixer until soft peaks form. Gradually add gelatin, beating until stiff peaks form. Pour in syrup slowly, beating constantly at high speed until mixture begins to lose its gloss. Stir in vanilla and pecans.

3. Drop from teaspoon onto waxed paper. Sprinkle with tinted coconut.

The Cincinnati Milacron Cafeteria

Midwest Menus Reflect Melting Pot

AS IF A MODERN city has not enough problems, Chicago suffers an identity crisis. Other people in other places remember Chicago for Mrs. O'Leary's cow—which burned the place down—or Al Capone—who shot it up.

A spiritual cousin of the industrialized Northeast, Chicago is surrounded by the fertile farms of the Midwest. At a national crossroads, the city gets input from vastly different cultures and cuisines.

Yet, beneath the firm hand of "Boss" politics, Chicago remains somehow unrefined. Different traditions rub shoulders without blending into a distinctly Chicago culture. The lack of a clearly defined personality makes the "Second City" moniker stick—and stick in Chicagoans' throats.

So, too, with Chicago foodservice. Natural riches within easy grasp inspire a broad range of dining experiences. Great Lakes fish rivals New England's fine seafood. And the "hog butcher to the world" taps a treasury of beef.

Chicago foodservice operators like to give their restaurants a homey feeling. Many of the best hold forth in old mansions. The old, ethnic neighborhoods maintain clusters of restau-rants that exhibit the dining traditions of the Old World. The thriving new neighborhoods create traditions of fast-paced dining.

Even if you are hard put to identify a uniquely Chicago cuisine, the city can dazzle you with its sprawling mix of ideas other cities can borrow, too.

Chicago's cuisine first became known to the world during the Columbian Exposition. The approach to food preparation at that time comes through in these instructions excerpted from the *Woman's Exchange Cookbook*.

Mrs. Roher, who presided over the Cooking School at the World's Fair, said in one of her talks, that to make a good pie, first, above all things, have everything cool, including yourself. Use a good, fine flour and the best of butter, a marble slab for pastry board, and a rolling pin with movable handles. Always use ice water or the very coldest of water. Paste is much improved by keeping overnight in a cold place, but never allow it to freeze as its lightness is ruined.

Mrs. Roher's talk was not all theory but practice; as she stood before the pastry table, queenly in her manner, working out with hand the ideas and suggestions as she went along, it would seem as if her pastry might become food fit for the gods.

A great improvement is made in pie crust by the addition of about a heaping teaspoonful of baking powder to a quart of flour.

Some Chicago favorites of the period:
PLUNKETS.

Four eggs, weight of eggs in powdered sugar, weight of eggs in butter, weight of eggs in rice flour, 1 teaspoonful of vanilla, or juice and rind of 1 lemon. Beat the butter to a cream, then add the sugar gradually, beating all the while; then add the yolks of the eggs, beat again, then add the whites beaten to a stiff froth, then, gradually, the rice flour. Add a teaspoonful of vanilla, or the juice and rind of a lemon. Now beat until fine and light, pour into greased, small scolloped tins (patty tins) and bake in a moderate oven about twenty minutes.
FUMBLES, NO. 1.

Half pound of butter, 9 ounces of flour, 1 teaspoonful of vanilla, half pound of powdered sugar, 2 tablespoonfuls of sherry, 3 eggs. Beat the butter to a cream; add the sugar gradually, beating until very light. Now beat the eggs all together, add to the butter and sugar, add the sherry, the vanilla, and last, the flour, sifted. Beat the whole well. Put the mixture into a pastry bag, and press it through the tube in small round cakes on the bottom of a baking pan lightly greased. If you have no pastry bag, you may drop by spoonfuls. Bake in a moderate oven until the edges are a delicate brown.
LADY FINGERS.

Take 8 eggs, whip the whites to a firm snow. In the meantime, have the yolks beaten up with six ounces of powdered sugar. Mix all together with six ounces of sifted flour; stir well, and add 1 teaspoon lemon extract; squeeze the mixture through funnels of stiff writing paper on sheets of well greased writing paper. Grate white sugar over each; let them lie till the sugar melts, and they shine, then put them in a moderate oven, until they have a fine color; when cool take them from the tins, and lay them together in couples, by the backs. These cakes may be formed with a spoon, on sheets of writing paper. Half this quantity will be trouble enough.

These were some of the Chicago food traditions during the period that followed the Chicago Fire.

The Palmer House

Exploiting civic pride as early as 1871, wealthy merchant Potter Palmer opened a queenly hotel. An unlucky 13 days later, the original Palmer House went up in the smoke of the Chicago fire.

The undaunted Palmer opened anew in 1875. This time, fortune smiled on the Palmer House; it became a glittering center in Chicago social life.

When the aging star was rebuilt in 1926, the old facilities kept running until the new were ready. Then—section by replaced section— they were torn down. A massive, $12 million renovation completed in 1967 gave the hotel its fourth incarnation.

Today's Palmer House occupies the heart of downtown Chicago. Heavy convention business (the hotel boasts one of the city's largest ballrooms) helps fill its 2,232 rooms. Its restaurants range from Trader Vic's Polynesian to the elegant Empire Room. Food/ Beverage Manager Jim Rice estimates that foodservice sales total $1 million a month.

Hilton Hotels, which bought the Palmer House for $19 million in 1945, revels in such continuing success. But it has also learned to respect the hotel's tradition.

When Conrad Hilton took over, he wanted to expand and improve service at the Palmer House. He noticed that chocolate was the only ice cream on the menu, offered every day. So he began to alternate exotic strawberry and mocha ice cream.

Hilton did not realize that the chocolate ice cream, specially made in the Palmer House kitchen, was an old favorite. After hordes of irate customers accosted the captain, Hilton restored the traditional dessert to its place of honor on the menu.

A local dairy, using the old recipe, has taken over ice cream production. Menu changes swirl around it. But it remains a symbol of the tradition of service pursued at the Palmer House.

The Berghoff

Beer may have made Milwaukee famous, but it enriched Chicago foodservice.

Herman J. Berghoff came from Germany to

found a brewery in Indiana. He could not get a wholesale license in Chicago. So, he checked out the World's Fair and opened a retail outlet on State Street, "that great street," in 1898.

From 1903 to 1915, Berghoff's grew. It added rooms on its western side, eventually abandoning the original corner. A spread of ham, sausages, and cheese was served free with a nickel beer or a 15 cent shot of whiskey.

Prohibition forced Berghoff's to expand its menu. It still has a German base but offers variety—40 hearty entrees a day, 75 to 100 entrees a week. With check averages of $3.40 for food and 55 cents for drinks, it attracts 3,200 customers to fill its 700 seats five times daily.

"Business is terrific," reports John Berghoff, third-generation manager. "Even though some of the theaters are closed and convention business is down, this January was our best in seven years."

But downtown business could not support a second Berghoff's. Located a few blocks away, under the "L" tracks, the unit closed a few years ago. The family has no thought of opening other units.

"If you have one place, you can concentrate on it and do a better job," John insists.

The restaurant serves up homey menu items in a warm atmosphere, enriched by wood paneling. The family breweries were bought out 20 years ago, but a private brewer now supplies a special beer.

Berghoff's uses the old-European waiters' system to keep its modern complex of bar, main dining room, and downstairs annex running smoothy. As waiters pick up orders, they pay for the food with house money. Then, they are responsible for collecting checks, so cashiers are not needed.

But though Berghoff's still operates on the basis of traditional factors of foodservice success, it is by no means resting on its edelweiss.

"Your reputation is only as good as your last customer," John advises.

The Blackhawk

The knack of finding and adapting new ideas has been raised to an art by Don Roth. Yet this master merchandiser has earned his place at the focal point of Chicago dining with showmanship all his own.

Roth's father opened the Blackhawk 54 years ago. Its live entertainment kept the restaurant a downtown hot spot. But by 1952, television killed the big bands.

Realizing the need for a new approach, Roth went looking for ideas on the West Coast. He started at the Benson Hotel in Portland and worked his way down to Lawry's in Los Angeles.

Flipping over the roast beef and salad menu, Roth got Lawry's permission to copy the concept in Chicago. He makes no bones about his indebtedness.

While Roth may be a borrower, he applies his own show business know-how to stir up dining excitement. In addition to merchandising the Blackhawk, he has opened Don Roth units with a stripped-down menu north of the Loop—even in the Chicago suburbs.

Yet Roth definitely is not giving up on downtown. He believes the West Coast concept of a glamorous deli might work and may convert his downstairs dining room. He is transforming a bar on the far side of the main room into a fast-food unit. And he expects to take full advantage of the foodservice possibilities when the city converts the alley behind the Blackhawk into a mall with a French theme.

"You have to swing with the times," Roth asserts. "That's the name of the game downtown."

The Como Inn

Chicago's heart belongs to beef. But its many neighborhoods savor a melting pot of ethnic cuisines.

Many Italians settled just north and west of downtown. Among them was Guiseppe Marchetti, who came from a small town near Florence. In 1924, at the age of 20, he opened the Como Inn.

Like so many other neighborhoods, Marchetti's changed. After World War II, expressways and urban renewal pushed the old Italian families out.

The Como Inn changed, too. A few blocks from its original site, the restaurant has grown from 13 seats to a cluster of opulent dining rooms, seating 450, with private rooms on the second floor. It has become big business, grossing $2 million a year.

But it maintains the family feeling. Four

Marchetti brothers—Joe, Stefano, Paul, and Larry—plus uncles Marcello and Peter share the management tasks. And Guiseppe comes in three or four times a week to visit with regulars.

Customer loyalty—often passed from one generation to the next—is inspired by the Como Inn's unabashed love affair with Italian foodservice. Interior designers Stefano and Paul keep a crew of Italian artisans to create ethnic settings that adapt with the seasons. Their next project, remodeling the oldest room to look like a country kitchen.

All the Marchettis visit Italy often to seek design and menu ideas. After their last trip, they introduced Osso Bucco (leg of veal), now a regular menu sell-out. But when they brought an espresso machine from Florence, they had to soften the Italian coffee for American tastes by adding some Colombian coffee beans.

The busy catering arm demands even more customizing. Recent tasks ranged from a benefit dinner for 750 at Chicago's Shedd Aquarium, prepared in a makeshift kitchen on the site, to finding a girl to jump out of a cake.

The Marchettis meet such challenges whenever they come up as part of their continuing effort to maintain the Como Inn's vitality.

Sirloin Room
The Stockyard Inn

You are in Mayor Daley country when you drive toward the Amphitheatre. But the "Boss" switched his favor from the grand old convention hall to McCormick Place. Prestigious exhibitions—including the National Restaurant Show—followed suit.

The fortunes of the Stockyard Inn reflect that change. Opened in 1912 as a haven for meat-packing chiefs, whose pictures still adorn its walls, the inn sits on land owned by William Wood-Prince. Two years ago he encouraged Nick Diaz and Howard Mitchell to take over the 60-room inn, dining rooms, and concessions at the Amphitheatre.

The center still books some big shows. During this year's Machine Tool Show, the Sirloin Room took in $12,000 to $15,000 a day—its best gross ever. Still, current shows often draw the kind of customers who do not understand tipping, forcing the Sirloin Room to tack on an automatic 15 percent service charge.

Without shows, the restaurant grosses $20,000 a week. It manages to hold menu prices down: the top luncheon steak costs $5.50.

"This place is a tradition," Diaz states. "But the thing is that, since the stockyards have moved out, a lot of people don't know the inn is still here."

Diaz and Howard are advertising on radio and in magazines to counteract that. And, even though it is hard to save an aging restaurant, they certainly understand beef. They own a cattle ranch in Florida and expect to serve their own beef at their recently opened Stockyard II in nearby Pensacola.

Cape Cod Room
The Drake Hotel

When regulars belly up to the weathered oak bar in the Cape Cod Room, they may quaff a few for Cape Cod Charlie.

Now Charlie was a goldfish, one of many pets who lived in a tank at the bar. On Sept. 18, 1964, a do-gooder cleaned the tank. And then he refilled it with chlorinated water. All the fish but Charlie died.

On Charlie's demise a couple of years later, a plaque was prepared in his memory. Mounted beneath a wooden duck, it now hangs just to the right of the old oak bar.

That bar, too, shows the clubby feeling of the Cape Cod Room. Architect Ben Marshall persuaded Edwin Brashears, Sr. to take over the bankrupt Drake family's hotel in 1933. For a seafood restaurant in one corner of the hotel's arcade, Peter Hunt helped capture the charm of a New England fishing village.

The long oak bar was part of the furniture when the room opened in 1936. Over the years, customers carved initials over its face. But when management replaced it with a shiny new bar, the regulars howled until they put the original back.

Thus, except for a few added accessories, the 153-seat Cape Cod Room looks basically as it did 40 years ago. But its prices have had to change, now $3.75 to $10.75 per item.

Heartland

It is a strange task, searching for professional foodservice in rural Indiana and Illinois. What one finds there is corn. Food, surely enough, but more appropriately "feed" for a less service-oriented aspect of the foodservice process.

The land is a sprawling agricultural patchwork from which its inhabitants reap their livelihood and sustenance. Generations of families have worked identical rows in the same fields and have, then, gathered for meat and potato meals. Home ties are strong, in part accounting for the lowest per capita restaurant expenditure of any region in the nation.

Still, these Americans are copious producers, a fact of which they are passionately proud. They combat a hard environment; their lives are hearty and their celebrations earnest. Small wonder that their culinary treasures include the likes of sorghum cookies and sarsaparilla jelly.

And there are places of beauty—physical, historical and human—where it has become appropriate to celebrate by breaking bread with one's neighbors. One such "place" is the Covered Bridge Festival held annually in Parke County, Ind. For 10 days each autumn, the county's 18,000 residents play host to 350,000 visitors, during what has been listed by the U.S. Department of the Interior as one of the top 10 tourist attractions in the U.S.

Ostensibly, the event honors the county's nation-leading total of 36 covered bridges. Actually, it is a nostalgic celebration of the charm of late 19th-century life, with the county residents themselves providing the attendant foodservice. During these colorful fall days, one may journey to the county seat, Rockville, and enjoy homemade persimmon ice cream, fried apple pies and crullers, whole hog sausage, roast corn, ham and biscuits, gingerbread with whipped cream, Covered Bridge Stew and Beans on Washday Soup— cooked in huge, cast-iron kettles on the courthouse lawn. Were all these cooked *inside* the courthouse, the result would be one of the most noteworthy country restaurants in America. Of course, the 20th century has changed Indiana. ("We'd like to have home-made ice cream all the time," says Parke County Executive Secretary Charles Felkner, "but it takes long enough to go to the store and get it.")

But along with all that corn, America's heartland appears to retain an equal amount of human spirit.

Turkey Run Inn
Marshall, Ind.

Sandstone gorges, meandering creeks, virgin forests. Hardly a standard Indiana scene. But the 2,182-acre Turkey Run State Park is an oasis of beauty, far from illusion.

Although the park is very much a favorite with the outdoor type, Indiana has handsomely provided for the less intrepid through the construction of the Turkey Run Inn. Opened three years after the formation of the park, in 1916, the inn is built on a site where fried chicken picnics were traditionally held by community members after church on Sunday. Despite certain radical changes in the spot's clientele, the foodservice has not changed all that much.

In what has become the key development in the history of the inn, the 72-room facility was enlarged by the addition of a modern convention hall in 1972. Since then, the inn has played host to groups representing such stellar companies as Caterpillar, Geigy and Monsanto. Such progressive companies have found that the area offers the minimum in the way of distractions and the maximum in terms of healthful relaxation.

"Whatever they want in terms of food," offers Manager William Engle, "we'll fix. But when we serve ham and cornbread and beans . . . well, these are things these fellas haven't had in years. The last time Caterpillar was here, they stayed for a week and never changed one menu."

Quite appropriately, however, the inn is in its true glory at Thanksgiving. Some families come back for generations to spend the November holiday at Turkey Run. What does this combination of industrial and family business mean to this "back woods" inn?

"Each year business is getting better," says Engle. "We've had no recession here."

New Salem Lodge
New Salem, Ill.

While a resident of New Salem, Abraham Lincoln worked as a miller, held a partnership in a grocery store and, for a brief period, distilled corn liquor. He did not succeed at any of these occupations, to be sure. But then, how many are really up to the challenges of the food world?

By his own admission, Paul Petersen was an equally unlikely candidate for foodservice. When he came to help manage the rambling rustic lodge at the entrance to New Salem State Park some 18 years ago, he "didn't know a hamburger from a sausage patty."

Unlike Mr. Lincoln, however, who had to settle for another line of work, Petersen quickly "learned by doing." He is now half-owner, as well as manager, of the New Salem operation.

Nowadays, he is also ably assisted by his wife Loretta and their four children. The proud papa states: "Everyone in the family seems to have a natural talent for making good food and giving good service. We come up with a lot of original ideas and never seem to have a problem with rising to an occasion."

"Occasions" are as many and varied as the people who come to see the reconstructed village. During the month of May, for example, the lodge serves special meals to 20,000 to 30,000 school children. These meals are frequently interspersed with gatherings of business people and distinguished foreign visitors.

Hosting a delegation of Russian business officials, the Petersens went all out with "a Russian menu, Russian music, and Russian liquor." The liquor was vodka, frozen to a syrupy consistency and laced with pepper. Many of the guests claimed it was the unscheduled highlight of their visit.

Currently, luncheon guests at the lodge's rough-oak dining room encounter a sandwich named Rachel. Described by its inventors as "the Lady Reuben," it gets its flare from a special sauce whose formula is a family secret. Petersen will gladly divulge where it can be purchased, however.

Even in New Salem, only some get the hang of this business.

Spring Green
Spring Green, Wis.

Near the northern border of Illinois, the land begins to undulate. The military-like formation of corn rows becomes interspersed with dairy cows, grain, and patches of green. Trees begin to appear in numbers and with a frequency that lifts the landscape to a lyrical level.

In this lovely, diverse, agricultural land, a great American artist was born, worked and is buried. His work, which spread throughout the American Midwest before embracing the world, is carried on here by people who proudly call themselves his disciples. Spring Green, Wis., is the home of Taliesin; Taliesin is the home of the famous architect, Frank Lloyd Wright.

When Wright designed and built Chicago's Midway Gardens in 1913, he not only created a vast, integrated scheme of indoor dining rooms, summer dining terraces, private dining rooms, and an outdoor cabaret, he also designed and executed all the service ware, furniture, linen, sculpture, paintings, murals, frescoes, windows, and planting urns. His restaurant theories were as "organic" as his other undertakings. All reflected an agricultural upbringing under a mother whose only concerns were, Wright once claimed, "whole wheat bread and religion."

In the 1940s, Wright began the construction, with his students, of a tea house a short distance from the Taliesin studios and living quarters in Spring Green. Due to numerous intervening factors, it was not until 1967 that Taliesin architects finished the project for the Wisconsin River Development Corporation, a group headed by Willard Leland, which is developing some 5,400 acres of land in the Spring Green area. The Spring Green restaurant is now the only foodservice operation in a building built specifically for that purpose by Wright.

Project Director Robert Graves and Restaurant Manager Art Berenbruch have no illusions about what brings the restaurant's patrons the three hours from Milwaukee or Chicago.

Although the restaurant serves an attractive Continental-American cuisine, it is dining amidst great art that makes the experience so special. Gazing at a sweeping bend of the Wisconsin River, restaurant guests become part of a panoramic interaction set up by a great artist and The Great Artist.

Yesteryear
Kankakee, Ill.

What happens, then, when someone takes a Frank Lloyd Wright house and makes a restaurant of it? According to Marvin Hammack and Ray Schimel, who are the proprietors of such an establishment, "what you have to do is treat your customers like neighbors."

And, in truth, dining at Yesteryear, located in a handsome residential area bordering the Kankakee River, is like visiting the home of delightfully wealthy and eccentric old friends —people to whom the kitchen is the heart of the house, and to whom the house is the heart of hospitality.

Hammack and Schimel worked hard to create this impression when they undertook their restaurant venture 23 years ago. For a while, they accepted only 50 or 60 customers per meal, "so we could really take care of everyone who came. We wanted a dining room, not a restaurant."

In addition to their painstaking work, they found that their out-of-the-way location, some 60 miles south of Chicago, became a major advantage.

"There was really no place to eat in southern Illinois between Chicago and St. Louis," explains Schimel. "We started to appear in travel brochures. People went home and talked about us."

Asked to characterize their menu, both agree "it's what we like to eat." Their selections reflect local agricultural production in combination with dishes garnered during extensive travels. (The partners also run a travel agency.) Each meal is served with apple butter, cottage cheese, home-baked sweet rolls, and an assortment of imaginatively prepared fresh vegetables.

Once again, however, it is the building which often ends up being the star.

"Yes," admits Hammack, "it's a fact we've never tried to hide."

Miss Hulling's
St. Louis

America's heartland has seen many groups pass by, each leaving a contribution to menus. From the blend emerged a distinctly American foodservice concept: good but simple food, served quickly, conveniently and inexpensively. A standard-bearer in this area: Miss Hulling's, St. Louis.

Heart of the whole $9-million operation is the cafeteria at 11th & Locust, started in 1929 by Miss Florence Hulling.

"My suppliers were great about helping then," she recalls "and they still are today."

Things have changed from that first 200-seat operation. Today the Miss Hulling's operations have a total of 2,315 seats; only 50 percent are for cafeteria service. All 10 facilities are in the St. Louis area.

Florence met and married Stephen Apted, meanwhile making her dream of good food served in a clean, attractive facility a daily reality.

"I never thought of giving up. We were successful," says Florence. Her son Stephen grew up in the business and now is involved in recreation facilities in the area.

Cafeteria foods have changed. In the '30s, pumpkin pie was reserved for Thanksgiving and Christmas. Today it is a daily menu item. Fresh vegetables, prepared in small batches as needed, are still on the menu. Now, many frozen and canned vegetables are also among the 11 featured daily. Ten entrees, including roast beef, fried catfish, and corned beef, rotate on the menu to give patrons a variety of choices. Homey desserts include fresh strawberries, offered plain or with whipped cream, and bread pudding with lots of raisins.

A retail section, just off the dining area, offers sandwiches, salads, and desserts for take-out. Baked goods, from the bakery upstairs, include decorated cakes, pies, candy, cookies and various breads. Some frozen prepared entrees are also for sale. The bakery alone uses about 68,000 pounds of butter each year.

Steve Gorczyca, general manager, describes Miss Hulling's as a comfortable place. Atmosphere and food are like home, but with a pleasant difference, he says. "The menu is All-

American; we have several nationalities of settlers in St. Louis, and each adds to the variety of foods offered here," Gorczyca notes. "Men do, indeed, eat here; more than 50 percent of the cafeteria customers are men.

They enjoy the fresh fruit, wide selection and choices of 'plain' or 'sauced' side dishes. Ladies seem to come for a chance to get ideas for foods to serve at home, as well as to enjoy Miss Hulling's.

Midwest Recipes

STONE FENCE*

Yield: 1 serving

Ingredients
APPLEJACK or RUM	1 ounce
HOT CIDER	6 ounces
BUTTER	1/2 teaspoon
CINNAMON STICK	1

Procedure
Mix first 3 ingredients together in a mug. Add cinnamon stick for use as a muddler.
*Colonial Tavern Drink

Foodservices Division
Milwaukee Public Schools
Thomas J. Farley
Gold Plate, 1970

CIDER MILL PUNCH

Yield: approximately 3 quarts

Ingredients
APPLE CIDER	1/2 gallon
ORANGE JUICE	2 cups
LEMON JUICE	1 cup
HONEY	1/4 cup
CINNAMON STICK, 2-1/2-inch	1
CLOVES, WHOLE	5
ALLSPICE, WHOLE	1/4 teaspoon
BUTTER	1-1/2 teaspoons

Procedure
Combine all ingredients in a saucepot and bring to a boil. Cover and simmer for 1 hour.

Pantry Shelf

CHICKEN GUMBO SOUP

Yield: 20 gallons

Ingredients
SHORTENING	4-1/2 pounds
FLOUR	5-1/2 pounds
PAPRIKA	6 tablespoons
CHICKEN STOCK	15 gallons
CHICKEN BASE	8 ounces
ONION, AP, minced	10 pounds
CELERY, diced	12 pounds
GREEN PEPPER, chopped	2 pounds, 8 ounces
TOMATOES, CANNED, crushed	2 No. 10 cans
TOMATO PUREE	1 No. 10 can
SALT	1-3/4 cups
PEPPER	1-1/2 teaspoons
SUGAR	2-1/8 cups
OKRA	1 No. 10 can
RICE, cooked	1-1/4 gallons
CHICKEN, cooked, diced	5 pounds

Procedure
1. Make a roux of the shortening, flour, and paprika. Cook 10 minutes.
2. Add chicken stock and chicken base. Stir until smooth. Bring to a boil. Add next 8 ingredients. Cook 30 minutes.
3. Add drained okra, cooked rice, and diced chicken. Heat thoroughly. Serve piping hot.
Note
Turkey meat may be substituted for the chicken.

Gimbels, Milwaukee

CHICKEN SOUP CREOLE

Yield: 21 gallons

Ingredients

ONION, EP, diced	2-1/4 gallons
CELERY, EP, diced	3-1/4 gallons
CHICKEN STOCK	18 gallons
CHICKEN BASE	8 ounces
OKRA	2 No. 10 cans
WHOLE TOMATOES, crushed	2 No. 10 cans
RICE, uncooked	3 pounds
GREEN PEPPERS, diced	17
CHICKEN, finely diced	6 pounds
SUGAR	2 cups
SALT	1-3/4 cups
PEPPER	1 teaspoon

Procedure

Cook onion and celery in chicken stock with chicken base, approximately 15 minutes. Add drained okra, and crushed whole tomatoes. Cook a few minutes. Add rice and cook until rice is almost done. Add green peppers, diced chicken, sugar, and seasonings. Cook 10 minutes.

Gimbels, Milwaukee

BOOKBINDER RED SNAPPER SOUP

Yield: 4 servings

Ingredients

FISH STOCK	2 pints
DICED ONION	1/4 cup
DICED CELERY	1/2 pint
DICED RED SNAPPER	1 cup
DICED GREEN PEPPER	1 cup
BUTTER	2 tablespoons
TOMATO SAUCE	1 pint
BROWN SAUCE	1 quart
SHERRY	1/2 cup

Procedure

1. Smother the onion, celery, and green pepper in butter and add fish stock; cook for 15 minutes.

2. Then add the diced red snapper and cook for 10 minutes.

3. Add 1 pint of tomato sauce and 1 quart of brown sauce. At the last moment before serving, finish with good sherry.

The Cape Cod Room

CLAM CHOWDER

Yield: 6 gallons

Ingredients

CLAMS, chopped	1 gallon
POTATOES, diced, steamed	16-1/2 pounds
ONION, MEDIUM-SIZED, diced	1
SALT PORK, finely diced	1/2 pound
THIN CREAM SAUCE	3-1/2 to 4 gallons
SALT	to taste
PEPPER	to taste

Procedure

1. Simmer clams until tender. Save broth.

2. Steam potatoes and onion 3 minutes.

3. Fry salt pork until lightly browned.

4. Combine all ingredients and add cream sauce. Season to taste.

Michigan State University

POTATO SOUP

Yield: 6 servings

Ingredients

POTATOES, MEDIUM-SIZED, peeled, diced	6
BUTTER	2 tablespoons
CARROT, MEDIUM-SIZED, diced	1
FINELY CHOPPED ONION	1/4 cup
FLOUR	2 tablespoons
MILK	1 quart
FINELY CHOPPED PARSLEY	2 tablespoons
SALT	1 tablespoon
SEASONED SALT	1/2 teaspoon
MONOSODIUM GLUTAMATE	1/4 teaspoon
RED PEPPER	1/4 teaspoon
CHICKEN BOUILLON CUBE	1

Procedure

1. Cook potatoes in boiling salted water until tender.

2. Melt butter in 3-quart kettle. Heat until golden brown. Add carrot and onion. Cover and cook until tender. Remove from heat.

3. Blend in flour. Stir in milk. Add half of potatoes.

4. Mash rest of potatoes and add with remaining ingredients. Serve steaming hot.

Pantry Shelf

CREAM OF LETTUCE SOUP

Yield: 50 portions

Ingredients

1. LETTUCE LEAVES,
       OUTSIDE   from 1 head
   CELERY LEAVES   from 1 bunch
   ONION, SLICED   1
   WATER   1 quart
   SHORTENING   1-1/4 cups
   FLOUR   2-1/2 cups
2. LETTUCE HEAD,
       SMALL   1
   WATER   1 quart
   MILK, WARM   1-1/4 gallons
   SUGAR   2-1/2 tablespoons
   SALT   3 tablespoons
   PEPPER, WHITE   1/4 teaspoon
   CHICKEN BASE (OPTIONAL)   1/2 ounce
   YELLOW FOOD COLORING   few drops

Procedure

1. Boil the first 4 ingredients 20 minutes. Strain.
2. Add hot water to make 1-1/4 gallons of stock.
3. Melt shortening; add flour to make a roux. Blend well.
4. Gradually add stock to roux, stirring constantly. Cook 10 minutes.
5. Cook chopped lettuce head in 1 quart water.
6. Add to the roux mixture the lettuce and stock in which it was cooked, the warm milk, sugar, salt and pepper.
7. Stir in the chicken base and yellow food coloring.
8. Heat to boiling point. Serve piping hot.

Note

For meatless stock, omit chicken base. In its place use onion base supplemented with minced celery and other vegetables.

Gimbels, Milwaukee

WISCONSIN CHEESE SOUP

Yield: 50 portions (2-1/2 gallon)

Ingredients

CELERY, DICED FINE	3 cups
CARROTS, DICED FINE	3 cups
ONION, DICED FINE	1-1/2 cups
STOCK	6 quarts
BUTTER	1-1/2 cups
FLOUR	1-1/2 cups
SHARP CHEESE, DICED	1-1/2 quarts
MILK, HOT	1-1/2 gallons
BAKING SODA	3/4 teaspoon
PAPRIKA	1-1/2 teaspoons
CORNSTARCH	1/2 cup
SUGAR	3 tablespoons
SALT	4-1/2 tablespoons
MILK, COLD	(approx.) 3/4 cup
WORCESTERSHIRE SAUCE	2 tablespoons
PARSLEY, CHOPPED	to garnish

Procedure

1. Cook celery, carrots and onion 10 minutes in 2 quarts of the stock.
2. Add the remaining 4 quarts stock and enough water to bring the stock up to the original 6 quarts.
3. Melt butter and blend in flour to make a roux. Cook 10 minutes.
4. Gradually add stock and vegetables to the roux, stirring to make a smooth sauce.
5. Add diced sharp cheese. Cook *very slowly* until cheese is blended into the sauce.
6. In meantime, heat milk.
7. Combine baking soda, paprika, cornstarch, sugar and salt. Add enough cold milk to make a thin paste.
8. Add with the worcestershire sauce to the cheese mixture.
9. Stir in the hot milk. Bring to simmering point. Taste for seasoning.
10. Serve sprinkled with chopped parsley.

Note

To prevent curdling, exercise care in the choice of cheese used in this recipe.

Heartland

Tranquility, beauty, and bounty are nowhere more evident than in America's heartland —rural Illinois, Indiana, and Wisconsin. The sandstone gorges, meandering creeks, and virgin forests (above left) that surround Turkey Run Inn in Marshall, Ind. seem the perfect background for the bountiful meals served there. Ham, corn bread, and beans are favorites that visitors cannot seem to get enough of, whether the dishes are familiar or being encountered for the first time. The Spring Green (Wis.) Restaurant displays desserts in the uniquely satisfying dining room designed by Frank Lloyd Wright and placed on a sweeping bend of the Wisconsin River in Wright's own country. Begun in 1940 by Wright, the restaurant was brought to completion by Taliesin architects who had worked with him.

Yesteryear, also designed by Frank Lloyd Wright, was a home that has been transformed into a restaurant. Because it began as a home, owners Marvin Hammack and Ray Schimel say, "What you have to do is treat your customers like neighbors." In addition to a sizable local clientele, "neighbor-customers" have made Kankakee a regular stop on the route from Chicago to St. Louis. Typical of the menu fare are the dishes pictured at right.

All of the dining areas at Yesteryear seem intimate because of Wright's way of creating a sense of smaller areas within the whole space. There is a feeling of seclusion, yet tables are easily accessible for service, a special advantage since every meal is accompanied by offerings of apple butter, cottage cheese, home-baked sweet rolls, and an assortment of imaginatively prepared fresh vegetables. The owners added their dimension to foods from the area.

Beans on Washday Soup is a central attraction at the Covered Bridge Festival held annually in Parke County, Ind. The traditional dish is prepared on the courthouse lawn in Rockville, Ind. as it was in pioneer days. Then a big cast-iron kettle was filled with water and beans at the same time the women of the community started heating water for washday. Seasoned with a locally-favored combination of spices and herbs, the hearty soup was ready for all comers when "nooning" time arrived.

Today, the county's 18,000 residents organize each autumn to play host to 350,000 visitors who come to the 10-day Festival. Odds are about even as to whether the chief attraction is the 36 covered bridges to be found in the county or the availability of this savory soup, plus homemade persimmon ice cream, fried apple pies and crullers, whole hog sausage, roast corn, ham, and biscuits, gingerbread with whipped cream, and Covered Bridge Stew.

Crisp fried fish with an extra portion of almond butter sauce is just one of the many menu attractions pictured at left as served at the rambling rustic lodge at the entrance to New Salem (Ill.) State Park. Travelers in Lincoln country usually make more than one visit to the New Salem Lodge dining room with its rough-hewn oak interior which is run by Paul Petersen and his family. Rachel, "the lady Reuben," is convincing proof that all of the family is truly "devoted to good food and good service." It is a sandwich with a special flair provided by a flavorful sauce whose formula remains a family secret.

VEGETABLE SOUP

Yield: 96 portions

Ingredients

BEEF STOCK	5 gallons
CELERY, E.P., DICED	4 quarts
LEEKS or ONION, E.P., DICED	1 quart
CARROTS, E.P., DICED	2 quarts
TOMATOES, CANNED, No. 10	1
SALT	1/2 cup
PEPPER	2 teaspoons
GREEN BEANS, CANNED or FROZEN	1 quart
GREEN PEAS, CANNED or FROZEN	1 quart
PARSLEY, CHOPPED	1 cup

Procedure

1. Add raw celery, leeks or onion, carrots, canned tomatoes, and seasonings to the beef stock.

2. Simmer until flavors are well blended and vegetables are tender. Add green beans and peas.

3. Simmer until all vegetables are tender.

4. Add chopped parsley just before serving.

Wesley Memorial Hospital, Chicago

OXTAIL SOUP

Yield: 48 portions (3 gallons)

Ingredients

OXTAILS	6 pounds
FAT	4 ounces
BEEF STOCK or WATER	1-1/2 gallons
ONION, sliced	2 cups
CARROTS, diced	3 cups
CELERY, diced	2 cups
POTATOES, diced	1 cup
BARLEY	1 cup
BAY LEAVES	4
TOMATOES, CANNED, No. 2-1/2	1
SALT	to season
PEPPER	to season

Procedure

1. Cut oxtails in pieces and brown in hot fat.

2. Add browned oxtail joints to hot stock. Cook 3-1/2 hours.

3. Strain stock from meat. Cool meat. Cut meat off joints, and in smaller pieces, if necessary. Return meat to stock. Bring to a boil. Add vegetables, barley and bay leaves. Simmer 30 minutes. Skim off fat.

4. Add canned tomatoes, salt and pepper. Taste for seasoning. Heat and serve piping hot.

Evanston Hospital, Evanston, Ill.

CORN CHOWDER

Yield: 50 portions

Ingredients

SHORTENING	1-1/4 cups
FLOUR	2-1/2 cups
CHICKEN BASE, (OPTIONAL)	1-1/2 ounces
STOCK	1 gallon
SALT	2-1/2 tablespoons
SUGAR	1 tablespoon
GREEN PEPPERS, DICED	2
ONION, DICED	2 cups
CELERY, DICED	2 cups
POTATOES, COOKED, CUBED	2 cups
PIMIENTO	1/4 cup
CREAM STYLE CORN	3 cups
MILK, HOT	1-1/4 gallons

Procedure

1. Melt shortening and blend in flour to make roux. Cook 10 minutes.

2. Combine chicken base and stock, and add to roux, stirring constantly.

3. Cook 15 minutes. Add vegetables and seasonings. Boil 10 minutes.

4. Add corn and pimiento and cook 5 minutes longer.

5. Stir in warm milk. Bring to a boil. Taste for seasonings. Serve very hot.

Note

For a meatless stock, use an onion base.

Gimbels, Milwaukee

CREAM OF CHICKEN SOUP WITH HARD-COOKED EGGS

Yield: 15 gallons

Ingredients

SHORTENING	1-3/4 quarts
FLOUR, sifted	4-1/2 quarts
CHICKEN STOCK	9 gallons
CHICKEN BASE	4 ounces
ONION, MINCED	1-1/2 quarts
GREEN PEPPERS, CHOPPED	7
CELERY, DICED	4-1/2 quarts
PIMIENTO, diced	1 cup
WHOLE PEPPERCORNS	1-1/2 teaspoons
SUGAR	1 cup plus 1 tablespoon
SALT	1-1/8 cups
MILK, WARM	5 gallons
YELLOW FOOD COLORING	few drops
EGGS, HARD-COOKED, CHOPPED	20
CHICKEN MEAT	3 cups
RICE, COOKED, DRY	5 quarts

Procedure

1. Make a roux of shortening and flour. Cook 10 minutes.

2. Add chicken stock and chicken base. Stir until smooth. Bring to a boil.

3. Add onion, green peppers, celery, pimiento, peppercorns, sugar, and salt. Simmer 30 minutes.

4. Add warm milk. Stir well. Do not boil.

5. Add food coloring, chopped hard-cooked eggs, diced chicken, and warm rice. Heat thoroughly.

6. Serve garnished with chopped parsley.

Gimbels, Milwaukee

SAUTE TENDERLOIN TIPS WITH MUSHROOMS IN SAUCE

Yield: 50 5-ounce portions

Ingredients

TENDERLOIN TIPS, trimmed, fat free	17 pounds
MUSHROOMS	3 pounds
SHALLOTS	1 pound
BUTTER	3 ounces
BROWN SAUCE, hot	1-1/2 gallons
BURGUNDY	6 ounces
SALAD OIL	1 pint
BUTTER, melted	for toast points
PARSLEY, chopped	6 ounces

Procedure

1. Slice tenderloin tips on the bias.

2. Wash mushrooms thoroughly and slice, lifting mushrooms from water rather than pouring water off. Fine particles of mushrooms will be avoided and dirt will also remain in bottom of pan.

3. Saute shallots and mushrooms in butter and combine with hot brown sauce. Add burgundy and adjust seasoning. Simmer slowly while preparing tenderloin tips.

4. Heat oil to smoke point and cook tenderloin tips quickly in large frying pan or sautoir. Brown nicely but do not cook well done.

5. Mix cooked tips (draining oil) with mushroom sauce. Bring to boiling point without scorching; remove from heat.

6. Serve in casseroles. Dip small toast points in melted butter and chopped parsley. Insert toast points deep into casserole, parsley end out. Provides both garnish and accompaniment.

BRAISED SHORT RIBS OF BEEF

Yield: 50 10-ounce servings

Ingredients

SHORT RIBS	
(about 10-ounces each)	50
ONION, peeled,	
medium cut	1-1/2 pounds
CARROTS, scrubbed,	
medium cut	1/2 pound
CELERY, cleaned,	
medium cut	1/2 pound
SALAD OIL	1 pint
SWEET BASIL	2 teaspoons
SAGE	1/2 teaspoon
THYME	1/2 teaspoon
BREAD FLOUR	1 pound
BEEF STOCK, hot	6 quarts
TOMATOES, chopped	1 No. 2-1/2 can

Procedure

1. Trim ribs; remove fat and tie meat to bone.

2. Put vegetables in lightly greased roasting pan and place short ribs on top. Pour 1 cup oil evenly over all. Combine spices and sprinkle as evenly as possible over top.

3. Brown in oven at 400°F., turning as necessary. Do not let vegetables burn.

4. When nicely browned, add remainder of oil and flour, blending well. Cook for 5 to 10 minutes. Add hot stock, stirring to mix well, until slightly thickened. Add tomatoes and blend.

5. Cover, return to oven and cook 2 to 2-1/2 hours or until tender. When ribs are cooked, remove to clean pan.

6. Strain sauce. Adjust seasoning and thickening. Remove excess fat. Pour sauce over ribs. Hold for service in warm place but do not continue to cook.

7. When serving, remove string. Serve one 10-ounce rib portion with 3 ounces sauce. A fresh vegetable garnish may be added.

LASAGNA

Yield: 120 servings

Ingredients

GROUND BEEF	14 pounds
COOKING OIL	as needed
CANNED TOMATOES	6-1/2 quarts
plus LIQUID	2 quarts
TOMATO PASTE	2-1/4 quarts
OREGANO FLAKES	3-1/2 tablespoons
SUGAR	1 tablespoon
ONION, chopped	1 quart
GARLIC CLOVES, SMALL	5
SALT	to taste
PEPPER	to taste
LASAGNA NOODLES	4-1/2 pounds
CHEESE, AMERICAN,	
sliced	7-1/2 pounds
COTTAGE CHEESE	7 quarts
CHEESE, PARMESAN,	
grated	2 quarts
CHOPPED PARSLEY	1/2 cup

Procedure

1. Brown meat in a small amount of hot oil. Stir to mix tomatoes, tomato paste, oregano, sugar, onion, and garlic. Add browned meat. Bring to boil; turn down heat; allow to simmer 1 hour. Add salt and pepper to taste.

2. Break noodles into 2-inch pieces and cook in rapidly boiling salted water as directed on package.

3. Cut cheese slices into quarters.

4. Spread 1-1/2 quarts tomato mixture on bottom of each counter pan. Over this, place a layer of noodles, a layer of 32 quarters American cheese, 1-1/2 cups cottage cheese and 1/2 cup parmesan cheese. Repeat this process 3 times. Top with remaining tomato mixture.

5. Bake in oven at 350°F. for 40 minutes, or until firm. Let stand 15 to 20 minutes. Chopped parsley should be sprinkled over top before serving.

Michigan State University

VEAL LIMONE
FROM THE COMO INN

Yield: 6 servings

Ingredients

VEAL TENDERLOIN, MEDIUM-SIZED	18 pieces
LEMONS, fresh	3
FLOUR	as needed
SALT	1/2 teaspoon
WHITE PEPPER	1/2 teaspoon
WHITE SAUTERNE	1 cup

Procedure

1. Preheat large skillet with olive oil.

2. Sprinkle both sides of veal with salt and pepper; lightly flour, shake off excess flour; place in skillet.

3. Saute until veal loses its pink color, but do not brown.

4. Add juice of two lemons; sprinkle with white sauterne, remove from heat.

5. Place a thin slice of lemon on each piece.

6. Cover and let simmer for 2 or 3 minutes. Serve at once.

MELTING POT STEW

Yield: 100 portions, 1 cup provides 2 ounces cooked lean meat and 1/2 cup vegetables

Ingredients

BONELESS STEW LAMB, cubed	19 pounds, 4 ounces
GARLIC, minced	4 cloves
WATER	3 gallons
ALL-PURPOSE FLOUR	1-3/4 quarts
SALT	4 ounces
PEPPER	1 tablespoon
POTATOES, SMALL WHOLE, halved or cubed	13 pounds
CARROTS, pieces or halved or cubed (1/2 inch)	7 pounds
ONION, quartered	2 pounds

Procedure

1. Brown lamb with garlic.

2. Add water; simmer, covered, about 1 hour, until tender.

3. When lamb is tender, remove about 2 quarts broth; cool.

4. Blend flour, salt, and pepper into broth. Add to hot meat mixture; stir constantly until thickened.

5. Steam vegetables. Combine with meat carefully.

American Lamb Council

SAUERBRATEN OR GERMAN POT ROAST

Yield: 25 portions

Ingredients

BEEF, CHUCK OR RUMP	10 pounds
SALT	to season
PEPPER	to season
MIXED PICKLE SPICES	1 ounce
GROUND GINGER	1 ounce
ONION, sliced	1 cup
BROWN SUGAR	1 cup
VINEGAR	1 quart
WATER	3 quarts
FLOUR for dredging	1 cup (approx.)
FAT	1 cup (approx.)
SOUR CREAM (optional)	1 cup

Procedure

1. Place meat in earthenware container. Add salt, pepper, mixed pickle spices, ground ginger, sliced onions and sugar.

2. Combine vinegar and water and bring to a boil. Pour hot vinegar mixture over meat and seasonings.

3. Cool. Cover and place in refrigerator for 3 or 4 days, turning meat every day.

4. At the end of the marinating period, remove meat. Drain thoroughly.

5. Dredge the meat with flour, and brown on all sides in hot fat in roasting pan. Add a small amount of the spice liquid with the onions.

6. Cover closely and cook in oven at 300°F. for approximately 3 hours, or until meat is tender.

7. Remove meat from pan.

8. Strain liquid and make gravy. Just before serving, add sour cream to gravy if desired.

Evanston Hospital, Evanston, Ill.

VEAL CUTLETS—WISCONSIN STYLE

Yield: 50 4-ounce portions

Ingredients

FLOUR	3 cups
SALT	1 tablespoon
PEPPER	2 teaspoons
VEAL CUTLETS	50
BUTTER	1 cup
GARLIC CLOVES	2
FLOUR	3/4 cup
MILK	2 quarts
WORCESTERSHIRE SAUCE	1/4 cup
SALT	2 tablespoons
CHEESE, CHEDDAR, grated	1 pound

Procedure

1. Combine the first three ingredients.

2. Dredge cutlets in flour mixture, and brown in hot fat in skillet. Place cutlets in baking pans. Cover and bake in oven at 325°F. for 1 hour.

3. Melt butter in skillet. Add chopped garlic and blend in the flour. Cook 5 minutes.

4. Add hot milk and cook until thickened.

5. Blend in Worcestershire sauce, salt and grated cheese.

6. Remove meat from oven. Pour sauce over meat, and return to oven at 300°F. for 30 minutes.

Institution Management Tea Room,
School of Home Economics
University of Wisconsin, Madison

BRAISED LIVER WITH ONIONS →

Yield: 50 4-ounce portions

Ingredients

FLOUR	3 cups
SALT	5 tablespoons
PEPPER	1 tablespoon
LIVER, BEEF	10 pounds (approx.)
ONION, SLICED	4 pounds
BACON FAT	2/3 cup
WATER	1 quart

BEEF—TOMATO—CORN SCALLOP

"We developed this recipe as a year-round item and it has proved very popular."

Yield: 24 6-ounce portions

Ingredients

SHORTENING	1/2 cup
ONIONS, chopped	2 (medium)
GREEN PEPPERS, sliced	4
BEEF, ground	2 pounds
SALT	1 tablespoon
PEPPER	1/4 teaspoon
EGGS, whole	4
WHOLE KERNEL CORN, canned	1 quart
TOMATOES, canned	2 quarts
BREAD CRUMBS	1 cup
CHEDDAR CHEESE, grated	4 ounces

Procedure

1. Saute chopped onions and sliced peppers in shortening until delicately browned. Add meat and seasonings.

2. Stir in the beaten eggs and mix well.

3. Into a greased steam table pan (20- by 12-inches) put a layer of the meat mix, then a layer of corn, followed by a layer of tomatoes. Repeat until all ingredients are used.

4. Top with crumbs. Dot with grated cheese.

5. Cook in oven at 350°F. for one hour.

The Wurzburg Company, Grand Rapids, Mich.

Procedure

1. Mix flour, salt and pepper. Dredge sliced liver in flour mixture and brown in hot fat. Place in baking pans.

2. Saute onion in bacon fat, and spread over liver.

3. Add a small amount of water to each pan.

4. Cover and bake in oven at 300°F. for 1 hour.

Note

This is a very popular entree in our Tea Room.

Institution Management Tea Room,
University of Wisconsin, Madison

CURRIED CHICKEN WITH BAKED TOMATO IN CROUSTADE

"This is a delicious and colorful entree—wonderful for women's luncheons or wedding breakfasts."

Yield: 25 portions

Ingredients

CHICKEN STOCK, HOT	2 cups
FLOUR	4 ounces
SALT	3/4 tablespoon
PEPPER	1/4 teaspoon
PAPRIKA	1 teaspoon
CURRY	2 tablespoons
CHICKEN STOCK, COLD	1 cup
BUTTER	1 cup
EGG YOLKS, large, beaten	8
CHICKEN, COOKED, DICED	2 pounds
MUSHROOMS, A.P., sauteed	5-3/4 cups
CELERY, minced	1/2 cup
PIMIENTO, minced	1/2 cup
BREAD SLICES, 2-1/2 inches thick	25
BUTTER, melted	1/2 cup
TOMATOES, MEDIUM	25
BUTTER SQUARES	25
WATERCRESS	to garnish

Procedure

1. Bring 1 pint chicken stock to a boil. Combine flour, salt, pepper, paprika, and curry. Add 1 cup cold chicken stock. Blend well. Then add hot chicken stock and butter. Cook sauce in steam-jacketed kettle or double boiler 15 minutes, stirring frequently. Gradually stir in the beaten egg yolks. Blend well. Add chicken, minced celery, pimiento, and sauteed mushrooms. Cook 15 minutes or until mixture is thoroughly heated and sauce is of the desired consistency.

2. Cut unsliced bread in 2-1/2-inch slices. Cut off crusts, or cut with a canape cutter half-through the slice. Hollow center out with a knife leaving sides and bottom about 1/2-inch thick. Brush entire surface with melted butter.

3. Arrange on rack in shallow baking pan.

4. Peel 25 medium-sized tomatoes. Cut in halves. Place one-half tomato in the hollow of each croustade. Top with a square of butter.

5. Bake in oven at 375°F. until tomato is tender and croustade is delicately browned.

6. Cut the other half of each tomato into 4 wedges. Set aside.

7. Top the tomato-croustade with a 4 ounce dipper of the chicken mixture. Space tomato wedges around bottom of croustade.

8. Generously sprinkle over all sharp cheese grated on a coarse grater. Place under broiler until cheese melts and sauce is bubbly. Serve on hot platter garnished with watercress.

Schuler's of Marshall, Inc., Marshall, Mich.

CHICKEN BECHAMEL

Yield: 50 portions

Ingredients

NOODLES, DRY	3 pounds
CHICKEN BROTH	2 gallons
SALT	1-1/2 tablespoons
CHICKEN FAT	1 cup
SIFTED FLOUR	1 cup
CHICKEN STOCK	3 quarts
CHOPPED CELERY, EP	1 cup
CHOPPED ONION, EP	1/2 cup
MUSHROOMS, CANNED OR	1 8-ounce can
MUSHROOMS, FRESH	3-1/2 cups
CHICKEN FAT	1/4 cup
LEMON JUICE	1 cup
OLIVES, STUFFED, chopped	1 pint
SLIVERED ALMONDS, toasted	2 cups
CHICKEN, cooked, diced	6 pounds

Procedure

1. Cook noodles in 2 gallons chicken broth or in boiling salted water. Drain.

2. Make sauce with 1 cup chicken fat, flour, and 3 quarts chicken stock.

3. Saute celery, onion, and mushrooms in 1/4 cup chicken fat.

4. Combine noodles, sauce, sauteed vegetables, lemon juice, stuffed olives, chicken, and 2 cups almonds. Blend well. Season to taste.

5. Turn mixture into steam table pans, and bake in oven at 350°F. for 1 hour.

6. Garnish servings with the remaining toasted almonds.

Note

Turkey may be used in place of chicken.

**University Hospitals and School of Home Economics
University of Wisconsin, Madison**

MUSHROOM CAPS STUFFED WITH CHICKEN AND RICE

Yield: 40 portions, 2 mushroom caps each

Ingredients

MUSHROOM CAPS	5 pounds
(1 ounce each)	
BUTTER	1 pound
CHICKEN FAT	12 ounces
ONION, CHOPPED FINE	6 ounces
GREEN PEPPER, 1/4 inch cubes	4 ounces
MUSHROOM STEMS,	
sliced 1/4 inch thick	8 ounces
FLOUR	4 ounces
CHICKEN BROTH	3/4 quart
CHICKEN BASE	4 tablespoons
SALT	3/4 tablespoon
MONOSODIUM GLUTAMATE	1/2 tablespoon
PAPRIKA	1/2 teaspoon
BLACK PEPPER	1/2 teaspoon
CHICKEN, COOKED,	2 pounds,
1/4 to 3/8 inch pieces	8 ounces
RICE, COOKED	2 pounds
CHICKEN GRAVY	1 to 1-1/2 cups

Procedure

1. Cook mushroom caps in butter with lid on the pan so that they are partially steamed.

2. Saute onion, green pepper, and mushroom stems in chicken fat.

3. Add flour to chicken fat and vegetables. Blend well.

4. Slowly add chicken broth to which has been added the chicken base.

5. Add salt, monosodium glutamate, paprika and black pepper, then the chicken, cooked rice and gravy. Blend well.

6. Using a No. 30 scoop, fill mushroom caps with this mixture.

7. Place in bake pan with 1/2 inch chicken broth.

8. Bake in oven at 300°F. for 15 to 20 minutes.

9. Serve 2 stuffed mushroom caps on toast points with rich Chicken Gravy. Garnish with parsley or watercress.

Note

If mushroom caps are smaller, disregard the count per serving, and allow 2 oz. raw mushroom caps for each portion.

Dayton's, Minneapolis

TURKEY DIVAN

Yield: 25 portions

Ingredients

1. *MORNAY SAUCE*	
CHOPPED ONION	3/4 cup
BUTTER	2-1/2 cups
FLOUR	2-1/2 cups
MILK, hot	5 quarts
EGG YOLKS, slightly beaten	15
PARMESAN CHEESE	3/4 cup
WHIPPED CREAM	1-1/4 quarts
COOKING SHERRY	1/4 cup
2. BROCCOLI, AP, cooked	10 pounds
TURKEY, WHITE MEAT,	
cooked, sliced	4 pounds
PARMESAN CHEESE	1/2 cup

Procedure

1. Saute onion in butter until golden, but not brown. Blend in flour; add milk. Simmer 15 minutes. Strain mixture. Divide sauce into half; keep one-half warm.

To remaining half, add beaten egg yolks and parmesan cheese. Cool. Fold in whipped cream and sherry.

2. Place 2 stalks of broccoli in greased shallow casserole. Pour Mornay Sauce (without the sherry) over the broccoli. Arrange 3 slices white meat of turkey (approximately 2-1/2 ounces) on top.

Spread Mornay Sauce (with sherry and whipped cream added) over turkey.

Top with parmesan cheese, allowing 1 teaspoon for each casserole.

Bake in oven at 350°F. for approximately 25 minutes or until sauce is bubbly and cheese is melted and lightly tinged with brown.

The J. L. Hudson Co., Detroit

DOUBLE BREAST OF CHICKEN MIDWEST

"This is a popular entree for special parties or banquets as it can be prepared in advance. It is also in demand in the main dining rooms at the Palmer House.

"The lid of the baking dish and the rim of dough are not removed until the dish is served at the table. As the dough is cut away, and the lid raised, the appetizing goodness that has been sealed in gives off an aroma fit for a king. Oh's and ah's echo forth from the hungry diner, and no time is lost in sampling this tempting fare."

Yield: 10 portions

Ingredients

1. BROILERS, eviscerated,

1 pound, 12 ounces each	10
WILD RICE, AP	1 pound
CHOPPED ONION	2 tablespoons
CUBED CELERY	1 cup
DICED CARROTS	1/2 cup
BUTTER	1/4 cup
FLOUR	1/2 cup
WHITE WINE	1/2 cup
CHICKEN STOCK	1/2 cup
SALT	to taste
PEPPER	to taste
STRIPS of BROWN PAPER,	
18 inches long by 1 inch wide	10
COOKING OIL	2 tablespoons

2.

BUTTER	1/4 cup
FINELY DICED	
CARROTS	1/2 cup
FINELY DICED CELERY	1/2 cup
SLICED ONION	1/4 cup
BAY LEAVES	3
WHITE WINE	1/2 cup
CHICKEN STOCK	1 cup
BROWN GRAVY	1 cup
TOMATO PASTE	1 tablespoon
SALT	4 tablespoons
PEPPER	1/2 teaspoon

3. SEEDLESS GRAPES,

CANNED	2 No. 1 cans
WHITE WINE	1 cup

4.

BREAD FLOUR, unsifted	3-2/3 cups
WATER, cold	2 cups

Procedure

1. Remove double breasts of chicken leaving on only the wing tips. Refrigerate until ready to use.
Cook wild rice. Drain.

Saute the chopped onion, celery, and carrots in 1/4 cup butter. When tender, add the 1/2 cup flour, then the wild rice. Blend well. Add 1/2 cup white wine and 1/2 cup chicken stock.

Season with salt and pepper, and simmer slowly a few minutes.

2. Spread double breasts of chicken on meat board.

Place equal parts of the rice mixture on top of each double breast as shown in Figure 1.

Fold the tip points of the breast over the wild rice.

Fold over the whole breast.

Oil strips of brown paper using the cooking oil. Roll strips of paper around each double breast.

3. In a 14-inch round skillet or baking pan, place 1/4 cup butter. When butter is melted, add finely diced carrots, celery, and onion, then the crumbled bay leaves. (These vegetables will form a flavorful bed for the chicken breasts, and later add flavor to the gravy.)

Place the double breasts over the vegetables. Cook in oven at 450°F. for 15 minutes. Remove brown paper. Cook 20 minutes longer or until breasts are brown and tender. Baste frequently.

Remove breasts from skillet and place in greased individual baking dishes, leaving the vegetables in skillet.

Add to the skillet 1/2 cup white wine, chicken stock, brown gravy, and tomato paste. Add pepper and salt.

Simmer until liquid is reduced to approximately 1 cup. Strain liquid over chicken.

Top chicken breasts with white seedless grapes. Pour over 1 cup white wine. Cover baking dish.

4. Make a stiff dough using the 3-2/3 cups flour and 2 cups water. Roll dough in form of a long sausage. Place dough around lid of each baking dish.

Bake in oven at 350°F. for 20 minutes.

Do not remove lid or rim of dough until entree is served at table.

Note

The chicken legs can be utilized in a menu item for another meal or the breasts may be bought cut as double fronts with wings on.

The Palmer House, Chicago

ESCALLOPED TURKEY ⟶

Yield: 350 portions

Procedure

1. Cook 175 pounds eviscerated turkey until tender.

2. Cool in stock. Remove turkey. Save stock.

3. Strip meat from bones. Cut into bite-sized pieces.

4. Make a regular celery dressing, using 30 2-pound loaves of bread. Season to taste.

5. Spoon dressing into deep bake pans, 10-inch by 16-inch, to a depth of 1 inch.

6. Cover with a generous layer of turkey pieces, mixing the dark and the white meat.

7. Using the turkey stock, giblets, heart and liver, make a rich gravy.

8. Pour gravy over turkey in pan. Cover with buttered and seasoned crumbs.

9. Bake in oven at 350°F. for 1 hour or until sauce is bubbly.

10. Serve with cranberry sauce or cranberry-orange relish.

11. Garnish with watercress.

**Department of Residence Halls and Commons,
University of Chicago**

WILD RICE DRESSING FOR ROAST CHICKEN, DUCK OR TURKEY

Yield: 50 portions

Ingredients

WILD RICE, uncooked	1 cup
WHITE RICE, uncooked, browned	2 cups
CHICKEN LIVERS, chopped	1 pound
CHOPPED CELERY	3 cups
CHOPPED ONION	1 cup
BUTTER or MARGARINE	6 tablespoons
SALT	3 tablespoons
PEPPER	1 teaspoon
MONOSODIUM GLUTAMATE	1 teaspoon
CHICKEN BASE	2 tablespoons
BREAD CRUMBS	1 cup

Procedure

1. Boil or steam wild rice until tender.

2. Brown white rice under broiler or in oven until golden, then boil or steam it until tender.

3. Combine the wild and the browned rice.

4. Saute chicken livers, celery, and onion in butter or margarine until chicken livers are cooked and vegetables are tender.

5. Add seasonings, chicken base, and bread crumbs; blend well with rice mixture.

6. Bake in oven at 350°F. for 45 minutes.

The Northern Trust Co., Chicago

TURKEY PIE

Yield: 250 4-oz. portions

Ingredients

TURKEY FAT and MARGARINE	7 pounds
FLOUR	3-1/2 pounds
TURKEY STOCK	7 gallons
SALT	5/8 cup
PEPPER	3-1/2 tablespoons
CARROTS, DICED FINE	5 pounds
FROZEN PEAS	5 pounds
MUSHROOMS, FRESH	5 pounds
BUTTER or MARGARINE	1/2 cup
TURKEY, COOKED, DICED	16 pounds
PASTRY TOPS, 3-7/8 inches in diameter	250

Procedure

1. Melt turkey fat and margarine. Blend in the flour.

2. Add turkey stock; bring to a boil stirring constantly. Add salt and pepper. Cook until mixture thickens and flour is well cooked, stirring occasionally.

3. Steam carrots and frozen peas. (Do not overcook.)

4. Slice and saute mushrooms in butter or margarine.

5. Add diced turkey and vegetables to thickened stock.

6. Fill casseroles with hot mixture. Cover with pastry tops. Bake in oven at 425°F. until top is golden brown—approx. 20 to 25 minutes.

Harper Hospital, Detroit

POMPANO PAPILLOTE DRAKE CHEF'S STYLE

Yield: 6 servings

Ingredients

FILLET of POMPANO	6
RED WINE	1/2 pint
BUTTER	2 ounces
COOKED LOBSTER, diced	2 ounces
JULIENNE MUSHROOMS	2 ounces
SHALLOTS, chopped	1/4 ounce
WATER	4 ounces

Procedure

1. Combine in a pot the red wine, lobster, mushrooms, butter, shallots, and water. In this mixture, poach the six fillets of pompano for 20 minutes.

2. After 20 minutes, thicken the mixture with arrowroot to the desired consistency.

3. Place each fillet with equal amounts of sauce in/on a sheet of paper, forming a paper bag, clamping all edges so that no air is allowed to escape. Bake until the bag begins to puff up.

GLAZED CANADIAN BACON AND SWEET POTATOES

Yield: 20 portions

Ingredients

CANADIAN BACON, 3/4-inch slices	5 pounds
SWEET POTATOES, 18-ounce cans	5
ORANGE JUICE CONCENTRATE, undiluted	1-1/4 cups
MOLASSES	1 cup
PREPARED MUSTARD	1 cup
GROUND CLOVES	1-1/4 teaspoons

Procedure

Heat oven to 350°F. Arrange canadian bacon slices in a shallow baking pan. Place sweet potatoes around bacon. Blend orange juice, molasses, mustard, and cloves. Pour over bacon. Bake 20 to 25 minutes.

New Salem Lodge

CHEESE SOUFFLE

Yield: 48 servings or 60 servings

Ingredients	**48 Servings**	**60 servings**
MILK	4 quarts	5 quarts
QUICK COOKING TAPIOCA	1 pound	1-1/2 pounds
SALT	1-1/2 ounces	2 ounces
CHEESE, SHARP	5-1/4 pounds	7-1/2 pounds
EGG YOLKS	45	56
EGG WHITES	45	56

Procedure

1. Heat milk and add tapioca. Cook, stirring, on low heat until thick.

2. Add salt and cheese; stir until cheese is melted. Cool mixture slightly.

3. Beat egg yolks until yellow and fold in.

4. Beat egg whites until stiff, not dry, and fold in.

5. Set in a pan of hot water and bake in oven at 350°F. for about 1 hour.

Michigan State University

FUN-TIME FONDUE

Yield: 6 to 8 servings

Ingredients

GARLIC CHEESE SPREAD	1 6-ounce roll
SHARP CHEDDAR CHEESE SPREAD	2 6-ounce rolls
BEER	3/4 cup
RYE BREAD, UNSLICED	1 loaf

Procedure

1. Melt cheese spreads in double boiler. Add beer and blend well.

2. Hollow out rye bread, leaving about 1 inch of bread on the sides and bottom. Put shell into oven to warm. Cut hollowed out bread into 1-inch squares.

3. Pour the hot cheese mixture into the warm bread shell. Arrange bread cubes around the bread.

4. With fondue forks, dip bread cubes into hot cheese mixture.

The Cincinnati Milacron Cafeteria

HAM-CHEESE GRITS

Yield: 150 servings

Ingredients

GRITS	1-1/2 gallons
WATER, boiling	6 gallons
EGGS, WHOLE	48
MARGARINE	6 pounds
CHEESE, SHARP, grated	16 pounds
SEASONING SALT	2/3 cup
SALT	1/3 cup
GARLIC POWDER	1 tablespoon
LIQUID HOT PEPPER SEASONING	1 tablespoon
WORCESTERSHIRE SAUCE	1/2 cup
CHEESE, PARMESAN	as needed
PAPRIKA	as needed
HAM*, diced (optional)	5 pounds

*Diced ham may be added to the dish or may be used to substitute for some of the cheese.

Procedure

1. Gradually stir the grits into the boiling water. Simmer, stirring often, for 25 to 30 minutes.

2. Add the next 8 ingredients. Divide evenly in 6 greased steam table pans. Sprinkle each pan with parmesan cheese and paprika.

3. Bake in oven at 300°F. for 45 minutes.

Myron Green Cafeterias

HAM, CHEESE, TOMATO CLUB SANDWICH

Yield: 1 sandwich

Ingredients

BREAD, buttered	2 slices
COOKED HAM	1 slice
HORSERADISH	1 teaspoon
CHEESE, cheddar or swiss	1 slice
LETTUCE	1 leaf
TOMATO	2 thin slices
WATERCRESS	as needed

Procedure

1. On one slice of buttered bread, place a slice of cooked ham. Spread ham lightly with horseradish, then add a thin slice of cheese.

2. On another slice of bread place a lettuce leaf, then thin slices of tomato and top with watercress.

3. Serve the sandwich open or use a third slice of bread to make a club sandwich.

PIZZA SANDWICH

Yield: 6 sandwiches

Ingredients

FRENCH BREAD, INDIVIDUAL LOAVES	3
GROUND BEEF	1 pound
CHEESE, PARMESAN	1/3 cup
FINELY CHOPPED ONION	1/3 cup
CHOPPED RIPE OLIVES	1/4 cup
SALT	1 teaspoon
WHITE PEPPER	1/4 teaspoon
OREGANO	1/2 teaspoon
TOMATO PASTE	1 6-ounce can
TOMATO SLICES	12
CHEESE, AMERICAN	6 slices

Procedure

1. Cut loaves of bread in half lengthwise.

2. Brown the meat.

3. Add the next 7 ingredients, mix well.

4. Spoon mixture on bread. On top of each sandwich, place 1 slice of tomato, then 1 slice of American cheese, cut diagonally, finishing with second slice of tomato. Broil until cheese melts. Serve with potato chips.

The Cincinnati Milacron Cafeteria

CINNAMON BUNS

Yield: 100 3-inch buns

Ingredients
DOUGH

ACTIVE DRY YEAST	2-1/2 ounces
WATER, 112°F.	7 cups
FLOUR	5-1/2 pounds
NONFAT DRY MILK	3 ounces
SALT	7/8 ounce
SUGAR	12 ounces
SHORTENING	7-5/8 ounces

BROWN SUGAR-CINNAMON MIXTURE

BROWN SUGAR	2 pounds
CINNAMON	1/4 cup
BUTTER, melted	1 pound

Procedure

1. Add yeast to water and let stand 3 minutes to dissolve.

2. Combine flour, dry milk, salt, and sugar in 20-quart mixer bowl for 1 minute on speed No. 1.

3. Add shortening and mix for 1 minute on speed No. 1.

4. Add dissolved yeast, and using a dough hook, mix on speed No. 1 for 3 minutes. Scrape. Mix on speed No. 2 for 3 minutes. Scrape. Continue mixing on speed No. 2 for 4 minutes or until dough leaves sides of bowl and gluten is developed.

5. Let rise in bowl until double or proof at 90°F. for 1 hour.

6. Punch down and portion into 1-1/2-ounce pieces. Round up and let rest 10 minutes.

7. Drop buns into melted butter and roll in brown sugar-cinnamon mixture. Place 1-1/2 inches apart on 18-inch by 26-inch bun pans.

8. Proof at 90°F. for 30 minutes.

9. Bake in oven at 350°F. for 30 minutes.

**Kansas Wheat Commission
Hutchinson, Kansas**

YESTERYEAR'S KUCHEN

Yield: 24 2-inch squares

Ingredients

ALL-PURPOSE FLOUR	3 cups
BROWN SUGAR	2 cups
BUTTER or MARGARINE	1 cup
BAKING SODA	1 teaspoon
SALT	1/4 teaspoon
NUTMEG	1-1/2 teaspoons
BUTTERMILK	1 cup
EGGS, WHOLE, well beaten	2

Procedure

Combine flour and sugar. Cut in butter or margarine until mixture becomes crumbly. Remove 1 cup of the mixture; set aside. Add baking soda, salt, and nutmeg to the remaining mixture; stir. Add buttermilk and eggs; mix until blended. Spread mixture into a greased 13-inch by 9-inch pan. Sprinkle reserved crumbs over top. Bake in oven at 350°F. for 35 to 40 minutes.

Yesteryear

MARINATED MUSHROOMS

Yield: 6 servings

Ingredients

FRESH MUSHROOM CAPS, MEDIUM-SIZED	36
SALT	to taste
BUTTER	1/2 pound
LEMONS	3
ALLSPICE	1 tablespoon
CHOPPED PARSLEY	1/2 cup
CHOPPED PIMIENTO	1/2 cup

Procedure

1. Melt butter in large skillet; do not brown. Add mushrooms and salt. Stir gently. Add juice of lemons and lemon halves.

2. Simmer uncovered for 5 minutes. Add allspice. Cover skillet and simmer 5 minutes.

3. Remove from heat. Stir in parsley and pimiento. Set aside to cool.

4. Remove mushrooms from skillet with slotted spoon just before serving. Serve at room temperature.

The Como Inn

POTATO SALAD

Yield: 60 4-1/2-ounce portions

Ingredients

POTATOES, cooked, diced 1/2-inch cubes	15 pounds, AP
ONION, grated	1/3 cup
CHOPPED PIMIENTO	3 tablespoons
CHOPPED PARSLEY	4-1/2 tablespoons
CHOPPED MIXED PICKLES	3/4 cup
SUGAR	1-1/2 tablespoons
VINEGAR	3 tablespoons
MAYONNAISE	3 quarts
SALT	1/2 cup
EGGS, hard-cooked, diced	9

Procedure

1. Cook potatoes, cool, and dice.
2. Combine all ingredients. Mix lightly.
3. Let stand to season one hour before serving.

The Chicago Bar Assn.

KIDNEY BEAN SALAD

Yield: 40 5-ounce portions

Ingredients

LARGE KIDNEY BEANS No. 10 can	2 cans
FRESHLY GROUND PEPPER	1 teaspoon
ONION, grated	1/2 cup
CELERY, cut in rings	3 quarts
PIMIENTO, chopped	1 cup
SWEET PICKLES, sliced	2 cups
AMERICAN CHEESE, cut in 3/4-inch by 1/2-inch cubes	3/4 pound
MAYONNAISE	2 cups
SALT	2 tablespoons

Procedure

1. Drain and rinse kidney beans in cold water. Drain again thoroughly.
2. Grind pepper; grate onion; cut celery in fine rings.
3. Slowly and carefully mix together all ingredients except the cheese.
4. Serve on nest of salad greens.
5. Top each salad with cubes of cheese.

CORN RELISH

Yield: approximately 5 pints

Ingredients

CORN, WHOLE KERNEL, YELLOW, drained	2 1-pound cans
TOMATOES, drained	2 1-pound cans
CHOPPED, UNPEELED CUCUMBER	1 cup
CHOPPED ONION	1-1/2 cups
CHOPPED GREEN PEPPER	1 cup
SUGAR	2/3 cup
CIDER VINEGAR	2/3 cup
MUSTARD SEED	1 teaspoon
CELERY SEED	1 teaspoon
SALT	1 teaspoon

Procedure

Mix all ingredients in large kettle. Bring to a hard boil. Remove from heat. Ladle at once into hot, sterilized jars. Seal.

Pantry Shelf

MOM'S BREAD AND BUTTER PICKLES

Yield: 8 pints

Ingredients

CUCUMBERS, unpeeled	6 pounds
ONIONS, thinly sliced	8
GREEN PEPPERS, thinly sliced	2
RED PEPPERS, thinly sliced	2
SALT	1/2 cup
CRACKED ICE	1 quart
SUGAR	5 cups
TURMERIC	1-1/2 teaspoons
MUSTARD SEED	1-1/2 teaspoons
CELERY SEED	1 teaspoon
GROUND CLOVES	1/2 teaspoon
WHITE VINEGAR	1 quart

Procedure

1. Slice cucumbers very thin to make a gallon. Put into 2-gallon stone crock with onion and peppers. Mix salt and ice. Pack on top of vegetables. Cover with weighted lid. Let stand for 3 hours; drain.
2. Mix rest of ingredients. Pour over vegetables in large enamel or aluminum kettle.
3. Bring to boil over low heat. *Do not cook any longer.* Ladle at once into hot, sterilized jars. Seal.

Note

A "must" in all worthy collections of pickle recipes.

Pantry Shelf

PERSIMMON PUDDING

Yield: 48 pieces (1 pan, 14- by 9-1/2- by 2-1/4-in.,
cut 6 by 4)   24 portions

Ingredients

EGGS	8
GRAHAM CRACKER CRUMBS	3-3/4 cups
BAKING POWDER	2-1/2 teaspoons
SUGAR	2-1/2 cups
MILK, WHOLE	2-1/2 cups
PERSIMMON PULP	3 cups
BUTTER, MELTED	1/2 cup plus 2 tablespoons
SALT	1/4 teaspoon

Procedure

1. Beat eggs until very light
2. Roll graham cracker crumbs fine. Add baking powder and sugar to the crumbs.
3. Add dry ingredients, alternately with the milk to the persimmon pulp.
4. Add beaten eggs, melted butter and salt.
5. Pour into lightly greased baking pan.
6. Bake in oven at 350°F. for 1 hour. Serve with Hard Sauce.

L. S. Ayres & Co., Indianapolis

OZARK PUDDING

Yield: 2 pans (9-inch by 15-inch by 2-inch)

Ingredients

EGGS, well beaten	8
GRANULATED SUGAR	5-1/3 cups
BAKING POWDER	1/4 cup
FLOUR	2-2/3 cups
SALT	1 teaspoon
PEELED, CHOPPED APPLES	1 quart
CHOPPED NUTS	3 cups
VANILLA	2 tablespoons plus 2 teaspoons
WHIPPED TOPPING	to garnish

Procedure

1. Beat eggs and sugar together. Beat until thick and creamy. Blend dry ingredients into the egg mixture. Add apples, nuts, and vanilla.
2. Grease bottoms of 2 9-inch by 15-inch by 2-inch pans. Pour mixture into pans.
3. Bake in oven at 350°F. for 45 minutes.
4. Cut into squares and top each portion with whipped topping.

Myron Green Cafeterias

SALEM VILLAGE PUDDING

Yield: 27 portions

Ingredients

EGGS	18
SUGAR	1 pound, 2 ounces
SALT	1-1/2 teaspoons
NUTMEG	1-1/2 teaspoons
MILK	3 quarts
VANILLA	to taste
RAISINS	3/4 cup
CINNAMON ROLLS, stale	9

Procedure

Mix the eggs, sugar, salt, and nutmeg until thoroughly mixed. Add the milk and vanilla and whip until well blended. Sprinkle raisins in bottom of three 8-inch square pans. Cover with approximately 1/4 inch thick slices of rolls. Pour the custard over the top of the rolls and the raisins. Sprinkle with a little ground nutmeg. Place pan in a water bath and bake in oven at 350°F. for about 1 hour, or until knife comes out clean. Let cool and cut each pan into 9 squares. Serve with cream or a tart dessert sauce.

New Salem Lodge

POACHED PEARS MILANESE

Yield: 6 servings

Ingredients

PEARS, BROWN-SKIN, SMALL	12
or MEDIUM-SIZED	6
DOMESTIC SAUTERNE	1 quart
SUGAR	2 cups
CLOVES	24
CINNAMON STICKS	12

Procedure

1. Pour wine into deep saucepan; add sugar, cloves, and cinnamon. Bring to boil. Simmer covered 15 to 20 minutes.
2. Wash and drain pears. Core pears from bottom and trim bottom of the pears so they will stand. Stems and leaves are left on.
3. Arrange pears in deep saucepan standing upright. Pour boiling wine, cinnamon, and cloves over pears. Cover and poach in oven at 350°F. for 30 to 40 minutes. Serve warm with flaming Grand Marnier.

The Como Inn

CRANBERRY COTTAGE CHEESE SALAD

Yield: 32 portions (Individual 4-ounce molds)

Ingredients

LEMON FLAVORED GELATIN	12 ounces
HOT WATER	3 cups
CANNED WHOLE CRANBERRY SAUCE	2-1/4 quarts
CELERY, finely diced	3 cups
PECANS, chopped	4 ounces
PLAIN GELATINE	1-1/2 tablespoons
COLD WATER	1/4 cup
SALT	1 teaspoon
LEMON JUICE	1/4 cup
CREAMED COTTAGE CHEESE	2 pounds

Procedure

1. Dissolve lemon gelatin in hot water. Add whole cranberry sauce, celery and pecans. Place mixture in refrigerator until it begins to congeal.

2. Soak the plain gelatine in cold water for 5 minutes. Then place over hot water or in steamer until it is completely dissolved. Add salt and lemon juice to this and stir into the creamed cottage cheese. Place this mixture in the refrigerator also.

3. When both mixtures are about to congeal remove from refrigerator and fill individual 4-ounce molds. Fill the mold 1/3 full of cranberries, cover this with layer of cottage cheese. Then finish filling with cranberries.

4. Chill until completely set. Unmold and serve on crisp lettuce with mayonnaise.

FLOATING ISLAND

Yield: 3-3/4 quarts, 24 portions

Ingredients

MILK	3 quarts
SUGAR	1-1/2 cups
CORNSTARCH	1/2 cup
SALT	3/4 teaspoon
EGG YOLKS	18
VANILLA	1/2 teaspoon
NUTMEG	1 teaspoon

Procedure

1. Scald milk in steam-jacketed kettle or double boiler.

2. Combine sugar, cornstarch and salt, and gradually add to scalded milk, stirring mixture with wire whip.

3. Cook until mixture thickens slightly.

4. Beat egg yolks. Add a little hot milk to yolks. Blend well.

5. Combine with rest of milk in kettle, and cook about 5 minutes or until mixture coats the spoon. Remove from heat and add vanilla.

6. Pour mixture into sherbet glasses. Sprinkle with nutmeg, and top with meringue.

Note

To cook meringues. Follow recipe for soft meringues. Drop by spoonfuls into pan of boiling water. Place in oven at 425°F. until golden brown.

University of Chicago Clinics
Billings Hospital, Chicago

CLEAR RASPBERRY TAPIOCA

Yield: 20 to 22 4-ounce portions

Ingredients

RASPBERRY JUICE, strained	2-1/2 quarts
QUICK TAPIOCA	1 cup
SUGAR	to sweeten
SALT	1/4 teaspoon
LEMON JUICE, FRESH	2 teaspoons
WHIPPED CREAM	

Procedure

1. Combine raspberry juice and tapioca and cook a few minutes. Add sugar—the amount will depend on the sweetness of the raspberry juice. Add salt and lemon juice.

2. Serve 4 ounces in sherbet glasses, alternating the raspberry tapioca with whipped cream.

Indian Trail, Winnetka, Ill.

CHESS PIE

Yield: 12 9-inch pies

Ingredients

MARGARINE	4 pounds
HARD WHEAT FLOUR	1 pound
CORN MEAL	1 pound
SUGAR	12 pounds
EGG YOLKS	4 pounds
WHOLE MILK	1 gallon
GROUND NUTMEG	1/4 ounce
PIE SHELLS, 9-inch, unbaked	12

Procedure

1. Cream the margarine.

2. Sift the flour and corn meal into the sugar. Add to the margarine and mix thoroughly.

3. Beat egg yolks slightly and add to the above mixture. Mix in milk slowly. Add the nutmeg. *Let the mixture stand 1 hour.*

4. Stir the mixture well and fill unbaked shells. Use 1 quart filling to each shell. Put filled shells in oven.

5. Add more of filling mixture until shells are as full as possible. Bake in oven at 350°F. for 45 minutes.

Myron Green Cafeterias

MINT CHIFFON PIE

Yield: 6 9-inch pies

Ingredients

GELATINE	2-1/2 tablespoons
COLD WATER	3/4 cup
EGG YOLKS	1-1/4 cups
SUGAR	1 cup
SALT	1 teaspoon
HOT WATER	1-1/2 cups
PEPPERMINT ESSENCE	1/2 to 1 teaspoon
GREEN VEGETABLE COLORING	1-1/4 teaspoons
EGG WHITES	2 cups
SUGAR	1 cup

Procedure

1. Soften gelatine in cold water.

2. Beat egg yolks slightly, and add sugar, salt and hot water.

3. Cook over hot water, or in small steam-jacketed kettle, until of a custard-like consistency.

4. Add softened gelatine to hot mixture.

5. Whip this mixture on third speed of mixer until thick and fluffy.

6. Add peppermint essence and green coloring matter, and mix well.

7. Beat egg whites until foamy; add sugar gradually and beat until whites will hold in peaks.

8. Carefully fold the egg whites into the gelatine-custard mixture. Pour or scale mixture into baked pie shells. Refrigerate.

Note

Just before serving, top each pie with whipped cream and garnish with chocolate "topettes," or shavings of unsweetened or semi-sweet chocolate.

Milwaukee, Wisconsin

BAKING POWDER SHORTCAKE BISCUITS

Yield: 100 biscuits

Ingredients

PASTRY FLOUR, unsifted	3 quarts
GRANULATED SUGAR	1-3/4 cups
SALT	1-1/2 tablespoons
BAKING POWDER	1/2 cup
SHORTENING	1-3/4 cups
EGGS	3/4 cup
MILK	3 cups

Procedure

1. Sift together the flour, sugar, salt, and baking powder. Add shortening and blend well.

2. Beat eggs and combine with some of the milk, and add to flour mixture.

3. Use additional milk to make as soft a dough as can be handled.

4. Turn on to a lightly floured board, and knead lightly.

5. Roll dough 1/2 inch thick. Cut biscuits with doughnut cutter.

6. Bake in oven at 425°F. for approximately 25 minutes.

Springfield Public Schools, Springfield, Mo.

VIRGINIA STRAWBERRY MOLD

Yield: 40 portions (2-1/2- by 2-1/2- by 2-inches)

Ingredients

BUTTER	1 pound, 8 ounces
SUGAR	4 cups
STRAWBERRIES, FRESH, HULLED	2 quarts
PECANS, CHOPPED	1-1/2 cups
EGG WHITES	6
VANILLA WAFERS, crushed	2 pounds
WHIPPED CREAM	For garnishing
STRAWBERRIES, FRESH, UNHULLED	40

Procedure

1. Cream butter. Add sugar gradually and mix well.

2. Cut strawberries in halves or thirds, and add with the pecans to the butter mixture. Fold in the beaten egg whites.

3. In a greased baking pan arrange alternate layers of crushed vanilla wafers and the fruit mixture—two layers each—ending with the vanilla wafer crumbs.

4. Chill 12 hours. Cut in squares; serve with whipped cream.

Southern Illinois University, Carbondale

CANDIED PARSNIPS

"Parsnips are a general favorite in this part of the country, and when candied in this way, they deserve the laurels."

Yield: 8 portions

Ingredients

PARSNIPS, AP	1-1/2 pounds
BUTTER or MARGARINE, melted	2 tablespoons
SALT	1/4 teaspoon
CINNAMON IMPERIALS	1/4 cup
BREAD CRUMBS, buttered	2 tablespoons

Procedure

1. Peel, core, and cut washed parsnips into strips approximately 2-1/2 to 3 inches long and 1/2 inch thick. Steam parsnips approximately 10 minutes—or until fairly tender.

2. Place steamed parsnips in half-size steam table pan. Sprinkle with melted butter or margarine, salt, and cinnamon imperials. Dust with bread crumbs.

3. Bake in oven at 400°F. for 30 minutes—until cinnamon imperials are melted and bread crumbs are well browned.

Note

Candied Parsnips should be fairly dry. Do not allow parsnips to float in excess fat or juice. Do not reuse syrup from one pan to make a second pan.

APPLE DUMPLINGS

Yield: 50 dumplings

Ingredients

FLOUR, all-purpose	2 pounds, 12 ounces
SALT	1 ounce
BAKING POWDER, double-acting	1-1/2 ounces
VEGETABLE SHORTENING	1 pound, 8 ounces
MILK	2-3/4 cups
APPLES, peeled and cored	50 (only)
SUGAR, granulated	6-1/4 ounces
FLOUR, all-purpose	2 tablespoons
SALT	1/8 teaspoon
CINNAMON	1 teaspoon
NUTMEG	1/4 teaspoon
BUTTER, melted	1 cup
APPLE JUICE	3-1/4 quarts
SUGAR, granulated	3 pounds, 12 ounces
CINNAMON	1/2 tablespoon
NUTMEG	1/2 tablespoon
BUTTER	12 ounces

Procedure

1. Sift together the first three ingredients.
2. Cut shortening into flour mixture.
3. Add milk all at one time, mix just long enough to dampen flour.
4. Toss dough on lightly floured board, and roll about 1/16 inch in thickness.
5. Cut dough in 5-inch by 5-inch squares.
6. Place an apple in center of each dough square.
7. Combine sugar, flour, salt, cinnamon and nutmeg, and place approximately 1 teaspoon of mixture in hollow of each apple. Place over this 1 teaspoon of melted butter.
8. Moisten edges of dough square, bring points up over apple, press edges together, and place in baking pan.
9. Combine the last 5 ingredients, and boil 5 minutes. Pour over dumplings.
10. Bake in oven at 350°F. for approximately 50 minutes.

Miss Hulling's Cafeterias, St. Louis, Missouri

APPLE CRISP WITH BLACK WALNUTS AND COCONUT

Yield: 100 portions

Ingredients

WHOLE EGGS	2 dozen
GRANULATED SUGAR	3 quarts
SIFTED ALL-PURPOSE FLOUR	2 quarts
BAKING POWDER	1/2 cup
SALT	1 tablespoon
SHREDDED APPLES	3 quarts
CHOPPED BLACK WALNUTS	1-1/4 quarts
VANILLA EXTRACT	1/2 cup
COCONUT	1-1/2 quarts

Procedure

1. Beat eggs until light and lemon-colored. Gradually add sugar and beat until dissolved.
2. Sift flour, baking powder, and salt and gradually add to egg mixture. Blend thoroughly.
3. Add apples, nuts, and vanilla.
4. Scale approximately 4-1/2 pounds into each greased and floured bake pan. Top with shredded coconut.
5. Bake in oven at 350°F. for 45 to 60 minutes.
6. Serve warm or cold topped with a mound of ice cream or whipped cream.

BREAD PUDDING

Yield: 48 1/2-cup portions (1-1/2 gallons)

Ingredients

BREAD, day-old	1-1/2 gallons
EGGS, whole	16 only
SUGAR, granulated	1 quart
SALT	2 teaspoons
BUTTER or MARGARINE	1-1/2 cups
MILK	1-1/2 gallons
NUTMEG, ground	1 teaspoon
LEMON RIND, grated	2 tablespoons
RAISINS	2-1/2 cups

Procedure

1. Cut day-old bread into 1/2-inch cubes. Place in a greased baking pan.

2. Beat eggs slightly, and add salt and sugar.

3. Heat butter or margarine in milk until melted. Add to egg mixture gradually, stirring constantly.

4. Add nutmeg, grated lemon rind, raisins. Blend. Pour over bread.

5. Bake in pan of hot water in oven at 350°F. for about 1 hour.

6. Stir twice during first half hour of baking. Pudding is done when a knife inserted in center comes out clean. Serve warm or cold with whipped cream or Lemon Sauce.

BREAD PUDDING VARIATIONS

1. Vanilla Bread Pudding: Omit nutmeg, grated lemon rind, and raisins from recipe. Add 2 tablespoons vanilla.

2. Chocolate Bread Pudding: Omit nutmeg, grated lemon rind and raisins from recipe. Add 12 ounces un-sweetened chocolate. Melt chocolate in milk before adding milk to egg mixture.

3. Jelly Bread Pudding: Use Vanilla Bread Pudding recipe. Dot with jelly before baking.

4. Meringue Bread Pudding: Use Vanilla Bread Pudding recipe. Spread meringue on top of baked Bread Pudding. Bake until meringue is a golden brown.

5. Honey Bread Pudding: Use Vanilla Bread Pudding recipe. Substitute 2-2/3 cups honey for the sugar. Stir honey into the eggs.

ORANGE BAVARIAN CHARLOTTE RUSSE

Yield: 12 portions (generous)

Ingredients

GELATINE, UNFLAVORED	1-1/3 tablespoons
WATER, COLD	1/3 cup
WATER, BOILING	1/3 cup
SUGAR	1-1/2 cups
LEMON JUICE	1/4 cup
ORANGE RIND, GRATED	1 teaspoon
ORANGE JUICE AND PULP	1 cup
EGG WHITES, beaten	3
WHIPPED CREAM	1 cup
LADYFINGERS	1-1/2 dozen

Procedure

1. Soften gelatine in cold water. Dissolve in boiling water.

2. Add sugar, lemon juice, orange rind, juice and pulp. Chill.

3. When of a jelly-like consistency pour into stiffly-beaten egg whites. Blend well. Fold in whipped cream.

4. Cube a few ladyfingers and fold into the mixture.

5. Pour into a pan that has been lined with split ladyfingers.

6. Chill. Garnish each serving with whipped cream and a mandarin orange section.

Note

This dessert may be made 24 hours before serving time.

Southern Illinois University, Carbondale

Ten-Gallon Salute to Texas Foodservice

ANYONE RETAINING AN unadulterated cowboy and cactus image of Texas would do well to visit Dallas. The Southwest's largest banking center, headquarters for more insurance companies than any other city in the U.S., Dallas is a financial giant. Metroplex, rather than mesquite, is the chief topic of conversation.

So it is that sophistication is no stranger to Big D. A truly cosmopolitan appreciation of the arts exists, and this most emphatically includes haute cuisine. Several of the city's restaurants are dining spots of unqualified distinction.

The Old Warsaw
Dallas

A few, such as the Old Warsaw, bear favorable comparison with any in the U.S., providing the kind of foodservice that merits a ten-gallon salute.

Phil Vaccaro, whose Universal Restaurants also include Arthur's and Mario's in Dallas, acquired the Old Warsaw some five years ago. The business has had an elegant reputation since its opening in 1951.

Vaccaro admits, however, that the introduc-

tion of classical dining in Texas was not without its difficult moments. He recalls that The Old Warsaw menu was originally printed entirely in French in a rather elaborate, handwritten script.

"One customer told the captain," recalls Vaccaro, "that he couldn't read the writing because it was too elaborate. 'The reason you can't read the writing,' replied the captain, 'is because you are a Texan, and the writing is in French.' After a battle, we decided to put in a translation."

"Fifteen years ago we had to do a lot of explaining," concludes Vaccaro. "Not any more."

The Zodiac Room, Neiman-Marcus
Dallas

A shopping excursion has long been the appropriate excuse for luncheon at Neiman-Marcus. This coming Bicentennial year, however, patriotism will make a mid-day visit to the Zodiac Room an obligation.

Throughout the weeks of 1976, the Zodiac Room plans palatial pageantry featuring authentic culinary bounty from every state in the union. Special menus will contain information about the week's featured state, together with recipes for each of the menu items. All of the information will be bound and published at the year's end.

Bob Jones, corporate foodservice director, is coordinating the project with the help of long-time Neiman-Marcus employee Ben Izner. Seasonal availability has had to take some precedence over historical priority, so that Florida will have the lead-off place of honor in their program.

Foodservice in the 68-year-old retail giant did not begin until 1940, in the form of a roof-top restaurant for employees. The store's first public restaurant actually opened in the suburban Dallas store in 1951, and the Zodiac Room was not in operation until 1957. Today, combined food sales in the chain's six stores exceed $3 million. All six—seven by next year—major Neiman-Marcus restaurants will participate in the Bicentennial program.

The Menger Hotel
San Antonio

In 1898, when Theodore Roosevelt needed a few hundred men worthy of the name "rough riders," he came to San Antonio to recruit and train them. Surely, the prowess of the frontier fighter and the spirit of the Alamo were strong enought inducements for that location. It did not hurt, of course, that next door to the Alamo was a very unique bar.

The Menger Hotel's public room was decidedly the place to be in 1898. A cherrywood copy of the House of Lords Bar in London, the room was a ruggedly elegant place where tough hombres could enjoy their mint juleps in silver goblets. Time has seen fighting men from Generals Grant and Lee to Roy Rogers succumb to the spirit of the place.

Opened in 1859 by a German brewer named W.A. Menger, the hotel has a distinct place of honor in the social history of Texas. Generations of famous guests, including Sam Houston, Lillian Russell, Sidney Lanier, Jenny Lind, Sarah Bernhardt, Oscar Wilde, and O. Henry, have enjoyed its comfortable elegance. According to an employee of the hotel, "There are a lot of mothers around here who don't think their daughters are officially married if they're not married in the Menger; they've been at it for so many generations."

The Menger continues to thrive by preserving the elegant old, while accommodating the comfortable new. The original 110 rooms have been joined by 240 modern units, and food and beverage service has grown commensurately. The tropical pool has been thoroughly emptied of the alligators which inhabited it prior to the days of outdoor swimming.

Taking its history to heart, the Menger adheres to a "speak softly . . . big stick" philosophy. Manager Art Abbott reports that, in spite of decidedly low-key advertising, the hotel enjoyed 91 percent occupancy through the first half of 1975.

Casa Rio
El Paseo del Rio, San Antonio

An unfortunate legacy of some World Fairs is the financial discomfort in which the host city finds itself sometime after the sale of the last waffle. Fiscal indulgence in super towers and futuristic parks elicits a sad toll as city fathers discover the pie in the sky is palatable but once a century.

On the other hand, there is San Antonio.

When 1968 brought a global extravaganza to this southern Texas city, a very sensible look was taken at the future. Seven years later, tourism remains the second largest industry in this city of a million inhabitants.

El Paseo del Rio ("the river walk"), which received a beautiful face-lift for the fair, remains the city's culinary and entertainment gold mine. Indian, Spanish, French, German, Irish, Italian, and Black influences exist side by side, each to the benefit of all. Texas history notwithstanding, the greatest influence of all is Mexican.

Franklin Hicks, co-owner and general manager of the business founded by A.F. Beyer in 1946, certainly makes a financial point in this direction. At his Casa Rio restaurant, more than 300,000 people paid over $850,000 in 1974 to enjoy Mexican food. The restaurant also operated the boat concession on the river and catered 1,150 "floating" Mexican dinner affairs, during the same year.

Claire Regnier, executive director of the Paseo del Rio Association, refuses to be complacent, however. Her task is to help develop the tourist trade, but not at the price of alienating the residents.

"It has been shown," comments Regnier, "that when the residents move out, everyone suffers."

San Antonio continues to look in the right direction.

The Cellar Door
Houston

Texans take their barbecue seriously. In Houston, they frequently take it at The Cellar Door, where sales came to $5 million in 1974.

In Texas, barbecue is roughly translated as "smoked meat." Anyone who thinks this merely includes beef and pork, however, is probably an Easterner. The smoking ovens of the Cellar Door have hosted an awesome lot of critters in their day: turkeys, goats, wild game, possums, snakes, zebras, and armadillos has graced a table or two. For a reasonable price, in fact, the Cellar Door will put green hickory smoke under just about anything that can be beaten, bullied or bagged.

The Cellar Door is a family organization with seven separate restaurants. Pride and imagination have made each unit unique, however, with decor and entertainment tailored to the taste of the neighborhood in which each is located. All food is prepared from scratch in a central commissary, where 40,000 pounds of beef, a ton of ribs and 1/4-ton of ham are smoked each week.

The first Cellar Door opened on New Year's Day in 1954 when a Texas cowman decided to complete the process begun on the ranch. A cowman, as opposed to a cowboy, raises beef for food consumption. E. M. Bell simply decided that the way to insure a better barbeque was to cook and serve it himself.

Since Bell's death in 1965, the business has been ably maintained by his wife Lillye Pattison Bell and daugher Virginia Clarady. With additional family help, the business and several successful offshoots continue to flourish. An ultimate goal is operational self-sufficiency, including the production and processing of all meat used by the restaurant.

Texas-size appetites can only be satisfied by Texas-sized aspirations.

Texas Recipes

SCALLOPED CUCUMBERS

Yield: 25 portions

Ingredients

CUCUMBERS, peeled, thinly sliced	1 gallon
BREAD CRUMBS, fine	3 quarts
SALT	3 tablespoons
BUTTER, melted	3 cups

Procedure

1. Arrange cucumbers and bread crumbs in alternate layers in buttered bake pan, ending with crumbs. Make 3 layers.

2. Sprinkle salt on each layer of cucumbers.

3. Over each layer of crumbs pour 8 ounces (1 cup) melted butter.

4. Bake in oven at 375°F. for 20 minutes.

Note

This makes a delightful accompaniment for fish entrees.

DEVILED PECANS

Yield: 50 servings

Ingredients

BUTTER	8 tablespoons
WORCESTERSHIRE SAUCE	4 tablespoons
PECAN HALVES	4 cups
SALT	dash
CAYENNE PEPPER	dash

Procedure

1. Preheat oven to 350°F.

2. Place butter in a skillet and add worcestershire sauce; blend while butter melts. Add pecans, salt, and cayenne. Stir until nuts are coated.

3. Roast in oven for 20 minutes, stirring occasionally. Drain on absorbent paper and sprinkle generously with salt.

Gerald Ramsey, SMU

POT OF HOT LAMB AND BARLEY

Yield: 25 portions

Ingredients

1. LAMB, SHOULDER or
      LEG, RAW   4 pounds
   ONIONS, A.P, MEDIUM
      CHOPPED   12
   WATER, COLD   1-1/2 gallons
   PEARL BARLEY   2 cups
   SALT   4 tablespoons
   PEPPER   1/2 tablespoon
   MONOSODIUM
      GLUTAMATE   1 tablespoon
   CELERY TOPS AND/OR
      HERBS, CHOPPED FINE   to season
   FLOUR   1 cup
   WATER, COLD   1 cup
2. TOPPING
   POTATOES, MASHED   3 quarts
   MILK, HOT   1 pint
   BUTTER   1/2 cup
   EGG WHITES, SLIGHTLY
      BEATEN   8
   SALT   2 teaspoons
   PEPPER   1 teaspoon

Procedure

1. Cut lamb in 1 inch cubes. Brown lamb and chopped onions in fat cut from the meat.

2. Add the next 6 ingredients, and simmer gently 2 hours or longer, if necessary.

3. Mix flour with cold water. Thin with a little of the hot liquid. Thicken stock with the flour mixture. Cook 10 minutes.

4. Arrange 5 ounces of lamb mixture in each french casserole.

5. Combine ingredients for topping and whip potatoes until very light.

6. Press whipped potatoes through a pastry bag tube to make an attractive topping for each individual casserole.

7. Place casserole under broiler until puff is delicately browned.

Texas

HAM LOAF WITH CURRANT SAUCE

Yield   200 portions

Ingredients

1. HAM, SMOKED, E.P.,
      GROUND   24 pounds
   VEAL, E.P., GROUND   12 pounds
   PORK, E.P., LEAN,
      GROUND   12 pounds
   CORNFLAKES   3 gallons
   ONION, CHOPPED   1 quart
   GREEN PEPPER,
      CHOPPED   2 cups
   PIMIENTO, CHOPPED
      FINE   2 cups
   PARSLEY, CHOPPED   2 bunches
   NUTMEG   4 tablespoons
   SALT   to season
   PEPPER   to season
   EGGS, BEATEN   48
   MILK   1-1/2 gallons
2. CURRANT SAUCE
   CURRANT JELLY, 13
      OUNCE JARS   12
   PREPARED MUSTARD,
      SMALL JARS   12

Procedure

1. Combine all ingredients for Ham Loaf and blend thoroughly. Pack mixture in greased loaf pans.

2. Place in bakepans with hot water. Cover and cook in oven at 300°F. for 1-1/2 hours.

3. Uncover and cook until Ham Loaves are browned.

4. In meantime combine currant jelly and prepared mustard.

5. Stir over hot water until jelly is melted and ingredients are blended. Serve with the Ham Loaves.

Southern Methodist University, Dallas

CHICKEN FINE CHAMPAGNE
IN CASSEROLE

Yield: 24 portions

Ingredients

CHICKENS, 2-1/2 pounds each	6
FLOUR	2-1/2 cups
SALT	1 tablespoon
PEPPER	1/2 teaspoon
BUTTER	12 ounces
OIL	1/2 cup
MUSHROOMS, diced	1 quart (4 cups)
SHALLOTS, chopped	3/4 cup
THYME	1 teaspoon
BAY LEAVES	2
WHITE WINE, dry	4 wine glasses
CREAM (18%)	3 quarts
EGG YOLKS	6
BUTTER	6 ounces
FINE CHAMPAGNE or BRANDY	4 liquor glasses
FINE NOODLES, uncooked	2 pounds
BUTTER	4 ounces

Procedure

1. Clean chicken and cut into 8 uniform pieces.

2. Season flour with salt and pepper, and dredge chicken in it.

3. Saute chicken to a golden brown in the butter and oil.

4. Add shallots, thyme, bay leaves, and mushrooms. Saute 5 minutes.

5. Add white wine, and cook gently over moderate heat until volume is reduced to two-thirds.

6. Add cream. Cook over very low heat until chicken is fork-tender.

7. Remove chicken and mushrooms from pan. Keep sauce hot over gentle heat.

8. Beat egg yolks. Pour some of the hot sauce over them, stirring constantly. Combine with the rest of the sauce, and cook 3 minutes.

9. Remove sauce from heat, and very slowly add the 6 ounces butter, stirring gently with spoon. Add the champagne or brandy.

10. Arrange chicken and mushrooms on large platter or in individual casseroles. Adjust seasonings in sauce if necessary. Pour hot sauce over chicken.

11. Serve on cooked buttered noodles with parsley or watercress.

Texas

BARBECUED TURKEY

Yield: 10 to 12 servings

Ingredients

TURKEY (12-pound)	1
CELERY	1/2 bunch
BARBECUE SAUCE	2 cups
OLIVE OIL	1/2 cup
GARLIC, minced	2 cloves
SMOKED SALT or LIQUID SMOKE	1/4 teaspoon
PORK BELLY or BACON, thinly sliced	1 pound

Procedure

1. Salt and pepper inside of drawn, cleaned, and washed turkey. Stuff with celery ribs (add one-half orange and one onion if desired). Place in roasting pan.

2. Blend barbecue sauce, olive oil, garlic, and smoked salt; mix well. Pour over turkey and marinate three hours, turning and basting bird frequently.

3. Cover the breast and back of the bird with thin slices of pork belly or bacon. Wrap in foil for first two hours of roasting. Roast in oven at 350°F., basting the bird frequently, for approximately four hours.

Gerald Ramsey, SMU

CHICKEN AND ALMOND SOUFFLE

Yield: approximately 35 portions

Ingredients

BUTTER	1 cup
FLOUR	1-1/2 cups
DRY MUSTARD	1-1/4 teaspoons
SALT	to taste
MILK	1-1/4 quarts
CHICKEN, chopped	2-1/2 quarts
SLIVERED ALMONDS	1-1/2 quarts
EGG YOLKS, slightly beaten	24
EGG WHITES, beaten	36

Procedure

1. Make a light roux with butter and flour. Add milk, salt, and mustard. Bring to a boil, stirring constantly, and boil one minute.

2. Add chicken and almonds. Cool.

3. Blend with egg yolks, then fold into beaten egg whites.

4. Pour into well buttered souffle cups (3/4ths full). Bake in oven at 375°F. until done.

Neiman-Marcus

VEAL PASTIES

Yield: 25 portions

Ingredients

ONION, E.P., CHOPPED	6 ounces
BUTTER or SHORTENING	4 tablespoons
VEAL, COOKED, DICED	4 pounds
PARSLEY, CHOPPED FINE	2 tablespoons
SALT	1 tablespoon
PEPPER	1 teaspoon
MONOSODIUM GLUTAMATE	1/2 teaspoon
CHILI SAUCE	1/2 cup
POTATOES, COOKED, DICED	4 ounces
WHITE TURNIPS, COOKED, DICED	4 ounces
BROWN GRAVY	1 quart
PIE DOUGH	

Procedure

1. Saute onion in butter until limp but not brown.

2. Combine all ingredients except pie dough. Blend well. (Turnips and potatoes are optional.)

3. Roll pastry in individual circles approximately 6-inches in diameter.

4. Place 2 tablespoons or 3 tablespoons of the meat mixture in the center of the lower half of circle. Wet edges of pastry. Fold over to form turnover and crimp the edges.

5. Bake in hot oven (450°F.) until pastry is cooked —approximately 12 to 15 minutes.

6. Serve with some of the Brown Gravy poured over the pastry with an underlining of a bouquet of vegetables.

Texas

BARBECUED SHRIMP

Yield: 2 to 3 servings

Ingredients

SHRIMP, JUMBO SIZE, 15/18 count	12
FLOUR	1/2 cup
EGG	1
SWEET MILK	1 cup
SALT	to taste
PEPPER	to taste
FINE CRACKER CRUMBS	1 cup
COOKING OIL	1 quart
SMOKY BARBECUE SAUCE	1 pint

Procedure

1. Shell and de-vein shrimp leaving shell on tails. Wash and clean thoroughly.

2. Dust shrimp with flour. Break egg into bowl, beat well. Add milk and salt and pepper to taste. Dip shrimp in egg and milk, then roll in fine cracker crumbs.

3. Pour oil into deep saucepan and heat to 350°F. Drop in shrimp and fry for 4 minutes to seal moisture in shrimp.

4. Remove from deep fat and saturate in hickory smoke sauce.

5. Put shrimp in shallow pan and place under broiler or in oven for 5 minutes, or until tails become brown and crisp. Shrimp are ready to serve. Serve a mild, tasty barbecue sauce with shrimp.

Look's Restaurant

CARNE ASADA SAUCE

Yield: 4 quarts

Ingredients

ONIONS, LARGE, chopped	3
GARLIC, chopped	3 cloves
BELL PEPPERS, chopped	6
CELERY, chopped	12 stalks
CHILES	1 No. 2-1/2 can
TOMATOES, crushed	1 No. 10 can
CHICKEN BROTH	2 No. 10 cans
MARGARINE	as needed
SALT	to taste
CUMIN	to taste
PEPPER	to taste
FLOUR	3 cups
OIL	as needed

Procedure

1. In saucepot, saute onions, garlic, pepper, and celery until limp. Do not brown. Add chiles, tomatoes, and chicken broth. Bring to boil.

2. Add enough oil to flour to make a smooth paste; incorporate with above ingredients.

3. Reduce to simmer and cook for 1-1/2 hours. Add seasonings to taste.

4. Serve in a small bowl as an accompaniment for charbroiled beef or chicken.

Casa Rio

JELLIED TOMATO MADRILENE

Yield: 4 quarts (32 1/2-cup portions)

Ingredients

PLAIN GELATINE	3 ounces
COLD WATER	1 pint
CHICKEN BROTH, fat free	2 quarts
TOMATO JUICE	1-1/2 quarts
SALT	1-1/2 tablespoons
PEPPER	1/4 teaspoon
MONOSODIUM GLUTAMATE	1 teaspoon
CELERY SALT	2 teaspoons

Procedure

1. Soak the gelatine in cold water for 5 minutes. Then dissolve in 1 pint of hot chicken broth.

2. Add the remaining chicken broth, tomato juice, and seasonings. Chill.

3. When congealed, cut into cubes and serve piled in bouillon cups.

4. Garnish with lemon wedge and parsley.

FRUIT PLATE

Yield: 1 portion

Procedure

1. Ahead of assembling time, place the following in a 7-ounce flat dish:

    7 sections grapefruit

    7 sections orange

    5 sections red apple

2. On a bed of boston lettuce on serving plate, place a 3/4-inch slice of unpeeled Hawaiian pineapple that has had the core and most of the edible portion removed.

3. Cut the edible pineapple in pieces and place in center of the ring.

4. Top with a 3/4-inch circle of canteloupe or other melon.

5. Invert the sectioned grapefruit, orange and red apple over the pineapple and canteloupe rings.

6. Encircle the inverted fruit with 2 sliced strawberries.

7. Place small bunches of assorted fruit on either side of the pineapple ring foundation.

8. Nestle 2 cream cheese balls rolled in chopped toasted pecans in the watercress garnish at the side of the plate.

9. Pull 4 flanges from top of pineapple and place at stated intervals in lettuce bed to add a note of interest.

10. Make dressing of whipped cream and frozen strawberries, adding enough juice to tint cream a delicate pink.

11. Top with watermelon ball or a fresh strawberry.

The Mayfair Room, Houston, Texas

SPECIAL HOUSE DRESSING

Yield: 1-1/2 pints

Ingredients

EGG	1
DRY MUSTARD	1/2 teaspoon
SALAD OIL	4 ounces
LIQUID HOT PEPPER SEASONING	1/4 teaspoon
LEMONS, LARGE, juice of	2
WORCESTERSHIRE SAUCE	1 teaspoon
SALT	1/2 teaspoon
WHITE PEPPER	1/2 teaspoon
AVOCADOS, medium-sized	2
FRESH SHALLOTS (use tops only)	3
GARLIC or GARLIC POWDER	to taste
ANCHOVY FILLETS	1 ounce
MAYONNAISE	4 ounces
SAFFRON	1/2 teaspoon

Procedure

1. Blend eggs and mustard together. Add oil and mix thoroughly. Add liquid hot pepper seasoning, lemon, worcestershire sauce, salt, and pepper. Mix well with above ingredients.

2. Remove stones and peel avocados. Cut shallots and peel garlic. Grind together with the anchovies into a smooth paste. Add to above, blending gently but thoroughly.

3. Add mayonnaise and saffron and mix thoroughly. Pour into a container and chill for two hours. Serve as a dip or dressing for green salad.

Look's Restaurant

PATIO DRESSING

Yield: 1 gallon

Ingredients

WINE VINEGAR	18 ounces
SALT	1 tablespoon
BLACK PEPPER	1 tablespoon
POWDERED GARLIC	1 tablespoon
MONOSODIUM GLUTAMATE	1 tablespoon
DRY MUSTARD	1 tablespoon
OLIVE OIL	3 quarts
CHEESE, grated	to garnish

Procedure

1. Make a paste of vinegar and dry ingredients. Add olive oil.

2. Refrigerate overnight.

Dean Hansen, The Menger Hotel

TOFFEE LAYER CAKE WITH TOFFEE ICING

Yield: 10 10-inch layer or 5 2-inch layer cakes

Ingredients

CAKE FLOUR	1 pound, 8 ounces
SALT	1/2 ounce
BAKING POWDER, double-acting	1 ounce
COCOA	3/4 ounce
INSTANT COFFEE	1/4 ounce
SUGAR, granulated	1 pound, 11 ounces
BUTTER	9 ounces
MILK	1 pound, 8 ounces
EGGS, whole	14 (only)

Procedure

1. Sift together the flour, salt, baking powder, cocoa, instant coffee, and sugar.

2. Add to the flour mixture the butter and milk. Mix on low speed of mixer until smooth—approximately 4 minutes total mixing time.

3. Add the beaten eggs, a little at a time. Mix at low speed approximately 4 minutes. Scrape down bowl several times.

4. Scale 13 ounces batter into greased and floured layer cake pans.

5. Bake in oven at 350°F. for 25 to 30 minutes.

6. When cool, put Toffee Icing between and on top of layers.

Note

Boiled Icing may be used in place of the Toffee Icing, if desired.

Houston, Texas

TOFFEE ICING

Ingredients

BUTTER	1-1/8 cups
POWDERED SUGAR, sifted	5 cups
INSTANT COFFEE	1 tablespoon
MILK	1 cup
BROWN SUGAR	4-1/2 cups
SALT	1/2 teaspoon

Procedure

1. Cream together the butter, sugar, and instant coffee.

2. Combine milk, brown sugar and salt, and bring to a boil.

3. Cool before adding to first mixture. Blend until smooth.

BOILED FROSTING

Yield: 4-1/2 quarts

Ingredients

SUGAR, granulated	3 pounds
CARMELIZED SUGAR	1 pound
BOILING WATER	2-1/2 cups
EGG WHITES, beaten	8
COFFEE INFUSION, strong	2 tablespoons
SALT	1/2 teaspoon

Procedure

1. Combine sugar, carmelized sugar and boiling water.
2. Stir over low heat until all sugar is dissolved.
3. Boil without stirring to 238°F., or until a little of the mixture dropped in cold water forms a soft ball.
4. Beat whites until they peak.
5. Add syrup slowly to egg whites while beating constantly.
6. Add coffee infusion and salt.
7. Frosting should now be of the consistency to spread.

STRAWBERRY MERINGUE
FOR CREAM PIE

Yield: Topping for five 9-inch pies

Ingredients

HULLED FRESH STRAWBERRIES, washed and well-drained	1 quart
SUGAR	1 pound
EGG WHITES	1/3 cup
PLAIN GELATINE	1 tablespoon
LEMON JUICE	3 tablespoons

Procedure

1. Soak the gelatine in the lemon juice.
2. Place the berries, sugar and egg whites in the mixing bowl and whip for about 3 minutes.
3. Place the gelatine over hot water until dissolved, then add slowly to the berry mixture and continue beating at high speed until stiff (about 15 minutes).
4. Pile lightly on top of cooled cream filling in pie shells. One pint of cream filling is enough for 1 pie.
5. Keep refrigerated until served.

BLACK BOTTOM PIE

Yield: 4 9-inch pies

Ingredients

SUGAR	3 cups
EGG YOLKS	12 (only)
SALT	1/8 teaspoon
VANILLA	2 teaspoons
GRANULATED GELATINE, unflavored	4 tablespoons
CHOCOLATE, melted	2 ounces
SHERRY	1/2 cup
RUM FLAVORING	1/2 cup
EGG WHITES	12 (only)
SUGAR, granulated	1-1/2 cups
PIE SHELLS, baked	4

Procedure

1. Add sugar and salt to well beaten egg yolks. Cook over hot water until of custard consistency.
2. Remove from heat; add vanilla and hydrated gelatine.
3. Separate the mixture into 2 equal parts.
4. To the first half of the warm mixture, add the melted chocolate. Cool. Add sherry.
5. To the other half of the mixture add rum flavoring.
6. Beat egg whites, add sugar and beat until stiff but moist.
7. Fold one-half of the egg whites into chocolate mixture, other half into white mixture. Pour chocolate mixture into pie shells. Let set.
8. Pour white mixture on top of chocolate mixture in pie shells.
9. Chill until very cold and filling is well set.
10. Top with whipped cream and shaved bitter chocolate.

Houston, Texas

TEXAS

The Menger Hotel, a venerable San Antonio, Texas landmark, has used its rotunda as a showcase for art objects and furnishings that date back to its opening in 1859.

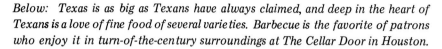

Below: Texas is as big as Texans have always claimed, and deep in the heart of Texans is a love of fine food of several varieties. Barbecue is the favorite of patrons who enjoy it in turn-of-the-century surroundings at The Cellar Door in Houston.

Below: Early elegance in Florida is exemplified in the opulent and imposing Breakers Hotel in Palm Beach. Guests enter a luxurious world of frescoes and vaulted ceilings reflecting the artistry of the Italian Renaissance, a favorite period in the early days of the resort.

Below: Mexican specialties are another mainspring of Texas menus. A sampler of the many popular South of the Border favorites served at Casa Rio, San Antonio, illustrates the range of the cuisine. Colorful umbrella-topped tables in background give a hint of the colorful surroundings enjoyed by Casa Rio patrons while they are eating.

The Alamo, a Texas landmark, is connected to The Hotel Menger (see preceding page) by century-old tunnels, one of which has been made into a wine cellar.

Above: The sophistication that characterizes Dallas today explains its several restaurants noted for serving haute cuisine of high distinction. Among those helping to establish Dallas as a fine dining city is The Old Warsaw with such entrees of distinction as the faisan en croute pictured here.

Below: Next to the Alamo, Neiman-Marcus probably spells Texas for more Americans than any other establishment. Noted for exceptional food, exceptionally well merchandised, their unique Bicentennial promotions were planned by Bob Jones and Ben Izner and adapted to their several

FLORIDA

Greenery creates a lush mood at Tampa's Columbia Restaurant founded at the turn of the century. Patrons relish authentic Spanish cuisine in the kind of courtyard associated with the native tradition.

BAKED CUSTARD WITH VARIATIONS

Yield: 25 portions

Ingredients

SUGAR	1-1/3 cups
SALT	1/4 teaspoon
EGGS, slightly beaten	10 (only)
MILK, cold	1 pint
MILK, scalded	2 quarts
VANILLA	1 tablespoon
NUTMEG	1 teaspoon

Procedure

1. Combine first four ingredients, and blend well.
2. Add scalded milk and vanilla. Sprinkle nutmeg over top of mixture.
3. Pour into custard cups or shallow baking pan. Place in hot water bath.
4. Bake at 320°F. for 45 minutes or until firm and blade of knife comes out clean.

FRENCH CUSTARD

Using Basic Custard Recipe—

Increase sugar by 2 ounces.

Use 2-1/2 quarts half and half cream in place of the cold and scalded milk. Omit the nutmeg.

After baking, chill. Then sprinkle custard liberally with brown sugar.

Drizzle maple syrup over all, and place under broiler until bubbly.

For a very deluxe dessert, serve with whipped cream.

CARMEL CUSTARD

Using Basic Custard Recipe—

Add 6 ounces sugar, caramelized.

Top custard with left-over cake crumbs.

ORANGE RUM SPANISH CREAM

Yield: 50 portions

Ingredients

UNFLAVORED GELATINE	1 cup
MILK	4 quarts
SUGAR	2 pounds
EGGS, separated	16
FRESH ORANGE JUICE	2-1/2 quarts
ORANGE RIND	6 tablespoons
FRESH LEMON JUICE	1/2 cup
SALT	1 teaspoon
RUM	2 tablespoons
FRESH ORANGE SECTIONS	to garnish

Procedure

1. Soften gelatine in 2 cups of milk for 5 minutes. Heat balance of milk in double boiler. Dissolve gelatine in hot milk. Add sugar and mix well.
2. Pour hot mixture into well beaten egg yolks, beating constantly. Cook in double boiler, stirring constantly until mixture thickens and coats the spoon.
3. Remove from heat and add orange juice, rind and lemon juice. Beat egg whites, with salt and rum until stiff. Fold into warm mixture. Pour in hot, 4-ounce glasses; chill. Garnish with orange sections.

Note

The Orange Rum Spanish Cream will form a layer of custard and one of jelly if the egg whites are added while mixture is hot. If a custard consistency throughout is desired, cool mixture. When it starts to set fold in stiffly beaten whites and flavoring. This dessert can be made into an Orange Bavarian by folding in one quart of whipped heavy cream.

Southwest Recipes

CARROT COOKIES WITH ORANGE ICING

Yield: 5 dozen (approximately)

Ingredients

BUTTER	1 cup
SUGAR	3/4 cup
WHOLE EGGS	2 (only)
CARROTS, cooked, mashed	1 cup
FLOUR, all-purpose, sifted	2 cups
BAKING POWDER, double-acting	1 teaspoon
VANILLA	1 teaspoon
SALT	1/4 teaspoon

Procedure

1. Cream butter and sugar.
2. Add one unbeaten egg at a time, and beat between each addition.
3. Add mashed carrots.
4. Sift flour, baking powder, and salt, and add to shortening mixture.
5. Mix well; add vanilla.
6. Drop on greased baking sheet, and bake in oven at 375°F. for 10 to 12 minutes.
7. When cool, ice with Orange Icing.

ORANGE ICING

POWDERED SUGAR	1 pound
ORANGE JUICE	1/2 cup
ORANGE RIND	Rind of 1 orange

Procedure

1. Sift powdered sugar, add orange rind and orange juice. Mix until smooth and of proper consistency.
2. Dip cookies in frosting, then place on rack to dry.

CARAMEL PUDDING

Yield: 27 portions

Ingredients

SUGAR ⎱ for syrup	3 cups
BOILING WATER ⎰	1/2 cup plus 1 tablespoon
EGGS, whole	18 (only)
VANILLA	1 tablespoon
SUGAR	1/2 cup plus 1 tablespoon
LIGHT CREAM	2 quarts plus 1 cup
SALT	1/4 teaspoon

Procedure

1. Melt sugar in an iron or heavy-bottomed skillet. When sugar is melted it will be a rich golden brown.
2. Gradually add boiling water, and cook until syrupy.
3. Beat eggs, add sugar and vanilla.
4. Stir in cream mixed with salt.
5. Coat the inside of the baking dishes with the caramelized syrup.
6. Pour cream mixture into the coated baking dishes.
7. Place baking dishes in pan of hot water, and bake in oven at 325°F. until pudding is set but not entirely firm. Cool slightly. Unmold, serve warm.
8. Garnish with candied fruit or blanched almonds.

ROSY SPICE LAYER CAKE WITH CREAM CHEESE ICING

Yield: 8 2-layer cakes (9-1/4-inch by 1-1/2 inch pan)

Ingredients

BUTTER	2 cups
VEGETABLE SHORTENING	2 cups
WHOLE EGGS	16 (only)
SUGAR	10-2/3 cups
CAKE FLOUR, sifted	16 cups
BAKING POWDER, double-acting	5-1/3 tablespoons
ALLSPICE	2-2/3 tablespoons
CINNAMON	2-2/3 tablespoons
SODA	2 teaspoons
PECANS, chopped	8 cups
RAISINS, cut up	8 cups
TOMATO SOUP, canned	2 quarts

Procedure

1. Cream butter and shortening on second speed of mixer. Add sugar gradually, mixing constantly.
2. Add unbeaten eggs, one at a time. Beat 1 minute after each addition.
3. Sift together the flour, baking powder, spices and soda.
4. Stir nuts and raisins into the flour.
5. Add flour mixture alternately with the tomato soup to the shortening mixture.
6. Mix only until smooth. Avoid overmixing.
7. Scale 1 pound, 2 ounces into each greased layer tin lined with waxed paper.
8. Bake in oven at 350°F. for 25 to 30 minutes.
9. When cool, put layers together with Cream Cheese Icing, and frost the top of cakes.

CREAM CHEESE ICING

Ingredients

CREAM CHEESE	1 pound, 8 ounces
MILK	1 cup
VANILLA	1-1/3 tablespoons
POWDERED SUGAR, sifted	16 cups
SALT	Few grains

Procedure

1. Blend cream cheese, milk, vanilla and salt until soft and smooth.
2. Add sugar gradually, beating well.
3. Spread between layers of Rosy Spice Cake, and on top of each cake.

Oklahoma City, Oklahoma

AVOCADO LIME CONGEAL

Yield: 2-1/2 gallons, 72 portions

Ingredients

GELATIN, LIME FLAVOR	2 pounds
WATER, boiling	1-3/4 quarts
GELATINE, UNFLAVORED	2 ounces
WATER, cold	1/2 cup
WATER, cold	1-3/4 quarts
AVOCADO, diced small (approximately 16)	4 quarts
LEMON JUICE (approximately 10 lemons)	1 pint
ONION JUICE	1 teaspoon
SALT	1 teaspoon
MAYONNAISE	1-1/2 quarts
ICEBERG LETTUCE	7-1/2 heads

Procedure

1. Dissolve lime gelatin in boiling water.
2. Soak plain gelatine in 1/2 cup cold water, add to gelatin mixture and stir well to dissolve.
3. Add 1-3/4 quarts cold water.
4. Combine avocado, lemon juice, onion juice, and salt, and let stand 5 minutes.
5. When gelatin mixture begins to thicken, add mayonnaise and whip well.
6. Fold avocado mixture into the gelatin mixture.
7. Place 2-1/2 quarts of mixture in each No. 165 steam table pan.
8. Chill until firm. Cut 18 orders to the pan.
9. Serve on lettuce leaves.

Florida, Fountain of Foodservice Ideas

IN THE 1500s, Spanish explorers seeking to conquer and exploit a new land, now known as Florida, did not realize the valuable food supply all around them. Reduced almost to starvation at many times in their search for gold and silver, they were forced to eat their horses and even their leather boots.

"Land of the Flowers," Ponce de Leon called the country—land of natural bounty as we know it today. Indian River citrus fruits, Miami stone crabs, terrapin from Key West, hearts of palm reaped from the Everglades—these edible resources abound in Florida today.

Floridians lay claim to a heritage rich in the picaresque adventures of Spain, France, England, Mexico, Venezuela. Perhaps the most flamboyant was Spain, whose impact still reverberates in restaurants around the state.

Columbia Restaurant
Tampa

At the Columbia restaurant in Tampa, a block-long series of 11 dining rooms, owner Cesar Gonzmart combines the quixotic razzle-dazzle of old and modern Florida. Gonzmart, a true afficionado of the musical arts, is his own star violin performer in a Spanish musical extravaganza staged nightly for the pleasure of guests.

The Columbia, founded in 1905 by the father of Gonzmart's wife Adela, is reputed to be the largest Spanish restaurant in the world. Guests enjoy authentic Spanish dishes, such as Paella Valenciana and Zarzuela de Mariscos (a seafood combination flavored with many spices and a hint of dry white wine).

The restaurant, which is on the Bicentennial trail in Florida, figures in the annual Fiesta Day in Tampa's Latin Quarter, Ybor City.

The Breakers
Palm Beach

Florida as a vacation playground was envisioned by Henry Morrison Flagler, self-made tycoon and partner to John D. Rockefeller. At the turn of this century, Flagler made Palm Beach into a resort of international acclaim.

The Breakers is the third structure to stand on the ground that Flagler chose as the site of an elaborate hotel venture.

"Flagler practically developed all of eastern Florida," says John Clifford, general manager of the Breakers. "He owned the Florida East Coast railroad all the way down to the Keys, and developed property all along the railroad's right of way."

A tribute to Flagler's lavish expenditures, the present Breakers opened in 1926, taking architectural inspiration from the famous Villa Medici in Rome.

The resort complex is still owned by Flagler System, Inc. Four restaurants at the Breakers serve lavish dishes that complement the gracious atmosphere of the hotel. Lobster Thermidor, a special recipe developed by food and beverage manager Henry M. Warren, is most popular.

During the spring and summer of 1969, Flagler System launched a dynamic expansion program for the complex. Kept uppermost in mind as plans were discussed was the need to retain the original flavor.

Ponce de Leon Lodge and Country Club St. Augustine

Ponce de Leon searched for the health and endless life attributed to the legendary Fountain of Youth—in the area now known as St. Augustine—to no avail. Today, St. Augustine claims that the fountain lies within its confines and will be found somewhere, sometime. In the meantime, vacationers enjoy today's life at the resort playground.

The Ponce de Leon Lodge and Country Club is another direct descendant of the Flagler empire. Until just a few months ago, it remained in the Flagler System. But Lawrence Lewis, owner, and John T. Morris, general manager, now preside over the 18-year-old property.

"The present Ponce de Leon retains a Moorish-Spanish influence in its architecture," notes Morris. "We have one valuable painting dating back to the mid-1800s. It's a focal point for our dining room, and shows an Arabic scene which complements the decor."

Seafood is quite popular at the Ponce de Leon. Serving fresh Florida lobster, most of which is caught by a fleet of boats off St. Augustine, the Ponce de Leon features a delectable Saturday night buffet—all you can eat, including fruits of the sea—for $7.

To celebrate the Bicentennial, the Ponce de Leon developed a special Colonial menu: creamy clam chowder, corn pudding, boneless fowl stuffed with wild rice. The fare is expected to entice banquets and will be featured on special flyers on the regular menu. Staff attire will be Colonial costumes—not the bright reds and greens depicting Florida's Spanish heritage, but the cool grays, whites and blacks of its English settlers.

Joe's Stone Crab Restaurant Miami Beach

Older than the city of Miami Beach, Joe's made its debut in 1913 in the home of Joe Weiss. Grandson Jessie Weiss now presides over Joe's.

Not a place for lavish decor, Joe's is strictly functional. It is geared to Miami's popular passion—the consumption of its native delicacy, stone crabs.

Not much to look at, the ugly crustacean has a taste that cannot be compared to other kinds of crab. Suffice it to say that Joe's biggest seller over the years has been the ornery-looking critter.

No carpeted floors adorn Joe's, no fancy wallcoverings or paintings. Old photographs of early 1900 scenes in Miami and an antique clock collection are about the only decorative elements in the interior.

But Joe's packs in the guests nightly during the five months (mid-May to mid-October) that stone crabs are legally ripe for picking. The typical meal joins stone crab with a cup of clam chowder and hash browned potatoes. Apple pie used to be the favorite dessert at Joe's, but Key Lime pie (a guarded recipe) now reigns supreme.

Fresh Florida pompano, broiled yellow-tail snapper, shrimp creole, and broiled lobster are other popular seafood delicacies at Joe's.

Named an historic landmark in April 1975, Joe's still sits on the site where Joe Weiss started the stone-crab dining craze in Florida.

Louis Pappas Riverside Restaurant Tarpon Springs

At one time the largest Greek colony in America, Tarpon Springs was best known for its sponge fishermen and brightly colored sponge-fishing fleet. Rubber and other substitutes for live sponges have depleted the trade. But the Greek colony remains, retaining its religious and cultural heritage. The busy, noisy waterfront is served by a family enterprise, the Louis Pappas Riverside Restaurant.

The 1926 Florida land crash affected Floridians with its subsequent financial disasters. One man affected was Louis Pappas. He was compelled to set up a restaurant business from his home. Slowly the business grew, and the facility was moved to a converted sponge warehouse built on stilts.

Now, 50 years later, Pappas' sons Michael, Jack, and Lucas, and Tony Houllis, a brother-in-law, have opened up the new Louis Pappas Riverside Restaurant—a 42,000-sq.-ft. building that seems to be many buildings in one.

The exterior is strikingly modern, similar in concept to a contemporary Greek village. The interior is devoted to Greek artifacts and driftwood panel paintings depicting ancient and contemporary Greek life and mythology. Antique statues of Greek mythological figures acquired by the family are interspersed.

Greek foods, as well as decor, delight Pappas patrons. The favorite, Greek salad, requires at least a thousand pounds of Greek feta cheese every week—plus hundreds of crates of lettuce, green peppers, tomatoes, cucumbers, radishes, avocados, and scallions.

Florida Recipes

SOUTHERN LOBSTER BISQUE

Yield: 64 portions

Ingredients

LOBSTER MEAT	5 pounds
STOCK FROM LOBSTER	10 quarts
BUTTER	1 pound
ONION, MINCED	1 pound
CELERY AND GREEN LEAVES, CHOPPED FINE	4 cups
BUTTER	1 pound
FLOUR	1 pound
SALT	to season
PEPPER	to season
CREAM (18%), HEATED	4 quarts
BAKING SODA	1/2 teaspoon

Procedure

1. Add 10 quarts cold water to lobster meat. Bring to simmering point and cook 15 minutes. Strain and save stock. Chop lobster meat. Saute onion and chopped celery in 1 pound butter.

2. Add chopped lobster and sauteed onion and celery to the lobster stock. Make a roux using 1 pound butter and 1 pound flour.

3. Add roux to boiling stock mixture. Stir until smooth.

4. Add heated cream and seasonings.

5. Do not let bisque boil once cream has been added.

6. Add baking soda to prevent separation.

7. Place over hot water or in bain marie to keep hot.

Miami, Florida

OYSTER AND HAM SOUP

Yield: 35 portions

Ingredients

BUTTER	1/4 cup
ONIONS, SMALL, MINCED	4
FLOUR	1/2 cup
HAM, FINELY CHOPPED	4 cups
STOCK	1 gallon
CELERY, CUBED	1 quart
RICE, UNCOOKED	1-1/3 cups
BAY LEAVES	8
OYSTERS AND LIQUOR	2 quarts
SALT	to season
PEPPER	to season
PARSLEY, SNIPPED	2/3 cup

Procedure

1. Saute onions in butter until tender. Add flour.

2. Cook until flour is delicately browned, stirring all the time.

3. Add ham, stock, celery, rice, bay leaves and liquor from oysters.

4. Cook gently until rice is cooked, and celery is tender.

5. Season with salt and pepper.

6. Add oysters, whole or minced, and cook until they are thoroughly heated.

7. Taste for seasoning. Add parsley and serve piping hot.

Note

If gumbo file powder is available, add 2 tablespoons to soup as it is removed from the heat.

Grandma's Kitchen, Miami, Fla.

SCOTCH BARLEY BROTH WITH LAMB SHANK HALF, PEASANT STYLE

When featuring a Peasant Luncheon in the Men's Grill, lamb shanks are used as the main meat dish. The lamb shanks are cooked in advance for the Scotch Broth, which forms part of the meal. The vegetables for the broth are cut in large pieces in keeping with the peasant style of the meal. The Scotch Broth is served in an 8-oz. soup bowl, and the lamb shank half on a separate plate. Peasant bread and sweet or salt butter completes the entree. This is a popular luncheon feature as the Scotch Broth is almost a meal in itself.

Yield: 25 portions

Ingredients

1. STOCK FOR SCOTCH BROTH
   LAMB SHANKS,
   AVERAGE WEIGHT, 12
   OUNCES, EACH ... 26
   WATER, COLD ... 2-1/2 gallons
2. BARLEY ... 1 cup
   BAY LEAF ... 1/2
   SALT ... 1-1/2 tablespoons
   PEPPER ... 1 teaspoon
   ONION, coarsely cut ... 8 ounces
   CARROTS, coarsely cut ... 8 ounces
   CELERY, coarsely cut ... 8 ounces
   POTATOES, coarsely cut ... 8 ounces
   ROUX ... 1 cup

Procedure

1. Wipe lamb shanks and saw in half. Brown in a 350°F. oven.
2. Remove to steam-jacketed kettle, cover with the 2-1/2 gallons cold water. Bring to a boil. Simmer until lamb meat is tender and the stock is reduced. Remove lamb shanks. Keep hot.
3. Drain off all stock in excess of 5 quarts. Reserve for other use. To remaining 5 quarts stock add barley, seasonings and vegetables. Simmer slowly 1 hour.
4. Add roux, and cook until of the desired thickness.
5. Serve Scotch Broth in 8-ounce soup bowl with lamb hock on side dish as a complete entree.

CHILLED TOMATO AND CUCUMBER SOUP

Yield: 25 portions

Ingredients

TOMATO JUICE, CANNED,
   46 ounce cans ... 3
OLIVE OIL FRENCH
   DRESSING ... 1-1/2 cups
CUCUMBERS, SHREDDED ... 3 cups
CROUTONS ... 3 cups

Procedure

1. Combine tomato juice and french dressing. Blend well and chill.
2. Shred cucumbers and chill.
3. Delicately brown croutons.
4. Serve 6 ounces tomato mixture in each bouillon cup.
5. Pass shredded cucumbers and croutons from the side.

Grandma's Kitchen, Miami

ROAST BEEF HASH

Yield: 20 6-ounce portions

Ingredients

ROAST BEEF,
   coarsely chopped ... 4 pounds
POTATOES, cooked, diced ... 2 pounds, 8 ounces
GREEN PEPPER, cooked,
   diced ... 3 ounces
ONION, small, diced,
   sauteed ... 4 ounces
SALT ... to season
PEPPER ... to season
STOCK ... 1 to 2 quarts
CHILI SAUCE ... 2 cups

Procedure

1. Combine the first 6 ingredients. Blend thoroughly.
2. Gradually add the stock. The amount required will depend on the moisture content of the other ingredients.
3. When mixture is well mixed, place in bake pan.
4. Cover with a layer of chili sauce.
5. Bake in oven at 350°F. for 20 to 25 minutes.

Miami

GERMAN SAUERBRATEN

The Germans have given us many of our favorite dishes. They are fond of foods cooked with vinegar, sugar, and spices. Sauerbraten is one of our most popular German meat dishes. Sauerbraten should be served with either Potato Dumplings or "Spaetzle," and to make this dish complete Sweet-Sour Red Cabbage is a "must."

Yield: approx. 25 4-ounce portions

Ingredients

1. BEEF RUMP	10 to 12 pounds
SALT	to season
PEPPER	to season
GARLIC CLOVE	1
ONIONS, medium, sliced	4
CELERY, diced	1 cup
CARROTS, medium, diced	2
LEEKS, diced	1 stalk
PARSLEY	few sprigs
BAY LEAVES	4
THYME	1/2 teaspoon
CLOVES	6
2. VINEGAR, WHITE WINE	3 quarts
WATER	1 quart
3. BUTTER	1 cup
FLOUR	1 cup
MARINADE	3 cups
BOUILLON *or* STOCK	3 quarts
TOMATOES, RAW, quartered	7
GINGERSNAPS	6
SUGAR	2 tablespoons
4. RED WINE	1 wine glass

Procedure

1. Cut meat in chunks suitable for slicing. Rub meat with salt, pepper, and garlic clove.

Into an earthenware pot (or preferably a small wooden keg) place the next 8 ingredients. Place the meat in the pot.

Bring vinegar and water to a boil, and pour over meat and other ingredients in the pot.

Marinate 5 days, turning frequently to insure even curing.

2. Heat butter in a large pot. Remove meat from marinade and brown on all sides in hot butter. Remove meat. Combine flour with butter in pot, and cook to a light brown.

Add 3 cups of the marinade and the bouillon or stock, stirring constantly until thoroughly blended. Return meat to pot. Bring sauce to a boil.

3. Add remaining ingredients with the exception of the red wine. Simmer beef slowly until tender. Remove meat from pot.

4. Add the red wine. Taste for seasoning and, if necessary, add salt and pepper. Slice meat into portions. Strain sauce. Serve over meat or pass sauce from the side.

Florida

ROAST SHOULDER OF LAMB WITH BARBECUE SAUCE

Yield: 25 portions

Ingredients

1. SHOULDER LAMB, OVEN-READY, boned, rolled, and tied	2 shoulders
2. BARBECUE SAUCE	
BUTTER	1 cup
ONION, minced	1 cup
VINEGAR	1 cup
BROWN SUGAR, packed	1/2 cup
GARLIC CLOVES, grated	1/4 cup
HORSERADISH, grated	1 tablespoon
WORCESTERSHIRE SAUCE	2 tablespoons
DRY MUSTARD	2 tablespoons
SALT	1 tablespoon
PEPPER, WHITE	1 teaspoon
CATSUP	1 cup
TOMATO PUREE	1 cup

Procedure

1. Wipe boned and rolled shoulder lamb. Roast in oven at 325°F. until internal temperature registers 180°F. on thermometer, or until meat is tender—approximately 2 to 2-1/2 hours. Slice meat into 1-1/2 ounce slices on meat slicer.

2. For Barbecue Sauce, saute onions in butter 5 minutes. Add remaining ingredients and simmer 30 minutes or longer.

Miami

SPANISH CHICKEN WITH YELLOW RICE

Yield: 12 portions

Ingredients

1. FRYER-CHICKEN, 3 pounds
   each, quartered ... 3
   LARD ... 4 ounces
   OLIVE OIL ... 3 ounces
2. GREEN PEPPERS,
   chopped fine ... 2
   ONION, chopped fine ... 12 ounces
   BAY LEAF ... 1
   NUTMEG ... a pinch
   SALT ... 1 tablespoon
   HOT STEAK SAUCE ... 7 drops
   GARLIC SALT ... 1 tablespoon
   TOMATOES, FRESH,
   small cubes ... 2
3. STOCK ... 1-1/2 ounces
   SAFFRON SOLUTION ... a sprinkle
   RICE, LONG-GRAIN,
   uncooked ... 1 pound,
    ... 8 ounces
   SAUTERNE WINE ... 1/4 cup

Procedure

1. Wash, dry and trim chicken. Cut in quarters.
2. Heat shortening and oil. Add chicken and cook until pieces are a golden brown. Turn to evenly brown pieces.
3. Remove chicken from pan. Add the next 8 ingredients, and cook in the fat until green peppers and onions are tender but not brown.
4. Stir vegetables occasionally to cook evenly.
5. Add stock made from wing tips, necks, and giblets. Cook until liquid comes to the boiling point.
6. Sprinkle with saffron solution.
7. Add rice. Stir until liquid reaches boiling point.
8. Add chicken. Cover pan and cook in oven at 350°F. until chicken pieces are fork-tender and rice is cooked—approximately 18 to 20 minutes.
9. Remove from oven. Sprinkle with sauterne wine. Cover. Let rest 10 minutes before serving.

Note

To make saffron solution, toast 1/2 ounce saffron on brown paper. Pulverize well. Add a small amount of water (1/4 cup) and bottle.

Water may be substituted for the stock if necessary.

Las Novedades Spanish Restaurant, Tampa

ROAST ROLLED SHOULDER OF LAMB WITH FRESH MINT SAUCE

Yield: 25 portions

Ingredients

SHOULDER LAMB, oven-ready,
   boned, rolled, and tied, E.P. ... 2 shoulders
SALT ... 1 tablespoon
PEPPER ... 1/2 tablespoon
ONION, chopped ... 4 ounces
PARSLEY, chopped ... 2 tablespoons
RED WINE ... 1 cup
WATER ... 1 cup

Procedure

1. Wipe lamb shoulders which have been boned, rolled and tied. Rub meat with salt and pepper.
2. Place lamb in open roasting pan. Cover with chopped onion and parsley. Roast in oven at 325°F. for approximately 30 minutes.
3. Begin basting every 15 minutes with a mixture of red wine and water.
4. If oven thermometer is used, cook lamb to an interior temperature of 180°F. Otherwise allow from 2 to 2-1/2 hours approximate cooking time.
5. Place cooked roast on slicing machine and slice in 1-1/2 ounce slices (approx.). Allow 2 slices (3 ounces) per portion.

LOBSTER THERMIDOR

Yield: 100 servings

Ingredients

BUTTER	6 pounds
ONION	6 pounds
ALL-PURPOSE FLOUR	3 pounds (3 quarts)
SALT	4 ounces (1/2-cup)
WHITE PEPPER	2 teaspoons
DRY ENGLISH MUSTARD	1 ounce
PARSLEY, chopped	2 ounces
MILK	6 gallons
CREAM SHERRY	1 gallon
BOILED LOBSTERS (or approx. 32 pounds cooked lobster)	100 1-1/2-pounds each
CHEESE, PARMESAN, grated	3 pounds
BREAD CRUMBS	3 pounds
BUTTER, melted	6 pounds

Procedure

1. Melt butter in saucepan. Add onion and cook until yellow (about 2 minutes). Then remove from pan.

2. Stir in flour and simmer until it bubbles. Add salt, white pepper, dry English mustard, and chopped parsley. Whip in milk and cream sherry until smooth. Fold in cut-up lobster.

3. Pour filling into lobster shells. Sprinkle with grated parmesan cheese, bread crumbs, and butter. Bake in oven at 450°F. until brown.

ST. AUGUSTINE CRABMEAT A LA ROBERT

Yield: 40 servings

Ingredients

FRESH MUSHROOMS, sliced	20 large
BUTTER	10 ounces
WHITE WINE	1 cup
SALT	as needed
WHITE PEPPER	as needed
MONOSODIUM GLUTAMATE	as needed
BREAD CRUMBS, toasted	1 quart
EGGS	8
WHITE CRABMEAT	10 pounds
PREPARED MUSTARD	1/4 cup

Procedure

1. Saute mushrooms in butter slowly until tender. Add white wine and cook slowly for 5 minutes. Add salt, white pepper, monosodium glutamate and remove from stove.

2. In a separate bowl, mix together the bread crumbs, eggs, crabmeat, and prepared mustard. Fold in slowly to avoid crumbling crabmeat.

3. Place in individual casseroles. Bake in oven at 350°F. for 10 to 15 minutes. Remove from oven.

4. Top with hollandaise sauce, or grated cheese as desired. Brown under broiler at time of serving.

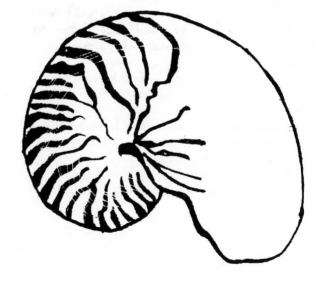

SPINACH SOUFFLE

Yield: 54 portions

Ingredients

SPINACH, frozen	12 pounds
BUTTER	6 tablespoons
FLOUR	6 tablespoons
SALT	to season
PEPPER	to season
NUTMEG	a dash
CHICKEN STOCK, hot	3 cups
or	
MILK, scalded	3 cups
PARMESAN CHEESE	1-1/2 cups
BUTTER	6 tablespoons
EGG YOLKS, well beaten	18
EGG WHITES, beaten stiff	24

Procedure

1. Chop frozen spinach. Add to butter in saucepan. Cover and cook until all the water from the spinach has boiled away. (Do not add any additional water.)

2. Combine flour, salt, pepper, and nutmeg, and mix to a paste with 1/2 cup milk or stock.

3. Add flour paste to hot liquid and cook as for white sauce—about 15 minutes.

4. Fold in spinach and blend well. Continue cooking until spinach is heated. Remove from heat.

5. Add 1/2 cup of the parmesan cheese and beaten egg yolks. Blend thoroughly. Cool slightly.

6. Fold in stiffly beaten egg whites.

7. Pour into ungreased 6 oz. molds. Smooth surface in shape of a dome.

8. Sprinkle the remaining cup of parmesan cheese over top of molds, allowing approximately 1 teaspoon per mold. Top each mold with 1/2 teaspoon melted butter.

9. Place molds in a pan of hot water.

10. Bake in oven at 350°F. for 20 to 25 minutes or until molds are set.

Miami

SEAFOOD-FILLED PINEAPPLE WEDGE

Yield: one portion

Ingredients

JUMBO SHRIMPS (22 to 1 pound)	4 (only)
FRESH PINEAPPLE SHELL	1/2 (only)
PINEAPPLE FANS	4 (only)
LUMP CRABMEAT	1 ounce
LUMP LOBSTER MEAT	1 ounce
LOUIS DRESSING	1/2 ounce
COCKTAIL SAUCE	1/2 ounce
RUSSIAN DRESSING	1/2 ounce
BLACK OLIVES (190 to No. 10 can)	3 (only)
PIMIENTO (4 to 7-oz. can—8 strips each)	1 strip
SHREDDED CHICORY	4 leaves
ESCAROLE	4 leaves

Procedure

1. Cook shrimp 15 to 20 minutes, or until done, in boiling water to which has been added salt, 2 lemons or limes, bay leaves, and sliced onion.

2. Cool, peel, and remove vein from shrimp.

3. Cut whole pineapple in half lengthwise, cutting through fronds.

4. Remove pulp in one piece from each half by cutting around edge of shell with sharp knife.

5. Slice pulp that has been removed into 15 fans for each half of pineapple.

6. Place a small quantity of shredded chicory in bottom of pineapple for build-up.

7. Place 1 ounce of crabmeat at one end of shell, 4 shrimps in center crosswise, and 1 ounce lobster meat at other end of shell. Cover crabmeat with Louis dressing, the shrimp with cocktail sauce, and the lobster with Russian dressing.

8. Place fans of pineapple along outer edge of shell, two on each side.

9. Garnish with leaves of escarole, black olives, one pimiento ring.

Miami, Florida

MOLDED AVOCADO SALAD

Yield: 32 4-ounce portions

Ingredients

GELATIN, LIME FLAVOR	1 pound
HOT WATER	1 quart
MASHED AVOCADO	2 quarts
SALT	2 teaspoons
LEMON JUICE	1/2 cup
CREAM, whipped	1 quart
MAYONNAISE	1 pint

Procedure

1. Dissolve the gelatin in hot water. Cool mixture before proceeding.

2. When gelatin begins to congeal fold in the other ingredients.

3. Mold. Chill.

4. For a "Christmas wreath" salad the above mixture is put into individual ring molds. When turned out, the ring is garnished by little sprigs of parsley. The bow on the wreath is pimiento.

SALAD SOPHISTICATE WITH HONEY-LIME DRESSING

Yield: 1 portion

Procedure

1. Arrange pineapple chunks, pear half, peach half, bing cherries and seedless grapes on a bed of bibb lettuce.

2. Garnish with watercress and maraschino cherry.

3. Serve with Honey-Lime Dressing made by combining equal parts of honey, lime juice, mayonnaise, and whipped cream, and blending well.

4. Serve dressing in a gooseneck from the side.

Grandma's Kitchen, Miami

LOUIS DRESSING

Yield: 1 quart (approximately)

Ingredients

CATSUP	1/2 pint
MAYONNAISE	3/4 quart
LIQUID HOT PEPPER SEASONING	1/4 ounce
DRY MUSTARD	1/2 ounce
SALT	1 teaspoon
RED PEPPER	1/2 ounce
LIMES	juice of 1/2 (only)
WORCESTERSHIRE SAUCE	1/2 ounce

Procedure

1. Blend all ingredients together. Mix thoroughly.

2. Pour into jar, cover, and keep in refrigerator.

3. Shake well before using.

Miami, Florida

FRUIT SALAD DRESSING

Yield: 3 quarts

Ingredients

FLOUR	1-1/2 cups
SUGAR	1-1/2 pounds
SALT	1 tablespoon
PINEAPPLE JUICE	1 quart
EGGS, yolk and white separated	12 (only)
MARSHMALLOWS	1/2 pound
LEMON JUICE	1 cup

Procedure

1. Mix dry ingredients, and add enough pineapple juice to make a smooth paste.

2. Heat balance of pineapple juice. Add sugar mixture, and cook in steam-jacketed kettle or double boiler until mixture is thick.

3. Beat yolks until thick and lemon colored.

4. Add some of the hot mixture to yolks, place with the balance of the mixture in kettle to cook for a few minutes.

5. Remove from heat. Add marshmallows.

6. When marshmallows are melted, and mixture cool, add lemon juice.

7. Fold in stiffly-beaten egg whites.

8. Store in covered containers in refrigerator.

9. Serve 1 part whipped cream to 2 parts dressing.

CHERRY PIE

Yield: 20 10-inch pies (30 pounds)

Ingredients

FROZEN CHERRIES,	
red, sour pitted	30 pounds
RED VEGETABLE	
COLORING MATTER	3 ounces
CORN SYRUP, white	3 pounds
CORNSTARCH	11 ounces
WATER, cold	1 quart
SUGAR	5 pounds

Procedure

1. Thaw cherries until 2-1/2 quarts juice are obtainable.

2. Mix together the cherry juice, corn syrup, and red coloring matter, and bring to boil.

3. Mix the 11 ounces cornstarch gradually with the water, and add to hot mixture stirring rapidly with wire whip; boil until mixture is clear and thick.

4. Add sugar, and just bring to a boil. If allowed to cook too long, the sugar will have a tendency to thin the mixture.

5. Pour the hot, thickened cherry juice over the partially thawed fruit.

6. Use a wooden spoon to fold the juice over the fruit.

7. Scale 24 ounces of cherry filling into each unbaked pie shell.

8. Top with latticed crust, with edges crimped upward to keep in the juice.

9. Brush top with slightly beaten egg mixed with oil.

10. Bake in oven at 400°F. for approximately 45 minutes.

Miami, Florida

ALMOND BISQUE

Yield: 30 portions

Ingredients

SUGAR	1-1/4 pounds
WATER	1-1/4 cups
EGG YOLKS	1-1/4 cups
PLAIN GELATINE	1/2 tablespoon
COLD WATER	2 tablespoons
CREAM, whipped	1-1/4 quarts
SLICED ALMONDS,	
toasted	2 cups
COCONUT MACAROON	
CRUMBS	2 cups
VANILLA	1 tablespoon

Procedure

1. Boil the sugar and water to the soft ball stage.

2. Pour this syrup over the beaten egg yolks.

3. Cook until thick, stirring constantly.

4. Soak the gelatine in 2 tablespoons cold water for 5 minutes. Add this to the egg yolk and syrup mixture. Stir until dissolved. Cool.

5. As the mixture thickens, add the whipped cream, toasted almonds, vanilla and macaroon crumbs. Freeze.

6. When serving, dip shallow portions with a large spoon.

FAMOUS GEORGIAN PECAN PIE

Yield: 18 portions (3 8-inch pies)

Ingredients

WHOLE EGGS	9 (only)
BUTTER or MARGARINE,	
melted	6 tablespoons
FLOUR	6 tablespoons
VANILLA	1 teaspoon
SALT	3/8 teaspoon
SUGAR	1-1/2 cups
CORN SYRUP, dark	4-1/2 cups
PECANS, broken halves	4-1/2 cups
PIE SHELLS, unbaked	3

Procedure

1. Beat eggs. Blend in the melted shortening, flour, vanilla, salt, sugar, and syrup.

2. Sprinkle nuts over bottom of unbaked pastry shell. Gently pour over the syrup mixture, dividing it evenly among the 3 pie tins.

3. Bake in oven at 425°F. for 10 minutes. Reduce heat to 325°F. and bake 40 minutes.

BANANA NUT LAYER CAKE

Yield: 7 pounds, approximately 4 10-inch layers

Ingredients

SUGAR	1 pound, 8 ounces
MARGARINE, melted	6 ounces
EGGS	4 (only)
PASTRY FLOUR, sifted	1 pound
BAKING SODA	2 teaspoons
BAKING POWDER, double-acting	1 tablespoon
SALT	1/2 teaspoon
BUTTERMILK	1/2 cup
PECANS, chopped	6 ounces
VANILLA	2 teaspoons
RIPE BANANAS, mashed	3 pounds

Procedure

1. Put melted margarine, sugar and eggs in bowl of mixer, and beat at No. 2 speed for a few minutes. Sift together the flour, soda, baking powder, and salt, and gradually add to the first mixture. Mix until well blended.

2. Add buttermilk, mashed bananas, and vanilla, and beat until batter is smooth. Add chopped pecans.

3. Scale 1-3/4 pounds of batter into each greased, floured 10-inch tin.

4. Bake in oven at 375°F. until cake shrinks slightly from sides of pan—approximately 20 to 25 minutes.

5. Cool, and put layers together with Banana Frosting.

Miami, Florida

BANANA FROSTING

Yield:

Ingredients

MARGARINE, melted	7 ounces
POWDERED SUGAR	4 pounds
BANANAS, mashed	2 cups
LEMON JUICE	1 teaspoon

Procedure

Blend the sugar and mashed bananas alternately into the melted shortening. Mix well, add lemon juice.

PAMELA JOAN'S CHEESE PIE

Yield: 24 servings

Ingredients

CREAM CHEESE (room temperature)	3 pounds
SUGAR	2 cups
EGGS	9
VANILLA	1 tablespoon
LEMON	1 teaspoon
ALMOND FLAVORING	1 teaspoon
TOPPING	
SOUR CREAM	3 cups
SUGAR	1 cup
VANILLA	1/2 teaspoon
ALMOND FLAVORING	1/2 teaspoon

Procedure

1. Whip all pie ingredients in mixer at No. 2 speed until well blended. Pour into three 9-inch pans. If pans are buttered, mixture will form its own crust. If you wish, however, use a graham cracker crust. With a graham cracker crust, use 10-inch pie pans. Bake in oven at 325°F. for 24 minutes only. Remove from oven; let cool 10 minutes.

2. To make topping, mix topping ingredients slowly by hand; pour over Cheese Pie. The pie will have made a rim to hold the topping. You may decorate top with unsweetened cherries. Put back in oven at 325°F. for 10 minutes only. Remove from oven; cool and refrigerate.

LEMON BAVARIAN CRUMB CRUST PIE

Yield: 12 8-inch pies

Ingredients
CRUMB CRUST

GRAHAM CRACKERS	3 quarts
BUTTER or MARGARINE	1 pound, 8 ounces
SUGAR	2 pounds

PIE FILLING

MARSHMALLOW BITS	2 pounds, 8 ounces
WHIPPING CREAM	3 quarts
GELATINE	3/4 cup
COLD WATER	1-1/2 pints
SUGAR	4 pounds, 8 ounces
COLD WATER	2-1/4 quarts
LEMON JUICE	1-1/2 pints

Procedure

1. Mix finely ground cracker crumbs with sugar and melted butter. Spread mixture over bottom and sides of pie tins. With the back of a spoon press mixture into the pie tin. Bake in oven at 375°F. for 7 to 10 minutes. Cool.

2. Soak marshmallow bits for 30 minutes in whipping cream. Soak gelatine in the 1-1/2 pints of cold water for 5 minutes. Add lemon juice. Bring sugar and the 2-1/4 quarts of water to a boil, and add to the gelatine and lemon juice mixture. Cool until mixture begins to stiffen.

3. In the meantime, beat whipping cream and marshmallow mixture until stiff. Fold into gelatine mixture until well blended. Fill pie shells and chill thoroughly. Just before serving decorate with whipped cream, if desired.

PINEAPPLE ORANGE SPONGE

Yield: 50 portions

Ingredients

PINEAPPLE JUICE	1 pint
EGG YOLKS, slightly beaten	1 cup
CRUSHED PINEAPPLE	1/2 No. 10 can
SUGAR	2 pounds
ORANGE JUICE	1-1/2 cups
ORANGE RIND, grated	1/2 ounce
UNFLAVORED GELATINE	1 ounce
COLD WATER	1 cup
EVAPORATED MILK, chilled and whipped (or whipped cream)	1 quart
EGG WHITES	3/4 cup

Procedure

1. Heat the pineapple juice and add it slowly to the egg yolks. Cook over hot water until thick.

2. Add the crushed pineapple, sugar, orange juice, and grated rind.

3. Soak the gelatine in cold water for 5 minutes. Heat over hot water until dissolved and then add to the pineapple mixture. Cool. When it begins to congeal, whip it and fold in the whipped evaporated milk and beaten egg whites. Chill until firm.

4. Serve in sherbets; top with fresh orange sections.

New Orleans Creole/Continental Cuisine

NEW ORLEANS AND environs is noted for the spicy character of Creole foods. However, the elegance of the continental cuisine featured in many of its landmark dining spots is an equally effective drawing card for tourists.

The appeal of jazz and the unique flavor of the Mardi Gras highlight the city's year-round appeal. Foodservice operations have taken full advantage of both elements in building successful enterprises.

Antoine's

"Ain't seen the races? Why say, mister, to visit Noo Orluns and not see the races is like not eating a meal at Antony's cafe."

The sentiment that the great American author William Faulkner penned a "scant" 50 years ago was even then anything but a fresh piece of advice. Since 1840, when a young Marseilles hotel apprentice named Antoine Alciatore began going down to the New Orleans wharves to drum up business for his boarding house, Antoine's has been one of the city's great landmarks.

Boarding house no longer, the restaurant moved to its present opulent quarters on St. Louis Street in the Vieux Carre in 1850. Today, it is proudly growing into its fifth generation of family ownership.

Roy Gust, Jr.—whose father, Roy Sr., and uncle, William Gust, nephews of the late Roy Alciatore, are the present proprietors—is devoting himself to maintaining the restaurant's venerability. And at Antoine's, that challenge not only includes the supervision of a great cuisine and the host of concerns attendant upon the management of any food operation—there is also some legitimate concern with ghosts.

"I am a firm believer," says Roy Jr., speaking appropriately enough in the restaurant's Mystery Room, from which the painting "All is Vanity" mysteriously vanished on the day his grandfather died. "Sometimes at 2 a.m., when the restaurant is closed, I sit at one of the tables with a glass of wine and they all . . . "

He breaks his reverie to sample a new batch of Oysters Rockefeller, of special concern to the restaurant as the dish was created by the Alciatores. Although the restaurant is famous for its Creole cuisine, described by Roy Jr. as the happy accident produced by African chefs working on European cuisines, its cuisine is more accurately described as French cuisine provencal.

Roy Jr. best describes his family's heritage, however, with the candor of "spiritual" intuition, when he says, "It's not classic, it's not anything else. It's Antoine's."

Elmwood Plantation

A relative newcomer in terms of New Orleans' restaurant longevity, the Elmwood Plantation is second to none when it comes to the history of the soil upon which it stands.

In 1719, a grateful King Louis XIV of France gave 8,500 acres of rich Mississippi Valley land to Minister Nicholas Chauvin de la Freniere. Chauvin, who became attorney-general of Louisiana and was later executed as a leader of French insurgents resisting the transfer of political power to the Spanish, built a lovely home on his plantation property in 1762. Later the residence of the first American to govern Louisiana, this property has long attracted the interest of Colonial scholars who have proclaimed it the oldest plantation in the Mississippi Valley.

When Joseph Marcelo Jr. and Nicholas Mosca purchased the home and the lovely remnant of land upon which it stands, they discovered that entry into the restaurant business put them simultaneously into the reconstruction business. Aided by students and professors from Louisiana State University, the work has resulted in a long scholarly article proving the authenticity of the land's artifacts.

Together with numerous New Orleans seafood specialties, the restaurant further celebrates the bounty of Louisiana by featuring a large assortment of game birds, served with wild rice and candied yams. Creole and Italian specialties are also listed in the menu.

There is not, interestingly enough, a single elm on the property. But 32 oaks, beautiful grounds, and a number of *definitely* Colonial artifacts make this establishment something beautiful to behold.

Commander's Palace

Thomas Jefferson doubled the territory of the United States when, in 1803, he authorized the Louisiana Purchase. Actually, he had sent his ministers to France for a more specific purpose—the purchase of a single city.

Vitally important as a port, and surrounded by wonderfully fertile agricultural land, the city's natural gifts further prompted the president to remark that "the position of New Orleans certainly destines it to be the greatest city the world has ever seen."

Certainly many 19th-century Americans agreed, for the Louisiana Purchase occasioned the migration of vast numbers of American merchants and businessmen to the thriving port city. Today, testimony to their success is evident in the beautiful manor houses and luxuriant gardens comprising the Garden District.

A popular reminder of this romantic era is the restaurant at the corner of Washington Avenue and Coliseum Street: Commander's Palace. Originally built and operated by sea captain Emile Commander, the beautiful Victorian building and lush gardens which comprise the restaurant have been, since 1969, the property and concern of Ella, Adelaide, Dick, and John Brennan. This famous foodservice family runs Commander's with their restaurant philosophy for all ages: "good food and fun."

Thus, the patrons who come to be enchanted by the area's historical beauty and the restaurant's superlative New Orleans' cuisine are also treated to warm-hearted hospitality.

Recalling the true story of a Northern waiter who resigned after three days on the job, Dick Brennan smiles the smile of New Orleans success. "He couldn't take it because the people were so friendly."

The Caribbean Room, Pontchartrain Hotel

Albert Aschaffenburg, president of the Pontchartrain Hotel, admits that concern is inevitable when a hotel annually generates $1 million in room revenue and $2 million in food and beverage sales.

"Our food is so well known," he laments, "people sometimes forget that we are a hotel."

Especially ironic is the fact that the Pontchartrain was opened in 1928 ("just in time for the crash," says Albert) as an apartment hotel and had no formal dining room until 1948. Lysle Aschaffenburg, co-founder-owner, and resident genius of the

Pontchartrain, created the Caribbean Room simply because he realized the need to accommodate the hotel's growing transient business.

After a difficult beginning, the restaurant found its key to success in featuring "the kind of cuisine New Orleans people would enjoy." That Creole/Continental cuisine, featuring fresh local seafood, prime meats, the hotel's own baked goods, and elegant attention, has earned the facility many of the world's top foodservice honors, as well as the undying affection of the people of New Orleans.

Even though the seating capacity of the restaurant has tripled while the relatively small kitchen has remained the same size, six special entrees are run every evening because, according to food and beverage manager John Mickelson, "so many of the same people eat here night after night."

T. Pittari's

Anyone who has had the pleasure of dining in New Orleans knows of the wonderful indigenous seafood. Oysters, shrimp, backfin lump crab, red snapper, flounder, and trout have a legitimate claim to being as fine here as anywhere in the world. Small wonder then that when Tom Pittari, Sr. told his wife that he was going to fly in Maine lobsters for their restaurant, she told him he was crazy.

One can only wonder how she felt when he added bear to the menu, or mountain lion or even, for a time, hippopotamus.

Yet Pittari has two good reasons for everything that is served in his 81-year-old establishment. First, each item provides a distinctive and enjoyable culinary experience for his customer. Second, according to the man who also heads his own advertising agency, the totality of a menu with dishes ranging from Long Island Duckling to Western Buffalo Steak proclaims the restaurant's desire to attract everyone at least once. Tom Sr. and his wife travel extensively to sample the best of American regional cuisines. If they like something, and can arrange to get it to New Orleans, then it has a good chance at being served at T. Pittari's.

"I've always tried something different from the competition," says Pittari. "Come to Pittari's 30 times, and you can have something different each time."

So it is that Pittari is a hard man to impress with something new. He does, however, recall one recent event with a fair amount of wonder. The week that New Orleans hosted the Super and Sugar Bowls, customers patiently waited three hours for a seat in the restaurant.

"Now that," he says, "was something."

New Orleans Creole/Continental Recipes

GRANDMA HOLDIN'S THREE-WAY COLD REMEDY

1 PINT ESSENCE OF TURPENTINE
1 PINCH CONCENTRATED MUSTARD
3 WINTERGREEN ROOTS
4 TABLESPOONS RED PEPPER
51 POWDERED RED ANTS
  GARLIC TO TASTE
  SIMMER 3 HOURS AND COOL.
  (a) RUB ON
  (b) DRINK
  (c) USE AS ENEMA

**1970
GOLD PLATE AWARD
AMERICANA ARCHIVES
THERAPEUTIC RESEARCH
Thos. Farley**

CHILI

Yield: 3 gallons

Ingredients

ONIONS, LARGE, chopped	3
GARLIC BUD, chopped	1
BELL PEPPER, chopped	1
SHORTENING	3 ounces
BEEF, GROUND (chili grind)	8 pounds
SALT	to taste
CHILI POWDER	4 tablespoons
TOMATO SAUCE	4 6-ounce cans
BLACK PEPPER	1 tablespoon
TOMATOES, CANNED, STEWED, sieved	1 quart
KIDNEY BEANS	1 No. 10 can

Procedure

1. Saute onions, garlic, and bell pepper in shortening. Add all other ingredients except kidney beans. Simmer 4 hours.

2. Add kidney beans. Heat through and serve.

**Minute Man of America, Inc.
Wesley T. Hall**

FAVORITE PEANUT SOUP

Yield: 25 portions

Ingredients

CELERY, cubed	2 cups
ONION, chopped	1/4 cup
GREEN PEPPER, chopped	1/4 cup
BOILING WATER	1 pint
FLOUR, all-purpose	1/4 cup
MILK, rich	3 quarts
PEANUT BUTTER	4 cups
SUGAR	4 teaspoons
SALT	to season
PEPPER	to season

Procedure

1. Simmer celery, onion, and green pepper in pint of boiling water 10 minutes. Drain, reserving the water.

2. Combine the flour with 1/4 cup of the cold milk. Stir to a smooth paste. Add to the remaining milk.

3. Combine milk and water in which vegetables were cooked.

4. Add vegetables, then the peanut butter and sugar. Season with salt and pepper. Blend peanut butter well into mixture.

5. Cook in steam-jacketed kettle or double boiler until mixture is well blended and thoroughly heated.

6. Serve garnished with chopped peanuts or chopped parsley.

Tuskegee Institute, Tuskegee, Ala.

SOUTHERN SEAFOOD GUMBO

Yield: 50 portions

Ingredients

OLIVE OIL	1/2 cup
ONION, minced	2-1/2 cups
CELERY, cubed fine	2 cups
GREEN PEPPER, chopped	1/2 cup
FLOUR, all-purpose	3/4 cup
TOMATOES, canned	2 cups
BROTH,	
BEEF or CHICKEN	1-3/4 gallons
PAPRIKA	dash
LIQUID HOT PEPPER	
SEASONING	1-1/4 ounces
PARSLEY	1/2 cup
WHOLE CLOVES	3
BAY LEAVES	3
THYME	dash
OKRA, frozen	5 pounds
GARLIC CLOVES, minced	1/4 cup
MONOSODIUM	
GLUTAMATE	1 tablespoon
SHRIMP, A.P., peeled	
and cooked	12 pounds
OYSTERS, raw	1 pint
CRABMEAT, canned,	
6-1/2 ounces	1
FILE POWDER	1 tablespoon

Procedure

1. Saute onion, celery and green pepper in a small amount of the olive oil.

2. Brown the flour in some of the olive oil.

3. Place sauteed vegetables and brown flour in steam-jacketed kettle.

4. Add tomatoes and broth, and blend well. Cook at simmering point 1-1/2 hours.

5. Add paprika, liquid hot pepper seasoning, parsley, whole cloves, bay leaves, and thyme.

6. Saute okra in the remaining olive oil.

7. Add minced garlic cloves and monosodium glutamate.

8. Cook 10 minutes.

9. Add okra, deveined shrimp, crabmeat, and oysters to the first mixture.

10. Simmer gently 1-1/2 hours. Add file powder.

11. Serve over fluffy rice.

Southeastern Louisiana College, Hammond, La.

SHRIMP BISQUE WITH FRENCH FRIED SHRIMP BALLS

Yield: 25 portions

Ingredients

1. SHORTENING	2 ounces
FLOUR	2 ounces
ONIONS, medium size	2
CELERY LEAVES	4
TOMATOES, canned	1 cup
SHRIMP STOCK	1-1/2 gallons
RICE, uncooked	8 ounces
SALT	to season
2. SHRIMP BALLS	
SHRIMP, E.P., boiled,	
shelled, deveined,	
ground fine	1 pound
BUTTER	2 ounces
SHALLOTS	1 bunch (small)
BREAD CRUMBS	1 cup
SHRIMP STOCK	1 cup

Procedure

1. Heat 2 ounces shortening in soup pot. Add flour and brown.

2. Add chopped onions and celery leaves. Cook 5 minutes or until all water is cooked out of vegetables, stirring well.

3. Add tomatoes and shrimp stock. Bring to a boil, stirring constantly. Add rice and simmer 1 hour.

4. Strain twice through a fine sieve. Taste for seasoning; save Shrimp Sauce.

5. Put cooked, deveined shrimp through fine grinder.

6. Saute shallots in butter until tender.

7. Remove saute pan from the direct heat. Add bread crumbs and ground shrimp meat. Blend well.

8. Add shrimp stock gradually. Cook over direct heat 5 minutes. Remove from saute pan and refrigerate.

9. When thoroughly chilled, roll shrimp mixture into balls the size of a marble.

10. Dust with flour. Fry in deep fat at 375°F. for 5 minutes.

11. To serve, place shrimp balls in individual soup bowls, and pour over the piping hot Shrimp Bisque. Serve immediately.

Pontchartrain Hotel, New Orleans

ROCK CORNISH GAME HEN FLAMBE

Yield: 1 portion

Ingredients

ROCK CORNISH GAME HEN	1
STUFFING	
BUTTER	4 tablespoons
CHICKEN LIVERS, chopped	4 ounces
GREEN PEPPER, chopped	1
SHALLOTS, chopped	3
OR	
CHIVES, SMALL BUNCH, chopped	1/2 bunch
GARLIC CLOVES, minced	2
WILD RICE, cooked	1 cup
PARSLEY SPRIGS, snipped	3
PIMIENTO, chopped fine	1/2
EGG	1
SALT	to season
PEPPER	to season
PATE DE FOIE GRAS	to garnish
RUM	to flame

Procedure

1. Prepare Cornish game hen. Wash and dry thoroughly.

2. Saute chicken livers, green pepper, and shallots or chives in butter. Add cooked wild rice, parsley and pimiento. Mix well.

3. Remove from heat and blend in egg. Season with salt and pepper. Stuff hen, cook in oven at 300°F. for 25 minutes. To serve, place a portion of pate de foie gras on opening by stuffing. Pour over rum and flame.

Arnaud's Restaurant, New Orleans

SHRIMP A LA CREOLE

Yield: 25 portions

Ingredients

ONION, diced	1 pound
CELERY, diced	1 pound
GREEN PEPPER, diced	1 pound
VEGETABLE SHORTENING	2 ounces
GARLIC CLOVES, minced	3
CANNED TOMATOES, NO. 10, solid pack	3-1/2 pounds
TOMATO PUREE	2 pounds
BAY LEAVES	6
WHOLE CLOVES	4
WHOLE ALLSPICE	4
SALT	to season
PEPPER	to season
RICE, long grained	2 pounds
SHRIMP, cooked, cleaned	3-1/4 pounds

Procedure

1. Cook onion, celery and green pepper in hot fat in skillet until onions are a delicate brown and vegetables are partially cooked.

2. Add minced garlic cloves, and cook slowly 5 minutes.

3. Add crushed tomatoes, tomato puree, and spices. Simmer slowly 30 minutes. In meantime, cook rice.

4. Add cooked shrimp to sauce; let simmer slowly 15 minutes.

5. Serve in preheated casserole with a mound of fluffy rice.

Pontchartrain Hotel, New Orleans

MIKE FINK'S MISSISSIPPI JAMBALAYA

Yield: 6 servings

Ingredients

SLICED BACON, cut 1-inch pieces	1/4 pound
CHOPPED ONION	1/2 cup
GREEN PEPPERS, MEDIUM-SIZED, seeded, cut 1-inch strips	2
RAW RICE (BLEACHED)	1 cup
GARLIC CLOVES, chopped	2
TOMATOES, WHOLE PACK, chopped	1 pound
THYME LEAVES	1/4 teaspoon
SALT	1 teaspoon
BLACK PEPPER	1/2 teaspoon
CHICKEN STOCK	2 cups
SMOKED HAM, cooked, cut 2-inch by 1/2-inch strips	1/2 pound
RAW SHRIMP, MEDIUM-SIZED, shelled, deveined	1 pound
CHOPPED FRESH PARSLEY	1 tablespoon
COOKED PEAS	3 ounces
MUSHROOMS, sliced	3 ounces

Procedure

1. Take a heavy skillet or pot large enough to hold 4 quarts. Fry bacon until brown but not crisp. Remove from the fat and retain.

2. Add the onion to the bacon fat and cook until glossy; add the cut green peppers. When green peppers are wilted and glossy, add the rice and fry until rice becomes glossy. Then add the garlic, tomatoes, bacon, thyme, salt, and pepper. Stir thoroughly. Add the chicken stock and ham strips. Bring to a boil. Cover pot and place it in oven at 350°F.

3. After mixture has cooked for 15 minutes, add the shrimp, pushing them into the rice mixture. Cook, covered, an additional 7 minutes, until rice is tender and has absorbed all of the cooking juice.

4. Saute the mushrooms.

5. Serve in a casserole garnished with freshly chopped parsley. If additional moisture is needed, add some chicken stock. Top with peas and sauteed mushrooms.

United Airlines Food Services Library

STUFFED BUFFALO ROAST

Yield: 1 4-pound roast

Ingredients

COOKING OIL	4 tablespoons
FINELY CHOPPED SHALLOTS	4 tablespoons
FINELY CHOPPED GARLIC	1 tablespoon
PARSLEY, finely chopped	1 bunch
WHITE ONION, SMALL, finely chopped	1
FRENCH BREAD, stale	1/2 loaf
BUFFALO MEAT, GROUND	3/4 pound
SALT	to taste
PEPPER	to taste
THYME	pinch
EGGS	2
BUFFALO ROUND	3 pounds

Procedure

1. In skillet, saute in oil, shallots, garlic, parsley, and white onion. When halfway cooked, add ground buffalo meat. Cook until meat is done.

2. Break bread into colander, wet, and knead.

3. Put cooked buffalo meat and seasonings in large pan. Mix with wet bread, then add raw eggs to bind.

4. Use meat maul to pat out buffalo round into a rectangle, 1/4 inch thick; add salt and pepper.

5. Spread buffalo dressing evenly over meat. Roll like jelly roll and tie with string. Saute in skillet until brown.

6. Put in baking pan and roast in oven at 350°F. for 30 to 40 minutes.

T. Pittari

SWEETBREADS CHASSEUR

"Veal sweetbreads are considered a great delicacy. They are more tender than lamb or beef sweetbreads, and are the highest priced. All sweetbreads should be precooked before being used in any way. Sweetbreads Chasseur is a favorite entree at The Pontchartrain."

Yield: 20 portions

Ingredients

VEAL SWEETBREADS	5 pounds
BACON, DICED	8 ounces
MUSHROOMS, FRESH, SLICED	1 pound
SHALLOTS, CUT FINE	1 bunch (small)
TOMATOES, MASHED	1 cup
BROWN SAUCE	1 pint
DRY SHERRY WINE	3 ounces
BRANDY	2 ounces

Procedure

1. Wash sweetbreads. Soak in cold water 20 minutes, if desired. Plunge into boiling water to which has been added 1/4 cup vinegar and 1-1/2 tablespoons salt. Simmer 25 minutes—do not boil. Drain.

2. Hold under cold water, and slip the thin membrane off with the fingers. With paring knife, remove fat and thick connective tissue. Split sweetbreads lengthwise in halves, if very thick.

3. Place sweetbreads in greased baked pan. Cook in a 400°F. oven until brown.

4. Saute bacon until crisp. Remove from pan.

5. Add mushrooms and shallots and saute in the bacon fat until tender, approximately 10 minutes.

6. Add tomatoes, brown sauce, dry sherry wine, bacon and sweetbreads. Simmer gently 20 minutes.

7. Remove from direct heat. Add brandy.

8. Serve at once. Sprinkle with snipped parsley, if desired.

Ponchartrain Hotel, New Orleans

EGGS HUSSARDE

Yield: 1 serving

Ingredients

HAM SLICES, grilled	2
RUSKS	2
MARCHAND DE VIN SAUCE (recipe below)	1/4 cup
EGGS, soft poached	2
HOLLANDAISE SAUCE	3/4 cup
PAPRIKA	to garnish

Procedure

1. Lay a slice of ham across each rusk and cover with Marchand de Vin Sauce.

2. Place eggs on rusks and top with hollandaise sauce. Garnish with sprinkling of paprika.

MARCHAND DE VIN SAUCE

Yield: 2 cups

Ingredients

BUTTER	3/4 cup
FINELY CHOPPED MUSHROOMS	1/3 cup
MINCED HAM	1/2 cup
FINELY CHOPPED SHALLOTS	1/3 cup
FINELY CHOPPED ONION	1/2 cup
MINCED GARLIC	2 tablespoons
FLOUR	2 tablespoons
SALT	1/2 teaspoon
BLACK PEPPER	1/8 teaspoon
CAYENNE PEPPER	dash
BEEF STOCK	3/4 cup
RED WINE	1/2 cup

Procedure

1. In a 9-inch skillet, melt butter, and lightly saute the mushrooms, ham, shallots, onion, and garlic.

2. When the onion is golden brown, add the flour, salt, pepper, and cayenne. Brown well, about 7 to 10 minutes.

3. Blend in the stock and the wine. Simmer over low heat for 35 to 45 minutes.

Commander's Palace

CRABMEAT REMICK

Yield: 6 servings

Ingredients

LUMP CRABMEAT	1 pound
BACON, crisp-cooked	6 strips
DRY MUSTARD	1 teaspoon (scant)
PAPRIKA	1/2 teaspoon
CELERY SALT	1/2 teaspoon
LIQUID HOT PEPPER SEASONING	1/2 teaspoon
CHILI SAUCE	1/2 cup
TARRAGON VINEGAR	1 teaspoon
MAYONNAISE	1-1/2 cups

Procedure

1. Divide crabmeat into 6 portions and pile into individual ramekins.
2. Heat in oven at 400°F.
3. Blend together mustard, paprika, celery salt, and liquid hot pepper seasoning. Add chili sauce and vinegar. Mix well. Blend with mayonnaise. Spread the warm crabmeat with this sauce.
4. Glaze under broiler.
5. Garnish with bacon strip.

Pontchartrain Hotel, New Orleans

CHICKEN CREOLE
FROM THE ENTERPRISE

Yield: 10 servings

Ingredients

ROASTING CHICKENS, 3-POUND	2
ONIONS, MEDIUM-SIZED, diced	2
GREEN PEPPER, LARGE, blanched, diced	1
MUSHROOMS, sliced	1 pound
TOMATOES, LARGE, diced	3
CHICKEN STOCK	1 pint
CORNSTARCH	1 tablespoon
SHERRY or WHITE WINE	1/2 cup

Procedure

1. Boil or roast the chicken until tender.
2. Remove meat from bones and cut into bite-sized pieces.
3. Place onions, green pepper, mushrooms, and tomatoes in a saucepan.
4. Add chicken and chicken stock and bring to a boil. Thicken with cornstarch diluted with wine. Season to taste.
5. Serve in casserole with Saffron Rice.

United Airlines Food Services Library

SWEET POTATO AND APPLE SOUFFLE

Yield: 50 portions

Ingredients

SWEET POTATOES, A.P.	25 pounds
SALT	1 teaspoon
GRANULATED SUGAR	3 pounds
BUTTER or MARGARINE	1 pound
MILK, SCALDED	1 quart
CINNAMON	1-1/2 teaspoons
NUTMEG	1-1/2 teaspoons
LEMON or ORANGE JUICE	1/2 cup
VANILLA EXTRACT	1 tablespoon
APPLES, RAW, DICED	5 only

Procedure

1. Steam potatoes in their jackets until tender but not soft. Peel and mash in power mixer with salt, sugar, butter and hot milk. Add seasonings and diced apples.
2. Place in a greased baking pan. Bake in oven at 350°F. for approximately 30 minutes.

Note

Orange juice may be substituted for the milk; the mixture placed in orange shells and baked. Garnish with miniature marshmallows and cook a few minutes longer—until marshmallows are delicately browned. Or garnish with pecans.

Southeastern Louisiana College, Hammond, La.

SHRIMP VENEZIANA

Yield: 6 servings

Ingredients

SHRIMP, cleaned, cooked, chilled	36
ITALIAN PARSLEY, finely chopped	1 cup
OLIVE OIL	1 cup
FRESH GARLIC, finely chopped	1 tablespoon
SALT	1 tablespoon
WHITE PEPPER	1 tablespoon

Procedure

1. Slit shrimp three-fourths of the way through the back with sharp knife. Place shrimp in deep mixing bowl; add salt and pepper, toss gently; add garlic, oil, and parsley. Mix thoroughly.
2. Marinate at room temperature for 30 minutes before serving.

The Como Inn

CANDIED SWEET POTATOES WITH ORANGE SLICES

Yield: 50 portions

Ingredients

SWEET POTATOES, A.P.	25 pounds
SYRUP	
BROWN SUGAR, LIGHT	2 pounds
GRANULATED SUGAR	1 pound
WATER	2 cups
BUTTER	1 cup
CINNAMON	1-1/2 teaspoons
NUTMEG	1-1/2 teaspoons
LEMON JUICE	1/4 cup
ORANGES, LARGE, WHOLE	3

Procedure

1. Wash and peel sweet potatoes. Cut in half lengthwise, or if large, in quarters. Steam until tender.

2. Boil syrup ingredients 10 minutes.

3. Arrange cooked sweet potatoes in greased baking pan.

4. Thinly slice unpeeled and washed oranges. Arrange slices on top of sweet potatoes in pan. Pour over hot syrup.

5. Bake in oven at 350°F. for 45 minutes.

6. Baste with syrup several times during the cooking until the potatoes are well glazed.

Southeastern Louisiana College, Hammond, La.

SHRIMP REMOULADE

Yield: 16 servings

Ingredients

TARRAGON VINEGAR	1/2 cup
TOMATO CATSUP	2 tablespoons
HORSERADISH MUSTARD (CREOLE)	4 tablespoons
PAPRIKA	1 tablespoon
SALT	1 teaspoon
CAYENNE PEPPER	1/2 teaspoon
SALAD OIL	1 cup
MINCED GREEN ONIONS, with TOPS	1/2 cup
MINCED CELERY	1/2 cup
SHRIMP, cooked, cleaned	4 pounds
LETTUCE, shredded	as needed

Procedure

1. In a small bowl combine vinegar, catsup, mustard, paprika, salt, and pepper. While beating this mixture, add oil gradually. Stir in green onions and celery. (If an electric blender is used, place all of the ingredients, except oil, in the blender and blend for 15 seconds. While blender is still in operation, tilt cover and add oil gradually.)

2. Pour sauce over shrimp and marinate in refrigerator for 4 to 5 hours.

3. For each serving, place 6 marinated shrimp on shredded lettuce.

Pontchartrain Hotel, New Orleans

CREOLE SHRIMP SALAD NEW ORLEANS

Yield: 12 portions

Ingredients

SHRIMP, cut in uniform pieces	1-1/4 quarts (1-1/2 pounds)
BOILED RICE, well drained	2-1/2 cups (5 oz. dry weight)
RAW CAULIFLOWER, diced	2-1/2 cups (1 medium head)
GREEN PEPPER, cut in thin slivers	3/4 cup
PIMIENTO, cut small	3/4 cup
SALT	1 tablespoon
PEPPER	1/4 teaspoon
MAYONNAISE	1/2 pint (approximately)
RIPE OLIVES, finely chopped	3 tablespoons
GREEN ONIONS, chopped	1/4 cup

Procedure

1. Combine cooked shrimp, rice, cauliflower, green pepper, and pimiento. Toss lightly. Add salt and pepper.

2. Add chopped olives to mayonnaise and add to salad. Avoid adding too much mayonnaise as the mixture will become soggy. Add only enough to hold mixture together.

3. Serve in lettuce cup. Garnish with ripe olive slices, a bunch of watercress, and two small green onions.

COLESLAW

Yield: approximately 50 servings

Ingredients

CABBAGE	6 heads (approx. 8 pounds total)
RADISHES	1 6-ounce package
CARROTS	2 (approx. 1/2 pound)
CHOPPED SWEET PICKLES	3 cups
VINEGAR	2 cups
MAYONNAISE	3 pints
SUGAR	2 cups
BLACK PEPPER	1 teaspoon
SALT	2 tablespoons

Procedure

1. Wash vegetables, chop, and refrigerate.

2. Combine dressing ingredients and add to vegetables one hour before serving.

Minute Man of America, Inc.
Wesley T. Hall

PINEAPPLE AND LOUISIANA YAMS FLAMBEE A LA GERMAINE

"Flaming desserts always intrigue our guests, and they are very popular in our restaurant."

Procedure

1. Use slices of canned pineapple and thick slices of boiled yams.

2. Roll yams and pineapple rings in flour, then dip in milk, and again roll in flour. Deep fat fry them until a golden brown.

3. Sprinkle generously with sugar. Place in oven at 350°F. for 5 minutes.

4. Arrange pineapple rings and yam slices on platter.

5. Place a maraschino cherry in the center of each pineapple ring.

6. Pour rum over all; light with a match, and serve immediately.

7. Add sherry, if desired.

APPLE PIE FLAMBEE A LA MAGDALENE

1. Place a small amount of rum in brulot bowl.

2. Add lump of sugar. Light with a match, and while flaming pour over Apple Pie a la Mode. Delicious eating!

Arnaud's Restaurant, New Orleans

SWEET POTATO CHIFFON PIE

Yield: 8 10-inch pies

Ingredients

SWEET POTATOES, boiled, peeled	3 pounds
SUGAR, granulated	3 pounds, 8 ounces
MILK	3 pints
CORNSTARCH	3 ounces
BUTTER	2 ounces
SALT	3/4 tablespoon
EGG WHITES	1 pint
VANILLA, pure	2 tablespoons
PIE SHELLS, baked	8 (only)

Procedure

1. Puree the sweet potatoes.
2. Dissolve the cornstarch in some of the cold milk.
3. Scald the rest of the milk with one-half the salt and three-quarters of the sugar. Add butter. Add pureed potatoes and bring to the boiling point.
4. Add cornstarch, stirring briskly with wire whip. Cook until mixture is thick, and all trace of raw starch has disappeared. Add vanilla.
5. Add remaining salt to egg whites, and beat to medium stiffness. Add remaining sugar gradually, and continue beating until mixture will form in peaks.
6. Fold hot cornstarch mixture carefully over egg whites. Do not overmix.
7. Fill pre-baked pie shells. When cool, place in refrigerator to chill. When chilled, filling is firm.
8. Serve with whipped cream or any suitable topping.

COFFEE WHIP WITH ALMONDS

Yield: 32 portions

Ingredients

GELATINE, UNFLAVORED	1 ounce
COLD WATER	1 cup
HOT WATER	1 pint
GRANULATED SUGAR	1 pound
MILK, hot	1 quart
INSTANT COFFEE	1/4 cup
HEAVY CREAM or EVAPORATED MILK, whipped	1 quart
VANILLA	1 tablespoon
SLICED ALMONDS, toasted	1/4 pound

Procedure

1. Soak gelatine in cold water for 5 minutes.
2. Add hot water and stir until gelatine is dissolved.
3. Melt the sugar in a heavy iron skillet over low heat. When it is medium brown remove from the heat and add hot milk.
4. Stir over low heat until sugar is all dissolved.
5. Add this mixture and the instant coffee to the gelatine.
6. Cool until the gelatine begins to congeal. Then whip until frothy and fold in whipped cream, vanilla, and toasted almonds.
7. Pile into serving dishes. Chill thoroughly before serving.

The Golden Land of Missions and Mobility

THE COLORFUL BEGINNINGS of California's foodservice/lodging occurred back in 1769. The famous Franciscan missionary, Father Junipero Serra, founded the first mission in San Diego.

His chain of inns, located just a day's journey apart, numbered 21 by 1823 when the last was built in Sonoma, just north of San Francisco. Serra's "multi-unit empire" stretched over 600 miles up the coast on a route still called El Camino Real. The missions often fed hundreds, or even thousands, of soldiers and Indians and accommodated traveling clergy or laymen overnight.

Each mission was a cluster of adobe buildings. It provided the padres with a place for prayer, a community-dining area, a kitchen where Indian women prepared food, and tiny cells for sleeping.

The central courtyard was planted with vegetables, fruits, herbs, and there California's first livestock was raised. It was the Spaniards who brought cattle, pigs, goats, and sheep to California via Mexico, together with the grapes that started America's wine industry.

Santa Barbara Mission
Santa Barbara

Continuing such traditions, the mission at Santa Barbara still operates, feeding and housing hundreds of persons each week. The old California kitchen pictured on the cover of this book was re-created at the Mission of Santa Barbara, one of California's oldest establishments still in operation.

An active religious community, the mission also maintains a museum displaying artifacts. Brother Mateo, curator, selected from the museum's collection authentic utensils from the mission's early days to show how one of the nation's first institutional kitchens operated. The mission traditions, together with techniques evolved from other early efforts at group feeding in other parts of the country, must be credited with providing the foundation for foodservice/lodging in America today.

St. Vincent's Medical Center
Los Angeles

By 1856 California's first health care facility, St. Vincent de Paul, was established in the pueblo of Los Angeles by six Sisters of

Charity—nuns who dedicated themselves to caring for the ill. Though it has been relocated and rebuilt four times, it has, without interruption, continued that task.

Today, St. Vincent's Medical Center, a nine-story 385-bed hospital, is one of the city's most advanced facilities, known particularly for open-heart surgery. Sister Michele, a poised, quiet little dynamo, presides over a foodservice department that feeds thousands of employees daily, focuses on pleasing patients, and runs varied catering activities for hundreds every month.

In her brand new facility, operating from a century-old tradition, Sister Michele exploits the most sophisticated kind of foodservice system: preparation cooking in a full-production kitchen, pre-plated foods, blast freezing, storage, holding, heating in convection ovens in patient floor galleys. She stresses excellence, economy, and education for patients on how to change eating habits to prevent recurring illness.

She gained her technical expertise primarily at Purdue University during a special course on convenience foods systems. To that she applied herself with particular zeal because her administrator had said, "If you get an 'A' in the course, we'll install whatever foods system you recommend."

University of Santa Clara
Santa Clara

All early California culture originated in the missions. The oldest school had its simple beginnings in 1777 when the Franciscan friars established the Santa Clara Mission and school just outside the state's first incorporated city, San Jose.

The school became a college when the Jesuits took over in 1851. By 1921 it had become a university.

The campus today is luxuriantly landscaped with an interesting mix of buildings. An 1822-vintage adobe that formed part of the first mission's granary (the only area in a mission that required a lock) still stands as an important element of the gardens.

The original church and mission buildings suffered from three fires. But an 1850s dormitory and classroom building is being remodeled as a residence/dining hall for the 64 Jesuits who teach on campus.

Foodservice is handled by Saga, under the direction of Ed Blair, a savvy manager who knows how to satisfy both clergy and students. An active, effective advisory committee meets each week to discuss menus and review problems. Such student interest helps Blair keep tuned in to student's attitudes.

"They're not so interested in theme parties and decorations; they care about the food," he observes. The most successful special dining events are simple hamburger cookouts or chicken barbecues held outdoors in the two-centuries-old gardens.

The university keeps in close touch with the community by catering civic, business, and social affairs. In spring and summer, the historic grounds around the Santa Clara Mission teem with activity every weekend, as seven or eight weddings take place. Receptions are catered by Saga or by the Faculty Club, a dining facility in the oldest structure on campus, part of the mission adobes.

Receptions are usually champagne buffets with hors d'eouvre and wedding cakes. Blair claims that consumption of the bubbly is not always so restrained as one might expect in such a sacred garden. He quips, "I wish I had the champagne in garden hoses so it would be easier to dispense!"

Influences from 200 years ago still affect the campus foodservice and maintenance departments. Most of those employees are Portuguese, who have remained in the same community adjacent to the Santa Clara Mission where they originally settled to be near their church or to Monterey's whaling industry. Portuguese traditions and language are everywhere apparent in the campus foodservice.

A. J. Bump's Saloon
Freeport

A close look at lesser-known places in California's tules (pronounced "too-lees"—bulrushes around the Sacramento River) reveals that fun, food, and history can mix well and make a popular restaurant. One booming reincarnation is A. J. Bump's Freeport Saloon, built in 1863 when the railroads connected with the river at the "free port."

The Saloon, general store and post office

was a rollicking headquarters for those who wanted goods—dry or "wet." But some straight-laced townsfolk disapproved of Mr. Bump's place, calling it a "festering moral canker in our midst."

Today, the joyful spot is owned by Terry Osmonson and Thomas MacMillan, two ambitious young men who restored the old building and developed an instantly successful steakhouse. Young and old, tourist and resident enjoy nostalgia, the finest meats, a super salad bar, and individual sourdough loaves.

Olvera Street
Los Angeles

Los Angeles offers many examples of the way California culture evolved from the traditions of service embodied in its missions. Los Angeles (the state's second city) was begun in the late 1700s by a little party of priests, Indian acolytes, and 11 families, who marched nine miles from the San Gabriel Mission. Its first thoroughfare was Olvera Street, today a festive, block-long market where Mexican foods are cooked to order in diverse operations—from taco stands to full-service restaurants, one of which is in Los Angeles' oldest brick house.

The 1849 Gold Rush offered fortunes to those who would cater to miners. Most who came to the Mother Lode country lived outdoors near the source of gold, eating sourdough bread or beef jerky.

Brown Derby
Los Angeles

Southern California boasts many old and famous (if not genuinely antique) restaurants. Memorable for its outrageous shape is the original Brown Derby.

It was 1926 when film star Gloria Swanson's husband, Herbert Somborn, and New York's Al Smith conceived the bizarre structure where hamburgers and blue-plate specials were sold. In 1929 the Derby was literally picked up and moved across the street to its present location on Wilshire Blvd. The Derby later added a coffee shop and, after Prohibition, a bar and lounge and a sidewalk cafe.

Bob Cobb was the popular maitre d' who invented the famous Cobb Salad. One day, one of his regular patrons said, "Fix me something easy to eat; I don't feel good today." Thus, the finely shredded, mild-flavored salad was born.

Two other Brown Derbys still prosper in the Los Angeles area, but they have split off from the original. That is still owned by Gloria Swanson's daughter and is now ably managed by veteran restaurateur Paul Sileo. He has renovated both front and back of the house and brought with him faithful associates who have helped restore the Derby.

San Francisco

But back in the boom towns and cities, such as San Francisco, the wealthy miners demanded the finest food and fancy accommodations. Such opulent landmarks as the Palace Hotel and the St. Francis in San Francisco offered fine French food to discriminating lumber and railroad barons as well as to nouveau riche miners. Also still operating in San Francisco are two great downtown dining establishments.

Tadich's Grill, the almost spartan lunch-counter seafood restaurant run by the Buich family, has been serving consistently good food for 119 years. It relies on devoted Yugoslavian immigrant employees.

Ritz Old Poodle Dog is as formal as Tadich's is informal. As its name implies, it is elegant, and formal, with high standards for its French cuisine. Established in 1849, the interior is so scrupulously groomed and timelessly decorated that it gives patrons a chance to relive champagne days.

A Variety of Ethnic Foods

Probably nowhere but in the tight microcosm of Manhattan can so many ethnic foods be found as in the diversified cuisine of this very large state—California.

Mexican foods brought by the padres were mixed with Spanish and Indian. French cuisine appeared after the Gold Rush when the wealthy imported their chefs, while Chinese cooks were brought in to feed railroad crews and mine workers. Sheepherders carried their native Basque dishes throughout the state. Armenians who settled in the central agricultural valleys contributed their specialties. Italians, originally connected with the

San Francisco fishing fleet, have kept their foods much in evidence. And Japanese, Korean, and Vietnamese dishes are gaining ground.

In the earliest days the padres and friendly Indians grew all the foods they needed—corn, the basic Indian staple, plus items the Spanish had first planted, such as lemons, oranges, black olives, grapes, avocados, chocolate. And the Franciscans were first to establish vast vineyards.

Creativity in Foodservice

More firsts and new trends in foodservice began in California than anywhere else in the nation. Among the concepts launched in the Golden State and still going strong: the drive-in—A&Ws began in 1919; the California coffee shop—Tiny Naylor's in the '30s, Norm's and Ship's in the '50s; do-it-yourself salad bar in the '40s; wine by the liter—Far West's Reuben's, '47; taco stands—Glen Bell's in '56; Polynesian themes—Don the Beachcomber and Trader Vic, '34.

And, of course, the original single beef entree concept, launched by Lawry's in '38. It was from this fertile spot on Los Angeles' Restaurant Row that the famous silver carts with built-in lights and heat originated (Lawrence Frank admitted copying them from a London restaurant, Simpson's), along with the salad bowl spinning on a bed of ice, mixed tableside, and served as an appetizer.

Another important trend developed in California: the restaurant as a "destination resort." By far the most successful and creative is the Ivy Award-winning Nut Tree Restaurant, started in 1921 as a highway stand halfway between San Francisco and Sacramento. Today it offers a unique dining experience in a totally controlled environment that satisfies gourmets, purist designers—and the general public.

Defying all the rules—poor location, no liquor, high prices—the restaurant complex is so beautifully run by the Power family with such intriguing additions—gift shop, toy store, train, coffee house, airport—that travelers stop in droves to enjoy and to spend. The Nut Tree has been copied in many ways, but none has matched its quality of food, service, and design excitement.

A few try. Pea Soup Anderson's in tiny Buellton has a gift shop, a children's zoo, and a booming business selling soup in supermarkets. Knott's Berry Farm was a jam and jelly maker that developed not just restaurants but an entire amusement park that continues to expand—playing a healthy second fiddle to Disneyland. Griswold's began as a superb restaurant in Claremont, added a smorgasbord, a motor lodge, and annexed an old Spanish-style schoolhouse for gift shops and restaurants—a miniature Ghirardelli Square.

It would be foolhardy to suggest that anyone could trace the first hamburger. But it is a fact that McDonald's was born in San Bernardino. The hot dog California leaves to Coney Island, fish 'n chips to jolly old England, but it still claims pie shops for its own, grateful to Marie Callendar's family for keeping that All-American dessert a superior delicacy!

California's agricultural riches make it the fruit, vegetable, and wine hamper of the nation. And its zestful spirit of innovation, combined with commitment to service, have made it a fountainhead of foodservice ideas.

California Recipes

TARANTINO'S CONEY ISLAND CLAM CHOWDER

Yield: 25 portions

Ingredients

CLAM MEAT, FRESH	
OR	
CANNED CLAMS	2 pounds
WATER	1 gallon
SALT	1 teaspoon
BUTTER	4 tablespoons
ONIONS, WHITE,	
chopped 1/4-inch	2
ONIONS, GREEN,	
chopped 1/4-inch	3
GREEN PEPPER, chopped	1
CELERY, chopped	8 ounces
FLOUR, all-purpose	1 cup
TOMATOES, canned, No. 10	1
POTATOES, E.P., diced 1/4-inch	2 pounds
THYME	a pinch
ROSEMARY	a pinch
SALT	to season
PEPPER	to season

Procedure

1. If fresh clams are used, wash, steam until shells open, and drain. Save clam liquor. Shuck clams. (There should be 2 pounds clam meat.) Chop clam meat and put in a 2-gallon kettle with 1 gallon water and 1 teaspoon salt.

2. Simmer until clams are tender. Drain and save stock.

3. In a separate pan, saute onions, pepper, and celery in the butter until tender. Do not brown.

4. Add flour to make a stiff roux. Cook 5 minutes.

5. Combine roux, clam broth and clam stock, chopped clams, tomatoes, raw potatoes, thyme and rosemary.

6. Season with salt and pepper.

7. Cook for 20 minutes, or until potatoes are tender.

8. Taste for seasoning. Serve piping hot.

Tarantino's, Fisherman's Wharf, San Francisco

SOUPE DE LAITUE, CAMEMBERT

Yield: about 3 gallons or 48 servings

Ingredients

BUTTER	1-1/2 pounds
FLOUR	12 ounces
CHICKEN BROTH, hot	3 gallons
ICEBERG LETTUCE,	
coarsely chopped	3 pounds
CELERY, sliced or diced	1-1/2 pounds
WATERCRESS, stemmed,	
chopped	1-1/2 bunches
SALT	to taste
PEPPER	to taste

Procedure

1. Melt butter; blend in flour. Cook over low heat about 5 minutes.

2. Blend into broth; cook and stir over low heat until thickened. Add lettuce, celery, and watercress. The soup may be served as soon as the vegetables are crisp-tender. Season to taste.

Western Iceberg Lettuce, Inc.

STUFFING FOR THE GOOSE

Yield: For one 10- to 14-pound goose

Ingredients

CHESTNUTS, A.P.	1-1/2 pounds
ONION, minced	1-1/2 cups
APPLES, diced	6 cups
GOOSE or CHICKEN LIVERS,	
chopped	8 ounces
BUTTER	1/2 cup
SALT	1 teaspoon
PEPPER	1/2 teaspoon
THYME	1/4 teaspoon
MARJORAM	1/4 teaspoon

Procedure

1. Peel chestnuts and simmer in veal or chicken stock until soft.

2. Saute in butter the onion, diced apples, chopped livers and chopped chestnuts.

3. Add seasonings and blend well.

Grison's, San Francisco, California

One of New Orleans' great dining traditions, Antoine's, was started in 1840 by Antoine Alciatore, newly arrived from Marseilles. Roy Gust, Jr., a member of the fifth generation of direct descendants of the original Alciatore, here raises a glass in memory of his great-uncle, Roy Alciatore, Sr., shown in portrait above in Antoine's Capitol Room.

NEW ORLEANS

Below: The flavor of New Orleans is captured in this scene showing street purveyors selling the prize fruits and vegetables that account in considerable part for the uniformly high quality food available in the city's restaurants.

Above: A menu that offers constant changes from familiar New Orleans foods keeps patronage high at T. Pittari's. One unexpected item on the 81-year-old establishment's menu is The Wild Game Skillet, featuring elk, venison, bear, and buffalo with corn bread. Buffalo steaks are another customer favorite.

Right: Commander's Palace, latest New Orleans restaurant site of the Brennan family, was selected because it made possible "the kind of restaurant we've always wanted to run."

Above Center: Creole sea-food gumbo as combined with the wizardry of the Commander's Palace staff results in a soup with sensory sorcery that's also colorful. See the closeup, left above.

Above: Dick Brennan surveys luncheon fare in the garden patio at Commander's Palace.

The view of the luxuriant inner court is enjoyed from guest rooms and restaurants alike at The Royal Sonesta Hotel. The Bourbon Street hostelry has several restaurants so dining choices can vary.

CALIFORNIA

Above: California food runs the gamut from delicately flavored fruit combinations to such protein rich dishes as Ranch Style Limas. The kettle full of beans and tomatoes is spiced with chili, garlic powder, and cayenne, sweetened with brown sugar and topped with bacon, then baked for two hours to assure a complete melding of flavors.

Right: Tamale Pie, made with corn meal, corn, tomatoes, black olives, and finely chopped beef is a classic dating from two centuries ago. The original recipe is still enjoyed by the brothers of the Santa Barbara Mission and visitors who come there for meals.

STEAK AND MUSHROOM PIE

Yield: 75 pies

Ingredients

BEEF, 1-inch squares	20 pounds
BROWN GRAVY (see below)	4 gallons
MUSHROOMS, 1/2 to 3/4-inch diameter	5 pounds (300 pieces)
WATER	1 gallon
VEGETABLE WHITENER	1 tablespoon
BUTTER, clarified	8 ounces
SHERRY	1/2 cup
PEARL ONIONS, FROZEN	5 pounds
CARROTS, 1-1/2-inch by 1/2-inch strips	5 pounds
PASTRY CIRCLES	75

Procedure

1. Braise beef until tender; add prepared Brown Gravy to beef.
2. Soak mushrooms for 1 minute in water to which vegetable whitener has been added. Drain.
3. Saute mushrooms in butter; add sherry.
4. Thaw pearl onions.
5. Steam carrots for 5 minutes in steam cabinet.

Note

See next column for instructions for assembling 1 Steak and Mushroom Pie.

Lawry's Associated Restaurants

BROWN GRAVY

Yield: 1/2 gallon

Ingredients

LAWRY'S BROWN GRAVY MIX	8 ounces
WATER	1/2 gallon
BURGUNDY	6 ounces
BUTTER, DRAWN	3 ounces

Procedure

1. Blend gravy mix and water together.
2. Bring to a boil. Simmer for 5 minutes.
3. Add wine and butter; blend thoroughly.
4. Serve hot.

Lawry's Associated Restaurants

PASTRY FOR STEAK AND MUSHROOM PIE

Yield: 38 pounds

Ingredients

ALL-PURPOSE SHORTENING	5 pounds
MARGARINE	5 pounds
FROZEN PUFF PASTRY DOUGH	2 pounds
BREAD FLOUR	8 pounds
PASTRY FLOUR	2 pounds
BREAD FLOUR	2 pounds
PASTRY FLOUR	2 pounds
ICE WATER	5 pounds, 10 ounces
SALT	9 ounces

Procedure

1. Combine first five ingredients and mix until barely blended (lumpy but no free flour present).
2. Mix last four ingredients well.
3. Combine two mixtures and mix until slurry is taken up.
4. Roll out and cut into 6-inch circles.

Lawry's Associated Restaurants

TO ASSEMBLE A STEAK AND MUSHROOM PIE

Yield: 1 serving

Ingredients

COOKED BEEF	3 to 4 ounces (9 to 10 pieces)
CARROTS	1 ounce (4 pieces)
MUSHROOMS, SMALL	1 ounce (4 pieces)
PEARL ONIONS	1 ounce (4 pieces)
BROWN GRAVY	9 ounces
PASTRY CIRCLE	1

Procedure

1. Place all ingredients except crust in 6-1/2-inch by 5-inch by 1-1/2-inch oval casserole.
2. Top casserole with crust.
3. Start pies in oven at 500°F. When crust begins to brown, reduce heat to 400°F. Bake for a total of 30 minutes.

Lawry's Associated Restaurants

TOAD-IN-THE-HOLE

Yield: 1 portion

Ingredients

DRAWN BUTTER	1/2 fluid ounce
YORKSHIRE PUDDING BATTER	4 fluid ounces
DRAWN BUTTER	1 fluid ounce
FILET MIGNON, thinly sliced	4 ounces
SALT	1/2 teaspoon
VEGETABLES*	3-1/2 to 4 fluid ounces
BROWN GRAVY (recipe, p. 157)	1 fluid ounce

*Mixture of 1 part chopped green pepper, 3 parts chopped onion, and 3 parts sliced mushrooms, sauteed together in butter.

Procedure

1. Heat yorkshire pan in oven at 500°F.
2. Pour 1/2 fluid ounce butter and Yorkshire Pudding batter into hot pan.
3. Bake in oven at 500°F. for 15 minutes.
4. Saute filet in 1 fluid ounce butter; season with salt.
5. Remove Yorkshire Pudding from oven; fill with sauteed filet and vegetables.
6. Return to oven at 500°F. for 5 minutes.
7. Product may be held at 200°F. with oven door ajar for up to 30 minutes.
8. Pour gravy over beef before service.

Lawry's Associated Restaurants

ADOBO OF LAMB

Yield: 24 servings

Ingredients

LAMB SHOULDER, BONELESS, cut in 1-inch cubes	8 pounds
THYME	1 teaspoon
OREGANO	1 teaspoon
BAY LEAVES	3
MINCED PARSLEY	1 cup
SALT	3 tablespoons
PEPPER, freshly ground	1 teaspoon
ONION, chopped	2 pounds
GARLIC CLOVES, minced	6
WATER	as needed to cover meat
ANCHO CHILES, DRIED	18
MULATO CHILES, DRIED	9
WATER, cold	as needed
WATER, hot	1 quart
TOMATOES, peeled, seeded, chopped	1-1/2 pounds
SUGAR	1 tablespoon
VINEGAR, DISTILLED	3 tablespoons
SALAD OIL	1/3 cup

Procedure

1. In a saucepot, place the lamb, thyme, oregano, bay leaves, parsley, salt, and pepper. Add half the onion and half the garlic. Cover with water and cook about 1 hour or until the lamb is tender. Drain, saving stock. Return meat to pot.
2. Meanwhile, wash chiles in cold water; remove stems and membranes. Tear chiles into pieces; cover with hot water and soak for one hour.
3. Puree undrained chiles in blender with remaining onion and garlic, tomatoes, sugar, vinegar, and 1-1/2 cups reserved stock.
4. Heat oil in skillet; "fry" puree in oil about 5 minutes.
5. If necessary, thin sauce with extra stock. However, the finished dish should be quite thick.
6. Pour sauce over lamb; cook over low heat about 30 minutes. If desired, garnish with onion rings and cilantro (Mexican parsley).

American Lamb Council

LAMB PIE

Yield: 35 portions

Ingredients

LAMB, SHOULDER AND NECK, boned, trimmed, cut in 2-inch pieces	12 pounds
TOMATO PASTE, canned	1 ounce
ONIONS, large, sliced	6
POTATOES, medium, sliced thin	12
CARROTS, cut in 2-inch pieces, canned or fresh	6
PEAS, canned	2 pounds
CUT GREEN BEANS, canned	2 pounds
FLOUR	5 tablespoons
CARAWAY SEED	1 teaspoon
PEPPER	to season
SALT	to season
CHEESE, nippy, grated	8 ounces

Procedure

1. Dredge lamb pieces with seasoned flour and saute until a golden brown. Add sliced onions and tomato paste and cook 5 minutes.

2. Add water to cover meat, and simmer gently until meat is tender.

3. Cook fresh carrots in a small amount of water, and add with liquid to meat mixture. (Canned carrots are added without any previous cooking.)

4. Add peas and green beans. Season to taste. Add caraway seed.

5. Fill individual greased casserole dishes. Cover with a thick layer of thinly-sliced potatoes. Sprinkle top with grated cheese.

6. Bake in oven at 300°F. until potatoes are soft and tender.

College of the Pacific, Stockton, Calif.

ROASTED BEEF HASH

Yield: approx. 35 pounds (93 6-oz. servings)

Ingredients

LEFTOVER ROAST BEEF, diced 1/4 inch	15 pounds
CORNED BEEF, diced 1/4 inch	5 pounds
COOKED POTATOES, diced 1/4 inch	8 pounds
ONION, diced 1/4 inch sauteed	8 pounds
BROWN GRAVY	3 quarts
WORCESTERSHIRE SAUCE	2 tablespoons
LIQUID HOT PEPPER SEASONING	1/4 teaspoon
SEASONED SALT	as needed
SEASONED PEPPER	as needed

Procedure

1. Brown all beef in oven at 500°F.

2. Reduce oven temperature to 300°F. when beef is browned.

3. Add potatoes, sauteed onion, brown gravy, worcestershire sauce, and liquid hot pepper seasoning.

4. Heat thoroughly, about 20 minutes.

5. Taste hash; add seasoned salt and seasoned pepper if necessary.

6. Cook 40 minutes longer in oven.

7. Place pan on serving counter.

8. When hash is ordered, brown 6 ounces on both sides in *very hot* skillet.

9. Serve with one fried egg on top of hash and 1/2 ounce Brown Gravy* along edge of mound of hash closest to the rim of the plate. Serve with 3 ounces cooked vegetables.

*Prepare 1 gallon of Brown Gravy mix according to package directions. Add 12 ounces Burgundy and 6 ounces drawn butter; blend well. Serve hot.

Lawry's Associated Restaurants

WESTERN PORK STEW

Yield: 24 or 72 servings, 6 ounces stew; 3 ounces potatoes

Ingredients	24 Servings	72 Servings
BOSTON BUTT, 1-inch cubes	5 pounds	15 pounds
CATSUP	1-1/2 cups	4-1/2 cups
BROWN SUGAR	2 ounces	6 ounces
CIDER VINEGAR	1/2 cup	1-1/2 cups
BLACK PEPPER	1/2 teaspoon	1-1/2 teaspoons
SALT	1 teaspoon	1 tablespoon
WORCESTERSHIRE SAUCE	2 tablespoons	6 tablespoons
CHILI POWDER	1 teaspoon	1 tablespoon
PREPARED MUSTARD	1 tablespoon	3 tablespoons
GARLIC GRANULES	1 teaspoon	1 tablespoon
GROUND CLOVES	1/2 teaspoon	1-1/2 teaspoons
WATER	3 cups	9 cups
FLOUR	1 ounce	3 ounces
CORNSTARCH	1 ounce	3 ounces
WATER	1/2 cup	1-1/2 cups
CARROTS, 1-1/2-inch chunks	1 pound	3 pounds
KIDNEY BEANS, CANNED, drained	2 pounds	6 pounds
ONIONS, CANNED BOILED, drained	1 pound	3 pounds
GREEN PEAS	3 ounces	9 ounces
RANCH STYLE POTATOES	4 pounds	12 pounds

Procedure

1. Place pork cubes in braising pan. Mix spices and liquids (next 10 ingredients) together and pour over pork. Cover pan and bake, covered, in oven at 375°F. for 1-1/2 hours or until pork is tender.

2. Mix water, flour, and cornstarch together. Add to cooked pork mixture and cook 5 minutes more.

3. Cook carrot chunks in salted water. Drain.

4. Add carrots, kidney beans, and small boiled onions to meat mixture. Place in deep steam table pan. Garnish with green peas.

5. Fry Ranch Style Potatoes. Place in deep steam table pan.

6. Serve stew on plate with potatoes next to stew.

Note

There should be 3-1/3 ounces of meat in each portion.

Mannings

VEAL BIRDS

Yield: 10 servings

Ingredients

DRY BREAD, cubed	10 ounces
PEPPER	1/8 teaspoon
POULTRY SEASONING	3/8 teaspoon
SALT	1/4 teaspoon
CHOPPED GREEN ONION	1/2 ounce
CHICKEN STOCK	1 cup
VEAL CUTLETS, cut 3 to 1 pound, approximately 1/2 inch thick	10
FLOUR	1/3 (plus) cup
SALT	1 teaspoon
PEPPER	pinch
CHICKEN STOCK	2-3/4 cups
FLOUR	3 tablespoons

Procedure

1. Combine bread and next 5 ingredients to make a moist, soft dressing.

2. Spread 2 ounces dressing on each cutlet. Roll and secure with a toothpick.

3. Season 1/3 cup flour with the salt and pepper. Roll birds in flour. Brown in hot fat and place in roasting pan. Pour remaining drippings over birds.

4. Add 2 cups of the chicken stock and bake, covered, in oven at 300°F. until tender, approximately 1 hour.

5. Remove from baking pan and make gravy from residue in pan by adding 3 tablespoons flour, cooking slowly to make a roux or paste. Add chicken stock (about 3/4 cup) and cook to make thin gravy. Pour over birds at time of service.

Michael Reese Medical Center

BROCCOLI PRONTO PIE

Yield: 24 servings

Ingredients

BROCCOLI, CHOPPED, FROZEN	2-1/2 pounds
BEEF, GROUND	4 pounds
ONION, chopped	12 ounces (2 cups)
TOMATOES	4 pounds (2/3 No. 10 can)
GREEN CHILIES	12 ounces
GARLIC SALT	3/4 ounce (1-1/2 tablespoons)
PEPPER	1/2 teaspoon
CORN CHIPS, SMALL	2-1/2 pounds
CHEESE, AMERICAN, shredded	1 pound (1 quart)

Procedure

1. Thaw broccoli; drain well.

2. Cook beef until it loses its color; drain off excess fat.

3. Add onion to beef; cook until limp. Add tomatoes, chilies, garlic salt, and pepper. Simmer 15 to 20 minutes.

4. Spread 1/3 of the corn chips in greased pan (20-inch by 12-inch by 2-1/2-inch); crush remaining chips. Add 1/2 crushed chips and the cheese to the meat mixture.

5. Spread 1/2 meat mixture in pan over chips; top with broccoli then remaining meat mixture and remaining crushed chips.

6. Bake in oven at 350°F. for about 1-1/4 hours. Let stand about 15 minutes before cutting 6 by 4.

California Frozen Vegetable Council

HALIBUT FLORENTINE IN CASSEROLE

Yield: 1 casserole (use 10-inch Welsh Rarebit dish)

Ingredients

HALIBUT STEAK	6 to 8 ounces
OR	
HALIBUT FILLET	5 to 6 ounces
WATER, hot	1/2 cup
LEMON JUICE	4 tablespoons
WHITE WINE	1 ounce
CREAM SAUCE, heavy, hot	1/4 cup
SPINACH	2 ounces
GREEN ONION, chopped	1 (1 tablespoon)
EGG YOLK	1
CHEESE, nippy, grated	1 ounce
SALT	to season
PEPPER	to season

Procedure

1. Place halibut in shallow casserole or saucepan. Add water and lemon juice.

2. Simmer gently 5 minutes. Add white wine. Simmer 2 minutes longer or until flavors are blended. (The simmering should reduce the liquid to about two-thirds its volume.)

3. Remove halibut from heat. Drain off the stock.

4. Combine stock with the heavy cream sauce; stir until thoroughly smooth.

5. Add chopped spinach and onion. Season with salt and pepper.

6. Bring sauce to boiling point. Remove from heat.

7. Pour some of the hot sauce over the beaten egg yolk. Combine with rest of sauce. (This is now Sauce Florentine.)

8. Pour Florentine Sauce over halibut. Sprinkle with grated cheese.

9. Bake in oven at 375°F. until cheese is melted and sauce is bubbly.

10. Serve hot in dish in which it has been cooked.

Tarantino's, Fisherman's Wharf, San Francisco

CRAB FLAKES AU GRATIN

Yield: 16 portions

Ingredients

BUTTER	1 cup
FLOUR	1/2 cup
MILK	1 quart
CREAM	2 quarts
SALT	2 teaspoons
CRAB FLAKES	3 pounds
SHERRY	8 ounces
CAYENNE PEPPER	few grains
PARMESAN CHEESE	4 ounces
BUTTER, melted	3 ounces

Procedure

1. Melt butter, add flour, and stir until a golden brown.

2. Add hot milk gradually and blend well. Add hot cream, and stir well.

3. Simmer gently 10 minutes, stirring constantly. Add sherry.

4. Add crab flakes and seasonings. Simmer gently 2 minutes.

5. Place mixture in greased individual casserole dishes.

6. Place 1-1/4 tablespoons grated parmesan cheese on top of each casserole. Drip melted butter over top.

7. Bake in oven at 350°F. until cheese is melted and sauce is bubbly—approximately 15 to 20 minutes.

Note

The Mission Inn suggests that chef's salad, grapefruit and avocado, or Princess Salad (torn lettuce, asparagus tips and pimiento with french dressing) be served with this casserole.

The Mission Inn, Riverside, Calif.

RIPE OLIVE TAMALE CASSEROLE

Yield: 100 portions

Ingredients

BEEF, GROUND, LEAN	14 pounds
COOKING OIL	1 pint
ONION, chopped	7-1/2 pounds
WHOLE KERNEL CORN	2 No. 10 cans
CORN MEAL	2 quarts
TOMATOES	2 No. 10 cans
SALT	1/3 cup
CHILI POWDER	1/3 cup
CANNED GREEN CHILES, diced (optional)	2 cups
DICED GREEN PEPPER (optional)	1 quart
CANNED PITTED CALIFORNIA RIPE OLIVES, drained	3 quarts
CHEESE, AMERICAN, shredded	2 quarts

Procedure

1. Brown beef in hot oil. Add onion; cook until wilted.

2. Combine liquid drained from corn with corn meal, tomatoes, salt, and chili powder. Simmer 10 minutes, stirring frequently. Add drained corn, meat mixture, and olives; add chiles and green pepper, if desired.

3. Pour into 4 baking pans (12-inch by 20-inch by 2-inch).

4. Bake in oven at 350°F. for 15 minutes.

5. Sprinkle with cheese; bake 15 minutes longer.

PRE-PREPARATION OF SPINACH FOR CREAMED SPINACH

Yield: for 6 gallons of creamed spinach

Ingredients

LEAF SPINACH, FROZEN	1 case (36 pounds)

Procedure

1. Thaw frozen spinach

2. Squeeze thawed spinach in a mop wringer lined with cheesecloth.

3. Grind spinach once, using fine blade on grinder.

4. Proceed with recipe for Creamed Spinach (recipe, next column).

Lawry's Associated Restaurants

CREAMED SPINACH

Yield: Approximately 6 gallons

Ingredients

SPINACH BASE (recipe below)	1 gallon
FLOUR	2 pounds
MILK	2 gallons
TABLE CREAM	2 quarts
SPINACH, GROUND	19 pounds

Procedure

1. Heat Spinach Base.

2. Add flour gradually; mix well. Cook 10 minutes.

3. Add milk and cream; mix thoroughly. Bring to a boil.

4. Add spinach; mix thoroughly. Heat thoroughly, about 20 minutes.

5. To serve, place 3 to 4 fluid ounces on dinner plate with roast prime rib of beef.

SPINACH BASE

Yield: 2-1/8 gallons

Ingredients

BACON ENDS, finely ground	5-1/4 pounds
GREEN ONIONS, finely ground	4-3/4 pounds
ONION, finely ground	10 pounds
GARLIC PUREE	2 teaspoons
SALT	1-1/4 cups
BLACK PEPPER, finely ground	1 tablespoon
MONOSODIUM GLUTAMATE	2-1/2 tablespoons
BUTTER, drawn	1-3/4 pounds

Procedure

1. Brown bacon until crisp.

2. Add green onions, dry onion, garlic puree, salt, pepper, and monosodium glutamate to bacon. Cook until vegetables are done.

3. Add butter and heat thoroughly.

Lawry's Associated Restaurants

RANCH STYLE LIMAS

Yield: 48 servings

Ingredients

FORDHOOK LIMA BEANS	10 pounds
TOMATOES	2 No. 10 cans
ONION, chopped	1-1/2 pounds
BROWN SUGAR, packed	2 cups
CHILI POWDER	3 tablespoons
SALT	2-1/2 tablespoons
GARLIC POWDER	1-1/3 tablespoons
CAYENNE PEPPER	2 teaspoons
PEPPER	1 teaspoon
BACON, sliced, halved	2 pounds

Procedure

In each of two baking pans (20-inch by 12-inch by 2-1/2-inch) combine half the limas, tomatoes, onion, brown sugar, chili powder, salt, garlic powder, cayenne, and pepper; mix well. Top with bacon. Bake in oven at 350°F. for about 2 hours.

HOBO BREAD

Yield: 3 loaves

Ingredients

RAISINS	2 cups
WATER, boiling	2-1/2 cups
BAKING SODA	4 teaspoons
BROWN SUGAR, packed	3/4 cup
GRANULATED SUGAR	1 cup
SALT	1/2 teaspoon
OIL	4 teaspoons
FLOUR	4 cups

Procedure

1. In the evening, put raisins, water, and baking soda in a bowl and cover.

2. The next morning, add the brown sugar, granulated sugar, salt, oil, and flour. Mix well.

3. Grease and flour 3 1-pound coffee cans. Fill cans half full of batter. Bake in oven at 350°F. for 1 hour. Let cool 15 minutes before removing from cans.

California Raisin Advisory Board

LIMA BEAN BREAD

Yield: 4 loaves, 1-1/2-pounds each

Ingredients

FORDHOOK LIMA BEANS, FROZEN	1-1/4 pounds
WATER	1 pint
NONFAT DRY MILK	1 cup
ALL-PURPOSE FLOUR	2 quarts
BAKING POWDER	2-1/2 tablespoons
SALT	1-1/2 tablespoons
BAKING SODA	1 teaspoon
GROUND CINNAMON	2 teaspoons
SHORTENING	1 cup
SUGAR	2 cups
EGGS	1-2/3 cups (8 large)
CARAWAY SEEDS	2 tablespoons
TOASTED SUNFLOWER SEEDS (optional)	1/2 cup

Procedure

1. Cook lima beans in water until soft, about 10 minutes. Drain, reserving liquid. Measure liquid, and restore volume to 1 pint. Place the beans and liquid in a blender jar and blend smooth. Add nonfat dry milk and blend 30 seconds. Turn out and cool.

2. Sift flour with baking powder, salt, soda, and cinnamon.

3. Cream shortening and sugar with paddle for 2 minutes at No. 2 speed. Add eggs and continue creaming 2 minutes more.

4. Using No. 1 speed, blend in flour mixture alternately with lima bean puree. Mix in caraway seeds (and sunflower seeds, if desired). Scale 1 pound 10 ounces per loaf into four greased pans (8-1/2-inch by 4-1/2-inch by 3-inch). Level dough in pan. Bake in oven at 325°F. for approximately 1 hour and 15 minutes.

California Frozen Vegetable Council

FRESH FRUIT MOUNTAIN

Yield: 50 portions

Ingredients

AVOCADOS	8
PINEAPPLES	4
APPLES	4 pounds
ORANGES	12
PEARS	12
BANANAS	10
STRAWBERRIES	2 quarts
SUGAR	2 cups
WATER	1 cup
FRESH ORANGE JUICE	1 cup
FRESH LEMON JUICE	2 tablespoons
WHOLE CINNAMON STICK	1/4 inch
RUM or BRANDY	1 cup
RUM or APPLEJACK	2 26-ounce bottles

Procedure

1. To prepare ice mold, invert a shot glass or 1/2 egg shell in bottom of mold. Cover with finely shaved ice, packing tightly, and freeze. To remove, wipe outside of mold with cloth wrung out in very hot water. Place serving plate on top and turn out.

2. To prepare fruit, cut avocados, pineapples, apples, and oranges into dice. Slice bananas and strawberries. Cut in large dice. Dip pears, apples, and bananas in lemon juice to avoid discoloration.

3. To prepare marinade, combine next 5 ingredients in saucepan and cook slowly 5 minutes. Cool and add rum or brandy. Marinate fruit in sauce 5 minutes before serving. Drain.

4. To serve, place toothpicks in fruit and stick into ice mold to form a colorful display. When ready to serve, pour rum or applejack in glass or eggshell in center of ice mold and ignite. Serve immediately.

AMBROSIA FRUIT SALAD

Yield: 25 portions

Ingredients

ORANGES, 150's	12
PINEAPPLE TIDBITS, FRESH or CANNED	1 pound
SHREDDED COCONUT	1 pound
SOUR CREAM	3 cups

Procedure

1. Peel and section oranges.

2. Prepare fresh pineapple—peel, core, and cut in cubes—or drain canned pineapple. Combine all ingredients, blend well.

3. Serve on lettuce leaf or endive liners.

4. Garnish with toasted coconut, chopped nut meats, or angelica strips.

CABBAGE SALAD

Yield: 36 servings

Ingredients

CABBAGE, shredded	4-1/2 pounds, E.P.
SALT	2-1/2 tablespoons
SUGAR, granulated	3 tablespoons
MIXED DRESSING*	1 quart (2 pounds, 2-2/3 ounces)

Procedure

1. Have ingredients in readiness. Mix in relays during serving. It is better not to mix too much at one time.

*MIXED DRESSING

Yield: 3 quarts (6 pounds, 8 ounces)

Ingredients

COOKED DRESSING	2 quarts
MAYONNAISE	1 quart

TROPICAL FRUIT SALAD

Yield: 1 entree salad

Ingredients

FRESH PINEAPPLE	1/2
LARGE LETTUCE CUP,	
paprika-tinted edges	1 (only)
ORANGE SLICES	3 (approx.
	1/2 orange)
BANANA, sliced	1/2
GRAPEFRUIT SECTIONS	6 (only)
DATES	2 (only)
PRUNES STUFFED WITH	
CREAM CHEESE	2 (only)
CREAM CHEESE, softened	3 ounces
NUT BREAD SANDWICHES	
cut in semi-circles	2 (only)

Procedures

1. Wash pineapple. Do not remove fronds.
2. Cut pineapple in half lengthwise, cutting through fronds.
3. Cut out core and discard. Remove pulp from each half by cutting around the edge with sharp knife. Leave a clean shell.
4. Dice fruit into large pieces.
5. Place pineapple shell on 10-1/2 inch plate in a large lettuce cup which covers most of the plate.
6. Refill shell with diced pineapple, sliced banana, and grapefruit sections.
7. Arrange orange slices on right side of shell near edge of lettuce cup.
8. Place stuffed prunes on left side of shell.
9. Place dates at bottom of pineapple shell.
10. With pastry tube, put a border of softened cheese on cut edge of shell.
11. Garnish with mint and a strawberry or parsley and a maraschino cherry.
12. Arrange sandwiches on each side of plate.

FIVE-CUP FRUIT SALAD

Yield: 10 portions

Ingredients

PINEAPPLE TIDBITS	1 cup
MANDARIN ORANGE SECTIONS	1 cup
FLAKED COCONUT	1 cup
MARSHMALLOWS, LARGE, diced	
or MINIATURE MARSHMALLOWS	1 cup
CULTURED SOUR CREAM	1 cup
LETTUCE CUPS	10

Procedure

1. Mix together the first five ingredients. Chill.
2. Arrange servings in lettuce cups.
3. Garnish with mandarin orange segments.

LORENZO SALAD

Yield: 6 servings

Ingredients

PEARS, LARGE, FRESH	
or CANNED	6 halves
LETTUCE	1 head
CREAM CHEESE	4 ounces
WATERCRESS	1 bunch

Procedure

1. Place one-half pear on nest of lettuce. Pipe a rosette of cheese at either end, and one in center.
2. Garnish with small bouquet of watercress.
3. Serve with the following dressing:

French dressing	1/2 cup
Watercress, chopped	1/4 cup
Chili sauce	1/4 cup

4. Combine and pour over salad just before serving.

Note

French dressing should be made with 3/4 olive oil, 1/4 tarragon vinegar, and seasonings.

SKILLET SALAD

Yield: 4 servings

Ingredients

WESTERN ICEBERG LETTUCE	1 pound (1 head)
BACON, cut into 1/2-inch pieces	8 ounces
VINEGAR	1/2 cup
SUGAR	1/4 cup
WATER	1/4 cup
DRY MUSTARD	1/2 teaspoon
DILL WEED (or OTHER HERBS)	1/4 teaspoon
SALT	1/2 teaspoon
PEPPER	pinch
CHOPPED GREEN ONIONS	1/2 cup
EGGS, hard-cooked, chopped	4

Procedure

1. Wash, core, and drain lettuce; shred coarse.
2. Fry the bacon pieces until crisp. Remove from fat and set aside.
3. Combine 1/2 cup of the bacon fat with the vinegar, sugar, water, and seasonings. Bring to a boil, stirring until sugar is dissolved.
4. Add lettuce, bacon pieces, onions, and egg to the pan and toss to mix or pour hot dressing over lettuce, bacon, onions, and egg in bowl and toss.

Western Iceberg Lettuce, Inc.

CABBAGE, PINEAPPLE AND GRAPE SALAD

Yield: 30 servings

Ingredients

CABBAGE, E.P., shredded	3 pounds
PINEAPPLE TIDBITS	1 pint
RED MALAGA or TOKAY GRAPES	1 pound
MAYONNAISE	1 cup
BOILED DRESSING	1 cup

Procedure

1. Halve and seed the grapes.
2. Toss the shredded cabbage, pineapple and grapes together in a bowl.
3. Add the mixed mayonnaise and boiled dressing.
4. Serve in lettuce cups and garnish with grapes or chopped nuts.

TOMATO SALAD WITH CHEESE STRIPE

Yield:

Ingredients

TOMATO, MEDIUM-SIZED, peeled	1
CREAM CHEESE	4 tablespoons
CREAM CHEESE, ROQUEFORT FLAVOR	2 tablespoons
SALT	1/4 teaspoon

Procedure

1. Cut tomato crosswise about one-third from top.
2. Mix cheese until smooth, add salt, and spread evenly on lower part of tomato.
3. Place other part of tomato over cheese. Smooth cheese with knife to make a uniform, thick stripe.
4. Place tomato on the side in a nest of greens—head lettuce accented with bibb lettuce and spinach leaves. Tuck watercress in the stem end of the tomato. Serve with french dressing

SEAFOAM SALAD RING WITH FRESH CRABMEAT

Yield: 6 servings

Ingredients

GELATIN, LIME FLAVOR	3 ounces (1 package)
WATER, boiling	1-1/2 cups
COTTAGE CHEESE, cream style	2 cups
GREEN PEPPER, chopped	1/4 cup
VINEGAR	1 tablespoon
ONION, grated	1 tablespoon
HORSERADISH	1-1/2 teaspoons
SALT	1/2 teaspoon
CRABMEAT	12 ounces or more

Procedure

1. Dissolve gelatin in boiling water in a medium-sized bowl, and chill until syrupy.
2. Combine cottage cheese, green pepper, onion, horseradish, vinegar and salt in another medium-sized bowl.
3. Blend cheese mixture into syrupy gelatin.
4. Pour into six individual molds, and chill until firm.
5. Unmold by running tip of paring knife around top of mold.
6. Place mold on bed of chicory or lettuce.
7. Fill center of mold with fresh crabmeat. Garnish crabmeat with wedges of ripe olives.
8. Serve russian dressing in a side dish.

CAESAR SALAD

Yield:	Serves 2	Serves 3	Serves 4
Ingredients			
ROMAINE, medium-sized heads (2)	8 cups	12 cups	16 cups
CROUTONS	1/2 cup	1/4 cup	1 cup
CODDLED EGG, pullet size	1 (only)	1(only)	1 (only)
PARMESAN CHEESE	1/4 cup	1/3 cup	1/2 cup
CAESAR DRESSING	4 ounces	6 ounces	8 ounces
ANCHOVY FILLETS	4 (only)	6 (only)	8 (only)

Procedure

1. Remove large outer romaine leaves.

2. Then cut lengthwise through romaine twice.

3. Break or cut romaine crosswise into pieces 1 to 1-1/2 inches.

4. Coddle egg *1 minute* in boiling water. Cool before using. Prepare eggs according to needs.

5. Place romaine in stainless steel bowl over shallow plastic bowl of shaved ice.

6. Combine the celery, eggs, green onion, and chopped artichokes.

7. Serve on chilled salad plates. Top with 2 anchovy fillets in crosswise fashion.

8. Do not mix salad for more than 4 orders at one time.

9. Place salad greens in bowls according to the servings desired.

Note

1. If prepared Caesar dressing is not on hand, substitute garlic-flavored olive oil and lemon juice in the proportion of 2 parts oil to 1 of lemon juice. Season with freshly ground pepper and a dash of salt.

2. Whether to add the egg raw or coddled is a controversial point. Some authorities claim that the greens are more easily coated with the dressing when the egg is coddled.

MINTED GRAPEFRUIT COCKTAIL

Yield: 10 to 12 portions

Ingredients

MINT JELLY	3 ounces
WATER	1 cup
SUGAR	1/2 cup
GRAPEFRUIT, 64's, sectioned	4

Procedure

1. Melt mint jelly in double boiler. Beat with rotary beater until smooth.

2. Make a thin syrup by boiling together the sugar and water approximately 5 minutes.

3. Add to the mint jelly. Chill.

4. Arrange sectioned grapefruit in cocktail glasses, allowing about 4 sections to each glass.

5. Pour over chilled mint syrup until glasses are three-quarters full.

LIME AND COTTAGE CHEESE MOLDED SALAD

Yield: 80 servings

Ingredients

GELATINE, UNFLAVORED	1-1/2 cups
WATER, cold	3 cups
SUGAR	5 pounds
WATER, boiling	1-1/2 quarts
FRESH LIME JUICE	3 pints
FRESH LEMON JUICE	2 cups
COTTAGE CHEESE	6 pounds

Procedure

1. Soften gelatin in the 3 cups of cold water. Dissolve over boiling water.

2. Dissolve sugar in the 1-1/2 quarts boiling water.

3. When sugar mixture is cool, add lemon and lime juices.

4. Add dissolved gelatine to the sugar and fruit juice mixture. (Green vegetable coloring may be added to the liquid if a deeper color is desired.)

5. When partially set, fold in the cottage cheese. Pour into individual molds.

6. Chill until firm. Serve on crisp lettuce leaf, and garnish with salad dressing, watercress, and radish rose.

FROZEN FRUIT SALAD

"Frozen Fruit Salad is an attractive item especially for summer as it may be served as a salad, dessert, or on cold plates. We make use of all the juice from the canned fruits in gelatin salads and desserts which are daily menu items."

Yield: 13 pounds

Ingredients

PINEAPPLE CHUNKS, CANNED, No. 10 can	1
PEARS, CANNED, No. 10 can, diced	1/2
PEACHES, CANNED, No. 10 can, diced	1/2
CANTELOUPE, MEDIUM-SIZED, diced	2
MARASCHINO CHERRIED, halved	1 cup
NUT MEATS	2 cups
WHIPPED CREAM	1 quart
POWDERED SUGAR	1 cup

Procedure

1. Combine fruit and nut meats.
2. Add sugar to whipped cream. Fold whipped cream into the diced fruit and nut meats. Pour into loaf pans and freeze.
3. Serve cut in slices.

DEVILED EGGS

Yield: 24

Ingredients

EGGS, hard-cooked	24
MAYONNAISE	1/3 cup
CAPERS, drained	1/4 cup
PREPARED MUSTARD	1-1/2 tablespoons
LIQUID HOT PEPPER SEASONING	few drops
PARSLEY, chopped	as needed

Procedure

1. Cut thin slice from bottoms of 24 hard-cooked eggs so they stand on end. Cut off tops of eggs.
2. Carefully remove yolks, saving whites. Blend with mayonnaise, drained capers, prepared mustard, and liquid hot pepper seasoning.
3. Stuff into egg cases; top with "lids." Sprinkle with chopped parsley.

SPINNING SALAD BOWL

Yield: 6 servings

Ingredients

ROMAINE, SMALL HEAD	1
ICEBERG LETTUCE, SMALL HEAD	1
ENDIVE, torn in pieces	1 cup
WATERCRESS, torn in sprigs	1/2 cup
SHOESTRING BEETS, well drained	1 cup
EGG, hard-cooked, sieved	1
SEASONED SALT	as needed
SEASONED PEPPER	as needed
SHERRY FRENCH DRESSING	3/4 cup

Procedure

1. Tear romaine and iceberg lettuce into small pieces.
2. Add endive, watercress, beets, and egg; mix well.
3. Sprinkle with seasoned salt and seasoned pepper.
4. Toss with Sherry French Dressing.

Lawry's Associated Restaurants

CHICKEN AND PINEAPPLE SALAD

Yield: 32 servings

Ingredients

CUBED STEWING CHICKEN	1 gallon
GREEN ONIONS, thinly sliced	4 bunches
MAYONNAISE	1 quart
PINEAPPLE CHUNKS, chilled	1/2 gallon
DICED CELERY, chilled	1/2 gallon
LETTUCE CUPS	32 (only)
PAPRIKA	as needed

Procedure

1. Stew chicken the day before, and leave overnight in broth in refrigerator.
2. Cube chicken and slice or dice onions, tops and all, if green.
3. Combine chicken, onions and mayonnaise. Allow to marinate in refrigerator for two or three hours.
4. Just before serving, add the canned, drained and chilled pineapple chunks and celery to the chicken mixture.
5. Serve in crisp lettuce cups, that have been dusted with paprika.
6. Garnish with deviled egg and radish roses.

CASTROVILLE CRAB SALAD

Yield: 12 salads

Ingredients

ARTICHOKES, LARGE	12
WATER	6 quarts
SALT	3 tablespoons
VINEGAR	6 tablespoons
SALAD OIL	2 tablespoons
CRABMEAT, cooked	1-1/2 quarts
CHOPPED CELERY	3 cups
EGGS, hard-cooked, diced	6
CHOPPED GREEN ONIONS	1/2 cup
MAYONNAISE	2 cups
PREPARED MUSTARD	2 tablespoons
LETTUCE CUPS	12

Procedure

1. Rinse artichokes; drain stems and leaves.
2. Heat water, salt, vinegar, and salad oil to boiling. Add artichokes. Cook until tender, about 45 minutes. Drain and cool.
3. Spread outer leaves of artichokes and pull out center cone. Cut off tender part of cone and chop fine.
4. With teaspoon, scrape out and discard fuzzy "choke" from center.
5. Dice large pieces of crabmeat.
6. Combine the celery, eggs, green onion, and the chopped artichokes.
7. Blend mayonnaise and mustard. Add to crab mixture.
8. Spoon into artichokes. Place artichokes in lettuce cup.

CALIFORNIA SALAD, STROGANOFF

Yield: 12 salads

Ingredients

LETTUCE	3 heads
BRUSSELS SPROUTS	3 cups
CAULIFLOWERETTES	4-1/2 cups
BEETS, sliced, drained	1/2 No. 10 can
MARINADE	
SALAD OIL	1 cup
WHITE WINE VINEGAR	4-1/2 tablespoons
DRY SHERRY	3 tablespoons
SEASONED SALT	1-1/2 teaspoons
DRY MUSTARD	1/2 teaspoon
DILL WEED	1/2 teaspoon
PEPPER	1/8 teaspoon
STROGANOFF	
MARINADE	4-1/2 tablespoons
SEASONED SALT	3/4 teaspoon
SOUR CREAM	1-1/2 cups

Procedure

1. Blend stroganoff ingredients.
2. Core, rinse, and drain lettuce; separate outer leaves. Refrigerate leaves and heart, to crisp.
3. Cook brussels sprouts and cauliflower in boiling salt water just until tender. Drain, cut, and halve.
4. Toss vegetables with 3/4 cup of marinade; chill.
5. Shred lettuce hearts.
6. To serve: line chilled salad plates with lettuce leaves. Fill with bed of shredded lettuce and brussels sprouts in ring inside. Ladle dressing into center.

COLE SLAW WITH FRESH ROAST'D PEANUTS

Yield: 6 gallons

Ingredients

LAWRY'S ITALIAN SALAD DRESSING MIX	14 ounces
WHITE VINEGAR	1/2 gallon
SALAD OIL	1 gallon
SUGAR	1 cup
SALT	1/2 cup
SHREDDED WHITE CABBAGE	20 pounds
SHREDDED RED CABBAGE	2-1/2 pounds
CHOPPED GREEN ONIONS	1-1/2 quarts
DICED CELERY	1-1/2 quarts
PEANUTS, unsalted, blanched	1 quart
LAWRY'S SEASONED SALT	2 tablespoons

Procedure

1. Combine Italian Salad Dressing Mix, vinegar, salad oil, sugar, and salt; mix well on No. 2 speed of mixer.

2. Combine cabbages, green onions, diced celery, and peanuts; sprinkle with seasoned salt.

3. Add dressing to cabbage mixture; mix well. Chill.

4. To serve, spoon 3 to 4 ounces into a small fruit dish.

Lawry's Associated Restaurants

COBB SALAD (ORIGINAL BROWN DERBY RESTAURANT)

Yield: 4 to 6 portions

Ingredients

LETTUCE, MEDIUM-SIZED HEAD	1
ROMAINE LETTUCE, MEDIUM-SIZED HEAD	1
WATERCRESS	1 small bunch
BREAST of CHICKEN	4 ounces
EGG, hard-cooked	4 ounces
BLEU CHEESE	4 ounces
TOMATO	4 ounces
BACON, fried crisp, crumbled	4 ounces
AVOCADO, MEDIUM-SIZED	1

Procedure

Finely chop all ingredients; put in wooden salad bowl; mix thoroughly with salad dressing.

SALAD DRESSING

SUGAR	1/2 teaspoon
SALT	1/2 teaspoon
BLACK PEPPER	1/2 teaspoon
DRY MUSTARD	1/8 teaspoon
WHITE WINE VINEGAR	1/2 cup
RED WINE VINEGAR	1/2 cup
SALAD OIL	3/4 cup
LEMON JUICE, fresh, from	1/2 lemon

Procedure

Mix above ingredients thoroughly and pour over salad. Serve on large chilled plate.

CANNED CHICKEN SALAD BOWL

Yield: approximately 35 portions

Ingredients

I. CHICKEN, canned,
        2-pound cans, diced   6 cans
    CELERY, white center
        only, diced   5 stalks
    ONION, large grated   1
    GREEN ONIONS,
        small, cut fine   1 bunch
    CUCUMBERS, peeled,
        diced   2
    POTATOES, medium,
        cooked, diced fine   4
II. Dice chicken, and toss all in-
    gredients together lightly.
    Add the following:
        VINEGAR   1 cup
        WORCESTERSHIRE
            SAUCE   2 tablespoons
        SUGAR, granulated   1 tablespoon
        SALT   2 tablespoons
        PEPPER, ground   1/2 teaspoon
        MAYONNAISE   5 cups

Procedure

Blend lightly. Serve on lettuce leaf garnished with sliced tomatoes, hard-cooked eggs cut in eighths, green onions and olives.

College of the Pacific, Stockton, Calif.

SALAD CROCK

Yield: about 16 1/2-cup servings

Ingredients

WESTERN ICEBERG   2 pounds (2 or
    LETTUCE   more heads)
SAUERKRAUT,   1 pound, 11 ounces
    drained   (No. 2-1/2 can,
                            about 3-1/2 cups)
CHOPPED TOMATO
    or PIMIENTO   2 cups
SALAD OIL   1 cup
VINEGAR   1/3 cup
SUGAR   1 ounce (2
                            tablespoons)
SALT   as needed
PEPPER   as needed

Procedure

1. Wash, core, and drain lettuce. Shred coarse.
2. Add sauerkraut and tomato.
3. Blend oil, vinegar, and sugar. Pour over lettuce mixture. Toss. Season to taste with salt and pepper. Chill.

CALIFORNIA CULTURE

Yield: 12 salad plates

Ingredients

FRESH CALIFORNIA
    NECTARINES, 60 COUNT   12
ICEBERG LETTUCE, crisped   2 heads
DEVILED EGGS   24
SARDINES,
    (3-3/4-ounce cans)   4
CUCUMBER, scored, sliced   2
GREEN ONIONS   24
RADISH ROSES   12
PARSLEY SPRIGS   as needed

Procedure

1. Cut 8 nectarines from pits lengthwise into wedges. Cut remaining 4 nectarines crosswise into rings and slip from pits.
2. You will need 24 rings to hold eggs.
3. Separate outer leaves from lettuce for lining salad plates. Shred remaining lettuce; spread into beds on lettuce leaves.
4. To prepare each plate: on lettuce bed, arrange 2 eggs on nectarine rings, nectarine wedges, sardines, cucumber, green onions, radish, and parsley sprigs.

A Heritage of Fine Food,
A History of Innovation

Firmly founded on a missionary heritage, California has led the nation in developing public foodservice/lodging. In the courtyard of the Santa Barbara Mission (left) travelers continue to find a place of rest and inspiration—as they have for hundreds of years. In the advanced foodservice system of the new St. Vincent's Hospital, Sister Michele (left below) carries on the dedication of the six nuns who started Los Angeles' first health care unit.

Taking an innovative approach to one of California's bountiful foods, the avocado, The Medallion Restaurant, Los Angeles, has created a menu star to match its elegant surroundings. They have found the avocado marries well with vegetables, crab, and shrimp, and also contributes a unique flavor to cold entrees, hot sandwiches, and hot and cold salads. Although the Medallion menu is 80 percent prime rib, steaks and lobster, it makes a specialty of unusual vegetables such as cheese-stuffed zucchini.

Above: California's natural bounty of foods—including a dazzling array of fruits and vegetables—makes possible lovely menu variations. Here nectarines are used to freshen a protein plate.

Right: Luncheon favorites at Los Angeles' Medallion Restaurant include (left) an open-faced Scandinavian sandwich of rare roast beef, cucumber, egg, tomato, tiny shrimp, dilled mayonnaise, and sliced avocado. The hot sandwich (right) combines breast of turkey, avocado, and sliced mushrooms, topped by Mornay sauce.

MACAROON FRUIT PUDDING WITH VANILLA SAUCE

Yield: 14 portions

Ingredients

PEACHES, FRESH	3 pounds
APPLES, RAW	2 pounds
LEMON RIND from	2 lemons
SUGAR	1 pound
NUTMEG	1/2 teaspoon
MACAROONS, dried, crushed	1 pound
BUTTER	4 ounces

Procedure

1. Wash, peel, and slice peaches and apples.

2. Add sugar, lemon rind, and nutmeg.

3. Arrange sliced fruit and crushed macaroons in alternate layers in buttered bake pan. Top with butter.

4. Bake in oven at 350°F. for approximately 30 minutes.

5. Serve with Vanilla Cream Sauce.

VANILLA CREAM SAUCE

Ingredients

SUGAR	12 ounces
CORNSTARCH	5-1/4 tablespoons
EGGS	2
MILK	1 quart
VANILLA	2 teaspoons

Procedure

1. Combine sugar and cornstarch. Stir in beaten eggs.

2. Add egg mixture to scalded milk, stirring constantly. Cook slowly until mixture thickens—about 15 minutes.

3. Remove from heat and add the vanilla.

FRENCH FRIED PEARS WITH LEMON SAUCE

Yield: 12 portions

Ingredients

1. PEARS, FRESH, LARGE		6
2. *BATTER*		
	FLOUR	1 cup
	SALT	1/4 teaspoon
	SUGAR	1 teaspoon
	BAKING POWDER	1 teaspoon
	EGGS, well beaten	3
	MILK	1 cup
3. *LEMON SAUCE*		
	SUGAR	1-1/2 cups
	CORNSTARCH	3-1/4 tablespoons
	SALT	1/2 teaspoon
	EGGS	2
	LEMON JUICE from	3 lemons
	LEMON RIND, grated from	1 lemon
	WATER	1 pint
	BUTTER	4 tablespoons

Procedure

1. Wash, peel, and cut pears in half. Remove core. Put pears in salted water to prevent discoloration.

2. Make batter by sifting together the dry ingredients, adding eggs and milk, and blending well.

3. Dip pears in batter, covering all sides. Fry in deep fat at 360°F. a few minutes. Drain and serve with Lemon Sauce.

4. For Lemon Sauce, combine the first 4 ingredients. Add boiling water, stirring to blend well. Boil 5 minutes. Beat eggs and add to hot mixture, first adding a little of the hot mixture to the eggs, stirring constantly. Cook 3 minutes longer. Remove from heat. Stir in the lemon juice and butter.

LEMON CHIFFON PIE

Yield: 16 9-inch pies

Ingredients

WATER, hot	3-1/2 quarts
GRANULATED SUGAR	2-1/2 pounds
SALT	1-1/2 ounces
YELLOW FOOD COLORING	1 teaspoon
CORNSTARCH	1 pound
WATER, warm	1 pint
LEMON JUICE	24 ounces
EGGS, WHOLE	12
LEMON RIND, grated	2 ounces
BUTTER	4 ounces
WATER, hot	1 pint
SUGAR	2-3/4 pounds
CREAM of TARTAR	2 teaspoons
EGG WHITES	2 pounds
PIE SHELLS, baked	16

Procedure

1. Combine first 4 ingredients and bring to boiling point.

2. Dissolve cornstarch in warm water and add to sugar mixture, stirring rapidly with wire whip. Boil until clear, stirring frequently. Remove from heat.

3. Combine lemon juice, beaten eggs, and lemon rind and add gradually to cornstarch mixture, stirring rapidly.

4. Add butter and let mixture cool to 120°F.

5. Bring the remaining sugar, water, and cream of tartar to a boil.

6. Add hot syrup to beaten egg whites. Continue to whip on third speed of mixer about 5 minutes or until cool.

7. Fold egg whites into lemon filling.

8. Dip evenly into 16 baked pie shells. Place pies in oven at 500°F. until a golden brown.

GINGER-FRUIT BAVARIAN PIE

Yield: 5 10-inch pies, 1-1/4 gallons filling

Ingredients

GELATINE, UNFLAVORED	2-1/2 ounces
WATER, cold	2-1/2 cups
GRANULATED SUGAR	1 pound
SALT	1 tablespoon plus 1 teaspoon
WATER, cold	1-1/2 quarts
MILK, cold	5-1/2 cups
CREAM, 18%	1-1/4 quarts
VANILLA	2 teaspoons
CREAM, 40%	1-1/4 quarts
GLACE CHERRIES	4-1/4 ounces
GLACE GINGER	3 ounces
GLACE PEEL	2-1/2 ounces
DATES, PITTED	3 ounces
FILBERTS, sliced	3 ounces
PIE SHELLS, baked	5

Procedure

1. Soften gelatine in cold water.

2. Heat together the sugar, salt, and water and pour over gelatine. Stir until gelatine is dissolved.

3. Combine milk and cream. Pour hot gelatine mixture over milk and cream. Let mixture set until of the consistency of soft jelly.

4. Beat on power mixer. This is essential to prevent curdling. Add vanilla.

5. Whip cream. Chop cherries, ginger, peel, and dates. Combine fruit.

6. Fold whipped cream into the gelatine mixture while it is still soft, then fold in the chopped fruit and nuts. Pour mixture into baked pie shells and set aside until well set.

ORANGE AND PINEAPPLE CHIFFON PIE

Yield: five 9-inch pies

Ingredients
CRUST

GRAHAM CRACKERS, rolled fine	1-1/3 pounds
GRANULATED SUGAR	10 ounces
BUTTER or MARGARINE, softened	10 ounces
ORANGE RIND, grated	1/2 cup

FILLING

UNFLAVORED GELATINE	2-1/2 ounces
COLD WATER	1 pint
HOT WATER	1 quart
SUGAR	2-1/2 pounds
SALT	1 teaspoon
ORANGE JUICE	1 quart
LEMON JUICE	1 cup
HEAVY CREAM, whipped	1-1/4 quarts
CRUSHED PINEAPPLE, drained	1-1/2 cups

Procedure

1. Combine ingredients for crust and mix well. Press into pie pans. Chill.

2. Soak gelatine in cold water for 5 minutes. Add hot water and stir until dissolved. Then stir in sugar, salt and fruit juices. Chill until it is partly congealed. Whip until fluffy.

3. Fold in whipped cream and crushed pineapple.

4. Pile into crumb crusts. Chill until firm.

5. Garnish with whipped cream and orange sections.

CHOCOLATE CREAM PIE

Yield: 3 10-inch pies

Ingredients

MILK	8-3/4 cups
SUGAR	1 pound, 14 ounces
CORNSTARCH	4-1/2 ounces
COCOA	3-1/2 ounces
SALT	1/2 teaspoon
EGGS, whole, beaten	6 ounces
MARGARINE	6 ounces
VANILLA	1-1/2 tablespoons

Procedure

1. Scald milk in small steam-jacketed kettle or double boiler.

2. Combine sugar, cornstarch, cocoa, and salt, and add to hot milk. Cook until thick, and all trace of raw starch disappears, stirring constantly.

3. Add beaten egg yolks to hot mixture, first adding some of the hot mixture to egg yolks. Cook 5 minutes. Add margarine. Remove from heat. Add vanilla. Cool.

4. Scale 2-1/2 pounds or 4-1/2 cups into each baked pie shell. Cover with meringue and brown in oven, or top with whipped cream.

Hotel and Restaurant Department
City College of San Francisco, Calif.

APPLE CRISP

Yield: 2 pans—approximately 11-1/2- by 17-1/2-inches

Ingredients

PIE APPLES, canned, No. 10, sliced	2 cans
BROWN SUGAR	1 pound, 12 ounces
FLOUR	1 pound
CINNAMON, ground	1-1/4 tablespoons
BUTTER or MARGARINE	10 ounces
LEMON JUICE	1/2 cup

Procedure

1. Layer apples in greased baking pan. Sprinkle with lemon juice.

2. Cream shortening and sugar. Add flour and cinnamon and beat until crumbly. Spread butter mixture over top of apples. Bake in oven at 375°F. for 30 minutes. Serve hot or cold with whipped cream or a la mode.

College of the Pacific, Stockton, Calif.

PEACH PIE FILLING

Yield: filling for three 9-inch pies

Ingredients

ELBERTA PEACH SLICES	1 No. 10 can
SUGAR	1 pound
FLOUR	4 ounces
CINNAMON	1 teaspoon
BUTTER	2 ounces
ALMOND EXTRACT	1-1/2 teaspoons
GRATED LEMON PEEL	2 teaspoons
LEMON JUICE	4 teaspoons

Procedure

1. Drain peaches well, saving syrup.

2. Combine reserved syrup, sugar, flour, cinnamon, and butter. Cook over medium heat until mixture thickens and boils. Add almond extract, lemon peel, and drained peaches. Cool.

3. When ready to make pies, ladle filling into pastry-lined tins. The pies may be baked open-faced with baked star or bell cut-outs added later. They may be streusel-topped and then baked. They may be lattice-topped or simply closed with a top crust before baking. Make them the way you like best!

4. With freshly baked peach pies, offer whipped cream, sour cream, or ice cream.

Glorietta Brand by Santa Clara Packing Company

ORANGE COCONUT DELIGHT

Yield: 25 portions

Ingredients

PINEAPPLE TIDBITS, FRESH or CANNED	1 pound
ORANGES, 150's	12
SHREDDED COCONUT	1 pound
MARSHMALLOWS, LARGE	1 pound
WHIPPED CREAM	1-1/2 quarts

Procedure

1. Drain pineapple, if canned.

2. Peel and section oranges.

3. Cut marshmallows in quarters.

4. Combine all ingredients and blend well. Chill thoroughly.

5. Serve in sherbet glasses and garnish each portion with orange section or toasted coconut.

FILLED MUSCAT STARS

Yield: 13 dozen cookies

Ingredients

MUSCAT FILLING	
SEEDED MUSCAT RAISINS, finely chopped	4 pounds, 12 ounces
CORNSTARCH	2 ounces
ORANGE JUICE	1 pound, 7 ounces
ORANGE PEEL, grated	1 ounce
SUGAR	1 pound, 12 ounces
PECANS, chopped	3 ounces
GROUND GINGER	3/8 ounce
BUTTER	4-1/2 ounces
DOUGH	
BUTTER and/or MARGARINE	4 pounds, 5 ounces
SUGAR, FINE GRANULATED	2 pounds, 4 ounces
SALT	1-1/2 ounces
BAKING SODA	1/2 ounce
LEMON PEEL, grated	1/2 ounce
LEMON JUICE	4 ounces
UNBLEACHED PASTRY FLOUR	5 pounds
EGG WASH	as needed

Procedure

1. To prepare the filling, combine all ingredients listed. Cook until it thickens. Cool.

2. Blend butter and/or margarine, sugar, salt, soda, and lemon peel thoroughly.

3. Add lemon juice and flour. Mix only enough to obtain smooth dough. Chill dough slightly prior to making up cookies.

4. Roll dough 3/16 to 1/4 inch thick. Cut into 3-inch discs.

5. Place on paper-lined (18-inch by 26-inch by 1-inch) dry sheet pans. Wash with light egg wash or water. Deposit 1 ounce filling on center of base cookie. Top with second disc with small star cut from center. (Stars may be baked separately and used as party cookies or may be re-rolled.) If desired, tops may be brushed lightly with egg wash, then topped with sanding sugar.

6. Bake in oven at 375° to 390°F. about 10 minutes.

California Raisin Advisory Board
(Reprint from Baking Industry Magazine)

CARROT CAKE

Yield: 1 cake

Ingredients

CORN OIL	1-1/2 cups
SUGAR	2 cups
EGGS	3
FLOUR	2 cups
CINNAMON	2 teaspoons
SODA	2 teaspoons
VANILLA	2 teaspoons
SALT	1 teaspoon
SHREDDED CARROTS	2 cups
CHOPPED NUTS	1 cup
CRUSHED PINEAPPLE	1/2 cup

Procedure

1. Combine all ingredients in a large bowl and mix until well blended.

2. Pour batter into a 9-inch by 13-inch buttered pan.

3. Bake in oven at 350°F. for 1 hour. Allow to cool.

4. Ice with Cream Cheese Icing.

CREAM CHEESE ICING

Ingredients

MARGARINE	1/2 cup
CREAM CHEESE	3 ounces
CONFECTIONERS' SUGAR	1-1/4 cups
CRUSHED PINEAPPLE	1/8 cup
CHOPPED WALNUTS	1/4 cup

Procedure

Cream margarine, cream cheese, and sugar until slightly fluffy. Mix in pineapple and walnuts.

**Mannings,
Chef Francisco**

PURPLE PLUM CRISP

Yield: 36 portions

Ingredients

PURPLE PLUMS, CANNED, No. 10 cans	3
LEMON JUICE	1/3 cup
SIFTED ALL-PURPOSE FLOUR	1 quart
SUGAR	2 cups
SALT	2 teaspoons
NUTMEG	2 teaspoons
BUTTER or MARGARINE	2 cups
GRAHAM CRACKER CRUMBS	2 quarts

Procedure

1. Drain and pit purple plums and arrange in greased baking pan. Sprinkle lemon juice over plums.

2. Combine flour, sugar, salt, and nutmeg.

3. Cut in butter or margarine until mixture is crumbly.

4. Add graham cracker crumbs.

5. Sprinkle graham cracker crumb mixture over purple plums.

6. Bake in oven at 350°F. for 40 minutes.

7. Serve warm cut in squares.

Note

Cake crumbs may be used in place of the graham cracker crumbs.

For a "company" dessert, serve the Purple Plum Crisp warm with plain or whipped cream, foamy or vanilla custard sauce, or topped with ice cream.

PEACH CRISP

Yield: 32 servings (2/3 cup each)

Ingredients

SIFTED FLOUR	1-1/2 cups
SUGAR	1-1/4 cups
BUTTER or MARGARINE	1-1/4 cups
CORN FLAKE CRUMBS	2-2/3 cups
SUGAR	1 cup
CORNSTARCH	1/3 cup
SALT	1 teaspoon
CINNAMON	1/2 teaspoon
NUTMEG	1/2 teaspoon
LEMON JUICE	3 tablespoons
SYRUP DRAINED from FRUIT	3-1/3 cups
CLING PEACH SLICES	1 No. 10 can

Procedure

1. Combine flour and sugar. Cut in butter until mixture is crumbly. Add corn flake crumbs, mix well. Set aside.

2. Mix sugar, cornstarch, salt, and spices in saucepot. Add lemon juice and syrup; stir until smooth.

3. Cook over low heat, stirring constantly, until thickened and clear. Stir in peach slices. Pour into greased baking pan, 20-inch by 12-inch by 2-1/2-inch. Sprinkle evenly with crumb topping.

4. Bake in oven at 400°F. for about 45 minutes. Serve in sauce dishes with cream, ice cream, or whipped topping.

Cling Peach Advisory Board

ROOT BEER PARTY TORTE

Yield: 1 torte

Ingredients

EGGS	4
YELLOW CAKE MIX (2 layer)	1 package
INSTANT VANILLA PUDDING MIX	1 package
ROOT BEER	3/4 cup
SALAD OIL	1/2 cup
CONFECTIONERS' SUGAR	1 cup
ROOT BEER	1/2 cup
WHIPPED TOPPING MIX	2 envelopes, 1-1/2 ounces each
ROOT BEER, ice-cold	as needed

Procedure

1. Beat eggs until thick and lemon colored; add cake mix, pudding mix, 3/4 cup of root beer, and oil. Beat 10 minutes at medium speed. Pour into 2 greased and floured 9-inch by 1-1/2-inch cake pans.

2. Bake in oven at 350°F. for 35 to 40 minutes, or until done. Cool 10 minutes; remove from pans.

3. Boil confectioners' sugar and 1/2 cup root beer together for 2 minutes. Spoon over cakes, puncturing top with long fork tines so that liquid will penetrate cake. Cool and chill.

4. At serving time, cut each layer in half horizontally, making 4 layers.

5. Whip topping mix as directed on package, substituting cold root beer for milk. Set aside about one cup of whipped topping for decorating the top.

6. Spread remaining topping between layers. Finish top with spooned dollops or make rosettes, using a pastry tube.

ROOT BEER PANCAKE ROLL-UPS

Yield: 12 pancakes

Ingredients

SUGAR	1/3 cup
CORNSTARCH	2 tablespoons
ROOT BEER	2 12-ounce containers
GRATED ORANGE RIND	1 teaspoon
PREPARED PANCAKE MIX	1-1/2 cups
EGGS	2
SHORTENING, melted	3 tablespoons
CREAM CHEESE, room temperature	1 8-ounce package
ORANGE MARMALADE	1/2 cup

Procedure

1. Mix sugar and cornstarch in saucepan; gently stir in one container of root beer.

2. Cook, stirring constantly, until thick and clear. Stir in orange rind. Keep sauce warm.

3. Combine pancake mix, eggs, shortening, and remaining root beer; beat until smooth.

4. Bake cakes on hot griddle, using 1/4 cup batter for each pancake. Turn pancakes when underside is brown and top is full of bubbles; cook second side.

5. Blend cream cheese and marmalade. Spread pancakes with cheese mixture and roll up jelly-roll fashion. Serve with hot sauce.

RAISIN APPLE SQUARES

Yield: 100 portions, 2-1/2- by 3-1/2-inches each

Ingredients

RAISINS, SEEDLESS	6 pounds
ALL-PURPOSE FLOUR	1 pound, 12 ounces
CORN MEAL	1 pound, 12 ounces
ROLLED WHEAT	2 pounds
SALT	1 ounce
BAKING SODA	1/2 ounce
BAKING POWDER	1-1/2 ounces
NONFAT DRY MILK	9 ounces
BROWN SUGAR	1 pound, 12 ounces
EGGS	12 ounces (6 large)
MOLASSES	2 pounds, 14 ounces (1 quart)
WATER	1-1/2 quarts
SHORTENING, melted	9 ounces
APPLES, pared, chopped	2 pounds, 8 ounces

Procedure

1. Cover raisins with water or fruit juice. Let stand several hours or overnight.

2. Combine dry ingredients in mixing bowl. Mix on low speed until blended.

3. Slowly add eggs, molasses, water, and shortening, mixing on low speed. Mix just enough to blend ingredients. *Do not overmix.* Blend in drained raisins and apples.

4. Spread batter in 2 greased sheet pans (18 by 26 inches).

5. Bake in oven at 375°F. for 50 to 55 minutes.

California Raisin Advisory Board

APRICOT SOUFFLE

Yield: 60 portions

Ingredients

APRICOT PUREE or CONCENTRATE	7 cups
GRANULATED SUGAR	1-1/2 quarts
EGG WHITES	3/4 cup
LEMON JUICE	6 tablespoons
SALT	1 teaspoon
PECAN PIECES	3 cups
CUSTARD or ICE CREAM SAUCE	as needed

Procedure

1. Combine apricot puree, sugar, and egg whites in mixing bowl. Beat 12 to 15 minutes.

2. Fold in lemon juice, salt, and pecan pieces.

3. Pour into 3 ungreased pans. Set pans in hot water and bake in oven at 325°F. for approximately 15 minutes. Serve with Custard or Ice Cream Sauce.

Note

For Ice Cream Sauce, combine vanilla ice cream with whipped cream and mix until fluffy.

SPANISH CREAM PIE

Yield: 5 10-inch pies

Ingredients

GELATINE, UNFLAVORED	5 tablespoons
WATER, cold	1/2 cup
WATER, hot	1-1/2 cups
WHIPPING CREAM	2 quarts
EGG YOLKS	10
SUGAR	2 cups
SALT	1 teaspoon
VANILLA	1 teaspoon
EGG WHITES	6
PIE SHELLS, baked	5
MERINGUE	
EGG WHITES	2-1/2 cups (20)
CONFECTIONERS' SUGAR	3-1/2 cups

Procedure

1. Sprinkle gelatine over 1/2 cup cold water. Let soften 5 minutes.

2. Add 1-1/2 cups hot water and stir until dissolved. Cool liquid.

3. Whip cream.

4. Beat egg yolks slightly and mix with sugar, salt, and vanilla. Blend well.

5. Fold egg yolk mixture into whipped cream.

6. Beat whites until stiff but not dry. Fold into whipped cream mixture.

7. Add gelatine, folding it gently into the mixture. Pour into baked pie shells. Top with meringue.

8. Slip under broiler to lightly brown meringue. Set pies aside until they are cool and filling is set.

Note

Allow 3-1/8 pounds pie dough for the 5 pies.

RAISIN MOLASSES PIE

Yield: 5 9-inch pies

Ingredients

SEEDLESS RAISINS	4 pounds
SUGAR	1-1/4 pounds
DARK MOLASSES	1-1/2 cups
MAPLE SYRUP	1 cup
WATER, hot	2-1/2 cups
SALT	2 teaspoons
CINNAMON	2 teaspoons
FLOUR	1-1/4 pounds
WATER, cold	2 cups

Procedure

1. Combine the raisins, sugar, molasses, syrup, hot water, salt, and cinnamon in the top of a double boiler. Stir well. Then cook for 15 minutes, stirring occasionally.

2. Add the flour and cold water mixture and cook another 15 minutes. Cool. Fill unbaked pie shells.

3. Bake in oven at 450°F. for 10 minutes, then

4. Pies may be baked without a top crust and gar-

FLUFFY YELLOW CAKE

Yield: 8 layers, 9-inch each or 4 cakes, 2 layers each

Ingredients

SHORTENING	3-3/8 cups
SUGAR	6-1/4 cups
EGG YOLKS	12
VANILLA	1 tablespoon
SIFTED CAKE FLOUR	2 pounds, 4 ounces
SALT	3/4 teaspoon
BAKING POWDER	3 tablespoons
MILK	3 cups
EGG WHITES, stiffly beaten	12

Procedure

1. Cream shortening and sugar on power mixer at low speed. Scrape down bowl and beater during the creaming process.

2. Add egg yolks and vanilla. Beat entire mixture until light and fluffy.

3. Sift flour, baking powder, and salt. Add alternately with the milk to the shortening mixture, keeping the batter smooth and of an even consistency.

4. Scrape down bowl and beater during mixing.

5. Fold in egg whites beaten stiff but not dry. Scrape down bowl and mixer, and remove from machine.

6. Scale approximately 1 pound, 3 ounces into each greased and floured layer cake pan. Bake in oven at 350°F. for 30 minutes.

7. Put layers together with Lemon Filling.*

8. Ice bottom and sides with Fluffy White Frosting.**

9. Cover top and sides with coconut.

LEMON FILLING

Yield: enough for four 2-layer cakes

Ingredients

FLOUR	2/3 cup
SUGAR	2-1/2 cups
SALT	1/2 teaspoon
BUTTER	2 tablespoons
WATER, boiling	2 cups
EGG YOLKS, beaten	6
LEMON JUICE	1/4 cup
LEMON RIND, grated	3 tablespoons

Procedure

1. Sift together flour, sugar, and salt. Add boiling water and butter.

2. Cook over low heat 10 minutes, stirring constantly.

3. Pour some of the cooked mixture onto the beaten egg yolks and add egg mixture to thickened mixture. Cook a few minutes longer. Blend in lemon juice and peel. Cool.

FLUFFY WHITE FROSTING WITH COCONUT

Yield: enough for four 2-layer cakes

Ingredients

GRANULATED SUGAR	2 cups
WATER, boiling	1 cup
CREAM of TARTAR	1/4 teaspoon
EGG WHITES	6
CONFECTIONERS' SUGAR	2 cups
VANILLA	1 tablespoon
COCONUT	1 pound

Procedure

1. Boil granulated sugar, water, and cream of tartar until syrup forms a soft ball (238°F.).

2. Beat egg whites until stiff, but not dry. Gradually add 2/3 cup confectioners' sugar. Beat until consistency of meringue.

3. Gradually add syrup, beating constantly until thick.

4. Add remaining confectioners' sugar. Beat until frosting will hold its shape when spread.

5. Spread on bottom and sides of cake. Cover with coconut.

Note

Any frosting left over may be kept in a covered container in refrigerator. Before using, a little hot water should be added to make the mixture smooth.

POPPY SEED CAKE

Yield: 32 servings (4 9-inch layers)

Ingredients

MILK	3/4 pint
POPPY SEED	3/4 pint
MARGARINE	12 ounces
GRANULATED SUGAR	1-1/2 pounds
SIFTED CAKE FLOUR	1-1/8 pounds
BAKING POWDER	3/8 ounce
EGG WHITES	8

Procedure

1. Pour milk over poppy seed. Allow to stand two hours.

2. Cream shortening. Add sugar. Continue beating until well blended and fluffy.

3. Then add flour (sifted with baking powder) alternately with milk and poppy seed mixture.

4. When all ingredients are well blended, remove from the mixer and fold in the stiffly beaten egg whites.

5. Scale 1 pound, 3 ounces of batter into each of 4 layer pans. Bake in oven at 350°F. for 25 to 30 minutes.

6. When layers are thoroughly cooled, slice in half. Spread bottom half with cold filling and replace the top. Cut each layer into 8 wedge-shaped pieces and sprinkle with powdered sugar before serving.

7. When serving in hot weather, take the same precautions as with any cream-filled pastries; keep refrigerated and serve the same day cake is made.

FILLING

Yield: Filling for 4 9-inch layers

Ingredients

EGG YOLKS	8
SUGAR	12 ounces
CORNSTARCH	4 tablespoons
SALT	1/2 teaspoon
MILK	3/4 quart
PECANS, chopped	4 ounces
VANILLA	2 teaspoons

Procedure

1. Beat the egg yolks. Gradually beat in the sugar, cornstarch, and salt.

2. Pour the scalded milk over these ingredients.

3. Cook over boiling water or over very low heat, stirring constantly, until mixture thickens.

4. When cool, add vanilla and chopped pecans.

5. Have filling thoroughly chilled before putting between cake layers.

ANGEL PIE

Yield: 5 9-inch pies, 30 portions

Ingredients

MERINGUE	
EGG WHITES	
(approximately 20)	2-1/4 cups
FINE GRANULATED SUGAR	1-1/4 quarts
CREAM of TARTAR	1-1/4 teaspoons
VANILLA	2 teaspoons
WHIPPING CREAM	1-1/4 pints
FILLING	
EGG YOLKS	
(approximately 20)	1-2/3 cups
GRANULATED SUGAR	1-1/4 cups
LEMON JUICE	1-1/4 cups
TOPPING	
WHIPPING CREAM	1-1/4 pints
GRATED LEMON RIND	2 tablespoons

Procedure

1. Beat the egg whites until stiff.

2. Add the cream of tartar and sugar very slowly, beating constantly.

3. Add the vanilla.

4. Continue beating for 10 minutes. Then spread the meringue in buttered pie plates, leaving the mixture higher at the edges.

5. Bake in oven at 225°F. for 1 hour. Cool.

6. When completely cooled, spread with whipped cream (1-1/4 pints).

7. Let stand in refrigerator overnight.

8. To make the filling, beat the egg yolks, add sugar and lemon juice, and beat until thick.

9. Cook over hot water until firm. Chill.

10. Fill meringue with filling; cover with a thin layer of whipped cream (1-1/4 pints).

11. Sprinkle with grated lemon rind.

ALMOND TOFFEE BARS

Yield: 2 sheet pans 12-inch by 18-inch, 64 bars approximately 2-inch by 3-inch

Ingredients

MARGARINE	1 pound
BROWN SUGAR	15 ounces
EGG YOLKS	2
VANILLA	2 teaspoons
FLOUR	1 pound, 3 ounces
SEMISWEET CHOCOLATE or CHOCOLATE BITS, melted	1 pound
ALMONDS, SLICED, toasted	4 ounces

Procedure

1. Cream the shortening. Add brown sugar and continue creaming until light and fluffy.

2. Add the egg yolks and vanilla. Beat well.

3. Add the flour and stir until well mixed.

4. Spread in oiled sheet pans. It will be a thin layer so spread it as evenly as possible.

5. Bake in oven at 325°F. for 20 minutes.

6. While still warm, spread with the melted chocolate.

7. Sprinkle with almonds. (Other nuts may be substituted.)

8. Cut while warm.

CHRISTMAS CAKE

Yield: 30 individual cakes

Ingredients

CARROTS, RAW, finely diced or shredded	1-1/4 pounds EP
SEEDLESS RAISINS, LIGHT or DARK	1-1/8 pounds
DATES, PITTED, chopped	1-1/8 pounds
SUGAR	2 pounds
WATER	1 quart
BUTTER or MARGARINE	3 ounces
CINNAMON	1 tablespoon
NUTMEG	1-1/2 teaspoons
ALLSPICE	1-1/2 teaspoons
SIFTED FLOUR	1-1/2 pounds
BAKING POWDER	2 tablespoons
SALT	1-1/2 teaspoons
PECANS, chopped	6 ounces

Procedure

1. Combine the carrots, raisins, dates, sugar, water, butter, and spices in a saucepan. Bring to a boil and cook for 20 minutes, stirring occasionally. Cool.

2. Sift the flour, baking powder, and salt together and add gradually to the cooled, cooked mixture. Add the chopped pecans.

3. Fill well-oiled individual gelatin molds or custard cups. Bake in oven at 325°F. for about 40 minutes. If the cake is baked in loaf pans, it will require about 1 hour in oven at 325°F.

4. Serve warm with vanilla sauce or hard sauce.

ALMOND TART SHELLS
WITH RUM CHIFFON FILLING

Yield: 32 individual tarts

Ingredients

GELATINE, UNFLAVORED	1 ounce
WATER, cold	1 cup
SUGAR	1 pound
EGG YOLKS	1 cup (approx. 12)
MILK	1 quart
RUM	3/4 cup
EGG WHITES	1-1/2 cups (approx. 12)
SALT	1 teaspoon
CREAM, WHIPPED	1-1/2 cups
CONFECTIONERS' SUGAR	1/2 cup
SWEET CHOCOLATE, grated	1/2 cup

Procedure

1. Soak the gelatine in cold water.

2. Beat the egg yolks and sugar, add the milk and cook over hot water until thick. Then remove from heat and stir in the soaked gelatine, stirring until it is completely dissolved.

3. Add the rum and allow the mixture to cool until it begins to congeal.

4. Then fold in the egg whites which have been beaten with the salt.

5. Fill the baked tart shells and chill until filling is firm.

6. Top with sweetened whipped cream and sprinkle with grated sweet chocolate.

7. To make the almond tart shells, add 1/2 cup finely chopped, lightly toasted almonds for each pound of flour used in making the pastry. Add almonds after the fat has been cut into the flour but before the water is added. Bake as any tart shells.

OATMEAL DATE BARS

Yield: 1 sheet, 12-inch by 20-inch

Ingredients

DATES, chopped	2 pounds
WATER, hot	2 cups
GRANULATED SUGAR	1 pound
OATMEAL	1 pound
FLOUR	1 pound
BROWN SUGAR	12 ounces
SHORTENING	1 pound
SALT	1 teaspoon
BAKING SODA	1 teaspoon

Procedure

1. Cook the chopped dates, hot water, and granulated sugar until well blended and thick. Cool.

2. Mix the shortening with all the dry ingredients until it is well distributed. Place one-half of this mixture in a well oiled baking sheet pan. Pat lightly. Spread the cooled date filling over this. Cover with the other half of the oatmeal mixture. Bake in oven at 325°F. for 45 minutes. Cut into bars while slightly warm. Serve plain or with whipped cream.

CALIFORNIA

A. J. Bump's saloon, built in 1873, has been rejuvenated by Terry Osmonson and Tom MacMillan (below, left and right.) Simple decor, highlighted by 15-ft. syrup label that covers most of dining room ceiling, helps sell salad and steaks. With only 65 seats, patron count averages 350 on Saturdays, an impressive performance.

The most distinctive exterior in Hollywood belongs to the original Brown Derby which has been selling hamburgers out of a hat since 1926. Recent restoration efforts have helped hold its position among leading Los Angeles restaurants.

BIG SKY

Right: Al Cook, owner of Dry Creek Lodge, Burris, Wyo., enjoys a duckling dinner served by Berenice Miller, a full-blooded Sioux. Dry Creek Lodge is located within a 2 million acre Indian reservation, an ideal take-off point for the camping and hunting trips organized by Al and Betty Cook.

Far Right: Typical of the sumptuous fish buffet featured on Fridays at the War Bonnet Inn in Butte, Mont., is this colorfully coordinated presentation. Container carved from ice holds fresh fruit for which Inn is noted. A varied selection of fresh and exotic fruits trucked in especially for the Sunday buffet has been an especially successful drawing card for Butte "brunchers."

PACIFIC NORTHWEST

Grilled halibut is a favorite with diners and chef alike at John Franco's Hidden Harbor, Seattle, Wash. because of its delicate flavor and ease of preparation.

Famous salads and Oriental deference to the customer's wishes are hallmarks of Canlis foodservice in both Seattle and Portland. Peter Canlis insists that salad ingredients be covered to maintain chill freshness to point of tableside assembly, just as broiled items are sizzling when served.

Above: Table games in a carpeted game room delight customers at The Iron Bull, Billings, Mont. Cook-it-yourself is the style for the steaks in several varieties kept in a reach-in refrigerator. Hot baked potatoes and a salad bar are kept at the ready on a side counter.

Left: Continental atmosphere and cuisine are keys to success at The Encore in Portland, Ore. Tureen of Marseilles style bouillabaisse is a specialty of the house.

COLORADO

Right: Colorado's Silver Rush legacy includes opulent Victorian decor. Denver's Le Profil offers backgammon and a special late-supper menu to the members who enjoy the club atmosphere.

Below: The crystal clear, icy water of mountain streams produces the Colorado mountain trout justly famous as prepared in the state's many restaurants.

Right: Pinto Bean Bake with Spareribs is good campfire or chuck wagon fare for Colorado mountaineers, whether native or just visiting. Long, slow baking in a spicy liquid assures moistness and unique flavor. Hearty servings are flanked by crisp, sauce-coated spareribs, a bouquet of parsley around spiced crab apples.

Below: Guardian of the high standards set for foods served at Denver's noted Brown Palace Hotel is executive chef Ira Dole.

Big Sky Country Builds Big Appetites

RUGGED MOUNTAIN MEN could not simmer intricate sauces. But they could savor the natural bounty.

Treading the Continental Divide in Wyoming, Montana, and Idaho, menus stress steak, potatoes, and ice cream. The steak is seldom rare, but it does come in a variety of cuts.

Fried chicken, barbecued ribs, shrimp, lobster, Alaska King Crab, and trout provide popular alternatives to steak. But most menus offer only one or two of these choices.

Potatoes—baked, fried, hashed, or mashed—team up with breakfast, lunch, and dinner.

Onions and beans, as well as potatoes, are grown in this region. Consequently, Westerners developed stick-to-ribs recipes to use them to the best advantage. Barbecued beans partner with ribs and steak; sliced raw onions add verve to salads or make a salad themselves when marinated; French fried onion rings spur a steak or snack.

No dinner away from home is complete without ice cream or pie. Dutch apple, peach, and pineapple win Western polls.

Tourists, condominium owners, and skiers have broadened the menus of Wyoming.

Lamb, beef, pork, fish and seafood—all add zest to menus in hotels, restaurants, and resorts. Skiers huddle around such *apres ski* dishes as fondue. And every chuckwagon caldron dishes up barbecued beans, beef stew, and high-country chili. Corn-on-the-cob in season, corn bread, and biscuits warm hands and hearts of hungry outdoors lovers.

Fry bread, an Indian specialty provides a treat at some banquets and community dinners. And for big-time Friday nights, buffets of seafood—shrimp, salmon, and trout— have a firm foothold in this Big Sky country.

Dry Creek Lodge
Burris, Wyo.

Broad vistas and rugged mountainscapes encourage appetites in Big Sky country. Even city dudes can get a taste of the gusty life at Dry Creek Lodge, where Al and Betty Cook organize camping and hunting trips.

"We tell the staff to watch but not laugh," Mrs. Cook says. "Then we ask ourselves what we are doing wrong, so guests can do things right."

To trek miles up into the Rockies, supplies

are loaded on pack horses. Kitchen gear and food go into panniers, wooden boxes with cubby holes. Frozen beef tenderloin goes out for the first evening meal. Most items are freeze-dried to save weight and space.

The Lodge is located amid a 2,000,000-acre Indian reservation. Formerly nomads, the Arapahoe and Shoshone Indians now live in villages scattered over the Wind River Reservation. Back in the early 1920s, a few Indians were persuaded to sell all or part of their acres.

"We bought this land from white people in 1965," remembers Al. "By 1970, we decided to build the lodge and guest houses."

The surroundings are rustic and majestic, but the dining room and lodge are sophisticated. Dinner menus include roast duckling on a bed of mixed rice, meringue shells filled with fruit, popovers and lemon meringue pie.

Soup, as a first course, may be cream of potato and celery or apple vichyssoise. Steaks offer an alternative to the eight-entree cycle.

In addition to duck, guests savor trout, ham, roast pork, prime rib, leg of lamb, beef tenderloin, and chicken.

"Our survival depends on our competency," reminds Al. "We cannot depend on suppliers delivering to our door; the nearest city is 60 miles away over mountain roads. We don't intend to do everything ourselves, but we must know how. That way our staff respects us more. It also increases our survival chances."

Walker's Family Restaurant
Rigby, Idaho

Most people in the community are Mormons. So Walker's serves no liquor—but bends by offering coffee and tea.

Clyde Walker, owner, grew up in the 200-seat restaurant, started by his parents in the early 1950s.

The salad bar is popular on weekends but family night is Monday. Fried chicken, served family style, is the featured entree.

It was scones that earned a statewide reputation for Walker's. Made of a yeasty, doughnut-type dough, they are cut in squares and deep fried to a golden brown. A whipped mixture of one part butter, one part honey, and one part margarine in a souffle cup accompanies an order of two scones.

Breakfast favorite is sourdough pancakes. A luncheon special is usually offered—priced under $2.

And, for the final touch, each table in the coffee shop section as well as the dining room has a special blend of spices and sesame seeds.

The Iron Bull
Billings, Mont.

"No problems with one customer taking another's steak," reports Steve Stochl, owner of a cook-it-yourself steak house.

A side counter holds the salad bar and hot baked potatoes. Steaks are kept in a reach-in at one end of the nearby bar. Customers enjoy the informal atmosphere.

Stochl says customers are 75 percent local, with regulars coming about three times a week. Menu is strictly steak and potatoes with beer and coffee to drink. New York strips, 10-, 15- or 20-oz. sizes, and top sirloin or T-bone steaks are offered. Microwave ovens back up regular ovens for baking the potatoes.

Labor costs are low, about 10 percent of the $435,000 gross sales for 1974. The crowd turns "about once" each evening in the 250-seat operation.

Apache Dining Room
War Bonnet Inn
Butte, Mont.

"Shrimp cocktail, steaks, and potatoes are as traditional as ice cream for dessert," says Herbert Leuprecht at the War Bonnet Inn. As chef-turned-resident-manager, he has taken the average food check from total disaster to about $4.95. He found a winning combination in fresh fruits and seafood.

"So long as we use the American English names for food, I can put items on the menu with assurance that they will sell," says Leuprecht.

Sunday brunch is a huge success. A display of fresh fruit, trucked in each week just for the occasion, is refilled several times each Sunday.

"We have citrus fruits, bananas, melons, grapes, and some unusual or exotic fruits, like papayas and fresh pineapples," says Leuprecht. "This is our drawing card, together with the bacon, eggs, ham, sausage, cereals, and hash browns."

Ice cream or sherbet must be included in the dinner price. Pie is a popular lunch dessert.

Big Sky Recipes

SUMMER DAY LUNCHEON STARTER

"This has proved a great favorite on a hot summer day as it makes a refreshing appetizer."... Chef Walter Blum

Yield: 1 portion

Procedure

1. Drop a small scoop (No. 24) Raspberry Sherbet into a sherbet glass.
2. Fill glass with Grape Juice.
3. Add a dash of Kirschwasser (optional).

Grand Teton Lodge Co., Grand Teton National Park, Jackson, Wyo.

TOMATO SOUP

Yield: 48 portions

Ingredients

TOMATO JUICE, canned	6 quarts
ONION, sliced	2 tablespoons
BUTTER	1-1/2 cups
FLOUR	2-1/3 cups
SALT	4 tablespoons
SUGAR	1 cup
MILK, cold	6 quarts

Procedure

1. Heat tomato juice and onion to boiling point.
2. Melt butter in saucepan. Add flour and stir until smooth.
3. Add enough hot tomato juice to make a mixture that will pour.
4. Add the flour mixture slowly to the remaining hot tomato juice, whipping thoroughly with wire whip.
5. Remove onion slices.
6. Bring tomato mixture to a rapid boil.
7. Add cold milk while beating constantly with wire whip.
8. Heat to boiling point.

Pennant Cafeteria, Topeka, Kan.

BROCCOLI CHEESE SOUP

Yield: 50 portions

Ingredients

BROCCOLI, A.P.	6 pounds
BUTTER, melted	1-1/2 cups
ONION, minced	1 cup
FLOUR	6 ounces
MILK	2 gallons
SALT	5 tablespoons
PEPPER	1 teaspoon
PAPRIKA	1 teaspoon
WORCESTERSHIRE SAUCE	2 tablespoons
CHEESE, SHARP, grated	1 pound, 4 ounces

Procedure

1. Prepare broccoli. Cook in 1 inch boiling salted water until crisp-tender.
2. Melt butter or margarine in saucepan. Add onion and cook until tender.
3. Blend in the flour, then the milk, stirring constantly.
4. Cook until smooth and thickened.
5. Add seasonings, worcestershire sauce and broccoli.
6. Set aside 3/4 cup grated sharp cheese for topping individual servings.
7. Add remaining cheese, and stir until it is melted.
8. Serve in heated soup bowls with a sprinkling of grated cheese on top.

Gold's of Nebraska, Lincoln, Neb.

VEAL FRICASSEE

Yield: 36 portions

Ingredients

I. LEG OF VEAL   10 pounds
    CARROTS, large pieces   12 ounces
    ONION, whole or large
        pieces   12 ounces
    BOUQUET GARNI
        CELERY STALK, cubed   1
        PEPPERCORNS   3
        BAY LEAF   1
        WHOLE CLOVES   3
        THYME   1/2 teaspoon
        PARSLEY SPRIG   1
    SALT   1-1/2 tablespoons
    CHICKEN BROTH or
        WATER   1-1/2 gallons, ap-
                                         proximately

II. FRICASSEE SAUCE
    CHICKEN FAT   1 cup
    FLOUR   1-1/2 cups
    STOCK FROM VEAL   1 gallon
    CREAM, 18 per cent   1 pint
    EGG YOLKS, beaten   6
    SALT   to season
    PEPPER   to season

Procedure

I.   Cut veal in 1-inch cubes. Cover with cold water. Bring to a boil.

2. Drain off water to remove any scum.

3. Cover with chicken stock or cold water.

4. Tie bouquet garni in cheesecloth bag, and add with carrots, onion and salt to the veal.

5. Bring to boiling point and simmer gently until meat is tender.

6. Remove carrots, onion, and bouquet garni.

7. Drain stock from meat to make the sauce. There should be 1 gallon.

II.   Make a roux of the chicken fat and the flour, gradually add the veal stock, stirring constantly. Then add the cream. Cook until sauce thickens.

2. Beat egg yolks. Pour over some of the hot sauce, and add to the remainder of the sauce.

3. Season with salt and pepper. Cook only a few minutes longer.

4. Arrange veal cubes over rice or noodles in serving dish and strain hot sauce over them.

Note

For Fricassee of Veal Shortcake, use 4 pounds veal for each gallon and 1 pint green peas. Serve over hot baking powder biscuit halves.

BARBECUED SPARERIBS

Yield: 100 portions

Ingredients

1. BARBECUE SAUCE
    GREEN PEPPER, diced   1 pound, 8
                                         ounces
    ONION, chopped   2 pounds, 8
                                         ounces
    GARLIC CLOVE, mashed   1
    TOMATOES, canned,
        crushed   1-1/2 quarts
    TOMATO CATSUP   1 quart
    TOMATO PUREE   1-1/2 quarts
    MUSTARD, dry   2 teaspoons
    CHILI POWDER   2 ounces (ap-
                                         prox.)
    SALT   4 teaspoons
    SUGAR   1/2 cup
    VINEGAR   1/2 cup
    BEEF STOCK   1 gallon
    RED PEPPER   1/2 teaspoon
    CORNSTARCH   4/5 cup
    WATER, cold   1/2 cup
2. SPARERIBS, A.P.   50 pounds
    SALT   4 ounces
    PEPPER   2 tablespoons

Procedure

1. Combine all ingredients for Barbecue Sauce except the cornstarch and water.

2. Blend well and simmer 1 hour, stirring frequently.

3. Mix cornstarch with cold water and add to sauce. Cook until mixture thickens.

4. Wipe spareribs with damp cloth. Cut in uniform pieces weighing 8 ounces each.

5. Season spareribs with salt and pepper. Place in greased baking sheets and brown in oven at 375°F.

6. Remove from oven, and with tongs place on edge in roasting pan. Pour Barbecue Sauce over spareribs. Cover.

7. Bake in oven at 325°F. for 1-1/2 to 2 hours or until tender.

8. Serve 1 piece spareribs with approximately 2 ounces sauce over the top.

SPRING LAMB STEW IN CASSEROLE

Yield: 25 portions

Ingredients

LAMB, NECK and SHOULDER	12 pounds
FAT	5 ounces
FLOUR	3-3/4 ounces
STOCK	4-1/2 pounds
TOMATOES, WHOLE, CANNED	2-1/2 pints
GARLIC CLOVES, chopped	2
WHITE ONION, small	2-1/4 pounds
CARROTS, cubed	2-1/4 pounds
WHITE TURNIPS, cubed	2-1/4 pounds
POTATOES	4-1/2 pounds
FRESH PEAS	8 ounces
FRESH STRING BEANS	8 ounces
BAY LEAVES	3
THYME	1 teaspoon
PARSLEY, chopped	1/4 cup
LEEKS, chopped fine	to season
PEPPERCORNS, whole	4
SALT	to season
PEPPER	to season

Procedure

1. Cut meat in 2-ounce pieces. Season with salt and pepper, and dredge lightly with flour. (The flour will hasten the browning process).

2. Put fat in skillet, and when hot, brown meat in it. When seared on all sides, place meat in saucepan.

3. Add rest of flour to skillet and mix to a smooth paste.

4. Add stock and bring to boiling point.

5. Add tomatoes, crushed garlic, bay leaves, thyme, leeks and peppercorns.

6. Pour stock over meat. Cover saucepan, place in oven at 300°F. and cook for 45 minutes. Remove any excess fat from top of stock.

7. Add carrots, onion, turnips sauteed in butter, and potatoes cut in small balls. Cover and cook in oven at 300°F. until meat and vegetables are fork tender—30 to 45 minutes. Add chopped parsley. Season with salt and pepper.

8. In meantime, cook peas and string beans separately and set aside for garnishing.

9. Pre-portion 13 ounces of stew, including 6 ounces meat, into preheated greased casserole dishes.

10. Garnish with peas and string beans. Serve very hot.

HAM A LA KING

Yield: 50 portions

Ingredients

HAM, cooked, diced	6 pounds
GREEN PEPPER, 1/4-inch cubes	1 pound
MUSHROOMS, FRESH, sliced	2 pounds
or	
MUSHROOMS, CANNED, sliced	1-1/2 pounds
BUTTER or SHORTENING	4 ounces
PAPRIKA	1/4 teaspoon
SHERRY	6 ounces
CREAM SAUCE (MEDIUM)	1-1/2 gallons
PIMIENTO, chopped	6 ounces

Procedure

1. Cut ham in 1/2-inch pieces.

2. Saute green pepper and mushrooms in butter or shortening. Do not brown.

3. Blend in the paprika. Add sherry and cubed ham. Cover and remove from the direct heat.

4. Let stand 5 minutes for the sherry flavor to permeate all ingredients.

5. Strain Cream Sauce over ham mixture. Add pimiento and mix gently.

6. Heat thoroughly. Taste for seasoning, and adjust, if necessary.

7. Serve on toast points in casserole or on plate.

SARATOGA CHOPS WITH CORN AND BREAD DRESSING

Yield: 25 portions

Ingredients

SARATOGA LAMB CHOPS	25
SALT	2 tablespoons
PEPPER	1 tablespoon
CREAM STYLE CORN	5 cups
SOFT BREAD CRUMBS	4 cups
MILK	1/2 cup
CHOPPED CELERY LEAVES	5 tablespoons
MARGARINE	8 tablespoons

Procedure

1. Brown chops slowly on both sides in large skillet.
2. Season with salt and pepper.
3. Combine remaining ingredients until well mixed.
4. Transfer dressing to well-greased steam table pan and place chops on top.
5. Bake in oven at 350°F. for approximately 30 minutes, or until done.
6. Serve one chop and top with No. 20 scoop of dressing.

Note

This is a moist dressing and has a very acceptable color.

TENDERLOIN TIPS IN CASSEROLE

Yield: 75 portions

Ingredients

TENDERLOIN TIPS	20 pounds
ONION, large	1
GREEN PEPPERS	10
MUSHROOMS	2-1/2 pounds
DRY BURGUNDY WINE	1 wine glass
BROWN SAUCE	3 gallons
SALT	to season
WORCESTERSHIRE SAUCE	to season
PEPPER	to season

Procedure

1. Dice lean, raw tenderloin tips into 1-inch pieces. Season with salt and pepper.
2. Brown meat in hot oil or fat in large skillet. Remove meat from skillet.
3. Add finely chopped onion, saute slightly. Then add mushrooms sliced, and green peppers diced in 3/4-inch pieces.
4. When vegetables are partially cooked, add burgundy wine, and cook at low temperature a few minutes longer.
5. Place the seared beef with the sauteed vegetables and liquid in large pot or pan.
6. Add Brown Sauce. (Use any good basic recipe for the Brown Sauce.) Heat to simmering point.
7. Cover pot or pan and place in oven at 350°F. Cook for 30 minutes. Avoid overcooking.
8. Remove from heat. Taste, and add more salt, pepper, and worcestershire, if necessary. Serve in preheated casseroles.

Note

If sirloin is substituted for tenderloin tips, allow one-half hour longer cooking time.

Camelback Inn, Phoenix, Arizona

BAKED GROUND BEEF AND ALMONDS

Yield: 24 portions

Ingredients

GROUND BEEF, ROUND or CHUCK	3 pounds
CELERY, cut in 1/2-inch pieces	2 cups
ONION, chopped fine	1-1/4 cups
GREEN PEPPER, sliced fine	2/3 cup
SALT	3-1/2 teaspoons
RICE, cooked	2 quarts
MUSHROOM SOUP, canned, 10-1/2 ounces	2
WATER	2 cups
CHICKEN GRAVY	2 cups
SOY SAUCE	1/4 cup
ALMONDS, blanched and sliced	2 cups
FRENCH FRIED NOODLES	2 cups

Procedure

1. Lightly brown ground meat in a small amount of fat. Pour off almost all of the fat. Add celery, onion, green pepper, and salt. Cook slowly until vegetables are tender, yet crisp.

2. Gently fold in the cooked rice, then add remaining ingredients.

3. Blend well, and spread mixture in two pans, 10-inches by 12-inches. Cover with french fried noodles.

4. Bake in oven at 350°F. for 30 minutes.

LAMB KABOBS

Yield: 32 to 35 portions

Ingredients

1. LEG OF LAMB, BONED	10 to 12 pounds
2. MARINADE	
ONION, chopped	2-1/2 cups
GARLIC CLOVES, minced	3
OLIVE OIL	1 cup
SHERRY	3 cups
BLACK PEPPER	1-1/2 tablespoons
OREGANO	4 teaspoons
THYME	2 teaspoons
SALT	1-1/2 tablespoons
3. TOMATOES, firm, medium, cut in 1/8's	5
GREEN PEPPERS, cut in 1-inch squares	3
BOILER ONIONS, parboiled	36
MUSHROOM CAPS	36

Procedure

1. Wipe lamb and cut into 1-1/2 inch pieces being careful to trim off gristle and most of the fat.

2. Combine ingredients for marinade and marinate lamb in it for several hours or overnight.

3. Thread skewers, alternating with the lamb and vegetables, allowing 2-1/2 ounces lamb per skewer. Allow space between for thorough cooking.

4. Broil 3 inches from the direct source of heat approximately 15 minutes, turning for even cooking, or bake in oven at 350°F. for 40 to 45 minutes. Baste frequently with the marinade. Allow 2 kabobs per serving. Serve on skewers, or slip from skewer when served.

HAM AND BROCCOLI IN CASSEROLE

Yield: 25 portions

Ingredients

MACARONI, uncooked	1-1/2 pounds
HAM, cooked, cut in 3/4-inch cubes	1-1/2 pounds
BROCCOLI, cooked	1-1/2 quarts
AMERICAN CHEESE, grated	2-1/4 cups
BUTTER	3/4 cup
FLOUR	1 cup
MILK	3 quarts
DRY MUSTARD	1 teaspoon
ONION, grated	1 tablespoon
WHITE PEPPER	1/4 teaspoon
SALT	1 teaspoon
VINEGAR	1/2 teaspoon
PARMESAN CHEESE	1/4 cup

Procedure

1. Cook macaroni in boiling salted water. Drain. Rinse.

2. Cut broccoli, slightly on the underdone side, in 1-inch pieces.

3. Using the butter, flour, milk, mustard, onion, vinegar and seasonings make sauce.

4. Add cheese and cook only until cheese is melted.

5. Lightly combine macaroni, ham and broccoli with the sauce.

6. Divide mixture evenly among 25 greased casseroles.

7. Sprinkle 1/2 teaspoon parmesan cheese over each casserole.

8. Bake in oven at 357°F. until cheese is melted and sauce is bubbly.

The Pennant Cafeteria, Topeka, Kansas

JOE BOOKER STEW

Yield: 6 servings

Ingredients

LEAN SALT PORK, diced	6 ounces
ONION, sliced	1/2 pound
BEEF CHUCK, cubed	2 pounds
FLOUR	1 ounce
BEEF STOCK	1 quart
THYME	1/8 teaspoon
SALT	to taste
BLACK PEPPER, ground	to taste
POTATOES, diced	12 ounces
CARROTS, sliced	12 ounces
WHITE RUTABAGA, diced	8 ounces

Procedure

1. In a heavy skillet, fry the salt pork over moderate heat until crisp. Remove the pork bits and discard.

2. Add onion to fat and cook until golden brown. Remove onion with slotted spoon and set aside.

3. Dust beef cubes with flour and brown sides in remaining hot fat. As the beef browns, add the cubes to the onion.

4. Pour 1 cup of beef stock into skillet and bring to a boil, stirring constantly and scraping in the brown particles that cling to the bottom and sides of the pan.

5. Return the onion and beef cubes to the skillet. Add remaining beef stock, thyme, salt, and pepper and bring to a boil. Reduce heat, cover tightly, and simmer for 1 hour.

6. Stir in potatoes, carrots, and rutabaga. Cover again and simmer for 30 minutes longer. Serve.

United Airlines Food Services Library

ORIENTAL CHICKEN

Yield: 24 portions

Ingredients

FRYING CHICKEN, 2-1/2 pounds, eviscerated, disjointed	6
SALT	1 tablespoon
GARLIC, minced	1/2 tablespoon
GREEN PEPPERS, medium, chopped	6
ONIONS, medium, chopped	4
PARSLEY chopped	1 cup
TOMATOES, canned, No. 10	1
SALAD OIL	1/2 cup
CAYENNE PEPPER	1/2 teaspoon
CURRY POWDER	2 teaspoons
CURRANTS, dried	2 cups
ALMONDS, blanched	3 cups

Procedure

1. Wash chicken; dry thoroughly, and cut in pieces.

2. Combine flour, salt and paprika in paper bag. Shake chicken pieces in mixture. Brown in deep fat.

3. Place chicken in baking pan; add 1/2 cup water; cover and place in oven at 300°F.

4. Saute garlic, green pepper, and onion in salad oil.

5. Add tomatoes, seasonings and currants. Cook until smooth.

6. Pour tomato mixture over chicken, and bake until tender.

7. Garnish with almonds. Serve with brown or wild rice.

Montana State College, Bozeman, Mont.

CARMEN'S TURKEY NEWBURG

"Carmen Lomastro, Camelback's noted chef for the past 7 years, suggests Turkey Newburg for a tasty and unusual luncheon or supper dish."

Yield: 24 portions

Ingredients

TURKEY, cooked, diced	4 pounds
BUTTER	1 cup
ONION, large, finely chopped	1
FLOUR, all-purpose, sifted	2 cups
PAPRIKA	2 tablespoons
MILK	2-3/4 quarts
SALT	to season
MEAT SAUCE, hot	1/2 teaspoon
WORCESTERSHIRE SAUCE	2 teaspoons
SHERRY WINE	1/2 cup

Procedure

1. Melt butter in saucepan. Add onion and cook until almost soft. Add paprika and one-quarter of the cubed turkey meat. Saute 5 minutes on moderate heat.

2. Add flour gradually, stirring until butter and flour are well blended. Slowly add the milk. Stir with wooden spoon until sauce reaches boiling point and is of the desired consistency.

3. Add remaining turkey, worcestershire sauce, hot meat sauce, and salt. Blend well. Add sherry wine, and cook 2 minutes longer. Serve on toast points, rusks, or in patty shells.

Note

Jellied cranberry sauce, whole-cranberry sauce, or spiced peach half stuck with blanched, toasted almonds and garnished with watercress make pleasing accompaniments for Turkey Newburg.

Camelback Inn, Phoenix, Ariz.

BEEF KIDNEY STEW

Yield: 25 portions

Ingredients

BEEF KIDNEYS	10 pounds
MARGARINE	8 ounces
ONION, minced	1/2 cup
CARROTS, sliced thin	1-1/2 cups
TOMATOES, canned	2-1/2 cups
BARLEY	1/4 cup
SALT	2 teaspoons
PEPPER	1/8 teaspoon
MONOSODIUM GLUTAMATE	2 teaspoons
FLOUR	1/2 cup
WATER	as needed

Procedure

1. Wash kidneys. Remove outer membrane. Split kidneys, and cut in 1/4-inch slices. Snip out fat and tubes with scissors. Soak in salted water 30 minutes. Drain well.

2. Saute in margarine 10 minutes, turning frequently.

3. Add the next 7 ingredients, and simmer 30 minutes.

4. Combine flour with enough water to make a paste. Add to kidney mixture. Blend well.

5. Simmer slowly 30 minutes, stirring occasionally.

6. Taste and adjust seasonings, if necessary.

7. Serve garnished with chopped parsley.

HAM LOAF ⟶

Yield: 250 portions

Ingredients

PORK, RAW, E.P.	30 pounds
SMOKED HAM, RAW, E.P.	30 pounds
CRACKER CRUMBS	1-1/2 gallons
SALT	2-2/3 tablespoons
PEPPER	1-1/2 teaspoons
EGGS, SLIGHTLY BEATEN	40
MILK	3-1/2 quarts
TOMATOES, CANNED, NO. 10	2-1/2

SWEDISH MEAT BALLS

Yield: 250 portions

Ingredients

EGGS	30
MILK	1-1/4 quarts
BREAD CRUMBS	5 quarts
PORK, GROUND	25 pounds
BEEF, GROUND	25 pounds
VEAL, GROUND	25 pounds
CELERY, DICED VERY FINE	1-1/4 quarts
ONION, MINCED	1 quart
SAGE	5 tablespoons
SALT	1 cup
PEPPER	to season

Procedure

1. Beat eggs in large mixing bowl. Add milk and bread crumbs and let mixture stand 5 minutes.

2. Add all other ingredients. Blend thoroughly.

3. Using a No. 16 dipper, shape into balls. Roll in flour.

4. Place on a greased baking pan and brown in oven at 425°F.

5. Remove to counter pans. Make a thin gravy using drippings in baking pan.

6. Pour gravy over meat balls. Cook in oven at 350°F. for 1 hour.

Montana State University, Missoula

Procedure

1. Grind pork and ham together. Mix with cracker crumbs, salt and pepper. Combine slightly beaten eggs and milk, and add to meat mixture. Blend thoroughly.

2. Weigh mixture into 5-pound lots. Shape into loaves.

3. Place in greased baking pans. Pour over crushed canned tomatoes. Bake in oven at 325°F. for 3 hours.

Note

Tomato Soup, or Tomato Puree may be used in place of Canned Tomatoes, if desired.

Montana State University, Missoula

JACKSON HOLE BARBECUE SAUCE

Yield: 12 12-ounce portions

Ingredients

DRY MUSTARD	1/2 teaspoon
CHILI POWDER	1 teaspoon
PAPRIKA	1 teaspoon
SALT	1 teaspoon
GARLIC SALT	1 teaspoon
ONION SALT	1 teaspoon
BLACK PEPPER, coarse grind	1 teaspoon
WORCESTERSHIRE SAUCE	2 tablespoons
STEAK SAUCE, HOT	dash
RED WINE, DRY	1 cup
OLIVE OIL	1 cup
VINEGAR	1/3 cup
WATER	1/2 cup

Procedure

1. Mix all ingredients for Barbecue Sauce.
2. One hour before cooking, baste meat with sauce. Let stand until time to cook. Baste meat frequently while cooking.

DEVILED EGGS AND ASPARAGUS IN CASSEROLE

Yield: 24 portions

Ingredients

EGGS, hard-cooked	24
MAYONNAISE	2-1/2 tablespoons
PREPARED MUSTARD	1 tablespoon
WHOLE MILK	2/3 cup
SALT	1 teaspoon
ASPARAGUS TIPS, canned, drained	1-1/2 pounds
CREAM SAUCE, thin	1-1/2 quarts

Procedure

1. Cut eggs lengthwise. Remove yolks and press through a fine sieve.
2. Combine egg yolks, mayonnaise, mustard, milk, and salt.
3. Using a pastry bag tube, refill egg whites with yolk mixture.
4. Cut asparagus in 1-inch pieces. Place 1 ounce in bottom of greased casserole dish.
5. Top with 2 halves stuffed eggs.
6. Heat in oven at 375°F. until yolks and sauce are slightly tinged with brown.
7. Garnish with parsley.

Note

Fresh or frozen asparagus may be substituted for the canned. For a less-expensive dish, canned cut asparagus may be used in place of the canned, fresh or frozen asparagus tips.

The Pennant Cafeteria, Topeka, Kansas

CREAMED SPINACH

Yield: 27 portions

Ingredients

FROZEN SPINACH	10 pounds
WHITE SAUCE, HEAVY	1-1/2 quarts
ONION, MINCED	1 cup
SALT	to season
PEPPER	to season
BUTTER	3 tablespoons

Procedure

1. Cook spinach in boiling salted water 3 minutes. Drain.

2. Cut spinach—do not chop.

3. Saute onion in butter until tender but not brown.

4. Fold spinach and onion into white sauce. Season with salt and pepper.

Note

For **Spinach** in Cheese Sauce, add 1/2 pound or 1-3/4 cups grated sharp cheese to the white sauce.

BROCCOLI-STUFFED BAKED TOMATOES

Yield: 24 portions

Ingredients

TOMATOES, large, firm	24
BROCCOLI, frozen, A.P.	2 pounds
BACON, A.P.	3 slices
SOFT BREAD CUBES, 1/2-inch	2 cups
ONION, chopped	2 tablespoons
SALT	to season
PEPPER	to season
BUTTER, melted	1/2 cup

Procedure

1. Remove slice from stem end of tomatoes. Scoop out pulp. Sprinkle inside of tomatoes with salt.

2. Cook broccoli. Drain and cut into small pieces. (There should be 4 cups cooked broccoli.) Saute bacon and crumble.

3. Combine tomato pulp with the other ingredients. Stuff tomatoes.

4. Top with 1 teaspoon melted butter. Bake in oven at 350°F. until tomatoes are soft—approximately 25 to 30 minutes.

Pennant Cafeteria, Topeka, Kansas

STUFFED YELLOW SQUASH

Yield: 24 portions

Ingredients

YELLOW SQUASH	24
BUTTER, MELTED	6 tablespoons
BREAD CRUMBS, FINE	3 cups
ONION, MINCED	1/4 cup
PARSLEY, MINCED	3 tablespoons
SALT	3 teaspoons
WHITE PEPPER	3/4 teaspoon
EGGS	3

Procedure

1. Parboil squash in boiling salted water until tender but not soft. Cool. Cut slice lengthwise off top of squash leaving the stem whole. Carefully scoop out the pulp from the center.

2. Stir crumbs into melted butter. Set aside 4 tablespoons crumbs for topping. Combine other 5 ingredients with crumbs, blend.

3. Mix together the mashed pulp and bread crumb mixture. Refill squash shells with crumb-squash mixture.

4. Sprinkle approximately 1/2 teaspoon reserved crumbs on top of each squash. Just before serving, place in oven at 400°F. until crumbs are evenly browned and squash thoroughly heated.

Gold's of Nebraska, Lincoln, Neb.

VEGETARIAN PLATE

Yield: 6 portions

Ingredients

1. CAULIFLOWER HEAD, fresh — 2 pounds
   SPINACH LEAVES — 6
   CARROTS, large — 2 pounds
   NEW PEAS — 2 pounds
   ASPARAGUS SPEARS, fresh — 2 pounds
   BUTTER, melted — 1/2 cup
   SALT — to season
   PEPPER — to season
2. POTATOES, large — 6
   EGGS — 3
   BUTTER — 3 tablespoons
   SALT — to season
   PEPPER — to season
3. MUSHROOMS — 6
   BUTTER — 6 tablespoons
   LEMON JUICE — 2 tablespoons
   TOMATOES, small — 4
   EGGS, poached — 6

Procedure

1. Clean cauliflower and spinach and soak 20 minutes in salted water.
2. Peel carrots. Shape in rounds with a parisienne spoon.
3. Clean asparagus.
4. Wash and peel potatoes. Wash mushrooms.
5. Scald tomatoes, peel, cut in quarters.
6. Cook the first 5 vegetables individually in boiling salted water. Drain.
7. Pour melted butter over each cooked vegetable, and season with white pepper, and, if necessary, salt. Keep hot.
8. Boil or steam potatoes. Mash and add 3 raw eggs, 3 tablespoons butter, salt and pepper. Beat until light and fluffy. Keep hot.
9. Simmer mushrooms in 2 tablespoons butter. When partially cooked, add lemon juice. Cook until mushrooms are tender.
10. Simmer the quartered tomatoes in 4 tablespoons butter. When partially cooked, season with salt and pepper.
11. Poach eggs.
12. Arrange hot vegetables on large platter paying special attention to the color arrangement. Force mashed potatoes through pastry bag tube to make a border around the other vegetables. Garnish asparagus with pimiento strips. Place a poached egg on the top of each serving of spinach.
13. Have vegetables very hot when served.

Note

If desired, serve the carrot balls, cauliflower, peas, and tomatoes in potato or noodle baskets, and surround with asparagus, potatoes, and spinach with poached egg.

The Brown Palace Hotel, Denver

HOT COLESLAW

Yield: 25 portions

Ingredients

CABBAGE, shredded	8 pounds
BAY LEAVES	3
CLOVES, WHOLE	4
BACON FAT	1 pound
STOCK	1 pint
GRANULATED SUGAR	5/8 cup
CIDER VINEGAR	1-1/2 cups
APPLES, RAW, peeled, diced	2 quarts
SALT	4-1/2 tablespoons
PEPPER	2 teaspoons

Procedure

1. Shred cabbage. Tie bay leaves and cloves in a gauze bag.

2. Melt bacon fat and add stock, cabbage, and sugar. Cook 8 minutes. Add vinegar and cook 5 minutes.

3. Add diced apples, salt, and pepper. Cook 10 minutes.

4. Remove spice bag and serve.

VEGETABLE RELISHES

Carrot Curls. Clean carrots and cut in very thin strips lengthwise with a vegetable parer. Roll up each slice tightly. Place close together in ice water. Place in refrigerator for several hours for the curl to set.

Carrot Sticks. Clean carrots. Cut in half. Slice lengthwise in broad strips and about 1/4 inch thick. Cut each strip again lengthwise into small sticks. Crisp in ice water. Serve "as is" or poke through a pitted olive.

Stuffed Carrots. Cut cleaned carrots in half crosswise. Remove core with apple corer. Stuff centers with a stiff creamed cheese mixture. Chill. Cut in thick cartwheels.

Celery Curls. Cut cleaned tender celery stalks in 2- or 3-inch pieces. Slash the ends into thin strips lengthwise, about 1 to 1-1/2 inches long. Or, slit both ends to within 1/2 inch of center. Leave in ice water approximately 3 hours for celery to curl. Drain thoroughly before serving.

Celery Sticks. Separate shoots from each stalk, and prepare in the same manner as carrot sticks.

Cucumber Scallops. Run the prongs of a fork lengthwise down the cucumber with or without the skin on. Slice thin and chill in ice water.

Fluted Vegetables. Press fluted vegetable cutter through one side of an oblong piece of vegetable, 3 inches long by 1 inch wide, then through the opposite side. This gives a waffled or fluted appearance.

Broccoli or Cauliflower Flowerets. Cut away green leaves and stalks from the head. Wash head well. Break into tiny flowerets, or slice into thin fans.

Radish Roses. Wash radishes and trim root and stem ends, leaving on 1 inch green stem. Beginning at the root end, with the tip of a sharp paring knife, cut the red skin into 4 or 5 sections to the middle of the radish to form petals. Chill in ice water to open petals.

Radish Fans. Wash radishes and trim root and stem ends, leaving on 1 inch green stem. Make deep circular cuts around radish but not all the way through it. Chill in ice water to spread fans.

TURKEY OR CHICKEN SALAD SUPREME

Yield: 35 portions

Ingredients

TURKEY or CHICKEN, cooked and cubed	3 quarts
CELERY, fine slices	3 quarts
PINEAPPLE, FRESH, diced	1-1/4 quarts
SALT	1-1/2 tablespoons
PEPPER, WHITE	1/2 teaspoon
OLIVES, BLACK, RIPE, sliced	1 cup
ALMONDS, BLANCHED, toasted	2 cups plus garnish
MAYONNAISE	2/3 pint
PIMIENTO, cut julienne	6
RIPE OLIVES, whole, pitted	36
PARSLEY	to garnish

Procedure

1. Mix lightly but thoroughly all ingredients except mayonnaise and garnishes.

2. Add mayonnaise. Blend well.

3. Chill. Serve in lettuce cups. Garnish each salad with 3 thin strips of pimiento, whole almonds, 1 ripe olive and a sprig of parsley.

Montana State College, Bozeman, Mont.

HUNTER'S PUDDING

Yield: 30 servings

Ingredients

BUTTER	13 ounces
SUGAR	1 pound, 10-1/4 ounces
GROUND CINNAMON	1 tablespoon
GROUND CLOVES	1-1/2 teaspoons
GROUND NUTMEG	1-1/2 teaspoons
EGGS	3
MILK	3-2/3 cups
BREAD CRUMBS	7 cups
CHOPPED NUTS	1 cup
RAISINS	3 cups
BAKING POWDER	2-1/2 teaspoons
BAKING SODA	2-1/2 teaspoons
SALT	1 teaspoon

Procedure

1. Cream the butter and sugar together.
2. Add the other ingredients in order as listed. Mix only long enough to combine evenly.
3. Place in a greased 12-inch by 20-inch by 2-inch pudding pan.
4. Bake in oven at 325°F. for 45 to 50 minutes.
5. Serve with hot RUM SAUCE.*

Oregon State University
Corvallis, Oregon

*RUM SAUCE

Yield: 1 quart (about 30 1-ounce servings)

Ingredients

SUGAR	6 ounces
CORNSTARCH	1-1/4 ounces
SALT	1/4 teaspoon
WATER, boiling	1 quart
RUM FLAVORING*	2 tablespoons
BUTTER or MARGARINE	1 tablespoon

*The flavor intensity of imitation rum may vary, so adjust rum flavor to taste.

Procedure

1. Mix dry ingredients. Add boiling water and cook until clear.
2. Add rum flavoring and butter or margarine.
3. Serve hot with Hunter's Pudding.

Oregon State University
Corvallis, Oregon

CAKE CRUMB SPICE CAKE

Yield: 12 pounds batter

Ingredients

EGGS, whole	1 pint
CAKE CRUMBS	3-1/2 pounds
COLD WATER	1 quart
SUGAR	1 pound, 8 ounces
RAISINS, soaked, drained	12 ounces
PECANS, chopped	4 ounces
VANILLA, pure	2 teaspoons
FLOUR, all-purpose, sifted	2 pounds
BAKING POWDER	2 ounces
CINNAMON, ground	4 teaspoons
CLOVES, ground	2 teaspoons
SALT	2 teaspoons
SODA	4 teaspoons
SOUR CREAM (18%)	1 quart

Procedure

1. Place cake crumbs, eggs and water in bowl of mixer, and mix at low speed until very light.
2. Add sugar, and continue mixing until well blended.
3. Add raisins, pecans and vanilla.
4. Sift together the flour, baking powder, spices and salt.
5. Dissolve soda in the sour cream.
6. Add flour alternately with the sour cream to the first mixture.
7. When all is added, continue beating at low speed 2 minutes.
8. Scale batter into greased and floured pans as follows: 12 ounces into loaf cake pans, 3-1/2 inches by 7 inches or 10 ounces into round layer pans, 7 inches in diameter or 3 pounds into sheet cake pans, 11 by 17 inches.
9. Bake in oven at 350°F. approximately 30 minutes.
10. When cool, ice with Boiled, Lemon Butter or Caramel Icing.

Menu Traditions from the Pacific Northwest

FUR TRADERS, GOLD MINERS, and mountain men blazed the way from the Plains of Kansas through the Rockies, the Cascades, and across the rivers of the Pacific Northwest. When they finally reached the coast of the Pacific, enterprising sea captains had already arrived.

Missionaries and determined settlers followed in the wake of Astor's fur traders. Dried and smoked meats and fish, shellfish, and game were the mainstay of rough-and-ready diets.

Loggers told tall tales of Paul Bunyan, and newspaper editors helped build the lore of prodigious feats of strength and a pancake griddle so big the cook tied slabs of bacon to his feet and skated around to grease the griddle.

Today, trade from Alaska's towns brings crab and other seafood to the Pacific Northwest. Fruits such as apples and pears grow in abundance. Grain from neighboring states on the other side of the mountains makes the breads and cereals so popular in this area.

Potatoes and onions come from the farms around the big towns. Much of the riches of produce are shipped to other parts of the United States. It is a meat and potatoes and fresh fruit kind of place, with salmon and shellfish also rating the front row.

Land companies failed right and left in the one-time orchards before the great Depression. Finally the engineer corps came and built dams; this meant irrigation and more and better farms.

Liars are the biggest and best in this Northwest country. The tales are long and complex and reflect only glory on the teller. So, of course, the biggest fish and best cooks can only be found in the Pacific Northwest.

Franco's Hidden Harbor
Seattle, Wash.

"I'm in the hospitality business to serve people," avers John Franco, owner of hidden Harbor Restaurant in Seattle.

Located in the center of Seattle's Marina Mart, a yacht mooring with slips for 120 yachts, burgees of clubs from up and down the coast fly in the breeze within this covered moorage.

Franco originated the idea of boating customers from his restaurant to football games at the nearby university stadium. "She's 65-foot, a converted ferry with twin decks and a dance floor," explains Franco. "We charter her each Saturday during football season. After brunch at Hidden Harbor, we board all the guests who want to go to the game. During the ride we serve popcorn and refreshments. We usually serve about 500 people on a football Saturday."

Franco sees a dilemma in hiring service people. "Our mature waitresses are good on side work, but not always good with customers. The young girls are bad about side work but are bright and enthusiastic with customers."

Business people make up the lunch crowd; check average runs about $3.50. The menu features fresh fish such as pan-size salmon, Quilcene oysters, and grilled halibut. Sandwiches, from clubhouse to Kasseri cheeseburger, still take a back seat to Dungeness crab in seven different guises.

James Chiarelli, architect, worked with Franco on the design of Hidden Harbor. An inside dining room seats 68, and a covered deck area seats another 50 to 70. The theme is nautical, with rope worked into unexpected areas to give texture.

Ivar's Acres of Clams
Seattle, Wash.

"While I was growing up here in Seattle, I played guitar and learned a lot of the regional folk songs. 'The Old Settler' was one that stayed with me," says Ivar Haglund.

"No longer a slave of ambition,
I laugh at the world and its shams,
As I think of my happy condition
Surrounded by acres of clams!"

And so it was that the fish bar Haglund opened on Pier 54 in 1938 grew into Ivar's Acres of Clams in 1946. Haglund still plays his guitar and sings "The Old Settler" on radio. "It has helped me sell a lot of fish and clams," he says.

The 250-seat restaurant juts out to the end of Pier 54. Latest decor addition is 100 feet of display area for Haglund's collection of china plates with fish designs and a series of framed scarves by a famous designer, brought back from Haglund's recent trip to Rome. The fish designs show up well; backing is mirror glass, with non-reflecting glass on top.

Haglund describes business in terms of dollar volume and customer count. Dollar volume was higher in 1974 than 1973; customer count was up. "Overall, 1974 was definitely better than the year before," declares Haglund.

Rosellini's Four-10
Seattle, Wash.

A landmark in Seattle dining since 1956, the Four-10 will soon pass into history when the building is razed for a new, bigger structure.

Victor Rosellini has one of the most extensive menus on the West Coast and prides himself on an international staff of seven in the kitchen. A big chalk board over the kitchen entrance informs service staff of specials for each day. "No clip-ons," says Rosellini. Waiters offer this daily item as "something special" to diners. Items are determined by what is fresh in the market and in season, perhaps salmon or abalone.

Lunch brings a crowd made up of 90 percent regulars, mostly business and professional people from the downtown area. "We are an 'in' spot for lunch," explains Rosellini. "Most diners know some of the other diners, many have special tables or waiters they prefer. We handle this just as I consider I want to be treated when I dine out. I'm interested in tomorrow, in having regular customers."

Wine sales in the Four-10 dining room were greater than liquor sales last year. Wine by the glass is extremely popular; 1974 sales were up 800 percent over a year ago.

Menu sales run about 50 percent table d'hote, and the rest a la carte. Lunch checks average about $7; dinner checks are about $15 per person. Veal is the most popular dinner entree.

Done in a "restrained rococo," the 140-seat dining room has snowy-white linen, clear-stemmed glassware, and heavy silver.

Robert Rosellini, Victor's son, is opening a new restaurant called The Other Place. Emphasis will be on French cuisine and fine wines with personalized service.

Longhorn Barbecue Restaurant
Spokane, Wash.

Barbecue—real, old-fashioned, open-pit barbecue—is the specialty of Longhorn Barbecue Restaurant in Spokane. Owned by five

Lehnertz brothers and their cousin, Duke Fette, the Longhorn serves hearty fare from sunup to past sundown.

"We started by serving beer and barbecue," says Manager Don Lehnertz. "All of us had a real liking for the Northwest; we came up here to harvest wheat when we were in school in Texas. So in 1956 we opened a barbecue place in downtown Spokane. It was too small within two years."

Today, after four remodelings, the waiting area extends from a 70-seat lounge, through a bench-lined hallway into the closed-in porch.

About 300 pounds of barbecued beef are sold each day.

Western breakfasts are popular. Check average runs about $2 for two eggs, meat, homemade hashbrowns marinated with bell peppers and onions, coffee specially blended for the Lehnertz brothers, and toast.

"Thick-cut toast is popular for lunch," Don says. "We run a special lunch each day. Chili is very popular in winter. A coarsely ground chuck, along with beans, makes a spicy chili people come back for."

And then there is homemade spiced wine. Spiced wine is served hot, in golden cups. Customers can "homestead" in the lounge or the dining room, or get real fast service if they are in a hurry.

Chic Lehnertz manages the drive-in and catering operation. Gene (Wishbone) Lehnertz is chief cook for catering on trail rides. This Argonne Branch may have 27 different parties to cater on one day, within a four-state area. Expo '74, the World's Fair in Spokane; company banquets; open house, and sporting events are some of the events catered.

"We pace ourselves," says Don. My brothers Gene, Dave, Chic, Claude, cousin Duke, and I have geared the menu at the Longhorn to the dishwasher, which fits into the schedule of turnover in the dining room and the seating capacity. It all works together, just like we do."

The Encore
Portland, Ore.

Roland Terry, designer for The Encore, created a Continental French atmosphere for owners Larry Hilaire and William Feasley.

The 165-seat operation includes the Chambre de Juges, or judge's chamber, a private dining room that began with a large round table where attorneys in the area gathered for lunch.

A brick wall along the side of the dining room where the stairway goes up was once an outside wall. During sandblasting to clean the bricks, they developed a sculptured look that Terry decided to leave. Other walls are covered with smooth panels painted a browned burgundy. Channel lighting behind banquettes highlights the sculpted brick and statuary.

The menu comes first at The Encore. "We have a small, intimate dining atmosphere," says Feasley. "Our meal is Continental."

Bouillabaisse, seafood, and a casserole of the day are specialties. Desserts and vegetables are offered on an a la carte basis. Lunch checks average $3; dinner runs about $8.50 per person.

The service staff changes. At lunch, there are mature waitresses; at dinner, waiters—often students at nearby university—are on the floor. "It adds a different touch," says Feasley. "Sometimes a customer is in for lunch and dinner within the same day or week."

Canlis
Seattle, Portland

Exemplar of the class house, operations owned by Ivy Award winner Peter Canlis feature the exotic seduction of the Pacific Isles. His Honolulu restaurant has been called the most beautiful restaurant in the world.

The first Hawaiian operation, in 1946, triggered a chorus of "come to Seattle"; two years later Canlis opened the doors of his first Stateside restaurant and moved his offices to Seattle as well.

By 1954 the first Hawaiian restaurant was replaced by that "most beautiful" award-winning, 230-seat operation in Honolulu. Roland Terry, designer and architect, set the pace for the Mainland restaurants.

The Portland restaurant, managed by Reza Rafati, is done in cool browns and greens with flashes of color provided by the kimonos of the waitresses and the warmth of golden wall decorations.

It took until 1965 for Canlis to open a 240-seat operation in the Fairmont Hotel in San Francisco.

Diners in each location can look out over the

city. Yet Canlis detests heights. In Portland, an Alaska King Scallop Chowder shares a menu insert with Hot Oregon Apple Pie.

That menu insert and the gowns of the waitresses are earmarks of Canlis' attention to detail. The insert is about one-third the size of the regular menu, attached by a golden cord; it features a table d'hote meal. Steaks and broiled foods are specialties.

Assistant managers sell wine and 40 percent of all customers buy wine. Employees have profit sharing, sick leave, a pension trust, and other benefits. Each operation has 35 to 50 employees. Dinner checks average $17.

With four restaurants doing better than $5 million yearly, Canlis can afford to be a snob—and enjoy it. "I'm nosey. I'm a perfectionist. I've built an empire."

Pacific Northwest Recipes

ENCORE CHINESE PEPPER STEAK

Yield: 1 serving

Ingredients

BEEF TENDERLOIN, TIP ENDS, thinly sliced	3 (approximately 5 to 6 ounces)
AU JUS	1/4 cup
ONION SOUP	1/4 cup
MUSHROOMS, cooked	2 tablespoons
BURGUNDY WINE	2 tablespoons
SALT	to taste
SOY SAUCE	dash
GROUND GINGER	to taste
CRACKED PEPPER	to taste
CLEAR GEL or CORNSTARCH	1-1/2 teaspoons
TOMATO WEDGES	4
GREEN PEPPER	4 strips
WHITE RICE, cooked	1 cup
WATER CHESTNUTS, sliced	1 ounce

Procedure

1. Saute slices of tenderloin in pan. Remove and set aside, keeping warm.

2. To the pan in which tenderloin was sauteed, add au jus, onion soup, mushrooms, Burgundy wine, salt, cracked pepper, ground ginger to taste, and soy sauce. Simmer thoroughly.

3. Blend Clear Gel or cornstarch with a little cold water. Add to ingredients in pan. Stir and cook until mixture is thickened.

4. Place tenderloin slices in casserole, add sauce, and garnish with tomato wedges, green pepper, and water chestnuts. Serve with white rice.

Hilaire's Encore

PORK STEW HUNGARIAN STYLE

Yield: 50 portions

Ingredients

PORK SHOULDER, BONELESS	12 pounds
FAT	1 pound
ONION, A.P., sliced	3 pounds
SAUERKRAUT, CANNED, NO. 10	2
PAPRIKA	1 cup
WHITE WINE, DRY	1 cup
BAY LEAVES	3
CLOVES, WHOLE	3
THYME, CRUSHED	a pinch
BEEF STOCK	1 gallon
SALT	to season
PEPPER	to season

Procedure

1. Wipe meat and cut in 1-inch cubes. Saute in hot fat until delicately browned.

2. Dust meat with flour and place in a hot oven at 400°F. for 10 minutes to toast the flour. Remove pan from oven. Mix flour well with meat.

3. Place meat in stew kettle. Brown onion in fat in pan and add to meat.

4. Combine paprika with the dry white wine and add to meat with the seasonings, stock and sauerkraut. Blend well. Simmer slowly 2 hours.

5. Serve with buttered noodles or spatzle (dumplings).

Hotel Benson, Portland, Ore.

SWEET AND SOUR RIBLETS

Yield: 25 portions

Ingredients

SALT	2 tablespoons
LAMB RIBLETS (CUT IN HALVES)	12 pounds
BOILING WATER	1-1/2 gallons
VEGETABLE OIL	6 tablespoons
GARLIC CLOVES, finely diced	3
SALT	1 tablespoon
MONOSODIUM GLUTAMATE	1 tablespoon
CORNSTARCH	3/4 cup
BROWN SUGAR	3/4 cup
SOY SAUCE	1/2 cup
VINEGAR	1/2 cup
COLD WATER	3 cups
PINEAPPLE JUICE	4 cups
BOUILLON CUBES	6
BOILING WATER TO DISSOLVE CUBES	1-1/2 cups
ONION, diced (approximately 2 small)	7-1/2 ounces
MEDIUM-SIZED CARROTS, thinly sliced	6
GREEN PEPPER, cut in 1-inch squares	13 ounces
SMALL SWEET PICKLES, sliced	24
PINEAPPLE CHUNKS	6 cups

Procedure

1. Add salt and lamb to boiling water in kettle. Cover and simmer slowly one hour or until meat is tender.

2. Drain, saving liquid for soup or sauces.

3. Brown the lamb riblets slowly in oil in a large skillet.

4. Mix together the next eleven ingredients for the sauce.

5. Transfer meat to stock pot and add the sauce mixture. Cook, stirring constantly, until sauce is transparent.

6. Add vegetables and pineapple.

7. Simmer mixture, covered, until vegetables are tender, but still a little crisp (approximately 20 minutes).

8. Serve over steamed rice or fried noodles.

CHILLED ALASKA KING CRAB AND CUCUMBER BISQUE

Yield: 50 portions

Ingredients

ONION, finely diced	1/2 pound
CUCUMBER, peeled, finely diced	1 pound
BUTTER	10 ounces
CAKE FLOUR	10 ounces
FISH STOCK	1 gallon
CREAM, LIGHT	1 gallon
ALASKA KING CRAB, finely chopped	2 pounds
SALT	to taste
WHITE PEPPER	to taste
RHINE WINE	4 ounces

Procedure

1. In soup pot, lightly saute cucumbers and onion in butter. Add flour to make roux; cook about 5 minutes, being careful not to brown.

2. Add hot fish stock and stir until slightly thickened and smooth. Incorporate hot cream.

3. Add crab; adjust seasoning. Chill well and serve ice-cold.

4. Garnish with 3 or 4 thin diagonal slices of Alaska King crab legs and a cucumber slice, with the peeling scored and twisted so as to stand on end.

5. Serve with hot, crusty french bread.

CHEF SPENCER'S FLAKED SHRIMP AND SEAFOOD AU GRATIN IN CASSEROLE

Yield: 24 portions

Ingredients

1. *CHEESE CREAM SAUCE*

BUTTER or SHORTENING	1 cup
FLOUR	2 cups
SALT	2 tablespoons
PEPPER	2 teaspoons
MILK	1 gallon
CHEESE, NIPPY CHEDDAR	1 quart

2. SHRIMP (PRAWNS or

ALASKA SHRIMP), cooked	1 pound
SALMON and HALIBUT, cooked	3 pounds
BUTTER or MARGARINE	4 tablespoons
ONIONS, LARGE, chopped	2
SHERRY	1/2 cup
BREAD CRUMBS	2-1/2 cups
BUTTER or MARGARINE	1/2 cup
PAPRIKA	3 teaspoons

Procedure

1. Melt shortening; stir in the flour and blend well. Add salt and pepper. Cook over low heat 5 to 7 minutes. Stir while cooking.

2. Add scalded milk, stirring constantly with wire whip. Cook until of the proper consistency. Add nippy cheese and stir until cheese is melted.

3. Chop shrimp and combine with the flaked salmon and halibut. Saute onions in the 4 tablespoons butter.

4. Add sauteed onions and sherry to the cheese sauce. Combine fish and cheese sauce. Place in individual greased casseroles. Top with buttered crumbs. Sprinkle with paprika.

5. Bake in oven at 350°F. for 20 minutes or until crumbs are delicately browned and ingredients are bubbly.

6. Serve topped with thick tomato slice or garnished with parsley and lemon wedge.

Note

The fish au gratin may also be put in greased baking pan.

Hilaire's Restaurants, Portland, Ore.

VEAL STEAK SAUTEED WITH NOODLES AND OYSTERS BERCY

Yield: 25 portions

Ingredients

VEAL STEAKS or CUTLETS,	
4 or 5 ounces each	25
SALT	to season
PEPPER	to season
FLOUR, ALL-PURPOSE	2 cups
SWEET BUTTER	1 pound
SHALLOTS, finely chopped	1/4 cup
CHICKEN BROTH, hot	1 quart
CREAM, 18%	1 pint
OYSTERS, RAW, blanched	8 dozen
DRY WHITE WINE	2 cups
CHIVES, chopped	2 tablespoons
PARSLEY, chopped	1 cup
LEMON JUICE	from 2 lemons
BUTTER	for topping
CRACKER CRUMBS, fine	3 cups
NOODLES, cooked, sauteed	4-3/4 pounds

Procedure

1. Roll the veal steaks in 1/2 cup of the flour which has been seasoned with salt and pepper.

2. Saute steaks in 1/2 pound hot butter until a golden brown on both sides and fork-tender.

3. Remove steaks from the pan. Add the other 1/2 pound sweet butter and saute shallots in it.

4. Add 1-1/2 cups flour. Stir until well blended.

5. Gradually add the hot chicken broth and cream. Blend well. Bring to boiling point.

6. Add blanched oysters and wine. Cook 10 minutes.

7. Add chives, parsley and lemon juice. Remove from heat.

8. In the bottom of a greased casserole, place a bed of sauteed buttered noodles.

9. Top with a veal steak.

10. Pour Oyster Sauce over all. Sprinkle with fine cracker crumbs. Dot with butter.

11. Place under broiler until delicately browned. Serve immediately.

CHEF CHITTENDON'S SALMON STEAK MARCHAND DE VIN

"This is very popular in our restaurants and is known as Hilaire's entree."

Yield: 1 9-ounce portion

Ingredients
BREADING MIXTURE

BREAD CRUMBS, soft	2-1/2 cups
SALT	1/2 teaspoon
PEPPER	1/8 teaspoon
LEMON JUICE	1 tablespoon
BUTTER, melted	6 tablespoons
SALMON STEAK	9 ounces
VERMOUTH, DRY	1/2 ounce

Procedure

1. Combine first 5 ingredients for breading steak.
2. Wipe steak with damp cloth. Dip steak in milk. Roll in seasoned bread crumbs.
3. Grill or saute until partially cooked.
4. Place steak in well-greased casserole dish. Sprinkle with vermouth.
5. Bake in oven at 375°F. for 10 to 15 minutes.
6. Serve in casserole with parsley and lemon or lime wedge.

Note

Be very careful not to overcook the steak as overcooking ruins it.

Hilaire's Restaurant, Portland, Oregon

TARANTINO'S LAZY MAN'S CIOPPINO

"This recipe is the outgrowth of customer requests. As is well known, the Italian fishermen's cioppino contains many shellfish in the shell. Due to the inconvenience to the customer in removing the meat from the shell as well as the accompanying messiness of the job, many of our patrons requested that we remove the crabmeat, oysters, shrimp, and clams from the shell prior to serving. So we term this "lazy man's" style. Our customers prefer it this way and assure us that the delicious sauce permeates the seafood and that the flavor of the cioppino is as inviting as though the meat were still in the shell."

Yield: 25 portions

Ingredients
CIOPPINO SAUCE

LEEKS	6
DRY ONIONS	3
GREEN PEPPERS	3
CELERY STALKS	6
GARLIC, chopped	1 tablespoon
WHOLE THYME	1/4 teaspoon
ROSEMARY	1/4 teaspoon
BUTTER	1/2 cup
DRY WHITE WINE	1 cup
TOMATOES, CANNED, solid pack	1 No. 10 can
WATER	1 quart
SALT	to taste
PEPPER	to taste
CRABMEAT	10 pounds
SHRIMP, LARGE, cooked	50
EASTERN OYSTERS	25
CLAMS (if available)	50

Procedure

1. Finely chop leeks, onions, green peppers, celery, garlic, and spices.
2. Saute in butter but do not brown.
3. Add wine, tomatoes, and water to the sauteed vegetables. Season with salt and pepper.
4. Simmer mixture 3 hours or until reduced one-quarter in volume. (This is the cioppino sauce.)
5. Add crabmeat, shrimp, oysters, and clams and simmer gently in the sauce 10 minutes.
6. Serve in casserole or deep dish with hot butter, garlic toast.

SWEETBREADS CHANTILLY WITH WILD RICE

Yield: 4 portions

Ingredients

WILD RICE, uncooked	4 ounces
SWEETBREADS	2 pairs
BUTTER	4 tablespoons
FLOUR	4 tablespoons
MILK	2 cups
WHITE WINE	2 tablespoons or more
BUTTER	2 tablespoons
MUSHROOMS, sliced	1 cup

Procedure

1. Wash rice. Cover with cold water. Bring to a boil and cook steadily for 25 minutes.

2. Drain, and dry rice in open kettle for a few minutes away from the heat. (Rice will remain light and fluffy if not stirred.)

3. Parboil sweetbreads. Remove outside tissue. Slice sweetbreads lengthwise.

4. In another saucepan make the sauce. Melt the butter, add the flour and blend well. Add milk. Cook until sauce thickens, stirring constantly.

5. Add wine and sauteed mushrooms.

6. Saute sweetbreads in 2 tablespoons butter.

7. Place a mound of hot rice on platter. Top with sweetbread slices.

8. Pour Wine Sauce over all. Serve at once, garnish with parsley.

POACHED FILLET OF HALIBUT AU GRATIN

Yield: 25 portions

Ingredients

HALIBUT, cut 4-ounce portions	25
SALT	to taste
PEPPER	to taste
MILK	1 quart
BUTTER	4 tablespoons
CHEESE, CANADIAN CHEDDAR, sliced	25 slices
PAPRIKA	as needed

Procedure

1. Fillet halibut in 4-ounce pieces. Season with salt and pepper.

2. Place fillets in well-greased bake pan.

3. Pour milk over fish. Dot with butter.

4. Cut cheese in pieces the size of the halibut fillets.

5. Top each fillet with a slice of cheese.

6. Sprinkle lightly with paprika.

7. Bake in oven at 375°F. for 35 minutes or until the fish flakes easily with a fork.

BRAISED VEAL

Yield: 185 portions

Ingredients

SHOULDER OR LEG OF VEAL, lean	38 pounds
FLOUR, PASTRY	4 pounds
STOCK	3 Imperial gallons
TOMATO PUREE, No. 10	1
TOMATOES, CANNED, No. 10	1
ONION	8 pounds
CELERY	10 pounds
CARROTS	12 pounds
POTATOES	7 pounds
PEAS, CANNED, No. 10	1
MONOSODIUM GLUTAMATE	4 tablespoons
CELERY SEED	1 tablespoon
PAPRIKA	3 tablespoons
SALT	14 ounces
PEPPER	2 tablespoons

Procedure

1. Dice lean veal into 1-1/2-inch cubes.

2. Place in greased bake pans, never more than 2 inches in depth.

3. Brown in oven at 400°F. for 30 minutes.

4. Remove from oven and stir in flour. Return to oven and continue browning for 15 minutes.

5. Remove from oven and mix well. Return to oven and brown 10 minutes longer.

6. Reduce oven temperature to 350°F.

7. Gradually stir in the stock, tomato puree and canned tomatoes. Mix well to prevent lumps from forming.

8. Continue cooking until meat is almost tender, stirring occasionally.

9. In the meantime, dice onion, celery and carrots in large pieces; potatoes in smaller pieces.

10. Add raw celery and onion to the meat mixture.

11. Steam potatoes and carrots until partially cooked, and add with seasonings and peas to other ingredients.

12. Continue cooking until vegetables are cooked and flavors are well blended.

CRABMEAT AU GRATIN

Yield: 25 portions

Ingredients

BUTTER	1 cup
FLOUR	2 cups
SALT	2 tablespoons
MILK, scalded	5 quarts
LIQUID HOT PEPPER SEASONING	4 dashes
EGG YOLKS	8
SHERRY	1/2 cup
CRABMEAT, FRESH	6 pounds
CHEESE, NIPPY, grated	1-1/2 cups
GREEN PEPPERS, cut in rings	5
MUSHROOMS, sliced, sauteed	15

Procedure

1. Melt butter. Stir in the flour and salt. Add scalded milk and liquid hot pepper seasoning. Stir until thickened.

2. Add a little of the hot sauce to the beaten egg yolks. Blend well.

3. Combine egg mixture with the remaining sauce. Stir in the sherry.

4. Add crabmeat. Adjust seasoning, if necessary.

5. Fill individual greased casserole dishes with the crabmeat mixture.

6. Top with grated cheese and green pepper ring filled with sauteed mushrooms.

7. Bake in oven at 350°F. until cheese is melted and sauce is bubbly.

8. Serve with french fried potatoes and tomato salad.

GRILLED FRESH SPRING SALMON STEAK

"This is one of our specialties at the Malahat Chalet and is always in demand."

1. Choose a 10- to 12-pound salmon. Cut 8-ounce steaks from the center of the salmon. (Use end pieces for salads and sandwiches.)

2. Dip steaks in milk, then in seasoned flour.

3. Pre-heat grill and oil well.

4. Place salmon steaks 2 to 3 inches from source of heat. Cook 4 minutes.

5. Turn and continue cooking for another 4 minutes.

6. Serve piping hot, garnished with lemon wedge and watercress.

Accompanying items chosen for this entree are: scalloped potatoes au gratin, buttered new beets or other colorful vegetable, tossed green salad with garlic dressing, hot roll and butter.

Note

Steaks may be pan fried, if desired.

LAMB FRICASSEE

Yield: 50 portions

Ingredients

LAMB STEW MEAT	15 pounds
FLOUR	for dredging
SALT	to season
PEPPER	to season
NUTMEG	1 ounce
BAY LEAVES	2 to 3
ONION, chopped fine	3 pounds
MINT JELLY	6 ounces
WATER	to cover meat

Procedure

1. Wipe meat and cut in 1-1/2 inch pieces.

2. Dredge meat with flour seasoned with salt and pepper.

3. Brown lamb in oven. Add nutmeg, bay leaves and chopped onion. Add mint jelly combined with just enough water to cover the meat. Cook slowly until meat is tender.

4. Adjust seasonings, if necessary.

5. Garnish each serving with steamed vegetables— carrots, peas, and potatoes.

HAMBURGER-ON-BUN

Preliminary Preparation

1. Cut Grade A, Boneless Beef Chucks in 3-inch pieces.

2. Use suet in the proportion of 1 pound suet to 5 pounds lean beef.

3. Combine lean beef and suet and mix well.

4. Grind only once through a 3/16 plate on food chopper.

5. Mold hamburgers in automatic machine using 1/4-inch plate, making 6 patties per pound. (As each patty is molded it drops on a piece of waxed paper separating the patties.)

6. Refrigerate until ready for cooking.

Final Preparation

7. Place patty on hot griddle and cook until juices show on the surface of the hamburger.

8. Turn patty over to finish cooking.

9. Once the patty is browned, season with White Spot's special seasoning.

10. Prepare bun. When patty is cooking, split bun and toast.

11. Place each bun half on griddle, face up. Dress each half with White Spot's special mayonnaise and relish.

12. On one half, place hamburger.

13. If ordered, top hamburger with cheese, onion, sauteed mushrooms, bacon, or lettuce and tomatoes.

14. Top with the other half of the toasted bun.

15. Cut bun in half. Garnish with a long slice of dill pickle.

16. Place bun on serving plate and serve at once.

17. If there is any delay in the bun being picked up, keep piping hot under infrared quartz lamp on counter.

White Spot's, Vancouver, B. C.

SEA GREEN PEAR SALAD

Yield: 36 4-ounce molds

Ingredients

LIME FLAVORED	
GELATINE	20 ounces
HOT WATER	1-1/4 quarts
PEAR JUICE	1-1/4 quarts
CREAM CHEESE	1-1/2 pounds
MILK	1 cup
GROUND GINGER	1 teaspoon
PEARS, sliced	1 No. 10 can

Procedure

1. Dissolve gelatin in hot water. Add pear juice. Pour enough in molds or pans to make a layer 1/4-inch thick. Chill until firm.

2. Chill the rest of the gelatine but only until it begins to congeal.

3. Soften the cream cheese with milk. Add the ginger and beat well.

4. Fold the cheese and drained pear slices into the whipped, cooled gelatine.

5. Finish filling the molds and chill until firm.

SOUR CREAM FRUIT SALAD

Yield: 28 4-ounce servings

Ingredients

PEAR HALVES, drained	
and cut	1 No. 2-1/2 can
PEACH SLICES, drained	2 No. 2-1/2 cans
PINEAPPLE CHUNKS,	
drained	2 No. 2 cans
APRICOT HALVES,	
drained and cut	1 No. 2-1/2 can
SMALL MARSHMALLOWS	8 ounces
FINE GRANULATED	
SUGAR	1/4 cup
COMMERCIALLY SOURED	
CREAM	1 pint

Procedure

1. Combine all fruits, marshmallows, sugar and sour cream. Let stand overnight.

2. Scoop or spoon out into lettuce cups. Garnish with maraschino cherries if desired.

PINEAPPLE CATAMARAN SALAD

Yield: 25 servings

Ingredients

LETTUCE, finely shredded	5 quarts
PAPAYA or MELON in	
season, cut in wedges	50 wedges
CANNED PINEAPPLE SLICES,	50 (1 No. 10
drained	can)
SHRIMP, cooked	100
FRENCH DRESSING	6-1/4 cups

Procedure

1. For each salad, place 3/4 cup shredded lettuce on lettuce leaves.

2. Place 2 papaya or melon wedges side by side on lettuce, about 2 inches apart.

3. Cut 2 pineapple slices in half and overlap crosswise on top of melon wedges.

4. Skewer 4 shrimp at one end and stick into center of pineapple half-slices to simulate sails.

5. Serve with 2 ounces of french dressing.

FILBERT CRUNCH DESSERT

Yield: 5 9-inch pies. Each can be cut into 6 or 7 pieces

Ingredients

EGGS	3 cups (about 15)
GRANULATED SUGAR	2-1/2 pounds
SALT	1 teaspoon
FILBERTS, chopped or sliced and toasted	10 ounces
GINGERSNAPS, finely crushed	1 pound

Procedure

1. Beat eggs thoroughly. Gradually beat in sugar and salt and continue beating for several minutes.

2. Fold in toasted nuts and gingersnaps.

3. Spread in greased 9-inch pie pans and bake in oven at 325°F. for 30 minutes.

4. Serve topped with ice cream or whipped cream.

ORANGE BAVARIAN CREAM

Yield: 25 servings

Ingredients

GELATINE, UNFLAVORED	2 ounces
WATER, cold	1-1/2 quarts
ORANGE JUICE	1-1/2 quarts
LEMON JUICE	1/2 cup
SUGAR	12 ounces
CREAM, WHIPPED	1 quart

Procedure

1. Soak gelatine in 1 pint cold water for 5 minutes. Then place over boiling water until dissolved.

2. Mix the orange juice, lemon juice, and sugar.

3. Stir this constantly while adding the gelatine. Add the rest of the cold water.

4. Allow to cool until almost firm. Then whip slightly and fold in the whipped cream. Chill.

5. When serving, garnish with fresh orange sections.

STEAMED CHERRY PUDDING

Yield: 20 servings

Ingredients

FLOUR	1 pound, 4 ounces
BAKING POWDER	1-1/4 ounces
SALT	1-1/4 teaspoons
SUGAR	1-1/4 cups
SHORTENING	6 tablespoons
MILK	2-1/2 cups
RED PITTED CHERRIES, FRESH, CANNED, or FROZEN, well drained	1-1/4 quarts

Procedure

1. Sift together the flour, baking powder, salt, and sugar.

2. Cut in the shortening (as for pastry).

3. Add the milk and mix lightly. Add the cherries.

4. Half fill well-oiled pudding dishes. Cover with waxed paper. Steam for 1 hour.

5. Serve with a sweet sauce.

LACY PECAN SHELLS

Yield: 24 shells

Ingredients

BUTTER	1/2 cup
BROWN SUGAR	2 cups
EGGS, whole	4 (only)
PECANS, finely chopped	1 cup
SALT	few grains
CAKE FLOUR, sifted	1 cup plus 5-1/3 tablespoons
VANILLA	1 teaspoon

Procedure

1. Cream butter. Add sugar. Beat for 2 minutes.

2. Add eggs and beat thoroughly. Add very finely chopped pecans.

3. Add remaining ingredients. Mix well.

4. Put 3 level tablespoons of batter on a very well greased cookie sheet. Spread very thin with spoon, using circular motion.

5. Bake in oven at 350°F. for 8 to 10 minutes.

6. Remove from sheet immediately. With broad spatula carefully lift off each cookie onto an inverted custard cup or glass to shape, or mold. This gives a cup-like shape.

Note:

Cook only two or three shells at a time, as you have to work very rapidly to mold shells before they become too cool. If smaller shells are desired, use only 2 level tablespoons of batter for each shell.

Because of the altitude differences, sugar and flour in this recipe may have to be adjusted.

RAISIN CORNSTARCH PUDDING

Yield: 32 servings

Ingredients

MILK, hot	2-1/2 quarts
CORNSTARCH	1 cup
BROWN SUGAR	1 cup
GRANULATED SUGAR	2 cups
SALT	1 teaspoon
MILK, cold	1 cup
SEEDLESS RAISINS	1-1/2 pounds
WALNUTS or PECANS, chopped	4 ounces
VANILLA	1 tablespoon

Procedure

1. Heat milk in double boiler.

2. Mix cornstarch, sugar, and salt with cold milk.

3. Add to the hot milk, stirring constantly until it thickens.

4. Add raisins and cook for 30 minutes, stirring occasionally.

5. Remove from heat, add nuts and vanilla, and pour into serving dishes. Chill. Top with whipped cream when serving.

BLACK CHERRY SAUCE

Yield: 2 quarts sauce (topping for approximately 32 desserts)

Ingredients

DARK SWEET CHERRIES, pitted	1 quart
CHERRY JUICE	1 quart
GRATED ORANGE RIND	1 tablespoon
HONEY	1-1/4 cups
RED FOOD COLORING	1 tablespoon
BUTTER or MARGARINE	4 ounces
CORNSTARCH	3 tablespoons
LEMON JUICE	1/2 cup

Procedure

1. Mix the cornstarch with 1/2 cup of cold cherry juice.

2. Combine the remaining cherry juice, orange rind, honey, coloring, and butter in a saucepan and bring to a boil. Add the cornstarch, stirring constantly.

3. When the mixture is thick, reduce the heat and cook 5 minutes. Then add the cherries and lemon juice.

4. Serve hot or cold. It is excellent over cream puffs (which have cream filling), on angel food wedges or on cottage pudding.

Silver Touch for Colorado Specialties

WITH THE MAJESTIC Rockies serving as a backdrop and the wealth of the silver miners as an immediate incentive, Colorado foodservice operators in the late 1880s needed menu fare that was robust, yet could be served in a manner that befitted the "struck-it-rich" silver royalty that patronized their establishments.

Opulent Victorian interiors were the fashion and Victorian furnishings are still to be found in some of today's establishments, maintaining the tone of earlier times. "Treat every customer like a silver baron" continues to be a standard for service in the Denver area.

Among the native foods available for the creation of menu specialties were fresh-caught mountain trout and Colorado beef and lamb. In this century, both of these are often featured items on menus far from the local scene, yet they continue to star where they were first served back in the days of the silver rush.

Brown Palace Hotel
Denver

"This hotel opened in 1892 to serve the successful silver miners, men who made their fortunes in the gold rush, and the cattle barons," says Karl Mehlmann, eleventh general manager of the Brown Palace and an Ivy Award winner.

"Today we are debating the wisdom of serving tea, complete with finger sandwiches and pastries, in the lobby each afternoon," he adds. "That lobby is sacred to the people of Colorado, no matter from how far away our guests come."

Mehlmann sees downtown hotels making great advances this year and for the next five years.

"We are getting more convention business, small and medium groups for meetings, as well as hometown people for a mini-vacation or a night out," he notes. "Bookings are in progress for the 1990s at the Brown Palace."

Gross sales for 1974 were up about 17 percent over 1973. The San Marco Room, Ship's Tavern, Gondola Bar and all other foodservice facilities account for 35 percent of the gross revenue, just on food sales.

The hotel maintains past elegance as it looks to the future. Executive Chef Ira Dole is proud of the Tiger Lily pattern silverware, which has been used since the hotel opened. Some of the Irish linen is still used in the dining rooms, but the china is new—only 40 years old.

Dole, who has been at the Brown Palace for 34 years, says, "We can do about any style of food desired, but our guests prefer steaks and chops. The hearty, simple fare is more in keeping with our traditions."

Dole is proud of his staff. Many have been with the Brown Palace for more than 10 years. All food preparation and sanitation are under Dole's supervision. Foodservice is one of six operating functions; the hotel is managed by a board of directors and owned by the Boettcher Foundation.

Named for a carpenter, the Brown Palace was designed by Frank E. Edbrooke, a Chicago architect. A series of artesian wells were drilled for the water supply; today, city water is still a backup in case of emergency. It took $2 million to build and furnish the hotel. Squares of onyx from Mexico were used in the floor of the lobby. The elegant Tower, a 300-room addition decorated by Havens-Batchelder of Denver, was completed in 1959.

Described as a rotunda, the original lobby resembles a series of eight verandas turned inside out so guests on each floor can look down over railings to the main floor. Its open effect preceded by several decades the dramatic atriums of such spectacular hotels as the Hyatt Regency group. Even with gold leaf from Colorado mines on the walls, priceless antiques and art objects in public areas, the Brown Palace atmosphere is hearty, simple and very good.

Le Profil
Denver

Coming to Colorado during the late 1800s with General George Custer, Ben Cook settled near Denver and took up a new trade as a plumber. Then he branched into building, finally building the apartment house which Le Profil occupies today.

T. Michael Cook, a grandson, manages the restaurant now. He capitalized on the ground swell of interest in backgammon by setting up a private club. Backgammon, a game which originated in ancient Egypt, is the raison d'etre for the club.

"The big thing is how members feel in the club and about the place," says Cook. "We can open up the room to seat 100, but it is more private and more comfortable when there are only 60 seats."

A special late-supper menu is available to club members. Omelets in four flavors, three other egg dishes, a beef burger, and steak bits for two are offered. Films are shown and special music played in the club. The sound system goes into the public areas of the restaurant, also.

The white-tablecloth dining room has 100 seats. In a style loved by Colorado's silver barons, crimson tufted banquettes and red plush chairs are set against walls of exposed pink brick and flocked wall covering. The dark paisley carpeting shows off plant stands of limed wood. One wall area has a softly lighted wine display set well above diners' heads. Tabletop items include thin crystal salt and pepper shakers, red candle bowls in gold-footed holders, and heavy silver sherbets holding sugar.

T. Michael, along with brothers Anthony J., Kenneth and Stan, formed Cook Enterprises in 1965. This group is responsible for the first swinging restaurant (with waitresses in hot pants) in Denver.

In 1960 Le Profil was redecorated by Harry Mecague of A. Parvin Co. A kitchen staff of French and Swiss, the Basque chef, a constantly bubbling stock pot, and fresh produce in season keep the set menu with weekly specials a constant attraction for local as well as tourist patrons.

A logo change gave the profile silhouette a cameo effect.

"It represents our concept and our own tradition," says T. Michael. "We respect tradition but want to keep only the parts of the past which are best for us and our customers. New ideas and new ways are necessary to enhance the excellence."

Le Petit Gourmet
Denver

Bill Bown, caterer, with a twinkle in his eye, vows that "children and dogs are a caterer's undoing." Although he tells of the kids who snitched all the croutons for one party and those who drank all the reception champagne another time, Bown's concern for perfection shines through the anecdotes and instructions.

"All employees are instructed to treat flambe liqueur and champagne corks just as respectfully as sharp knives." Bown says service people, often referred to as servants, are carefully trained in serving techniques for buffets, sit-down dinners and passing trays at receptions. As for himself, Bown uses the term "food designer." He has files of magazines with food pictures and recipes. He takes one or two staff members to Europe each year to tour kitchens, restaurants and museums for new ideas.

Analyses—of staff, of food at the pre-prepared stage before loading for a party, and again before service, of comments from guests and of notes that accompany payments—are a key to Bown's mania for perfection.

"I put so much of myself into these parties; my staff works so long and so hard to give satisfaction. It's a big show each time, with only opening night—no repeat for any event," he says. Bown also takes special care of his equipment. Specially adapted gas deck ovens hook onto the back of panel trucks. Each truck interior has special grooves and shelves to hold racks, containers of food, equipment, and linens.

Decorations are the magic that create theatrical quality for any catered affair. After 14 years, Bown still gets a kick out of seeing a bare barn of a room transformed into a glittering backdrop for an elegant dining experience.

"Call it my 'ego trip'," he says.

The Broadmoor Hotel
Colorado Springs, Colo.

"I am Norwegian. Our baker is from Honduras. We communicate because we both understand food," states Edmond Johnsen of the Penrose Room in The Broadmoor Hotel.

Opened in 1918, The Broadmoor catered to "the younger set who held many dansants (dinner dances)," says the official history book for the hotel. First play on the golf course was July 4, 1918.

Today, the hotel remains one of the great resorts. The Main Dining Room carries on the service tradition in the original building. The Tavern and adjoining Garden Room are flanked by Broadmoor South, with the Penrose Dining Room on the top floor, and Broadmoor West, to be completed in 1976.

A great pub, with interior decorated by W. & J. Sloane, Inc., is turn-of-the-century English. Called the Golden Bee, it has a pressed-metal ceiling, carved African mahoga-

ny bar, and chairs taken from an old British schooner.

Food in each operation suits the atmosphere. The Tavern offers entree salads, hearty sandwiches and such entrees as shrimp curry or Welsh rarebit. The Ramos Fizz, Cherry Flip, and Broadmoor Cooler are featured drinks.

The Golden Bee, with honky-tonk piano and a bartender with a real handlebar mustache, features the Banana Bee, sidecar, and other cocktails—with sandwiches, beef-and-kidney pie, and pickled eggs. Menu cover has a "picnic party disturbed by bees" and tells the story of the first English pub.

Fashion luncheons are featured in the Penrose Room. Jellied Madrilene and cream of cauliflower soup are some of the first courses offered to accompany entrees of Colorado lamb shanks, fresh vegetable plates with shrimp tempura and other delights.

Dinner menus offer a greater selection of first courses, including caviar and foie gras. Entrees may include beef Wellington, done in the manner of Escoffier, or "vol au vent of turkey," veal sweetbreads, and quenelles. As the list of awards grows for the Penrose Room, more and more diners have reason to recall glories of the table brought forth from Chef Johnsen's kitchen.

Chef George Ferrand presides over banquets and the Main Dining Room.

"I also take care of the guest who brings back the fish or fowl from his expedition into 'nature'. We are very careful because of all the regulations. But guests who are successful in hunting or fishing are so proud that we cannot bear to deprive them of their trophy," explains Chef Ferrand.

Catering Manager William Roub adds, "We make a point of being hospitable. Life is too short to not enjoy your work as well as your recreation."

About 60 percent of the special parties are arranged through Roub's office. The remainder come through sales.

"We communicate with the guest," Roub stresses. "The most important part of any function is to give the customer what he wants. Just as Chef Johnsen works at knowing food and pleasing diners, we work at selling what people want—and are willing to pay for."

Colorado Recipes

BRAISED BEEF WITH MUSHROOMS IN CASSEROLE

Yield: 25 portions

Ingredients

BEEF TRIM or TIPS	12 pounds
SHORTENING	1 pound
ONION, sliced	2 pounds
GARLIC CLOVES, minced	2
SALT	3 tablespoons
MUSHROOMS, sliced	3 pounds
TOMATO PASTE, 6-ounce cans	2
BEEF STOCK	1-1/2 gallons
FLOUR	1 pound
FAT FROM STOCK IN PAN	1 pound
PEPPER	to season
SALT	to season

Procedure

1. Cut meat in 1-inch cubes, and braise in shortening in oven at 375°F.

2. Add minced onion and garlic combined with the salt. Cook until onion is tender and transparent.

3. Add sliced mushrooms and tomato paste. Cook for approximately 15 minutes.

4. Add beef stock and cook in oven approximately 1 hour.

5. Remove from oven. Drain stock from meat. Strain stock and skim off fat. Save fat for roux.

6. Make a roux by combining the flour and the fat in the proportion of 1 pound fat to 1 pound flour. Add a small amount of the roux to the stock to make a thin sauce.

7. Gradually add the balance of the roux and cook until of a medium thick consistency. Add meat combined with other ingredients. Simmer gently until the beef is tender. Taste for seasoning. Serve on buttered noodles in casserole.

BAKED PORK CHOPS STUFFED WITH APPLE AND ONION DRESSING

Yield: 50 portions

Ingredients

1. APPLE AND ONION STUFFING

SALT PORK, finely chopped	4 ounces
CELERY, finely chopped	2 cups
ONION, finely chopped	1 cup
APPLE, TART, coarsely chopped	1-1/2 quarts
BREAD CRUMBS	5 cups
EGGS, slightly beaten	2
SALT	1 tablespoon
MONOSODIUM GLUTAMATE	1/2 teaspoon
THYME, powdered	1/4 teaspoon
STOCK or MILK	as needed

2. PORK CHOPS, cut 1 inch thick

PORK CHOPS, cut 1 inch thick	50
PORK FAT TRIMMINGS, rendered	1 cup
SALT	1 tablespoon
BLACK PEPPER	1/2 teaspoon
MONOSODIUM GLUTAMATE	2 teaspoons

Procedure

1. Render salt pork. Saute celery and onion in the fat until soft. Cool.

2. Combine all ingredients for the stuffing. The fat, apples and eggs should provide enough moisture to blend mixture together. If not, add a little stock or milk.

3. Wipe pork chops with damp cloth.

4. Cut halfway through each chop from fat to bone making a pocket for the stuffing.

5. Stuff loosely with apple-onion mixture. Pin to keep stuffing in place.

6. Sprinkle seasonings over stuffed chops. Brown chops on both sides in hot fat. Place in roasting pan in oven heated to 350°F.

7. Cook 45 to 60 minutes, or until chops are tender.

Note

This is a favorite entree in the 150 Greyhound Post Houses from Coast to Coast.

VEAL CHOPS SAUTE BROWN PALACE

Yield: 25 portions

Ingredients

VEAL CHOPS, from young veal	25
SALT	to season
PEPPER	to season
PAPRIKA	1 teaspoon
BUTTER	1 pound
SHALLOTS, chopped	8
DRY WHITE WINE	2 cups
CREAM, 30%	1 quart
MUSHROOMS, cut in half	2 pounds
LEMON JUICE	from 1 lemon
SALT	to season
PEPPER	to season

Procedure

1. Season chops with salt, pepper and paprika. Saute in butter in a heavy-bottomed pan until tender. Remove from pan. Keep hot.

2. Pour off some of the butter from the pan in which the chops were cooked.

3. Add chopped shallots. Cook until fairly tender. Do not brown.

4. Add dry white wine. Simmer until liquid is reduced in half. Add cream. Simmer until the liquid is again reduced in half or until mixture thickens. Strain.

5. In another pan, saute the mushrooms in butter. Add to sauce.

6. Add juice of 1 lemon. Bring to a boil and cook 1 minute.

7. Season with salt and pepper.

8. Arrange chops on hot platter. Pour sauce over them.

9. Place Broccoli Milanaise as a garnish around the chops. Pop into a very hot oven (450°F.) for a few minutes.

BROCCOLI MILANAISE

1. Clean and boil one 2-pound bunch of broccoli. Drain.

2. Make 25 small bunches by cutting the broccoli stems and placing the broccoli florets around the chops.

3. Season with salt and pepper. Sprinkle with grated parmesan cheese. Pour over some of the brown butter.

4. Place in oven at 450°F. with chops until cheese is melted and slightly browned.

Brown Palace Hotel, Denver

VEAL SWEETBREADS WITH CREAMED MUSHROOMS A LA ROYAL

Yield: 25 portions

Ingredients

VEAL SWEETBREADS	10 pounds
FLOUR, ALL-PURPOSE	to dust lightly
PANCAKE BATTER	to coat
FRENCH TOAST	50 slices
CREAMED MUSHROOMS	
MUSHROOMS, canned, sliced	4 cups
BUTTER	4 tablespoons
GARLIC SALT	to season
CREAM SAUCE	1 quart
SHERRY WINE	4 ounces
YELLOW FOOD COLORING	a few drops
ASPARAGUS, FRESH, extra fancy	3 bunches
CARROTS, FRESH	1 bunch

Procedure

1. Cook veal sweetbreads 15 minutes in boiling salted water to which has been added a few mixed spices.

2. Remove from boiling water, and cool in crushed ice.

3. Remove skin and membrane, and cut in uniform pieces.

4. Dust sweetbreads lightly with all-purpose flour, then dip in pancake batter.

5. Fry in deep fat at 360°F. similar to fritters.

6. In meantime prepare Creamed Mushrooms. Saute mushrooms in butter. Season with garlic salt and add to Cream Sauce. Blend well.

7. Add sherry wine and yellow food coloring.

8. Prepare French Toast by dipping bread in egg batter and pan-frying in butter.

9. To serve, arrange 2 slices French Toast in middle of plate. Top with approximately 5 ounces cooked sweetbreads. Arrange 3 cooked fresh asparagus tips on one side, and a few fresh cooked sliced carrots on the other side. Top the sweetbreads with the Creamed Mushrooms. Garnish with parsley and serve immediately.

SQUAW DISH

Yield: 24 servings

Ingredients

BACON, diced	3 pounds
EGGS, well beaten	24
CORN, WHOLE KERNEL, CANNED, drained	1 No. 10 can
SLICED PIMIENTO-STUFFED OLIVES	1-1/2 cups
PEPPER	1/4 teaspoon

Procedure

1. Fry bacon until crisp; drain off excess fat.
2. Combine beaten eggs, corn, olives, and pepper.
3. Pour egg mixture over bacon. Cook over low heat, stirring lightly until tender-firm.
4. Serve hot.

VEAL CUTLETS IN WINE SAUCE

Yield: 25 portions

Ingredients

VEAL CUTLETS, 6 ounces each	8 pounds
SALT	1 tablespoon
PEPPER	2 teaspoons
BUTTER	1 pound
MINCED ONION	6 ounces
MUSHROOMS, diced	1 pound
PARSLEY, minced	1/4 cup
FLOUR	1/2 cup
BEEF STOCK	1-1/2 quarts
WHITE WINE	1 pint (2 cups)
LEMON JUICE	1/4 cup

Procedure

1. Sprinkle cutlets with salt and pepper. Saute in butter on both sides. Transfer cutlets to greased baking dish.

2. Place onion, mushrooms, parsley and flour in the butter and brown slightly. Add stock, wine and lemon juice, stirring constantly. Blend well. Cook sauce until thick and all trace of raw starch has disappeared. Pour sauce over cutlets. Cook in oven at 300°F. for 1 hour.

VEAL CARLOS

Yield: 1 portion

Ingredients

VEAL STEAK	3 ounces
HAM STEAK	3 ounces
THYME	to season
SALT	to season
PEPPER	to season
GARLIC CLOVE, small	1/2
TOMATO SLICE, thick	1
BUTTER	2 ounces
NOODLES, uncooked	1-1/2 ounces

Procedure

1. Cut veal steak 1/4-inch thick.

2. Cut ham steak 1/4-inch thick from boned and rolled ready-to-eat ham.

3. Season veal steak with thyme, salt and pepper and a small amount of garlic.

4. Put veal and ham steaks together. Secure with toothpicks.

5. Dip steaks in flour, then in egg wash. Saute in hot fat until delicately browned. Cook veal steak 10 minutes, and ham steak 4 minutes.

6. In meantime cook noodles in boiling salted water until tender. Drain.

7. Saute thick slice of tomato in butter.

8. Arrange a bed of hot noodles in greased casserole.

9. Top with veal and ham steaks, then with sauteed tomato slice.

10. Pour over natural juices or a little broth.

11. Place in oven at 375°F. for 10 minutes.

12. Garnish with parsley or watercress.

BANQUET TENDERLOIN

"This is an excellent way to use less-expensive tenderloins."

Yield: approximately 24 portions

Ingredients

BEEF TENDERLOINS, A.P.	12 to 15 pounds
RED WINE, DRY	2 to 3 cups
OLIVE OIL	2 cups
GARLIC BUDS, SLICED	1/3 cup
BLACK PEPPER, COARSELY GROUND	1 tablespoon

Procedure

1. Strip off all fat, tough fiber, sheath from tenderloin.

2. Secure tail and loose flaps with thin skewers so that tenderloin is well shaped and of the same thickness from end to end.

3. Place meat in deep baking pan. Cover with the remaining ingredients.

4. Marinate meat 4 to 6 hours, turning frequently so that all sides are well marinated.

5. Remove tenderloins from marinade. Place on wire racks in shallow roasting pan.

6. Place in oven at 450°F. to sear the outside. Reduce heat to 350°F. and continue cooking until meat is done, basting frequently with the marinade. (The cooking time can only be an approximation as this will depend on the thickness of the meat. The center of the meat should be rare when done.)

7. Slice meat quickly in 1-inch slices. Serve on hot plates.

Note

Vegetables that add interest to this dish are Potato Puffs Amandine or Brazil Nut Potatoes (*INSTITUTIONS*, Sept. 1957, Pg. 140) and Broccoli or Asparagus Tips with Pimiento Butter.

BEEF STEAK AND KIDNEY PIE

Yield: 15 portions

Ingredients

CHUCK STEAK, choice, lean	4 pounds
SEASONED FLOUR	for dredging
BUTTER or MARGARINE	1/4 pound
ONIONS, medium, sliced	4
BEEF STOCK	to cover
WORCESTERSHIRE SAUCE	to season
VEAL KIDNEYS, approx. 6 ounces each	4
CARROTS, finger length, cooked	as needed
POTATO BALLS, cooked	as needed
MUSHROOMS, sliced	as needed
PARSLEY, chopped	to garnish
BRANDY	6 tablespoons
PASTRY, rich	as needed

Procedure

1. Cut steak in 1-1/2-inch squares. Dredge in seasoned flour. Saute in hot fat until delicately browned.

2. Add sliced onions and cook a few minutes.

3. Add enough beef stock to cover meat. Cook in oven at 350°F. until meat is tender.

4. Thicken sauce slightly, if necessary, and flavor with worcestershire sauce.

5. In meantime remove tubes from veal kidneys. Separate kidneys into sections, and cut in 1-1/2-inch cubes. Dredge cubes in seasoned flour. Saute in hot fat and cook until meat is tender.

To Make Pies

1. Divide the steak and kidney cubes evenly among the individual pot pie dishes.

2. Add 3 or 4 carrot pieces, 3 potato balls and a few sliced mushrooms.

3. Top with chopped parsley. Pour the beef sauce from pan over all. Top with rich pastry rounds. Bake in oven at 425°F. until crust is delicately browned and filling is piping hot—about 20 minutes.

4. Just before removing pies from oven, pour 1 teaspoon brandy through funnel into pies.

COWBOY'S BBQ BEEF
(Barbecued Brisket of Beef with Barbecue Sauce)

Yield: 6 servings

Ingredients

DEFATTED BRISKET of BEEF	2-1/4 pounds
DICED ONION	1 tablespoon
CARROT, SMALL, diced	1
DICED CELERY	1/2 cup
GARLIC CLOVE	1/2
WATER	1/2 cup
SALT	to taste
PEPPER	to taste
BAY LEAVES	2

Procedure

1. Preheat oven to 350°F.

2. Place brisket of beef in roasting pan. Add onion, carrot, celery, garlic, water, salt, pepper, and bay leaves.

3. Roast in oven for 2 hours.

4. After 2 hours, turn the oven down to 300°F. and, if necessary, add water, basting and turning meat frequently until meat is fork-tender.

United Airlines Food Services Library
Duri Arquisch

BARBECUE SAUCE
(for Cowboy's BBQ Beef)

Yield: 6 servings

Ingredients

VEGETABLE OIL	1 tablespoon
BRUNOISE of CELERY, CARROTS, and ONIONS	1/4 cup
GARLIC CLOVE, pressed	1/2
CHILI SAUCE	1/2 cup
DRY MUSTARD	pinch
BROWN SUGAR	1/2 teaspoon
HONEY	1 tablespoon
BROWN SAUCE	1 cup
WORCESTERSHIRE SAUCE	dash
APPLE CIDER VINEGAR	1 teaspoon
LEMON JUICE	to taste
SALT	to taste
CAYENNE PEPPER	to taste
SMOKE FLAVOR	1 drop

Procedure

In a heavy pan, heat the vegetable oil. Add the brunoise and garlic. Stirring frequently, cook for about 5 minutes, or until soft and translucent, but not brown. Stir in next 6 ingredients. Cook briskly, uncovered, until the sauce is of desired thickness. Remove from heat and season with salt, cayenne pepper, lemon juice, and smoke flavor.

United Airlines Food Services Library
Duri Arquisch

SPARERIBS WITH APRICOT SAUCE

Yield: approximately 50 servings

Ingredients

SPARERIBS	50 pounds
APRICOT HALVES	1 No. 10 can
CHILI SAUCE or	
CATSUP	1 quart
PREPARED MUSTARD	1/2 cup
PREPARED HORSERADISH	1/3 cup
GARLIC POWDER	1-1/2 tablespoons
WORCESTERSHIRE	
SAUCE	1/3 cup
LIQUID HOT PEPPER	
SEASONING	1/2 teaspoon
CIDER VINEGAR	1/2 cup

Procedure

1. Arrange ribs in single layer in shallow roasting pans. Roast, uncovered, in oven at 400°F. for 1 hour.

2. Meanwhile, drain syrup from apricots; set aside fruit. Add remaining ingredients to syrup; stir until blended.

3. Remove ribs from oven; discard drippings. Reduce oven temperature to 350°F.

4. Pour apricot sauce over ribs; continue roasting for 20 minutes, basting with sauce several times.

5. Add apricot halves, turning them in the sauce. Continue roasting for 10 minutes.

PINTO BEAN BAKE WITH SPARERIBS

Yield: 48 servings

Ingredients

PINTO BEANS	6 pounds
WATER	as needed
BACON or HAM RINDS	2 pounds
ONION, thinly sliced	1 pound
BAY LEAVES	4
TOMATO PUREE	2 cups
TOMATO CATSUP	2 cups
LIGHT MOLASSES	1-1/2 cups
BROWN SUGAR	2 cups
CIDER VINEGAR	1/2 cup
DRY MUSTARD	2 tablespoons
LIQUID SMOKE	1/2 teaspoon
SALT	to taste

Procedure

1. Cover beans with water and soak according to preferred method.

2. Combine beans, rinds, onion, and bay leaves; cover with water and place over heat. Bring to a boil and simmer slowly 1 hour until beans are tender but not split.

3. Drain and reserve liquid. Remove bay leaves.

4. Combine bean liquid with remaining ingredients and heat to boiling. Place beans in baking pan and stir in liquid mixture to cover beans by 1/2 inch.

5. Bake, covered, in oven at 325°F. for 5 to 6 hours, adding reserved liquid mixture as needed.

6. Remove cover last hour of baking to allow beans to brown.

7. Serve 3/4 cup of beans with baked spareribs. Garnish with a bouquet of parsley and spiced crab apples.

TROUT SAUTE AMANDINE

Yield: 25 portions

Ingredients

TROUT, FRESH, 10 ounces each	25
SALT	to taste
EGG DIPPING MIXTURE	
EGGS	20
CREAM (20%)	1 quart
PEPPER	to taste
SALAD OIL	1 cup
BUTTER	2 cups
FLOUR	4 quarts
AMANDINE	
ALMONDS, blanched, slivered	1-1/2 quarts
BUTTER	4 cups
LEMON JUICE	1/4 cup
LEMON SLICES	25

Procedure

1. Dress trout; clean and bone. With the skin side down, sprinkle inside with salt and pepper.

2. Combine eggs and cream to make dipping mixture.

3. Put flour in an 8-inch by 10-inch pan. Roll trout in flour, then dip in egg mixture and again in flour.

4. In an 18-inch frying pan, place 1 pound butter and 1 cup salad oil. Heat to 360°F. Place 4 trout skin side up in hot fat at one time. Fry 6 minutes until underside is a golden brown. Turn fish and cook 7 minutes longer.

5. In meantime, make amandine. Heat butter to 350°F. in a 12-inch frying pan. Add blanched and slivered almonds. Cook until a golden brown, turning constantly. Remove from heat and add lemon juice.

6. Serve each individual fish with 1 tablespoon amandine and 1 slice lemon.

BROOK TROUT SAUTE

Yield: 1 portion

Ingredients

BROOK TROUT	1
SALT	to taste
PEPPER	to taste
FLOUR	to coat
MUSHROOM CAP, LARGE	1
TOMATO SLICE, 3/4 inch thick	1
LEMON, thinly sliced	1
PARSLEY, FRESH	to garnish

Procedure

1. Wipe fish with damp cloth and dry thoroughly.

2. Dust fish with seasoned flour. Remove all surplus flour by shaking fish.

3. Place fish in hot frying pan with just enough fat to cover the bottom of the pan.

4. Cook until delicately browned and crisp. (Do not overcook fish, and never allow the fish to stand once it is cooked or it will lose its crispness and become soggy.)

5. While fish is cooking, saute mushroom cap, then the tomato slice.

6. Place cooked trout on hot serving dish. Top with tomato slice. Place mushroom cap in center of tomato slice.

7. Pour over all sizzling hot meuniere butter, made by utilizing the browned butter in which the fish was cooked and adding to it lemon juice and chopped fresh parsley.

8. Garnish with lemon slices and parsley and serve immediately.

GOOSE WITH APRICOT CORN BREAD

Yield: 24 servings

Ingredients

GEESE	
(12 pounds each)	2
BUTTER or MARGARINE	1 cup
CHOPPED ONION	3 cups
CHOPPED CELERY	1 quart
SALT	2 teaspoons
PEPPER	1/4 teaspoon
APRICOT HALVES	1/2 No. 10 can
PECANS, toasted	2 cups
CRUMBLED CORN BREAD	1 gallon
WATER	2/3 cup
BUTTER or MARGARINE, melted	1/2 cup
GOOSE DRIPPINGS	1/2 cup
FLOUR	1/2 cup
CHICKEN BROTH	3 cups
PARSLEY	to garnish
DRIED APRICOTS	to garnish

Procedure

1. Cook onion and celery in butter or margarine until tender. Add salt and pepper.

2. Drain apricots; reserve 1 cup of syrup for gravy. Dice apricots and chop pecans.

3. Combine onion mixture, apricots, pecans, and corn bread; toss lightly. Gradually add water until stuffing is just moistened.

4. Pack stuffing lightly into neck and body cavities of geese; fasten with poultry pins. Brush geese with melted butter. Roast in oven at 325°F. for 5 hours or until meat thermometer (inserted in thickest part of thigh) registers 185°F.; baste geese occasionally with drippings.

5. Remove geese from pan. Pour drippings from pan; skim off excess fat.

6. Pour 1/2 cup of drippings into roasting pan. Stir in flour until blended. Gradually stir in reserved apricot syrup and chicken broth; boil for 1 minute. Place geese on serving platter; garnish with parsley and dried apricots.

BIG SKY BAKED BEANS

Yield: 50 3/4-cup servings

Ingredients

DRY NAVY BEANS	6 pounds
WATER, cold	as necessary
BACON, diced	1 pound
WATER, boiling	as necessary
CHOPPED ONION	1-1/2 cups
MOLASSES	1 cup
BROWN SUGAR	1 cup
DRY MUSTARD	1 tablespoon
SALT	3 tablespoons
SWEET PICKLE JUICE	1/2 cup
CHOPPED SWEET PICKLES	2 cups
CATSUP	1 quart

Procedure

1. Pick over beans and wash them thoroughly; cover with cold water; bring to a boil; boil 2 minutes; remove from heat; cover and let soak for 1-1/2 to 2 hours.

2. Fry chopped bacon until crisp; reserve bacon and fat.

3. Add enough boiling water to beans to cover them; add onion; bring to a boil; reduce heat and simmer about 1 to 1-1/2 hours, or until tender but not mushy.

4. Add bacon and bacon fat, molasses, brown sugar, mustard, salt, pickle juice, and catsup to beans; pour into roasting pan. Bake in oven at 350°F. for about 1-1/2 hours or until browned. Serve hot or cold.

THE PERFECT BAKED POTATO

Scrub potatoes under running water. Let dry. Brush potatoes with oil; place on tray. Bake in oven at 400°F. for about 55 minutes for 9-ounce potatoes. To hold, puncture skin of each potato in one or two places, with fork.

IDAHO BAKED POTATO BONUS

Add 1 cup sliced pimiento-stuffed olives to 1 quart cheese sauce. Spoon 2 tablespoons sauce over split baked Idaho potato.

POTATOES O'BRIEN

Yield: 20 servings, 4 ounces each

Ingredients

HASH BROWN POTATOES, FROZEN, thawed	2-1/2 pounds
GRATED PROCESS AMERICAN CHEESE	2-1/2 cups
CHOPPED GREEN PEPPER	5/8 cup
CHOPPED ONION	5/8 cup
CHOPPED PIMIENTO	1/2 cup
FLOUR	3 tablespoons
SALT	1-1/2 teaspoons
WHITE PEPPER	1/4 teaspoon
HALF-and-HALF or LIGHT CREAM	3-1/2 cups

Procedure

1. Combine all ingredients except half-and-half in a half-size steam table pan. Pour half-and-half over the mixture. Cover with foil.

2. Bake in oven at 400°F. for 30 minutes.

3. Remove foil. Continue baking for 50 to 60 minutes or until browned.

SUN VALLEY STUFFED POTATO

Yield: 24 servings

Ingredients

IDAHO POTATOES	12
WHITE POTATOES	1-1/2 pounds
BUTTER or MARGARINE	1/4 pound
MILK, hot	1 pint
SALT	2 teaspoons
PEPPER	1/2 teaspoon
CHOPPED ONION	3/4 cup
SHREDDED CHEDDAR CHEESE	2-1/4 cups
CHOPPED PIMIENTO-STUFFED OLIVES	1-1/2 cups
SLICED PIMIENTO-STUFFED OLIVES	as needed

Procedure

1. Bake Idaho potatoes in oven at 400°F. for 1 hour.

2. Cut potatoes in half lengthwise. Scoop out pulp and place in mixer bowl. Reserve shells.

3. Boil white potatoes 25 minutes, or until tender Drain and add to baked potatoes.

4. Melt butter or margarine. Add butter, hot milk, salt, and pepper to potatoes; whip until smooth.

5. Add chopped onion, 3/4 cup of cheese, and chopped olives; mix well.

6. Mound mashed potato mixture into potato shells. Top each half with 1 tablespoon grated cheese and stuffed olive slices.

7. Place in baking pans and heat in oven at 350°F. for 20 minutes.

SCALLOPED POTATOES SUPREME

Yield: 40 servings, 4 ounces each

Ingredients

HOME FRIES, FROZEN	5 pounds
CREAM of CHICKEN SOUP	1 No. 5 can
MILK	3-1/3 cups
SALT	1-1/2 teaspoons
WHITE PEPPER	1/2 teaspoon
INSTANT CHOPPED ONION	1/2 cup
CHEESE, PROCESS AMERICAN, shredded	1 pound

Procedure

1. Combine soup, milk, onion, and seasonings; heat until hot. Add shredded cheese, stirring until melted.

2. Place potatoes in a 12-inch by 20-inch by 2-1/2-inch steam table pan. Add sauce mixture, stirring thoroughly.

3. Bake in oven at 400°F. for 60 to 70 minutes until lightly browned.

GREAT NORTHERN BEAN SALAD

Yield: 24 servings

Ingredients

DRIED GREAT NORTHERN BEANS, cooked	3 quarts
SLICED CELERY	1 quart
CHOPPED SWEET PICKLES	3 cups
TOMATOES, RIPE, SMALL, chopped	4
MINCED ONION	1/2 cup
SALAD OIL	3 cups
CIDER VINEGAR	1 cup
SALT	1 tablespoon
SUGAR	1 tablespoon
PAPRIKA	2 teaspoons
WORCESTERSHIRE SAUCE	1 tablespoon
GROUND CLOVES	1/2 teaspoon
GREENS	as needed
SWEET PICKLES,	24

Procedure

1. Mix beans with celery, pickles, tomato, and onion. Blend salad oil, vinegar, salt, sugar, paprika, worcestershire sauce, and ground cloves.

2. Pour salad dressing over bean mixture. Marinate overnight.

3. Serve salad on salad greens. Garnish with pickle fans. (Slice pickles several times lengthwise without cutting all the way through and spread the slices to form a fan shape.)

MOUNTAINOUS APRICOT MOUSSE

Yield: about 32 servings

Ingredients

APRICOT HALVES, drained	1 No. 10 can
GELATINE, UNFLAVORED	1/2 cup
SUGAR	2 cups
SALT	1/2 teaspoon
EGGS, LARGE, separated	12
MILK	1-1/4 quarts
GRATED LEMON PEEL	1 tablespoon
LEMON JUICE	1/2 cup
SUGAR	1 cup
CREAM, HEAVY	2 quarts

Procedure

1. Puree enough apricots to make 1 quart puree. Reserve remaining apricots for garnish.

2. Combine gelatine, 2 cups sugar, and salt in top of double boiler.

3. Beat together egg yolks and milk; add to gelatine mixture. Cook over boiling water, stirring constantly, until gelatine is dissolved.

4. Remove from heat; beat in lemon peel, juice, and apricot puree. Chill until mixture begins to thicken.

5. Beat egg whites until frothy; gradually beat in 1 cup sugar.

6. Whip cream until stiff; fold into egg white mixture.

7. Pour into 2 prepared 9-inch springform pans, or 4 greased 6-cup molds. Chill at least 6 hours.

8. To serve, invert each mousse onto plate. Remove sides from springform pan. Run spatula carefully under inverted bottom before lifting off. To remove mousse from mold, loosen edges with knife and shake gently. Garnish with remaining apricot halves.

FRESH STRAWBERRY TART

Yield: 24 servings

Ingredients

EGG YOLKS	20
SUGAR	3 cups
CRUSHED STRAWBERRIES, FRESH or FROZEN*	3 pints
LADYFINGER or BREAD CRUMBS	1 quart
VANILLA	4 teaspoons
EGG WHITES	20
WHIPPED CREAM	as needed
SLICED STRAWBERRIES	to garnish

*If frozen strawberries are used, drain slightly.

Procedure

1. Beat egg yolks. Add sugar and beat until light and fluffy.

2. Add strawberries, crumbs, and vanilla extract; mix thoroughly.

3. Beat egg whites until stiff but not dry. Fold into strawberry mixture.

4. Butter a 12-inch by 20-inch baking pan; dust lightly with sugar. Pour mixture into it.

5. Bake in preheated oven at 275°F. for 35 minutes, or until firm.

6. Serve cold with whipped cream garnished with sliced strawberries.

APRICOT SAUCE

Yield: 100 1/4-cup servings

Ingredients

CANNED APRICOT HALVES	3 No. 10 cans
CORNSTARCH	1/2 cup
WATER	3/4 cup
LEMON JUICE	1-1/2 quarts

Procedure

1. Puree undrained apricots until smooth.

2. Blend cornstarch and water in kettle; stir in apricot puree. Cook, stirring constantly, until sauce boils; simmer 10 minutes. Cool.

3. Stir in lemon juice; chill.

INDEX